BUSINESS HISTORY SERIES

GRADUATE SCHOOL OF BUSINESS ADMINISTRATION

NEW YORK UNIVERSITY

Thomas C. Cochran, Editor

THE PABST BREWING COMPANY

The History of an American Business

FREDERICK PABST

THE PABST BREWING COMPANY

》》》　》》》　》》》　《《《　《《《　《《《

THE HISTORY OF AN AMERICAN BUSINESS

THOMAS C. COCHRAN, Ph. D.

Professor of History, New York University

NEW YORK
New York University Press · Washington Square

LONDON
Geoffrey Cumberlege · Oxford University Press

1948

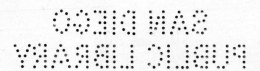

PRINTED IN THE UNITED STATES OF AMERICA

FOREWORD

BUSINESS is the work of the world. In peace or in war, it is humanity's chiefest task. It touches all our lives at myriad points. We cannot escape its influence by sitting on the sidelines and merely watching the world plunge by. Its reach extends into our holiest cloisters and our most easeful retreats.

The history of American business, in a very real sense, is the basic history of these United States. Yet, until recent years, it has been largely neglected. Politicians, generals, clergymen, and "intellectuals" of established professional status have claimed and won the spotlight in much or most of the historical writings to the exclusion of the less articulate but equally important men of business.

To some extent this phenomenon has been the result of the prestige of the military, priestly, and political orders—a prestige inherited from feudal Europe and from our own colonial past. Undoubtedly, too, it has been in part the result of the preoccupation of our economic historians with broad over-all trends that lend themselves in sweep and scope to classification or generalization. But more than a little it is the direct result of the fact that historical business records have not been easy to find and to use.

Business records, of course, are formidable in bulk. Moreover, they are seldom stored and preserved with any thought of scholarly use. And all too frequently business managements, in a generally unjustifiable fear of "airing the past," are prone to refuse to open their business records for historical appraisal.

Happily, modern business is saying goodbye to all that. As business enterprises come of age and grow old they begin to see the value in a true historical picture of their past activities. They recognize the importance of acquainting their newer executives with the policies and practices that in earlier days made for successes or for mistakes. They come to realize that

v

new policies very often gain tremendous force either by being explicitly identified with past experience or by departing from such experience. And in the course of such historical re-examinations, business often becomes acutely and tragically conscious of the shortness of "memory" of its elder statesmen to say nothing of the chaos, the confusion, and the losses that soon develop among business records that repose in the wastes of cellars and warehouses.

With the purpose of being of assistance in the important task of recovering and preserving the actions and thoughts of our earlier business executives, the New York University Graduate School of Business Administration is inaugurating a business history series. The projected volumes, of which two are now ready, will be limited to objective and scholarly studies of business companies, businessmen, or business situations. In sum, the editor of the series, Professor Thomas C. Cochran, will attempt to guide the projected volumes and their respective authors in the direction of an expanding picture of the realities of business entrepreneurship. In dealing with companies, men, and situations, it is hoped to avoid both the unrestrained praise of friend and the unwarranted damnation of foe.

The first volume of this series, presented herewith, is the history of a manufacturing company over one hundred years old, with a record of genuine achievement in its contributions to technology, market distribution, and business leadership.

G. ROWLAND COLLINS
Dean

PREFACE

THE Pabst Brewing Company is one of the oldest of the great American brewing concerns. Founded in 1844, it has, from the late sixties to the present day, maintained a leading position in its industry. Rich material for the study of successful entrepreneurship and the adjustment of a business firm to changing conditions in technology, markets, and competition is to be found in the Pabst records. As editor of the New York University Business History Series, it was my privilege to study these records and from them prepare this history of the Pabst Company as the first volume in our series.

The Pabst material tends to fall into four periods. For the first of these, from the founding of the enterprise as a partnership to its incorporation in 1873, there are few remaining company records. Thus the account had to be based largely on local newspapers, Wisconsin censuses, and other "outside" sources. The core of the study is the second period: from 1873 to the coming of prohibition in 1919. For these years the company records are fairly complete and my assistants and I had free access to them. In one sense, the present history ends in 1919. In the third period, the thirteen years of prohibition, new business problems arose that were not connected with brewing. To study these situations properly would require another book dealing with the history of prepared foods and soft drinks. Furthermore, in this prohibition era as well as in the fourth and last period of Pabst history, the years since 1933, full or interpretive writing is impossible because executives still active are the chief characters, and a highly competitive marketing situation produces many trade secrets. For the years after 1919, therefore, the study is not based on a complete examination of the company records.

Since 1933 the modern brewing industry has been different in many respects from the old industry that we analyzed from 1873 to 1919. Changes have been due to prohibition, the First World War, and new technology. The net effects of several innovations, such as the fast motor truck and the beer can, are not yet clear. The historian of brewing in the most recent period, therefore, may chronicle events, but he must reserve judgment on them. I hope, however, that there is enough detail in the last three chapters to permit the reader to see general changes and trends.

The officers of the Pabst Brewing Company headed by Mr. Fred Pabst, chairman of the board, and Mr. Harris Perlstein, president, greatly facilitated our research. We made particularly heavy demands on the time of Mr. E. L. Morris, vice-president of the Pabst Sales Company, and Mr. R. C. Zimmerman, assistant vice-president in charge of the Milwaukee division, and Dr. Alfred J. Schedler, chief brewing technologist. Without their assistance in overcoming the problems that inevitably develop in business research, our task would have been much harder. We wish to thank also Mrs. Frederick Best, Mr. George Bruce, Mr. W. O. Goodrich, Mr. A. Cressy Morrison, Mr. Theodore Mueller, and Mr. C. D. Williams for devoting time to this project. The Milwaukee County Historical Society and the library of the Schwarz Laboratories in New York City supplied much of the material that we used to supplement the Pabst Company records. In correcting the proofs, we were greatly aided by Professor Bayrd Still's extensive knowledge of Milwaukee history.

I, personally, wish to thank Arthur H. Cole for aid in choosing my objectives, William Miller for editorial advice, and Rosamond B. Cochran and Ferdinand Schultz for assistance in research. They all demonstrated that there need be no difficulty in co-operative research.

THOMAS C. COCHRAN

New York University
March 1948

CONTENTS

		Page
Foreword		v
Preface		vii
Illustrations		x
Tables		xi
I	The Bests Move to Milwaukee	3
II	Establishing the Business in Milwaukee	11
III	Prelude to Greatness	43
IV	The Captain Runs the Company	70
V	Brewing Becomes More Scientific	102
VI	Winning a National Market	129
VII	A National Sales Organization	160
VIII	Quality and Prestige First	180
IX	Holding a Quality Market	210
X	Pabst in Milwaukee	249
XI	Bargaining with Labor	271
XII	The Prohibition Movement	302
XIII	Fred Pabst Takes Control	325
XIV	Premier and the Merger	355
XV	The Revival of Brewing	366
XVI	The Campaign for the National Market	384
	Appendixes	400
	Bibliography	407
	Chronology	422
	Index	430

ILLUSTRATIONS

Frederick Pabst . . . . Frontispiece

Jacob Best, Sr. . . . . *facing page* 22

Phillip Best 48

Gustav G. Pabst 192

Fred Pabst 326

Harris Perlstein 362

TABLES

	Page
Milwaukee Breweries in 1850	27
Milwaukee Breweries as Reported in the Wisconsin Census of 1860	54
Production of Leading Milwaukee Breweries, 1866 to 1872	56
Production of Leading American Breweries of 1871-1872	56
Largest Brewers in 1877	73
Largest Brewers in 1895	74
Total Barrels Purchased or Manufactured by Pabst	75
Population and Beer Production, Chief Brewing Centers	79
Condensed Financial Statement, 1873-1893	84
Improvements in Relation to Sales, 1875-1893	87
Highest Salaries Paid Monthly	94
Monthly Salaries of Officers of the Company	94
Labor and Production at Empire and South Side	99
Expenses for Natural and Machine-Made Ice	109
Pabst Bottled-Beer Statistics, 1881-1893	124
Advertising Contracts (April 1879–May 1880)	130
Advertising Expenditures, 1878-1893	136
Salary Ledger of the Chicago Branches in 1883	172
Branches	173
Price of Beer and Net Return from Branches in 1886	175
Sales by States in 1888	176
Export Beer Sales	178
Pabst Sales and Domestic Consumption, 1893-1919	180
Financial Statistics	183
Trading Profits, 1904-1918	186
Stockholders in 1894	189
Highest Salaries Paid Monthly at the Empire Brewery	194
New Investments in Real Estate for Selling Purposes	197
Suds Brewed by the Month	203
Advertising Expenditures, 1897-1902	215
Sales of Brands	216
Advertising Expenditures, 1897-1919	219
Special Selling Expenses	227

Page

Home-Office Traveling Men in 1902 239
Profit on Branch Bottled and Keg Beer 242
Estimated Average Beer Sales by Area and State, 1909-1913 . . 243
Export Sales 247
Rates at Issue in Wage Dispute 279
Wages Paid, 1905-1918 299
Stockholders as of December 29, 1921, and August 8, 1922 . . 329
General Financial Data, 1921-1927 331
Profit and Loss and Surplus Account, 1926-1929 337
Plant Employees 338
Selling Expenses, 1921-1924 342
Selling Expenses, 1929-1931 348
General and Financial Data, 1928-1932 350
Results by Divisions, 1928-1932 351
Balance Sheet as of July 31, 1932 353
Capital, Surplus, and Physical Equipment, 1933-1946 . . . 375
Beer Sales in the United States 392
Appendixes
    Directors of the Phillip Best Brewing Company, Pabst
        Brewing Company, Pabst Corporation, 1873-1932 . . . 400
    Directors of the Premier-Pabst Corporation, Pabst Brewing
        Company, 1933-1946 401
    Number of Directors Constituting the Board 401
    Number of Officers, by Sample Years 401
    Number of Employees, 1878-1901, 1933-1946 402
    Seasonal Variation in Employment, 1907-1908 402
    Salaries of Office Staff, 1880 403
    Bank Loans, 1882-1893 404
    Syndicate Breweries 405

THE PABST BREWING COMPANY

The History of an American Business

CHAPTER I

THE BESTS MOVE TO MILWAUKEE

THE history of the Pabst Brewing Company begins before the use of the name Pabst or the founding of the city of Milwaukee. While the business that acquired the Pabst name in 1889 was moved to Milwaukee in 1844 by a German family named Best, this family's connection with brewing began at a date that is lost in the history of the Rhineland. The first available records are of Jacob Best, Sr. (the great-grandfather of the present Frederick Pabst), who in the early nineteenth century owned a brewhouse and winery in the small town of Mettenheim, Rheinhessen. Jacob Best, Sr., trained four energetic sons in the arts of brewing and wine making, and, as they reached maturity at the end of the 1830's, they hoped for more than was promised by the old and rigid communities around them. The Rhineland was not prospering at that time and a local brewery or winery was not likely to produce sufficient profits to satisfy four ambitious boys. Expansion of the business to new regions was the solution that seemed most appealing, and America was the land of promise.

The first attempt to expand the business to America seems to have been made by Phillip, the third son, who tried to develop an export wine business with the United States. In 1838 and 1839 he toured the French wine districts, spending several weeks in Paris.[1] His plan may have been to study French wines in order to develop better wines at Mettenheim, and then set up an agency for selling them in New York. This venture was not pursued for long, perhaps due to some bad wine years in Germany,[2] although, according to his sister-in-law, Phillip came to

[1] Information from Phillip Best's passport of 1838. There is evidence that Phillip also signed his name Philipp, and many secondary sources list him as Philip.
[2] Marcus Lee Hansen, *The Atlantic Migration*, p. 220.

New York in the early forties to sell the family wine.[3] The family's second American venture began with the journey of Jacob, Jr., the oldest son, and Charles, the second son, to Milwaukee in 1842. There they set up a vinegar factory.[4] This venture prospered so well that in less than two years Charles returned to Mettenheim to persuade his father and two other brothers to move the whole family business to the United States.

THE DECISION TO MOVE

There must have been long and serious arguments around the family table in the Best house in Mettenheim while a boy in his twenties tried to persuade his fifty-eight-year-old father, a well-established small-town businessman, to sell out and try a fresh start in an unknown city nearly five thousand miles away. But all forces were working in Charles's favor. His father's trade was largely among the farmers around Mettenheim, and, in 1844, these farmers were badly off with little prospect of improvement. The agricultural depression in Rhineland Germany was not simply a matter of a turn of the business cycle. Agricultural prices had been moving downward ever since the Napoleonic Wars, and the subsequent division of the old communal holdings into small individual farms had worked to the disadvantage of the peasants. If anything, the father's market for beer would get worse and worse. There seemed every reason to sell out; and an upswing of the business cycle in 1843 probably gave Jacob, Sr., a chance to unload his factory at a moderately good price.

While conditions in Germany thus gave many incentives for moving, conditions in the United States practically demanded that if any move were made it should be to the New World. Even there Wisconsin offered unusual attractions, and none more inviting than in the Milwaukee region. Cheap farm land was attracting thousands of German and American settlers to

---

[3] As reported in letter, Chris and Margaret Best to Mrs. George Blanke, May 4, 1943. [Copy in the possession of Mrs. Frederick Best, Oconomowoc, Wis.]

[4] Rudolph A. Koss, *Milwaukee*, p. 132.

the country around the Milwaukee port. This assured future brewers a growing supply of both barley and customers.[5] Moreover, taxes were unusually low, for Wisconsin had been a virtual wilderness during the frantic state-aided canal boom of the middle thirties and it had not contracted a burdensome debt like its more settled neighbors, Illinois and Michigan. Even without canals, Wisconsin offered first-rate transportation, for the port of Milwaukee was open to navigation during the entire beer-drinking season, and the Great Lakes provided cheap and easy water routes to Chicago and the East.

Not least among the factors which persuaded Jacob, Sr., to move must have been the many letters from Germans in Wisconsin that were passed from hand to hand in the Rhineland, or published in the local papers. These fully corroborated Charles's enthusiastic statements. Franz Neukirch, for example, had written of Milwaukee County to his wife in Hessen-Darmstadt at the end of 1839.

The soil produces everything that grows in Germany, but with the difference that it produces more with less cultivation. . . . . The people, though of many nationalities, are generally very agreeable and hospitable; jealousy and ill-will are unknown and everyone is delighted when others achieve success. . . . . Everything here is still in the process of becoming, yet none can deny, that this land will soon be one of the most populous and wealthy of the free-states, as immigration mounts every year, for since my arrival well over a thousand Germans, mostly Prussians, have come here. . . . . You would be surprised to see how much work I have accomplished all by myself, surely with much flow of perspiration, albeit it falls upon my own property and for you. . . . . Labor wages are generally high and the ordinary daily wage is one dollar. . . . . Meanwhile the necessities of life are not so expensive, and stand in a much better relationship to wages than in Germany, for one can dine in the largest restaurant in the city for a quarter of a dollar per meal.

[5] Wisconsin was selling its "school lands" cheaply in order to attract settlers, and United States Government land was still available a few miles from Milwaukee at $1.25 per acre.

2

.... One would be inclined to think that the prevailing high wages and low produce prices would make agriculture unprofitable, yet such is not the case because more is produced with less labor here than in Germany, and stock-raising costs nothing at all. Under these circumstances one would advise every poor and, in Germany, superfluous wage-earner to come to this country where most Germans quickly pay for their land by the labor of their hands and thus achieve an independent and care-free existence. I could write to you at great length concerning this land of freedom, where all things seem so different from what they are in Europe, but my letter would become too long.[6]

Less compelling, even to the freethinking, liberal Bests, than the vision of exciting economic opportunities in the lake cities of the United States, but, nevertheless, an added incentive to migration, was the freedom of thought in America. In Germany, freedom of speech, the press, and assembly had been rigorously curtailed for over twenty years in all the despotic principalities by laws and decrees modeled on those of Prince Metternich of Austria; it was neither a pleasant nor a safe country for liberals. By 1844, men such as the Bests had become disciplined to keep their ideas to themselves; no one but the father could think back to the time when things had been different. As Phillip wrote later, "The freedom to which every human being is born no one in Germany knows how to value, only here in America can he experience it." [7] Charles's description of how he and his fellow Germans ran their affairs in Milwaukee must have awakened old memories of a freer age for Jacob, Sr.

Prosperity had returned to the American West with a rush of business activity in the latter part of 1843, and Charles had left for Germany with the big talk of American boomers going through his mind. He probably believed most of it and it was fortunate that he did, for this time the optimists were right.

[6] Wilhelm Hense-Jensen and Ernest Bruncken, *Wisconsins Deutsch-Amerikaner, biz sum Schluss des neunzehnten Jahrhunderts,* II, Appendix I, 291-95 and passim. All translations from the German are by Ferdinand Schultz.
[7] Phillip Best to William Muth, May 10, 1847. Translated from the German. [Letter in the possession of Mr. Fred Pabst, Oconomowoc, Wis.]

Had the Bests been serious students of the business cycle, which most economists had not yet even recognized, they could scarcely have chosen a better period for initial investment than 1844. Had they carefully studied location theory, not yet even heard of, they could scarcely have chosen a better locality for a brewing business than Milwaukee.

Even without theory Charles knew this and, more important, he communicated his knowledge and feelings to the whole family. Jacob, Sr., his wife and her father, the two daughters, the sons, Phillip and Lorenz, and Phillip's young wife would all join Charles and Jacob, Jr., in America.[8] Clearly this was not a case of poor immigrants struggling to establish themselves in a new land, but of the moving of a business by its proprietor from one location to another. Jacob, Sr., sold his beer and wine factory in Mettenheim in order to invest his capital in a similar enterprise in Milwaukee.

MILWAUKEE IN 1844

To travelers on the little transatlantic packets in the summer of 1844 all of Germany must have seemed to be moving to the United States. During the summer, Rhinelanders and other Germans came to Milwaukee at the rate of over a thousand a week, most of them headed farther west.[9] Some of these migrants from an old and formal civilization were rudely shocked by Western Americans. Christian Preusser, a young watchmaker from Nassau, who was a shipmate of the Bests but did not reach Milwaukee until a couple of months later, wrote:

When I arrived here in October, 1844, I was disappointed and almost disgusted. . . . . I landed at the foot of Huron Street and by the time I reached Trayser's little tavern, where I took up my abode, my boots were all covered with clay. Trayser's little tavern was located at the southwest corner of Martin and Market streets and was a great hangout for newly arrived Germans.[10]

[8] *Milwaukee Sentinel*, Dec. 9, 1894.
[9] Albert Bernhardt Faust, *The German Element in the United States*, I, 470.
[10] *Sentinel*, Dec. 9, 1894, and Oct. 16, 1895.

Ambitious businessmen like the Bests, however, must have received a quite different impression of this bright wilderness city of sixty-five hundred people. As Postmaster Jackson observed of the local kilns "those fellows were making bricks out of sugar and cream." [11] In the days before coal smoke blackened their light clay, these houses must have made an impressive contrast to the crude wooden structures seen by the travelers at other lake ports. Milwaukee's trim, light houses ended at Huron Street,[12] the road leading west from the lake-front wharf; and to the south the bay was edged by miles of tamarack swamp. To the passing visitor this was undoubtedly an ugly jungle, and to the boosters of neighboring Racine and Kenosha it was "the swamp that never could be filled," [13] but, to smart businessmen familiar with the lower Rhine, it must have offered infinite possibilities of cutting channels and creating new building land.

The Milwaukee River, a gently flowing stream that a little dredging soon made deep enough for paddle-wheel steamers, came down from the north on the west side of the earliest settlement leaving a peninsula about a mile wide between itself and the lake. Below the old town, the Milwaukee was joined by the Menomonee from the west and the Kinnickinnic from the south to form a natural interior basin that opened to the lake about two miles below the end of the high ground at Huron Street. The land to the west, between the confluence of the three rivers, rose to a small plateau topped by a cluster of cream-colored brick houses. This suburban village known as Walker's Point, largely settled by Irish families, was not included in Milwaukee until a year before the city charter of 1846.

The German area where the Best brothers, Charles and Jacob, Jr., lived and worked was along the west bank of the Milwaukee River, in what had been called Kilbourntown before it joined in 1839 with east-bank Juneautown to form Milwaukee.

---

[11] Western Historical Company, *History of Milwaukee, Wisconsin*, p. 1611.

[12] Huron Street is now named East Clybourn Street.

[13] Letter, A. J. Langworthy to Captain Pabst, Sept. 10, 1896. Where no location is specified, the reader may assume that letters quoted are in the company archives.

In 1843 a bridge had been built over the river from Division Street on the east to Chestnut Street [14] on the west bank, and, as the Bests crossed the bridge en route from their landing at Huron Street, Jacob, Jr., or Charles undoubtedly pointed to their small vinegar factory that could be seen a few hundred yards up the river with all the pride of managers showing off a new branch to the chief executive.

In spite of its muddy streets and crude outskirts, the new city must have been exciting to the Bests. It was much bigger than Mettenheim, and the people worked with a fresh energy unfamiliar to the Rhinelanders. Milwaukee supported both a daily and a weekly newspaper. Twenty-seven "hotels" were kept busy taking care of new arrivals. Forty lawyers were well occupied with land titles, partnership agreements, and the ensuing disputes. The three breweries were unable to meet the increasing demand for beer.[15] Milwaukee was already extending its trade to the back country by means of a plank road to Waukesha, and at the Huron Street wharf the grains from the interior were being shipped out on the lake boats that brought in a steady stream of new settlers and manufactured goods. A contemporary writes of this new entry port to the West:

The magnificent Side Wheelers the only practical means of reaching the East during the season of navigation in Milwaukee's early days, landed at docks running out in the bay, in the 3rd Ward; as the river had not been made navigable at that time, and the mouth of the river was about half a mile below the present entrance. In the winter months our mail was usually fourteen days from New York, there being little railroad facilities West of Buffalo. The steamers came daily during navigation to bring 1000 to 1500 people mainly from a foreign shore, and they scattered from here all over the country but were of great service to the merchants in buying supplies for their trip. These people brought with them the gold and silver of their locality and it was of infinite and puzzling variety. Alexander

---

[14] Division Street is now named East Juneau Avenue, and Chestnut Street is now West Juneau Avenue.
[15] *Milwaukee Leader*, Jan. 30, 1929.

Mitchell's bank was then on the corner of Main (near Broadway) and Wisconsin Sts., where is now the office of the Central Wisconsin R.R. Mitchell issued a sheet giving the value of these coins, receiving them all in deposit. It was the greater part of our circulation, though causing much trouble to those not acquainted with their values.[16]

It would seem that almost any good businessman arriving in Milwaukee when the Bests did would be bound to succeed to some degree. The city's great period of growth was just beginning, and the increasing influx of Germans assured a dependable supply of both workers and consumers; but success on the scale of the Best organization, which within about thirty years was to represent the largest investment of any Milwaukee business, called for something more than merely average good luck in a good situation.

[16] A. J. Langworthy to Pabst, Sept. 10, 1896.

CHAPTER II

ESTABLISHING THE BUSINESS IN MILWAUKEE

As wise businessmen, the Bests spent some weeks of the summer of 1844 deciding where to locate their brewery. From the standpoint of later transportation needs it would have been best to build on West Water Street near the vinegar factory, but land values were relatively high there, and probably none of them at this time thought in terms of other than local customers who could be reached by horse-drawn wagon. The brothers also feared that if they dug the deep storage cellars necessary to keep lager beer cool, in the days before the general use of ice, the river might flood them. There was high land close by. Four blocks westward from the river at the edge of the settlement, where the Prairieville Road left Chestnut Street, the ground rose to a level ridge. Just below the summit of this ridge, which commanded a beautiful view of the river and the city, the Bests decided to build their brewery.

THE PROBLEMS OF BREWING

The Bests brought to their new establishment advanced European knowledge of the difficult art of brewing fine beer. Since no one yet understood the chemistry of beermaking at any point in the process, experience was the principal guide. Centuries of experience in Germany had routinized most of the procedure, and the Bests knew practically all there was to know about it.

The making of beer is as old as recorded history, going back at least to Egyptian times. By the early Middle Ages, beer was so standard a commodity of Western civilization, clerical as well as lay, that it was accepted for church tithes. Beer was also required in the conduct of higher education. Each college at Oxford had its brewhouse, and each fellow had his tankard, wine bowl, stoop, salt, and spoon. The famous scholar, Erasmus, complained of one Oxford brew that it was "raw, small, and windy." [1] In the earliest days of Harvard College the house mistress, called before a committee of investigation, pleaded:

For beer and bread, that it was denied them by me betwixt meals, I truly do not remember. . . . . And for their wanting beer, betwixt brewings, a week or half a week together, I am sorry that it was so at any time, and should tremble to have it so, were it in my hands to do it again, ... [2]

Shortly after the drawing up of the Federal Constitution, both Massachusetts and New Hampshire exempted breweries from taxation for limited periods in order to substitute beer for rum, whisky, and other strong liquors. Brewing moved westward with the early settlers. Chicago, for example, had a brewery in 1833 when there were scarcely a thousand people in the whole area. [3]

The English and American brews up to 1840 were all of the type known as top-fermentation beer in which the yeast stayed on top of the brew until skimmed off. This type included ale, porter, and what was generally called strong or common beer. Brewed according to English practices, the alcoholic content of such beer ran high, yet it did not keep for very long periods. It could be made well into the summer in northern areas, with the result that its manufacture and consumption was usually a hand-to-mouth affair, with as little as two weeks elapsing between the beginning of the brew and its sale to the customer.

The increased German immigration beginning in the late thirties brought to America men who understood the making of bottom-fermentation or lager beer of the Bavarian or South German type in which a yeast is used that sinks to the bottom of the brew. John Wagner of Philadelphia is generally conceded to have brewed the first bottom-fermentation beer in America in 1840, [4] but by 1845 it was being introduced into other parts of the country.

[1] Samuel Eliot Morison, *The Founding of Harvard College,* p. 98.
[2] Morison, p. 233.
[3] *One Hundred Years of Brewing,* pp. 182-83, 202.
[4] *One Hundred Years of Brewing,* p. 207.

In the early stages of preparation there is little difference in the making of the various kinds of beer and ale. They all start with barley malt as their principal ingredient, with the exception of some beers made from wheat which have never gained wide acceptance in this country. The malting of barley was the first step in the process at most of the early breweries; for the demand for malt in most sections had not as yet produced specialized malthouses, and, in any case, the larger brewers generally preferred to prepare their own malt. Carefully selected barley of uniform size and age, preferably of the two-row or Chevalier variety, as far as the Germans were concerned, was thrown into a large vat of water known as the steeping tub. After one to two and one-half days of steeping, during which time the light grains and other impurities floated to the surface and were skimmed off, the wet barley was spread over the stone or cement floor of the malthouse. Here the grain germinated for from three and one-half to as much as twenty-one days, depending upon the practice of the particular brewer. The main purpose of germination was to modify the barley by natural growth and to produce an enzyme, called diastase, that could convert the insoluble starch of the barley into soluble sugars necessary for brewing. Frequent stirring and turning over were necessary at this stage in order to produce uniform results. The process was generally regarded as completed when a little sprout on each barley grain, known as the acrospire, had grown to the length of the barley kernel itself.

The germinated barley, called green malt, was then shoveled onto a perforated iron floor above a kiln for drying. The hot air from the kiln, which had to be kept under 160 or 170 degrees F. so as not to darken the germinated barley if light beer was to be made, dried the grain within two to three days. This finished the process, and the barley, now called malt, was removed from the kiln, and conveyed by buckets or wheelbarrows to a storage place where it was allowed to age some weeks before being used in a brew.

The aged malt was next taken to the brewhouse for mashing or mixing. In small nineteenth-century establishments like that of the Bests, brewhouse and malthouse were all one. Mashing by the German system of decoction in use at this time was a tedious process. The malt, having first been broken or ground to a proper texture, was poured into water heated to about 120 to 130 degrees F. Some of this mash was then drawn off and boiled in the big brew kettle which was often the only vessel for boiling purposes. The boiled mash was then readded to the mash tub, and the process repeated a number of times. The process involved here, only partially understood, was that of changing the starch of the barley malt to malt sugar and dextrins and dissolving these to form a syrupy liquid called the wort, from which the beer would be made. During the course of this process the mash was continually stirred with long paddles and rakes until the wort, as shown by a saccharometer, a special type of hydrometer for ascertaining specific gravity, had dissolved most of the sugar and other extractable substances from the malt. The "spent" grain was now strained off, and additional warm water was run through it to extract still more sugar and also to dilute the wort. This process was known as sparging and the water used was called sparge water.

One can readily understand why a writer looking back on these early days could say,

The work required for the production of one brew of beer was exceedingly protracted and difficult. The hauling, dipping, pumping, breaking, stirring and boiling were tiresome work for the laborers, indeed, requiring from 15 to 17 working hours every day, and making the brewer's occupation one of hard toil and almost unbearable labor.[5]

The brewing itself, although this is also the name usually given to the whole process of beermaking, involved boiling the wort in a large open metal receptacle of over a hundred gallons capacity. Small quantities of hops were added from time to time

[5] *One Hundred Years of Brewing*, p. 86.

and the wort stirred by hand. Regulating the fire under the brew kettle must have been a difficult task in the Best brewery. Coal was not to be had in Milwaukee in the earliest years, and hence wood was used as a source of heat. Anyone who has tended a wood fire knows how difficult it is to keep an even temperature above it, yet if the wort were heated too fast it would be burned or scorched and the beer would acquire an unpleasant flavor. The wort was first boiled for some hours to concentrate it, and to coagulate albuminous substances which were then strained off. Brewers differed as to whether the wort with hops added should next be boiled for as little as twenty minutes or for several hours, but, in any case, after the boiling, the hops were strained off by a device known as a hop jack and the wort passed into cooling vats to prepare it for fermentation. It was at this point that the difference in process between ales, top-fermentation beers, and bottom-fermentation beers became marked, and where in those days the principal worries of the brewmaster began.

Today we know that there are dozens of types of cultivated or cultured yeasts, many more types of wild yeasts, and numerous bacteria that act somewhat like yeast. But in 1844 there were only two major distinctions recognized in brewing yeasts: top-fermentation ycast and bottom-fermentation yeast. Each brewery had its own yeast of one or both varieties, which it raised itself and endeavored to keep "pure." Actually the brewery's stock of "pure" yeast was undoubtedly made up of many varieties, and keeping it pure meant simply that wild fungi and other bacteria were eliminated as far as possible. All yeast is a unicellular fungus which in the course of growth through budding, or partition, secretes an enzyme known as zymase that, depending upon the type of yeast, converts the various sugars such as maltose, fructose, dextrose, and glucose into alcohol. As brewers already knew, and as Pasteur was to demonstrate a few years later, without the presence of yeast or some similar fungi, bacterial organism, or enzyme, fermentation will not take place.

None of these biochemical operations was understood in the 1840's. In fact, there were widely varying theories as to why the yeast brought about fermentation, and as to just what fermentation was. The misgivings with which any brewer tried a strange yeast in this period is well illustrated by the following story told by the Bests' first brewmaster, Max Fueger. One of the Milwaukee brewers, named Wagner, ordered some bottom-fermentation yeast from Bavaria which was so long delayed in transit that he doubted whether the culture would still be pure enough for fermentation purposes. Thinking over the risks involved, he offered to sell the yeast to Phillip Best for the cost of transportation alone.

Phillip hesitated for a time, but, after thinking it over for a day or two, he finally decided that he would make the attempt to brew lager beer if the yeast were good enough to warrant the efforts. Finally the yeast came. It was packed in a strong wooden box about a foot and a half square. The yeast was packed in a sort of sawdust around which were wound several folds of strong hop-sacking. The wrapping was carefully taken off, and to the astonishment of all of us, the yeast was found to be in good condition. We took it to the top of the main building and allowed it to dry out thoroughly. Then we dissolved the whole mass in a pail and allowed it to run through a sieve, which withheld the sawdust and permitted the yeast to pass into a proper receptacle below.

The capacity of our kettle in those days was just eighteen barrels, and we calculated that the yeast we had was just about enough for one brew. Neither Phillip nor I slept very much while we were trying the new yeast, but it was a success, although we did make better lager beer after six months than we did the first time. After our first trial, we brewed top fermentation beer in one brew and the next brew was a bottom fermentation beer.[6]

The old brewmaster did not mean that they made top-fermentation beer every other time from the same yeast. Rather, he refers to the fact that they were also making ale at this time,

[6] *One Hundred Years of Brewing,* p. 224.

which is a top-fermentation product. Undoubtedly some top-fermentation beer was made occasionally for immediate consumption as good lager takes many weeks for the brewing and fermenting or lagering processes.

The preparation of top-fermentation beer, or ale, from the cooling wort was much simpler than lager. This top fermentation could go on at ordinary temperatures of 65 to 70 degrees F., the general rule being not to allow the temperature to exceed 75 degrees F., since above that temperature lactic acid tends to form in the beer. When the wort had cooled to the temperature required for fermentation the yeast was added, or was "pitched" as the brewers' expression goes. Top-fermentation ales might ferment in four days or even less, whereas beer generally takes considerably longer.

For bottom-fermentation beer the wort had to cool to about 45 degrees F. before the yeast was added. This meant that without ice or artificial refrigeration it was only possible to brew bottom-fermentation beer during months when normal cellar temperatures could be kept this cool. In Bavaria the period was fixed by law as from September 29 to April 23, but in areas like Milwaukee where ice was plentiful in the winter the brewers may well have extended this time, even in the early days, by icing their cellars or floating ice on the beer in metal containers called "swimmers."

During the first or principal stage of fermentation of lager beer, an increasingly thick white froth appears on the surface of the fermenting tub, covering the entire surface by the end of the first or second day. At this stage the fermenting brew is said to be "in kraeusen." In a few hours the kraeusen disappears and the first stage of fermentation is finished. Even at this early period, however, the good brewer tested the amount of fermentation with a saccharometer to measure the change in the specific gravity of the wort. This varied according to the simple principle that the alcohol in the wort weighs less than the sugar that it replaces, and therefore the degree of fermentation can be measured by this change in the liquid.

Up to this stage, except for the difference in temperature, there was relatively little difference in the preparation of top- and bottom-fermentation beer. But at the end of this first fermentation, the top-fermentation beer or ale required only the removal of the yeast by skimming to be ready to be put into casks for delivery, whereas the bottom-fermentation or lager beer still had to go through a secondary or "ruh" (rest) stage of slow fermentation.

The lager was now strained and drawn off, just above the settlings, into what were called ruh casks that were placed in the coolest part of the cellar, an ideal temperature for this stage being only a degree or so above freezing. The ruh fermentation in which certain substances settle out and the alcoholic content increases slightly might take anywhere from ten days to several weeks, depending upon the practice of the brewer and the amount of time before the brew was needed on the market.

From the ruh or secondary fermenting casks, the beer was put into storage tanks of a capacity of from 17 to 35 barrels, also in as cool a place as possible. During the latter part of the storage period at least, the tanks were kept closed in order to accumulate additional carbonic gas, or if this was not done young beer from the kraeusen stage of fermentation was added to the barrels of old lager in the ratio of about one part of new to four parts of old in order to provide fresh carbonation. This process is known as kraeusening. In the old days the beer was next drawn off into 31-gallon barrels or fractional barrels for sale. These barrels were tightly bunged and kept in the coldest part of the cellar until sold. As the production for the heavy summer drinking had to be made in the winter or early spring months, large storage cellars were necessary.[7]

FOUNDING AND MANAGING THE BREWERY

Such was the state of the brewing art in the fall of 1844 when the four Best brothers, Jacob, Jr., Phillip, Charles, and Lorenz,

---

[7] For additional information, see *One Hundred Years of Brewing*, pp. 102-4.

joined their father in starting the brewery on Chestnut Street Hill. The small capital necessary for such a business was probably supplied by Jacob, Sr., from the proceeds of the sale of the Mettenheim property.[8] There is no record of what agreement the brothers had reached with their father, at this time, regarding the division of profits. Information about the personalities of the partners other than Phillip is also lacking. Phillip was a born leader of a fiery, imperious type. His sharp nose and chin gave an appearance of unusual perspicacity to an otherwise rather normal looking blond-haired, gray-eyed German. Phillip was only slightly larger than the average man, but his love for dramatic speech and action made him a commanding figure in any gathering.[9] His father and older brother were apparently able to work with Phillip in reasonable harmony, and Lorenz was too young at the start to assert himself, but Charles, being perhaps too much like Phillip, chose to resume his former business of vinegar making in the spring of 1845, and withdrew from the family company.

Capital investment began on September 10, 1844, when the partners purchased from Christian and Carolyn Rolle for $190 lots 13 and 14 in block number 127 on Chestnut Street Hill.[10] These two adjoining lots, making a plot of about a hundred feet square, provided space for the combined brewery, malthouse, and dwelling that the Bests speedily erected. It was a high, one-story, L-shaped building with a ventilated cupola on top for the kiln-drying of the malt. It must also have had a large cellar underneath for the fermentation and storage of beer.

Even this modest beginning seems to have strained the family resources, already depleted by the expensive voyage from Europe and many months of enforced idleness. A. J. Langworthy, a

---

[8] Victor S. Clark, *History of Manufactures in the United States,* I, 167, says: "Some country breweries represented an investment less than $1,000, and what were accounted considerable establishments sold for twice or three times that sum."

[9] His physical details are taken from his passport of 1838.

[10] See deed.

Milwaukee ironmaker, wrote of the difficulty the Bests had in finding the money necessary for manufacturing equipment.

In the summer of the year mentioned [1844] Phillip who was the businessman of the firm, came to my office on the canal, and asked me to make him a steam boiler to be used in the manufacture of "Lager Beer." I told him that I was familiar with their construction, it being a part of my business while in New York, but I disliked very much to have the noisy things around, and did not wish to do so. After considerable urging however I consented to make it, as I found a machinist in my employ that was used to riveting. I could only find two sheets of boiler iron in Milwaukee and went to Racine and Kenosha who were then in earnest rivalry with us, as to a metropolitan seat on the Lake Shore, each declaiming their superior advantages over each other, and over Milwaukee, a village in the swamp, which never could be filled. Both Racine and Kenosha were as sanguine as young roosters before their first defeat, and it is laughable to contrast the situation today. From Kenosha I went to Chicago and in all four of these towns there was not enough iron to make a single section of the boiler. On my way home with Captain Walker one of the old time Sidewheeler Captains, I made arrangement with him to get the iron for me in Buffalo and on his return he did so, and in four weeks thereafter the boiler was ready for delivery. I planned its construction and helped to do the riveting, mainly done on the dock out of doors, and the inhabitants of Milwaukee hearing the music of riveting all came to see it and I think if the roll had been called at that time that every man, woman, and child except the invalids, would have answered "here." It was the first boiler made in the territory of Wisconsin, four years before she was admitted to statehood. . . . . When the boiler was completed Phillip came with a red handkerchief loaded with these various coins taken in his business, which I think it took more time than an hour to count, and proved a great deal less than the amount due. At that time credit was unknown, all goods were spot cash. I could see that Phillip was dejected and in trouble. He said, "I had made the arrangement and had the promise of some money today on a mortgage of the premises where the boiler was going, but was disappointed. The man could not raise the money. I will leave the boiler until I can make money to pay the balance." I said to him, "Phillip, take the boiler, get to work as soon as possible and pay as soon as you can conveniently." He had not expected this and dare not ask it. I may say that he was filled with great joy, and ever after my most ardent friend. He then said, "The first keg of beer I put up will go to your house," and it came. He also said, "You shall have free beer as long as you live," and you can bear evidence that I never abused the promise, although in the 80's am still in excellent health, and am not likely to do so. Schandein told me after the noble-hearted Phillip went to Europe where he left his mortal remains, that in a serious mood he reminded him that the promise he made to me must not be forgotten.[11]

Judged by the breweries of a later day, the Bests' beginning was on a very small scale. But it was customary for nineteenth-century American business to start on a "shoestring," and the Best works were probably not far from the average size of the breweries of the 1840's. They are reported to have started their production at around 300 barrels of beer per year, and statistics show that there were many breweries in the United States producing as little as 100 and 150 barrels a year.[12] Furthermore, the Bests did not limit themselves to beer during the first couple of years; ale, porter, and rye and corn whisky were also manufactured by the partners. This diversification over five different products was probably an experimental undertaking until experience proved what the local demand was, and with operations on a small scale it may also have provided a more steady utilization of the family labor than would concentration on lager beer which could be brewed only during the cool months of the year. Except for a still for whisky, the same equipment probably served for all of these products.

Lager brewing must have begun not later than November or early December of 1844, as the first of Best's bottom-fermenta-

[11] Letter to Captain Pabst, Sept. 10, 1896.

[12] *Milwaukee Journal,* Apr. 21, 1939. Since Phillip Best, writing in 1847, called 16-gallon containers "kegs," it may be that production was in reality about 150 barrels. There is a similar question regarding barrel size and price on page 25.

3

tion beer was advertised for sale on February 22, 1845, together
with a notice of their whisky and also their vinegar. At the same
time, they offered to buy barley at 44 cents a bushel.[13] We have
no record of the price they put on their secondary products, but
beer sold for $4.50 per "keg" at the brewery and $5.00 delivered,
often by oxcart, around the town. After Charles's withdrawal
in 1845, Jacob, Jr., and Phillip apparently became equal partners with their father in the firm of Best and Company while
the young Lorenz remained an employee.[14] In 1850 Lorenz left
to join Charles and G. Fine in establishing the Plank Road
Brewery, the ancestor of the present Miller Brewing Company
plant.

The first record of a written partnership agreement between
the Bests on Chestnut Street Hill is a long document dated
August 6, 1851, that states in part:

It is therefore agreed by and between the parties to this agreement,
that they will be and remain partners in business as heretofore for
the space of three years from this date and until the death of one of
the parties. . . . .

And in case either the said party of the second part or the said party
of the third part shall die before the expiration of said three years,
and before the death of the said party of the second [sic] part, then
the wife of such deceased party shall have the right to continue said
business as partner assuming the place, rights and liabilities of her
deceased husband for the unexpired term of said space of three years
as aforesaid or she may at her option elect to secure five thousand
dollars for the share and interest of said husband in said partnership
property hereinbefore described . . . . plus one third of the incre-
ment of company property over and above the valuation of same at
the date of agreement.[15]

In 1853 at the age of sixty-six, Jacob Best, Sr., decided to withdraw from the business and leave the conduct of affairs to his

---

[13] Advertisement, *Wiskonsin-Banner*, Mar. 8, 1845. Date of first appearance noted
on advertisement.

[14] Endorsements on a short-term loan of 1846.

[15] See agreement. The company owed Jacob, Jr., $733 and Phillip $302 at this time.

JACOB BEST, SR.

sons. On January 14 of that year, Jacob, Jr., and Phillip gave a mortgage to their father for $5,500 representing his share in the business, the payment of which was to be spread over a number of years with installments coming due as follows: $1,500 coming due by October 1, 1853; $600 on October 1, 1854; $1,202.92 on October 1, 1855; and $38.45 every three months for the lifetime of Jacob, Sr., and his wife, Eva Maria. In addition, the brothers were to take over a personal note of Jacob, Sr., for $1,200 at 12 per cent interest, owed to Morgan Carpenter.[16] The father and mother were to have free use of the house and the well on the brewing property so long as either should live.

The brothers now entered into a partnership agreement of unlimited duration in which Jacob, Jr., was credited with an $8,249 share, and Phillip with $7,509.[17] Ironically, Jacob, Sr., retired on a modest basis just at the start of the nearly five years of profit making that must have far surpassed the total earnings of the business up to 1853.

EXPANDING THE BUSINESS

The business could only grow through the reinvestment of earnings plus such loans as could be negotiated in a frontier community where moderate interest rates ran to 10 or 12 per cent. A means resorted to, in 1846 at least, was to borrow to meet additional outlays required at the height of the selling season, and to repay the loan from the summer profits.[18]

As the records for this period are incomplete, there is no way of telling how often such loans were made. They must have been made more than once, however, for Phillip, particularly, pressed continuously for expansion. In the summer of their first producing season, when their volume was at the rate of perhaps 400 barrels a year,[19] the Bests invested in their first additional

---

[16] See mortgage and bond.

[17] See agreement.

[18] Mortgage loan negotiated July 21, 1846, paid off Oct. 21, 1846.

[19] There is no volume figure for 1845. Initial volume is generally set at 300 barrels, and by the spring of 1847, they were selling 28 to 30 barrels a week. (See p. 25.)

property. Byron Kilbourn, pioneer promoter of the area, and his wife sold the Bests the southwest corner of Ninth Street and Prairieville Road [20] for $125.[21] For the next two years the family worked away, probably more than doubling production without having to purchase additional property. By May 1847, with beer selling at the rate of 28 to 30 barrels a week, Phillip was sure of the family's success. He communicated his optimism to his wife's whole family, urging them to come from Hessen-Darmstadt to Milwaukee.

MILWAUKEE, May 10, 1847

DEAR MOTHER-IN-LAW, BROTHER-IN-LAW AND SISTERS-IN-LAW,

It is now high time that I reach for the pen myself, it was a great mistake on the part of Jacob that he was silent for so long. . . . . Therefore you must make up your minds all the more quickly, for he has written fully about what you must take along. For one perceives from all newspapers and letters that times are very bad. . . . . One beholds here how the farmer lives without worries, one seldom finds a farmer who doesn't have a newspaper in his house every week, the taxes he has to pay are about 5 to 8 "Gulden" on 100 hessian "Morgen." [22] In Germany no one knows how to appreciate the liberty to which every human being is entitled by birth, only here in America can he experience it. Here the farmer may speak as freely as the nobleman and the scholar, everyone may express his opinion in accordance with his knowledge and judgment, for all the laws depend upon the people, and all the officials as well; that is, the people get together and elect them the way the burgomasters are elected in Germany, and they receive no more remuneration than they need for a reasonably good living. There is a tremendous difference, here the officials and priests are dependent upon the people, and in Germany the people are dependent upon the officials and priests. The preachers' trade is a poor business here, they have to toil at it in the sweat of their brows.

I also want to write something to you about the Mexican War, it

---

[20] Prairieville Road is now named Winnebago Street.
[21] See deed.
[22] A gulden equals a Dutch guilder or about forty cents. A Hessian morgen was about 1.6 acres.

might frighten you somewhat if you should hear something about it and that without any definite basis. It is just about as far from here as it is from here to you, in keeping with liberty there is no compulsion to join in the war, only those who join voluntarily for pay. There were recently recruited again in the United States ten regiments, in the course of which two companies were shipped out from here also, one German and one American, they go directly to the capture of the capital of Mexico. Everyone receives nine dollars and board, and when he comes back again 160 acres of land, or if he is shot to death and has wife and children or parents they get it, if these are in Germany then they get half the value of the land sent to Germany. They believe that the Americans will win the war against the Mexicans very soon, for they have already conquered some of the major fortresses, whereby the American armies, which include many Germans, proved themselves very valiant. Many a German has lost his life in this wonderful region of Mexico. A great deal of money has been collected in the United States (and still is) to give partial support to the unfortunate poor Europeans. You cannot imagine how much flour and wheat is already being produced in this young state. A great deal of this flour (packed in light barrels) goes to Europe, I believe most of it remains in the Netherlands, Ireland and France. For here there is most excellent wheat land, and it will become one of the best states in America, and Milwaukee is and remains the first city in the state, for it already numbers 12,000 inhabitants. The property of people who bought places for themselves here three years ago and built thereon rises tremendously in value and likewise the land. For we see that in our own business, it goes so well now, that I could never have imagined that it could develop as far in ten years as it is now. Every week now we brew 28 to 30 kegs of beer, a keg is 64 quarts, the price thereof is when fetched from our house 4½ dollars per keg, if we deliver it ourselves with our conveyance then it costs 5 dollars.

We have three horses and want to buy another one, for the delivery of beer in the city and in the country, and at the same time we grind our malt with horsepower, we grind about 8 "Hessian Malter," [23] in 1½ hours with two horses, and it is very easy for

---

[23] One malter equals about eight bushels.

them. We use 20 to 25 "Malter" barley every week. The grain prices are at present, wheat 8 Gulden per Malter, corn 4 florins 30x.,[24] barley 4 florins, oats 3 florins.

Well dear friends, if you want to decide upon this important step, then the sooner you do it the better. For that very reason I am sending this letter by steamer via England, if only you could get ready so as to commence your journey in the first days of August, I would not advise it with children at a later time in the year, and don't you go on any other vessel than a mail-ship from Havre to New York. For these make the fastest and safest crossings and have good water. You do not need any passports. Make your contract with Streiker in Mainz, carry your contract-paper, and Streiker will provide for your maintenance. You could be ready for the journey in 14 days or three weeks. Further I want to call your attention to one very important matter. If only one of you brings with him 2500 to 3000 Gulden to begin farming here, then you may safely and assuredly sell your property without any further concern. If one brings in less then he must go quite far out of the city by this time and work very hard in order to make a few acres tillable. Now if you intend to come, be so kind as to bring along enough of the best sort of black cloth for two pairs of trousers and two coats and one side of velveteen vest, may it cost what it will. Don't take any silver money along, but everything in Netherlands 10 franc pieces and 20 franc pieces, and then the wife must carry half of it well concealed on her person, and the husband the other half; but no money in a trunk.

Now I conclude my writing with many cordial greetings from our entire family. I also greet you cordially and wish you much good fortune on your journey.

PH. BEST

Postscript: But it is safer if you take passports along.

MARIA BEST

Greet for us all our good friends and acquaintances.

PH. BEST [25]

At the end of 1847 the partners bought the lot in the northwest corner of Ninth and Chestnut Streets for $100 from Gran-

[24] "X." presumably means "pfennig" or penny.
[25] Translated from the German. [Letter in the possession of Mr. Fred Pabst.]

ville E. Williams,[26] giving the Bests the entire west side of the block between Chestnut and Winnebago (formerly Prairieville Road).

By 1850 Best and Company was fourth largest of the twelve breweries reported in the Wisconsin census.

MILWAUKEE BREWERIES IN 1850 [27]

Name	Capital	Production	Value Products	Em- ployees	Average Monthly Pay Roll
R. G. Owens	$12,000	4,000 bbls.	$20,000	9	$225
John Braun	3,000	4,000 bbls.	18,000	5	70
L & A Blossom	14,000	3,900 bbls.	11,350	12	180
Best & Co.	7,400	2,500 bbls.	11,250	4	62
Henry Bevering	2,000	1,500 bbls.	6,750	5	100
Best & Fine	4,220	1,200 bbls.	5,400	2	200
Stols & Schuder [sic]	2,000	1,000 bbls.	2,800	3	75
Henry Nunnemacher	3,000	800 bbls.	3,600	3	50
Aleizt	1,500	600 bbls.	2,400	3	40
John Engleheart [sic]	2,000	520 bbls.	2,362	4	80
W. L. Hopkins (beer and soda)	1,000	3,000 doz. bottles	1,125	6	64
Taylor & Bros. (small beer)	800	33,333 bottles	1,000	..	...

According to the quite unreliable figures supplied to the census collector, the company used two and four-fifths bushels of barley and two and one-fifth pounds of hops to make a barrel of beer. The cost per barrel for material and hired labor came to $1.29, and the average barrel sold for $4.50. On the basis of sales of 2,500 barrels, this left some $8,000 to cover fuel, feed, plant overhead, and remuneration to the three partners.

During the nationwide boom of the 1850's, Milwaukee beer and ale production increased from about 20,000 barrels a year in 1850 to over 100,000 barrels by 1857.[28] While we have no figures for individual company production, as one of the four largest breweries, Best's share should have risen from the 2,500

[26] See deed.

[27] United States Census Bureau, manuscript form, "Wisconsin Census" [1850]. The report is incomplete; Neukirch & Melms and D. Gipfels, for example, are not included although there are many proofs of their existence at this time. See W.P.A., "Notes on Milwaukee Brewing," MSS.

[28] Milwaukee City Directory [1857-58], p. xv.

barrels reported in the former year to over 10,000 barrels by the latter. Judged by the 1850 calculations, profits may well have reached over $20,000 a year before the panic of 1857.

The rapid increase in production was accompanied by new construction. A lot on Market Street between Biddle and Martin,[29] in the heart of the city of 20,000 people, was purchased in 1850,[30] and in 1854 the Bests built there a brick building with a beer hall on the ground floor. Then in 1857, as sales mounted beyond the fondest hopes of the early days, a new main brewery with exceptionally large "caves" or storage cellars was erected on the north side of Chestnut Street, between Ninth and Tenth. The *Milwaukee Sentinel,* a paper not generally enthusiastic about brewing at this time, had this to say of the new building:

One of the most prominent buildings in the Second Ward is Best's new brick brewery on Chestnut Street Hill. It is situated a little to the left of Chestnut Street as you reach the top of the hill, and it may be seen from almost any part of the city. The building is a fine looking one, and were it not for a life-sized figure of a sturdy Teuton which is perched on top, in the act of sipping a glass of lager, one would never suspect its being a brewery. It has much more the appearance of a public building of some sort. Under and about this building are the extensive subterranean apartments where the beer is kept. They extend under the hill a great distance, and we believe are the deepest cellars in the city. The quantities of beer manufactured by Messrs. Best and Company are almost fabulous. They send a great deal to Chicago, as well as other places, and the demand for it at home is very large, and constantly increasing. Everybody has tasted Best's beer, and it's very generally acknowledged to be the best in the country.[31]

Had the new building not been started in 1857 it might not have been built for the next ten years, as that year marked a peak of prosperity for the Milwaukee brewers that was not to

[29] Biddle Street is now named East Kilbourn Avenue, and Martin Street is now East State Street.
[30] See deed.
[31] *Sentinel,* Oct. 9, 1857.

be achieved again until after the Civil War. The description of
the brewery given in the Wisconsin census of 1860, therefore,
would presumably apply to the plant in 1857, as no additions
were made during the depression years of decreased production.
According to this report the brewery was valued at $50,000, em-
ployed eight men, used ten horses for delivery and a steam
engine for power. Coke was the most important fuel consumed,
with wood second, and coal last.[32]

MARKETING BEER

The pioneer period of expansion up to the panic of 1857 provided the kind of market of which modern businessmen may
only dream. The market expanded so steadily that, if a firm
merely maintained its competitive position, each year's sales
could be counted on to exceed those of the year before. The
population of the city of Milwaukee grew from 6,500 [33] when
the Bests started in 1844 to nearly 40,000 by 1857.[34] The growth
of the market for beer was even more rapid than these figures
indicate, for during the great immigration of the fifties the German drinking habits spread to the rest of the population.

One result was a mushroom growth of new breweries. A few
thousand dollars would set up a brewery, and a good brewmaster was the most essential factor for success. The stage of development of marketing and technology gave no great advantage to the large organization as against the small. With hand
operations and a little advertising, the brewery with a 500-barrel
output could compete locally with one of 10,000 barrels. When
the Bests began, there were already five establishments making
beer and liquors. By 1850 the number had increased to fourteen
or fifteen, and by 1857 to twenty five [35]—and there was ample
room for all.

[32] "Wisconsin Census" [1860].

[33] *Leader,* Jan. 30, 1929.

[34] Estimate for 1857 based on Federal census figures for 1850 and 1860. Of 31,077
people in Milwaukee County in 1850, 18,622 were foreign born.

[35] W.P.A., "Notes on Milwaukee Brewing," as checked for 1857 by the *Milwaukee
Directory* [1857-58], p. xv.

Even at the 1857 level, the number of brewers was small enough to allow the tacit operation of monopolistic competition to maintain price without resort to any formal association. That is, a cut by any one of them would immediately have been met by a general cut, and each brewer knew, therefore, that he could not benefit from such tactics.[36] The increase of the local market and the opening up of new outside markets by better transportation also lightened the pressure on prices. Beer and ale production of about 20,000 barrels in 1850 grew to 75,000 barrels by 1856, and an estimated 100,000 barrels by 1857.[37] The result of all these factors was a rise in price during the boom of the fifties from $4.50 in 1850 to $7.00 by 1857.[38] At this point the annual value of Milwaukee brewery products passed that of the flour mills, and was exceeded only by the total of all forms of iron manufacture.

The most important marketing distinction in the brewing business has been between firms that depend for a major portion of their income on selling beer in markets reached only by long-distance transportation, and those that depend on local markets served by their own trucks. The firms selling regionally or nationally are called "shippers" or "shipping brewers." Success in this far-flung business depends on the maintenance of a large volume in the distant markets. As a local country brewer said even in the 1930's:

The little fellow can make a go of it, if he stays in his own backyard. That's the brewer whose output runs between 1000-1500. But if he starts branching out to Chicago and Milwaukee, in competition with the financially strong shipping brewer, the little fellow finds himself with too much overhead in trucks, barrels, and bottles.

A couple of trucks and a neighborhood clientele is the answer.[39]

[36] See examples of rigidity of brewers' price structure in the 1860's, p. 65.
[37] "Wisconsin Census" [1850]; *Milwaukee Directory* [1857-58], p. xv.
[38] Customers' Accounts—Day Book, 1849-1852; Milwaukee Chamber of Commerce, *Annual Statement of Trade and Commerce* [1859], p. 35.
[39] *Journal*, Dec. 31, 1937.

Continuous large-scale shipping from Milwaukee to Chicago and other out-of-town markets began in 1852 and, by the next year, 3,639 barrels were "exported." [40] A hot summer which exhausted the Chicago local supplies during the seasonal shutdown of lager brewing in 1854, and the completion of the Chicago and North Western Railway to Milwaukee in 1855 gave a further boost to the Milwaukee product.[41] At the top of the boom in 1857, beer was being shipped from the Cream City at the rate of 25,000 to 30,000 barrels a year.[42] Valentin Blatz, who succeeded John Braun, and Charles T. Melms were the chief competitors of Best and Company in the shipping business of the fifties. In local opinion the three companies seem to have ranked about equally in size and prestige. Although no reliable figures are available on the shipping sales of any of the triumvirate, we know that Best and Company, with an office on Randolph Street in Chicago by 1857, was beginning the drive for a national and world-wide market that was to be the most distinctive feature of the history of the company.

The importance of the colorful, far-flung shipping business that was to send Best's and later Pabst's beer to the most remote parts of the earth must not obscure the fact that in the early days the local Milwaukee County area was still the major market. Except for the operation, up until 1848, of a beer hall at the brewery no effort was made during the first six years to set up direct retail outlets in the city. After the brewery hall was closed, retail customers were directed to near-by Becker and Lehmann's. During the 1850's, however, family rivalry, as well as increasing production, gave Best and Company a fresh interest in retail selling. From 1850 to 1854 Charles and Lorenz Best, operating the Plank Road Brewery, were active local competitors. On April 27, 1851, they opened a beer hall in Dr. Jung's building, 247 East Water Street, at Market Square.[43] This may

[40] *Directory* [1854], p. 310.
[41] *Sentinel,* Sept. 12, 1854. The local beer ran out early in September.
[42] Milwaukee Board of Trade, *Annual Report of Commerce* [1856], p. 29.
[43] *Wisconsin Banner,* Apr. 1, 1851.

have been the immediate cause of the resumption of retailing, less than two months later, by the elder Bests. On June 18, 1851, the latter opened their beer hall on their newly purchased lot on Market Street between Biddle and Martin, "built according to the Philadelphia manner." On July 13, they also reopened the hall above the brewery.[44] The hall between Biddle and Martin seems to have been operated for some years after the completion of a third beer hall, the brick one on Market Square in 1854, but there is no mention of it in the records after 1856. The period of competition between the Bests ended in 1854, when, Lorenz having died, Charles closed the Plank Road Brewery. Two years later Charles sold his property and moved to Illinois.[45]

Retail selling seems to have been regarded by the Bests as the principal reason for advertising. From the closing of the brewery beer hall in 1848 until the opening of the Market Street hall in 1851, advertising was discontinued, presumably on the assumption that the saloonkeepers knew all the brewers and, unless one were trying to reach the general public, there was little to be gained from such expenditure. The attitude was shared by most businessmen in this period; the idea of strengthening dealers by direct factory advertising was not generally accepted.

Even when they operated beer halls, neither Best and Company nor any of the other brewers of the early days spent much on advertising. One suspects that the rather frequent Best advertisements in the *Wiskonsin-Banner* during this period may have been due largely to the fact that Moritz Schoeffler, the editor, married Margaret Best, Jacob, Sr.'s, daughter, on October 12, 1845. This German-language weekly, which became a daily in 1850 and changed its name to the *Wisconsin Banner und*

---

[44] *Wisconsin Banner,* June 23 and July 12, 1851.

[45] Western Historical Co., *History of Milwaukee, Wisconsin,* p. 1458. Charles returned in 1865 and operated a vinegar factory on Tamarack Street [now named West State Street] which burned in 1866. After the fire he operated the Caspar Meyer Saloon where he sold Best beer. *Wisconsin Banner und Volksfreund,* Feb. 26 and Mar. 9, 1866.

Volksfreund upon absorbing the latter in 1855, seems to have been the only medium employed by the Bests for direct advertising. Save for the years 1848-1850, their notices appeared in its columns rather regularly during the first ten years of the partnership, but, after that, indirect methods through paying for saloon advertisements of particular beers seem to have become the general practice among brewers. The good sellers' market from 1854 to 1857 may also have made direct advertising seem less necessary.

The following single-column factual statements appeared with slight variations in most of the weekly issues of the *Banner* from early in 1845 through 1847, except for the deletion of vinegar from the list of wares offered in 1846, and corn and rye whisky in the following year.

Best & Company, Beer Brewery, Whiskey Distillery & Vinegar Refinery on Prairieville Street, south side of the summit of the hill above Kilbourntown. . . . . Herewith we give notice to our friends that henceforth we will have bottom fermentation beer for sale, also good corn whiskey and vinegar by the barrel. We will endeavor to give our worthy customers prompt and satisfactory service. For barley we will pay 44¢ per bushel.

February 22, 1845.

Later this was shortened to:

Beer Brewery, Whiskey Distillery & Vinegar Refinery on Prairieville Street, South side of the summit of the hill above Kilbourntown. . . . . We wish to announce to our friends and well-wishers that we always have good bottom fermentation beer as well as good corn whiskey and vinegar for sale by the barrel.[46]

With the opening of the Market Street hall in June of 1851, more colorful advertisements appeared in the *Banner*.

The Beer Hall of Best & Co. Brewery on Market Street. Business Opening—Ale and Bock beer in bottles, Lager beer by the pint

[46] Advertisements from the *Wiskonsin-Banner*, Mar. 8 and July 12, 1845.

(Seidel)—Wednesday, the 18th of the month, we open our beer hall, built according to the Philadelphia manner. In order to be able to serve our guests with good Ale, Bock and Lager beer from our home brewery. . . . . Our establishment is fully equipped to meet all requirements which can reasonably be expected of a brewery. We have excellent cellars on hand so that our friends may be served as from a spring, and

> When the glasses loudly ring,
> All the waiters quickly spring,
> Serving promptly all the guests
> With the "bestest" of the Bests.
>
> And to Green as well as Grey
> Render service equally,
> If, as custom doth decree
> Each one pays the proper fee.[47]

Smaller notices followed the original announcement:

The Beer Hall of the brewery of Best & Company, Market Street. . . . . Ale and Bock beer in bottles! Lager beer by the pint.

The reopening of the hall at the brewery was also advertised:

Another Beer Hall! Tomorrow we open our beer hall on the hill in the 2nd Ward, above our brewery, where we will serve our visitors with the best of the "Bests." Also, we will serve genuine Swiss cheese, etc., as may be desired.

Lively advertising continued in the *Banner* during the summer:

Swiss cheese and Rhine wine in the beer hall of Best & Co. We have just received a large shipment of genuine Swiss cheese which we offer for sale by the pound, likewise, we have genuine Rhine wine available in bottles and by the glass. Our Lager beer spring bubbles as fresh and clear as ever—for our benefit and the good and refreshment of thirsty mankind.[48]

[47] The Greys were the Germans who came before 1848. The Greens were the forty-eighters. Carl Frederick Wittke, *We Who Built America, The Saga of the Immigrant,* p. 190.

[48] Advertisements from the *Wisconsin Banner,* June 20 and 30, July 12, and Aug. 30, 1851.

For the Fourth of July celebration of 1852, the company produced its first display advertisement consisting of a two-column spread picturing the brewery and announcing, "Next Sunday, July 4th, we begin the tapping of our Bock beer which has been brewed according to the Munich fashion." [49] The end of direct newspaper advertising in 1854 marks the beginning of a period of some thirty years during which Best's selling efforts were directed more toward the dealer than the ultimate consumer.

THE BESTS BECOME COMMUNITY LEADERS

The same qualities of intelligence, enthusiasm, and boldness that made Phillip Best a leader in his business also fitted him for leadership in his boom-frontier community. Even before he could secure his citizenship papers, he was taking such an active part in defense of the Jacksonian democratic state constitution of 1846, that Best's beer came to be called Constitution beer, as against Neukirch's, the chief anti-Constitution beer. To please all their customers, saloons claimed to stock both, even though the supply in truth might originate from the same barrel. Politically, Phillip's campaign was a failure for the liberal constitution was defeated by the voters, chiefly because of its Jacksonian clause against banks, and a more conservative document was approved the next year; but the advertising given Best's beer was of lasting value.

By the early 1850's the Bests had become recognized leaders of the German community. Jacob, Sr., was elected Second Ward assessor in 1850, and in the following year, Phillip, who had recently received his final citizenship papers, was rewarded for his vigorous support of the Democratic ticket, by Governor Nelson Dewey, with a commission as second lieutenant in the Milwaukee Dragoons. [50] In 1853 he was made a first lieutenant, and it was natural that he should be a member of the fifteen-man

---

[49] *Wisconsin Banner,* July 1, 1852.
[50] Information from citizenship papers and commissions.

committee to arrange the May festival.[51] When the Carnival Verein was formed in 1857, Phillip was selected to act as first Carnival Prince.[52]

The Republican party, organized in 1854 mainly over the issue of the exclusion of slavery from the territories of the United States, gained many adherents among the Germans along the Great Lakes, among them, Phillip Best. The latter's conversion from Jacksonianism may have been influenced by the skillful oratory of his fellow countryman, Carl Schurz, who settled in Watertown, Wisconsin, about this time, and started organizing German Republicans. Furthermore, as a liberal, Phillip was undoubtedly shocked by the Kansas-Nebraska Act of 1854, the Democratic bill opening these territories to settlement by slaveholders. He must have used his strong influence with the Milwaukee Germans to help elect the Republican ticket in 1858, as he was quickly rewarded by the new Republican governor with the brigadier generalship of the First Division of the state militia, and thereby became one of the military leaders of Milwaukee.[53] As a ranking officer of the city, he led parades and reviews such as the elaborate affair staged for Washington's Birthday in 1859 and the homecoming reception of the Ninth Regiment when it returned from the Civil War battle fronts in November of 1864.

After their retirement, both Jacob, Sr., and Jacob, Jr., were active in local political affairs. Less than two months before his death on January 28, 1860, Jacob, Sr., was chosen local school commissioner for the Second Ward. Jacob, Jr., became a Second Ward alderman in 1861.[54]

The liberalism of the Bests carried them into the ranks of the freethinkers. Charles and Phillip, together with their journalist brother-in-law, Moritz Schoeffler, and Charles's partner,

[51] See *Milwaukee Daily News and Review*, Aug. 13, 1890, for other activities of Phillip Best.

[52] *Sentinel*, Feb. 26, 1857.

[53] *Sentinel*, Feb. 19, 1858.

[54] *Sentinel*, Apr. 8, 1861.

G. Fine, formed in 1848 a mutual-aid society or lodge of a free-thinking complexion known as the Hermanns-Soehne, for sickness and death benefits, the seventh such lodge in the United States.[55] But there is no indication that such activities produced any hostility toward them on the part of the more religious Germans.

THE EARLY PROHIBITION MOVEMENT

One movement which neither the Bests nor the other Germans joined was the growing prohibition movement. The leaders in Milwaukee were the members of those "Yankee" religious communities whose teetotaling zeal was undoubtedly aggravated by their association with the Germans who openly enjoyed their drinking and flourished nonetheless for it. These native elements came largely from New England, and from the "burned-over" section of upper New York famed for its religious fanaticisms during this period. Northeastern Puritanism and southern German love of good living were bound to come into more or less violent conflict. Each civilization had its merits, but they were different and conflicting. While the first temperance society in Milwaukee was the Catholic Total Abstinence Society, started in 1842, the German or Irish Catholics never supplied any real impetus to the prohibition movement. The total abstinence groups sponsored by the Protestant church, such as the Washington Temperance Society formed in 1843, the Sons of Temperance, Wisconsin Division No. 1, founded in 1846, and other similar societies that mushroomed all over southern Wisconsin, were far more active. It was in opposing this prohibition movement that the Germans became important in the political life of the state.

At first the Germans and their liberal allies were not numerous enough to check the movement. In 1849, a unique license law passed the legislature requiring the posting of a $1,000 bond by each liquor vendor on which he might be sued for damages

[55] Koss, p. 277.

4

to individuals or the community arising from the sale of liquor. This law, and an amended version the following year, was fought by the Milwaukee Germans. On the fourth of March 1850, a large group of men and boys went to the house of Senator Smith and gave him a charivari with pans and other percussion instruments because of his action in procuring the passage of the liquor law.[56] While the group serenading Senator Smith was only about three hundred strong, they doubtless represented the feeling of a goodly part of the citizens of Milwaukee. Such opposition led to the repeal of the obnoxious laws in 1851 and to the establishment of the principles that were to govern the liquor trade for many years. The new Act provided for local option, and where the local authorities agreed to allow the sale of liquor, a $50 annual license fee was to be collected, and a $500 bond posted against gambling. The money from this Act was to be applied solely for the purpose of defraying pauper expenses unless the amount received exceeded the amount required for this purpose.

The enactment of complete prohibition by Maine in this same year inspired the Prohibitionists of other states to double their efforts. The largest temperance meeting ever held up to that time in Milwaukee assembled on February 12, 1852, and resolved, "That we firmly believe that a law similar to the Maine Liquor Law *can be enforced in this city;* that we respectfully request our Legislature to enact such a law at its present session." [57] The evening before, an anti-Maine Liquor Law meeting of smaller size sent a humorous petition to the legislature to prevent the immoderate use of cold water, of which the "Free Democrats" observed, "We presume if nobody drank any more cold water than its authors, such a law would occasion very little inconvenience." [58] In July of the following year, Jacob Best, Jr., Edwin D. Baker, and a number of other citizens inter-

[56] *Sentinel,* Mar. 3 and 6, 1850.
[57] *Sentinel,* Feb. 14, 1852.
[58] *Sentinel,* Feb. 14, 1852.

ested in preventing prohibition formed the Wisconsin Free
Trade Society whose constitution read:

The primary object of this organization is the perpetuity and defense
of the principles of *Free Trade* in all the departments of legitimate
commerce and the extension and formation of the same by the use
of every honorable and proper means, and especially the suppression
of *Temperance Fanaticism,* which involves the destruction of a
principle vital to the best interests of commerce.

It shall be the duty of each member of this Society first to attend the
primary meetings of the political organizations respectively, to oppose the nomination of any person for office whose views and policy
are not known to be in consonance with the objects of this organization; and again if such are put in nomination, to appear at the polls
on the day of election, to participate in labor for their defeat, and the
success of those who have pledged themselves uncompromisingly to
oppose the enactment by the Legislature of this State of a prohibi-
tionary liquor law, or any other measures calculated to impose *partial*
and *unjust* restrictions upon trade, and also to recommend and encourage the formation of similar societies throughout the State.[59]

Baker was elected president and Jacob, Jr., one of the vice-
presidents.

The results of the contest in the election of 1853 were confusing. The Prohibition candidates in most cases were defeated;
but on a referendum on the issue of complete prohibition, the
people of the state voted 27,000 to 24,000 for a prohibition law.
The legislature in view of this equivocal result took no action,
but a new legislature in 1855 gave way to the prohibition pressure; and, in March, one of a number of laws that had been introduced in the legislature was finally passed and sent to the
governor. This law did not prohibit the manufacture but simply
the public sale of intoxicating liquors. Democratic Governor
Barstow vetoed the bill on the strictly constitutional grounds
that it would permit forfeiture of property without sufficient
proof of the guilt of the individual, but the prohibition forces

[59] *Sentinel,* July 13, 1853.

insisted that the governor would have signed a complete prohibition bill if it had been presented to him in place of this partial measure. To celebrate the governor's veto, Jacob, Jr., and his fellow "Free-Traders" organized a great antiprohibition demonstration. A cannonade was fired, bonfires were lit in the streets, and a torchlight procession bore banners denouncing the *Sentinel* for favoring the prohibition bill.[60]

This ended the prohibition excitement in Wisconsin for the time being. The growing strength of the Republican party and its refusal to allow the prohibition issue to interfere with the more important one of exclusion of slavery from the territories, and the general public acceptance of this point of view, as well as the increasing size of Milwaukee in relation to the rest of the state, all stifled the early prohibition movement.[61]

GERMANS SHAPE MILWAUKEE CULTURE

Though German beer halls and gardens were deplored and denounced by the moralists of Yankee Hill, the competition between brewers to establish such places was the source of the most important contributions to the early social life of Milwaukee. These beer gardens and lager-beer halls were among the first centers of singing, instrumental music, and drama, and it was in these fields that Milwaukee reached Midwestern eminence by the 1850's.

Although the Germans were less than a third of the total population of the city by the 1850's, they made the largest contribution to its early culture. Literature and poetry, for which New Englanders and New Yorkers were famed in their own regions, did not flourish on the frontier, and participation in music and drama seems to have been discouraged by the Northeasterners' religious traditions. But Milwaukee by 1853 came to be called the "German Athens" and, although it may have lacked something of the literature, sculpture, and painting of

[60] *Sentinel*, Mar. 30, 1855.
[61] Joseph Schafer, "Prohibition in Early Wisconsin," *Wisconsin Magazine of History,* VIII (1924-25), 298.

the ancient city in its Golden Age, Milwaukee tried to compensate for this by a lusty enthusiasm for the livelier arts. Certainly it was one of the gayest cities of the West, and continued to be for many decades.

Music was the greatest love of the Germans. In 1843, when the town was little more than two villages on each side of the Milwaukee River, a Beethoven Society was organized. German quartets, not unassociated with the beer halls, were formed, then a German singing society in 1847, and finally a Musik Verein, or Milwaukee Musical Society, on May Day, 1850. Under the able direction of Hans Balatka, this group, within a year, gave a creditable performance of Haydn's *The Creation*. Amateur dramatic groups, also performing in the beer halls and gardens, led to the opening of a German theater by the Kurz brothers in 1852 that was the direct predecessor of the Pabst Theater of the 1890's. In the next year German operatic concerts were being given by the "Stout Singer" H. Heide, a famous tenor, at the Milwaukee Garden, at Best's Hall, and finally at Market Hall where complete scenes from German operas were acted out in costume, and where Adelina Patti's traveling company performed the *Czar und Zimmermann*. Two competent bands, which, by including strings as well as brass, could be used for chamber music, trios, and quartets were playing for German carnivals, May dances, and other folk celebrations by the middle fifties as well as for the outdoor concerts in the beer gardens of some of the larger brewers.

The old-fashioned German saloon, according to local historian William George Bruce, "exemplified in Milwaukee as Bier Wirthschaft, had its definite place in the social life of the community, and served a useful purpose. It possessed special value to the immigrant as an introduction to new-world conditions." [62] It also bred equality and democratic feeling among the Germans.

---

[62] William George Bruce, "Memoirs of William George Bruce," *Wisconsin Magazine of History*, XVI (1932-33), 367.

BREWING BUILDS ECONOMIC PRESTIGE

But in Western America of the mid-nineteenth century it was the economic power that brewing brought to Milwaukee, rather than the music and drama it sponsored, that seemed to be its most important contribution. From the early 1850's on, brewing was usually the second or third Milwaukee industry in value of product, and in some years it was first. Even during the period from the 1860's to the middle seventies when Milwaukee was the greatest primary wheat market, brewing came to represent a larger invested capital than flour milling, and whereas Milwaukee mill products and iron manufactures were scarcely to be distinguished from those of Chicago, Pittsburgh, or St. Louis, Milwaukee's beer became famous throughout the world within the course of the first three decades of its manufacture.

The city was a natural distributing point for goods and settlers going to the back country, and the shipping point for back-country products. The telegraph connected Chicago and Milwaukee as early as 1848 but, due to the competition of steamers on the lake, the first railroad organized in Milwaukee in 1849 was built not along the lake shore to Chicago but inland to reach the hinterland. Aided by a bond issue of $234,000 from the city, the railroad was opened to Waukesha in 1851. In the great flurry of railroad building resulting from the discovery that land mortgages could be converted into railroad stock subscriptions, a rail connection with Chicago was completed in 1855. A board of trade for grain dealing was opened in 1849, a corn exchange in 1855, a livestock market in 1856, and a chamber of commerce was organized in 1858. When a manufacturers association was formed in 1863, Phillip Best became one of the eleven directors, but no brewer was invited to be a member of the predominantly "Yankee" chamber of commerce during its first six years.

CHAPTER III

PRELUDE TO GREATNESS

PHILLIP BEST's leadership in the community and the popularity
of his products alike were powerless to hold trade in the depression that hit Wisconsin from 1857 to 1863. Workers might
applaud General Best as he led Civil War parades, but they had
little money to spend on beer.

Following an orgy of credit inflation by unsound banks in
the early fifties, Wisconsin was now paying the price of too
rapid expansion in railroads and other "production goods." The
same price had been paid earlier by Illinois, Indiana, and Michigan which were the chief sufferers from the panic of 1837.
Later, in the panic of 1873, Kansas, Nebraska, Minnesota, and
the Dakotas suffered most. In 1857, Iowa, Missouri, and Wisconsin were hardest hit. This panic was not felt so keenly in
some of the older sections of the country, where expansion was
slower and banks more conservative, but it partially paralyzed
the economic life of the newest states. On top of the financial
panic came secession and the Civil War, and the combination
of these events reacted on the Western credit system so ad-
versely as to reduce employment and income in the new areas
for nearly seven years.

The panic was started by the collapse of the New York security market in the fall of 1857. When their ability to float new
securities to get more capital ended, all the Wisconsin railroads
failed. Construction stopped, work crews were disbanded, and
farmers, who had bought railroad stock by mortgaging their
farms for over $4,500,000, found their securities worthless. The
depression made the mortgages practically worthless, too, and
caused the failure of many banks that held such mortgages.
Serious as this was, the effects of secession and the Civil War
were far more severe. As reserves against their note issues, many
state banks in Wisconsin and neighboring states held Southern

state bonds, which had been purchased because of their higher interest yield in relation to their market price. The secession of these states in 1860 and 1861 made their securities unmarketable at any reasonable price and put the weaker banks in a position where they could not possibly redeem their notes. The Wisconsin law empowered the state comptroller to levy assessments against institutions whose security for their notes had depreciated. In the spring of 1861 it was quite impossible for most of the Wisconsin banks to pay these assessments. The resulting bank failures, and the contraction of note circulation by the banks that did not fail, reduced the amount of state bank notes circulating in Wisconsin from $4,580,000 on January 1 to $1,591,000 at the end of the year.[1] Deflation on such a scale affected the already depressed business conditions so badly that prosperity did not return to Wisconsin until well into the year 1863. While Illinois and some of the older Western states did not suffer quite so severely as Wisconsin, even in those areas business remained depressed and market conditions poor.

In these early days beer was consumed mainly by the working population, for whom it was a luxury that had to be curtailed in hard times. The sensitivity of beer and ale sales to the level of employment and real wages was clearly shown after 1857. The available estimates placed Milwaukee sales at an estimated 100,000 to 125,000 barrels in 1857.[2] In 1858 they had slumped to 50,000 barrels and in 1859 to 42,000 barrels.[3] It appears probable that sales did not again reach 60,000 barrels until after the war. Furthermore, Best and Company and the other beer brewers suffered even more than these figures would indicate, for one ale company maintained its sales at the expense of beer during the first part of this period and hence its proportion of the total sales rose from 10 to 20 per cent between 1857 and 1859.[4]

[1] Frederick Merk, *The Economic History of Wisconsin During the Civil War Decade,* p. 208.
[2] Milwaukee Board of Trade, *Annual Report* [1856], p. 29.
[3] *Directory* [1857-58], p. xv; *Sentinel,* Jan. 24, 1860.
[4] *Sentinel,* Jan. 24, 1860.

In the midst of these competitive and financial difficulties, the retirement of Jacob Best, Jr., put a further strain upon the resources of the firm. As a result of paying off his share, the business headed into a trying period with depleted working capital. There is no record as to why Jacob, Jr., decided to end his partnership with Phillip toward the close of 1858. Perhaps he found it difficult to get along with Phillip's fiery temper during these adverse times, or wanted to guard his failing health. If he thought, as most Western businessmen did, that the depression would be merely an incident of a few months duration, he probably did not regard his withdrawal as a serious handicap to the firm; he did not foresee the election of Lincoln, the secession of the South, and the resulting Western collapse.

In December the brothers arranged to terminate the partnership on October 1, 1859, but Jacob, Jr., retired at once and left for a trip through Germany.[5] As far as the brewery business was concerned, Jacob, Jr., may have sold out cheaply. He received $9,500 plus the Market Square beer hall for his half of the business that Phillip reported in the census of 1860 as worth $50,000. Census reports of value are often exaggerated, however, and the downtown hall, a substantial brick building with saloon and restaurant fittings, may have been worth ten to twenty thousand dollars. Furthermore, early 1860 was the one time between 1857 and 1863 when prosperity seemed about to return to Milwaukee and this may have colored Phillip's estimate. If the brewery had a true market value of $30,000 in 1858 and the beer hall $10,000, Jacob, Jr., received about his fair share. He rented the beer hall, first to Frederick Heinemann and then to Grassmann and Orth, but, as the depression deepened in Milwaukee, he failed to secure a tenant and had to operate it himself in December of 1862.[6]

The $9,500 due Jacob, Jr., was secured by a mortgage on the brewery property which was to be paid in two equal install-

[5] *Sentinel,* Dec. 16, 1858.
[6] *Banner und Volksfreund,* Dec. 6, 1862.

ments on October 1, 1860, and October 1, 1861.[7] The continuing bad conditions made it difficult for Phillip to provide working capital for the business and still meet these payments. On October 11, 1859, he replenished his cash by borrowing $2,300 at 10 per cent from his father, and on November 8, 1860, he paid Jacob, Jr., only $2,500. Not until July 2, 1868, did Phillip pay the one-year note due to his father. On October 8, 1861, he was able to pay Jacob, Jr., only $2,700.21, to which he added $2,458.12 on August 15, 1862. Not until January 8, 1864, was the entire debt to Jacob, Jr., paid and the mortgage canceled.[8]

The period from 1859 to early 1864, during which time Phillip ran the brewery alone, were years when no Milwaukee brewer could do more than cut expenses to the minimum and wait for better days. The sales of Best and Company declined from a level of 7,000 barrels, reported in the census of 1860, to 3,677 for 1863. The latter figure, however, is an exact amount based on tax returns, and is not strictly comparable to the 1860 figure that may have been set with an eye to favorable publicity. Meanwhile, Phillip's health was declining, and he wished to retire, but there was no one in the immediate family to take over the business. The solution to his problem came through the marriage of his daughter, Maria, to the man who was to provide, in brewing, the most brilliant leadership of his generation, Frederick Pabst.

FREDERICK PABST

Pabst was the kind of man about whom legends gather, and in describing his early life a selection must be made of those stories best substantiated and most widely accepted. There is an unconfirmed report that the Pabsts were descended from a noble Dutchman, Paul Pabst von Ohorn, who established himself in Saxony in 1470.[9] Accounts generally agree that Frederick Pabst's father, Gottlieb, was foreman of a large estate at Nichol-

[7] See mortgage papers.
[8] See records of loans and mortgage papers.
[9] *One Hundred Years of Brewing*, p. 224.

ausreith in Thuringia where Frederick was born on March 28, 1836.[10] Frederick's father and mother, Fredericka, came with their child to the United States in 1848, not apparently for political reasons but because friends had praised the opportunities in America and particularly in Milwaukee. The elder Pabst, however, found no opportunities to his liking in the Cream City and, having exhausted his savings, he and his family were forced to go to work in a boardinghouse in Chicago. The death of the mother in the cholera epidemic of 1849 ended their arrangements at the boardinghouse, and Gottlieb became a cook at the Mansion House where young Fred waited on tables for $5.00 a month and board.

This was obviously no job to satisfy a boy with the spirit of Frederick Pabst, and, after two years, he gave up hotel work and took to the sea as cabin boy on one of the Goodrich Line steamers plying Lake Michigan. There is a widely repeated story, often told by Frederick Pabst himself, that illustrates his forcefulness and determination at this early age. As a cabin boy it was his job to collect the tickets of passengers as they left the ship. One day at Chicago, Captain Ward, one of the owners of the Line, tried to leave without a ticket and was stopped by Pabst. Refusing without proof to credit Ward's story regarding who he was—Pabst had never seen him before—he forced the disgruntled officer to return to his cabin and wait for proper identification. One of the interesting parts of the legend, revealing Pabst's personality, is that he did this in such a way that Captain Ward did not hold it against him later, but rather made it a reason for greater respect.

By using his spare time to study navigation, and offering pilots relief at the wheel, Pabst became a first mate on the Goodrich Line "Traveler" at the age of twenty. Soon after, he distinguished himself by rescuing the captain and several passengers from the burning steamer, "Niagara." [11] He used his

---

[10] Except where otherwise noted, material on Frederick Pabst's early life is from the W.P.A., "Notes on Biography of Captain Frederick Pabst," MSS.

[11] John Goadby Gregory, ed., *Southeastern Wisconsin; A History of Old Milwaukee County*, II, 1213.

spare time the next winter to take a course in bookkeeping that must ultimately have been of great value to his business career.[12] In 1857, he was made captain of the Goodrich steamer "Huron." As it was customary with the Line to have captains own a share in their ship, Pabst became a part owner at one time or another in several of the Goodrich Line's vessels, and ended as a shareholder in their newest and finest ship, "The Seabird."

Phillip Best liked to travel by boat, and was frequently on Captain Pabst's ships. In 1860 the twenty-four-year-old Captain met Phillip's fifteen-year-old daughter, Maria, either by fishing her out of the water when she fell off a gangplank when boarding his ship, "The Comet," or in the more prosaic fashion of being invited to the Best's home in Milwaukee. On March 25, 1862, they were married.

After this, when he was not on the lake, the Captain lived with the Bests. In 1863 he was elected a Second Ward alderman,[13] proof not only of Phillip Best's standing in the community, but also, and more important, of young Pabst's winning personality.

Because of the demands of increasing business and Phillip Best's wish to retire, home ties undoubtedly would have drawn the Captain into brewing in a few years in any case. This decision was hastened, however, by a shipwreck, which undoubtedly made it easier for him to quit the sea. Caught too near the shore in December of 1863 by one of the sudden storms which are so frequent on Lake Michigan, he skillfully beached "The Seabird" on the sands of Whitefish Bay without casualties.[14] As the vessel was not moved until mid-July, and the repairs cost approximately $20,000, the Captain undoubtedly had to pay over most of his share in her to the Goodrich Line.[15] Whether he had anything left to invest in the brewing business is impos-

[12] *Milwaukee Free Press*, Jan. 2, 1904. Scrapbook clipping.
[13] *Sentinel*, Dec. 9, 1863.
[14] *Sentinel*, Dec. 19, 1863.
[15] *Banner und Volksfreund*, July 9, 20, 27, and Aug. 24, 1864. "The Seabird" was destroyed by fire in 1868. James S. Buck, *Pioneer History of Milwaukee*, I, 145.

PHILLIP BEST

sible to tell, but, in any case, the business needed managerial help as much as additional capital and Phillip seems to have been glad to take him in as an equal partner at the beginning of 1864.

The marriage of Phillip's younger daughter, Elizabetha, or "Lisette," to Emil Schandein on May 16, 1866, added the other member of the team that was to run the business so brilliantly for the next twenty years. Schandein, who had attended a scientific and technical school in Germany, contributed knowledge that Frederick Pabst lacked, and he shared with the Captain the ability to make friends and to command the respect of the community.

PHILLIP BEST RETIRES

Phillip Best now felt able to indulge in his wish to retire from business. On October 15, 1866, the partnership between Best and Pabst was dissolved by Phillip Best, paying Frederick Pabst $21,057.95 for his share in the business. Then a new agreement was entered into whereby Pabst and Schandein each paid Best $21,057.95 for a half interest, $6,057.95 down, and the remaining $15,000 in quarterly installments over six years. This sale did not include any of the brewery property or buildings, but merely the business itself and the movable equipment used in it. For the use of the property, Pabst and Schandein were to pay Best $4,800 per year.[16] These figures would indicate that the value of the entire business, including property and equipment, was by then, due largely to the general advance in prices, probably $100,000.

Shortly before his retirement, Phillip Best became president of the Fifth Ward Savings Bank, and also a director in the Second Ward Savings Bank.[17] But he had only a few years in which to enjoy his new honors and leisure. While in Germany in the spring of 1869, he became seriously ill, and Schandein

[16] See papers concerning dissolution of partnership, bill of sale, articles of agreement, and lease agreement.
[17] Chamber of Commerce, *Annual Statement* [1865], p. 72; *Sentinel,* July 19, 1869.

and other members of the family left to join him in June. He died at Altenglan, Germany, on the seventeenth of July 1869, and was buried in accordance with his dying request in the cemetery of his native village of Mettenheim.[18]

ORIGIN OF THE UNITED STATES BREWERS' ASSOCIATION

The changes in the Best partnership that transferred control of the business to young men untrained in brewing coincided with momentous developments in the organization of the brewing industry. Up to this time, the twelve hundred or more separate producers had never been organized for co-operative action. While the threat of prohibition had led to ~~ ~r propaganda by local groups, the fact that this was a st   r discouraged joint action by out-of-state brewers even wh   y were as near to each other as Chicago and Milwaukee or Newark and New York. But with the passage of the Act of Congress of July 1, 1862, effective September 1, placing a $1.00 per barrel tax on beer sold, and a $100 license tax on brewers producing over 500 barrels per year, the brewers realized that they must get together for the purpose of representation in Washington.[19] The five cents a gallon duty on imported malt liquors, passed on July 14, 1862, opened new possibilities of protecting the home market from German imports through a really effective tariff, and this further underlined the value of collective action. The brewers of New York City, which has always been the largest consuming center, led the way on August 21 by forming a local association that summoned a national congress to meet there on November 12.

While the Milwaukee brewers were not represented as an organization at the first meeting, Charles T. Melms, at that time the city's largest producer, was appointed to a committee to draft amendments for the internal revenue act.[20] The national

---

[18] *Sentinel*, June 11 and Aug. 16, 1869.

[19] Factual details for this section are largely drawn from *One Hundred Years of Brewing;* and Gallus Thomann, *Documentary History of the United States Brewers' Association.*

[20] Thomann, *Documentary History,* I, 114.

movement, however, led to the speedy formation of local brewers associations all over the country, and the following year Milwaukee was represented.

The brewers were disappointed at being taxed at almost as high a rate per gallon of alcohol as the distillers, but the discussion at the first meeting, conducted in German, centered mainly upon the operational defects of the law and its enforcement by the Internal Revenue Department. While the tax was on barrels sold, the law provided no means for determining this quantity, and the Internal Revenue Department insisted upon examining the brewers' books and adopting the German practice of using bushels of barley consumed as a check on probable production. This measurement made no allowance for beer drunk by workers, given to guests, or lost through accidents. Furthermore, the tax collected on beer contracted for before July 1, 1862, but not delivered until after September 1, had to be borne entirely by the brewer.

The committee, of which Melms was a member, brought sufficient pressure in Washington during the winter to bring about a reduction of the tax to 60 cents a barrel from March 3, 1863, to April 1, 1864; but as the war was still in progress at the latter date, and federal revenues were more than ever inadequate, the amount was again set at $1.00 per barrel. In fact, a threat of much higher taxation had to be met and defeated in the latter year. The outraged attitude of the brewers and their friends of German origin to such proposals is well illustrated by this article from the *Baltimore Wecker,* a German-language newspaper.

Such a tax would raise the price of beer, which at present is being sold at $8 per barrel despite the existing beer tax, to the exorbitant rate of $30 per barrel and the saloon-keepers would not be able to sell even the present small glass of beer for less than 15 cents if it is enacted.

The local brewers are fully justified in uniting nowadays to counteract such unenlightened intentions of the committee in question. If the gentlemen in Washington need money, let them take it from where it can be had, not levy a tax upon the poor man's drink. Coaches, riding horses, dogs, champagne and for all that also brandy and whiskey they may encumber with additional taxes; but beer, which is already overburdened, they ought to spare a trimming. The Germans don't tolerate any finagling on this point.[21]

The Second Annual Brewers Congress established a system of finance to provide permanent funds for its activities through a $2.00 per member initiation fee and monthly brewery dues of 20 cents per 100 barrels of beer sold. The local brewers associations were to act as agencies for checking local sales. The fourth meeting in Milwaukee adopted the official name, United States Brewers' Association. A standing committee on "agitation" was set up to work for a better revenue law, and another committee undertook a survey of European methods of tax collection. As a result of the findings of the latter committee, the present stamp system was enacted by Congress on July 3, 1866. The brewer buys the stamps from the Internal Revenue Department in advance, sticks them on the barrels in a special place, and cancels them as the beer is sold. A 10 per cent allowance for loss in shipment was granted which more than covered lager-beer wastage, although it fell short of that ordinarily sustained in ale shipping. In 1868 the Internal Revenue Department issued a necessary clarifying decision that free beer drunk in the brewery was tax exempt.

The Civil War had so thoroughly quieted the prohibition agitation of the fifties that the issue was not even discussed by the assembled brewers until the St. Louis convention in 1866. Their more serious grievances at this time were the threat of closer supervision, a bill for which was defeated in 1870, and the 15 cents per bushel tariff on barley which raised costs substantially by allowing the domestic producer to get a higher price as well as increasing the price of the essential Canadian imports. A minor compensation in the tariff system was the tax of 20 cents

21 As quoted in the *Sentinel*, Jan. 10, 1864.

per gallon on imported keg beer, and 35 cents per gallon on bottled beer, enacted in 1864.

National organization, by creating permanent local associations, stimulated many kinds of co-operation among brewers. A Brewers Fire Insurance Company of America, for example, was formed in the Middle West with early policyholders in Chicago, St. Louis, and Milwaukee.[22] When prohibition again threatened in the Wisconsin legislature in the form of the Graham Bill of 1872, the brewers as a group were able to swing into prompt and united action in contrast with the indirect and rather fumbling efforts of the Free-Trade Association of the 1850's.[23]

THE NEW PARTNERS AND THEIR COMPETITORS

National activity and national thinking suited the larger Milwaukee brewers, particularly Frederick Pabst. Before he left the lakes, the fame of Milwaukee beer had already begun to spread in the West. As early as 1862 the *Louisville Anzeiger* noted:

Yesterday our neighbor received some Milwaukee beer of which it is impossible to drink but one glass. One must exert great effort to stop with the second glass. We assert that no one can ever drink too much of it, even when one does drink too much of it.[24]

Before Lee had surrendered at Appomattox, Phillip Best had already entered the foreign market.

From Metamoras in Mexico, whence a shipment of 100 barrels was sent via New York by order of Mr. Dietz some time ago, Mr. Phillip Best recently received the very pleasing news that the beer had not only arrived in excellent condition, but that it had far surpassed any that had ever arrived in the city. This is good news not only for Mr. Best but also for all the other local brewers, for through it the already Union-wide reputation of Milwaukee beer will pervade all of Mexico.[25]

[22] *Sentinel,* Apr. 14, 1871.
[23] *Sentinel,* Mar. 19, 1872.
[24] As quoted in the *Sentinel,* June 11, 1862.
[25] *Banner und Volksfreund,* May 27, 1865.

5

Shipping was confined to the largest brewers in Milwaukee. From 1860 to 1866, this meant Melms, Blatz, Best, and possibly Schlitz.

MILWAUKEE BREWERIES AS REPORTED IN THE WISCONSIN CENSUS
OF 1860

Firm	Capital	Production in Barrels	Value Products	Employees	Average Monthly Pay Roll
C. T. Melms	$60,000	15,000 *	$30,000	10	$250
Valentin Blatz	50,000	8,000	32,000	8	240
Phillip Best-Empire Brewery	50,000	7,270	37,900	8	200
Joseph Schlitz	30,000	7,500	36,500	6	180
J. G. Sand	60,000	5,000	40,000	11	350
Stoltz & Schnider	20,000	4,500	18,000	6	144
Bast & Clingler	4,000	3,000	15,000	4	90
Richard G. Owens	10,000	2,000	12,000	8	200
Meyer & Co.	20,000	2,000	10,000	4	100
Johann Lenne	2,000	800	4,000	3	75
Bosch & Buol	1,500	700	3,500	3	50
Peter Gerstner	5,000	700	3,500	3	70
Calgeer & Co.	1,200	600	3,000	2	50
Charles Gopfel	5,000	600	3,000	3	75
John P. Englehardt	7,000	520	2,080	2	36
Otto Zwietusch	.....	500	3,000	2	40
Weber & Peck	3,000	500	2,500	2	50
Simon Meister	.....	450	1,850	2	50
Schwartz & Co.	200	450	1,200	2	40
Philipp Altpeter	1,000	400	2,000	2	50

* Presumably an error in the census report.

Resumption of heavy German immigration after the war, the increasing tastes of native-born Americans for beer, and the great boom from 1868 on, that provided the working man with spending money, increased the national consumption of beer by 140 per cent between 1864 and 1873. But the increase in the sales of Milwaukee brewers left national averages far behind. After relatively moderate progress for the Milwaukeeans from 1865 to 1868, sales increased 260 per cent in the next five years! [26]

[26] Chamber of Commerce, *Annual Statement* [1870], p. 63; [1872], p. 24; [1873]. p. 103.

Such an increase could be due neither to Milwaukee nor to Wisconsin alone. Diligently as the Germans of the Cream City might have consumed, a town with only 70,000 inhabitants in 1870 had its limitations, and rural Wisconsin was not a heavy beer-drinking area. The increase was due to sales outside of the city and its environs, probably as much as 30 to 50 per cent of the production of the three largest breweries being "shipped." By 1872 the relatively small city of Milwaukee had overtaken such great brewing centers as New York, Philadelphia, and St. Louis as the greatest beer exporting center in the nation.[27] Not unconnected with this latter achievement was the Chicago Fire of 1871. The conflagration started by Mrs. O'Leary's cow was so devastating that hard-pressed insurance companies were unable to cover losses, and many of the Chicago brewers were ruined. Milwaukeeans coming to the aid of thirsty Chicago increased their total sales 44 per cent in the following year.[28] But the truly remarkable factor in this business expansion was that almost half the increase after the Civil War was accounted for by one firm: Best and Company. While total Milwaukee sales went up 191,000 barrels from 1866 to 1873, Best's sales alone increased approximately 86,000 barrels.[29]

In 1864, when Captain Pabst entered the business, Best's sales were under 5,000 barrels. From that year to the next, sales increased 123 per cent and rose over 30 per cent the following year. It was at this point that Best felt so certain of the ability of his young son-in-law that he retired. The increase continued at nearly the same rate in 1867. In 1867 Valentin Blatz, by the margin of a couple of hundred barrels, was still the largest brewer in Milwaukee, but from 1868 on, Best and Company completely outdistanced its local rivals. Never again in the nineteenth century was a Milwaukee brewer to sell as much as Best or Pabst. By 1871, Best was selling more than its two nearest rivals com-

---

[27] Merk, p. 155.

[28] Chamber of Commerce, *Annual Statement* [1872], p. 24.

[29] Chamber of Commerce, *Annual Statement* [1870], p. 63; [1872], p. 24; [1873], p. 103.

bined, or 60,668 barrels against about 34,000 for Blatz, and 12,000 for Joseph Schlitz, who was also forging rapidly ahead in these days of nationwide prosperity. Although the latter had about a 165 per cent increase in business the following year, Best still held its commanding lead.

PRODUCTION OF LEADING MILWAUKEE BREWERIES, 1866 TO 1872 [30]

Brewer	1866	1867	May 1869-May 1870	1871	1872
Best	14,139	18,078	23,507	65,000	94,000
Blatz	18,139	18,244	18,383	34,000	41,224
Melms	11,737	13,157	8,542	.....	.....
Falk	5,468	5,546	5,574	7,000	12,050
Schlitz	3,882	5,580	7,181	12,000	32,000
Miller	1,606	.....	3,292	5,000	8,702
Obermann	1,416	.....	1,545	2,000	3,959

Viewed from the national angle Best's rise was almost equally spectacular. With sales of 23,000 barrels in 1869, it was already a relatively large brewery but still well behind such big city firms as Seipp & Lehmann of Chicago, Bergner & Engel of Philadelphia, and Kaufmann & Company and Windisch, Muhlhauser and Company, both of Cincinnati. By the period from May 1871 to May 1872 it had become second in the nation and, by 1874, it had overtaken Seipp, the leading firm.

PRODUCTION OF LEADING AMERICAN BREWERIES OF 1871-1872
(With Production Figures for 1872-1873 and 1873-1874) [31]

	May 1871-1872 Barrels	May 1872-1873 Barrels	May 1873-1874 Barrels
Seipp & Lehmann (Conrad Seipp) Chicago, Illinois	81,930	103,697	98,552
Best & Co. Milwaukee, Wisconsin	73,585	90,133	100,593

[30] Figures for 1866 are from the *Sentinel,* Mar. 30, 1867; 1867 from Chamber of Commerce, *Annual Statement* [1867], p. 49; 1869-1870 from the *Sentinel,* May 11, 1870; 1871 and 1872 from Chamber of Commerce, *Annual Statement* [1872], p. 24.
[31] Figures for 1871-1872 are from the *American Brewer,* IV, No. 3 (Mar. and Apr. 1873), 22, 32, 33; 1872-1873 and 1873-1874 from the *American Brewer,* V, No. 6 (June 1, 1874), 118, 119; V, No. 8 (Aug. 1874), 182; V, No. 11 (Nov. 1874). 254.

PRODUCTION OF LEADING AMERICAN BREWERIES OF 1871-1872
—Continued

	May 1871-1872 Barrels	May 1872-1873 Barrels	May 1873-1874 Barrels
Bergner & Engel			
Philadelphia, Pennsylvania	63,639	68,927	79,249
Kaufmann & Co.			
Cincinnati, Ohio	55,641	41,215	41,603
Windisch, Muhlhauser & Co.			
Cincinnati, Ohio	49,532	49,674	44,966
Bernheimer & Schmid			
New York, New York	47,020	46,590	46,361
Downer & Bemis			
Chicago, Illinois	44,236	.....	.....
F. & M. Schaefer			
New York, New York	43,847	45,800	48,547
George Ehret			
New York, New York	43,611	57,040	79,477
Bergdoll & Psotta			
Philadelphia, Pennsylvania	43,540	40,154	44,004
Anton Hüpfel			
New York, New York	40,172	.....	.....
Christian Moerlein			
Cincinnati, Ohio	39,979	43,985	56,897
Hauck & Windisch			
Cincinnati, Ohio	35,974	43,375	42,666
John Schneider			
Brooklyn, New York	34,057	.....	.....
Schalt Bros.			
Newark, New Jersey	33,121	39,320	32,228
Schaller & Gerke			
Cincinnati, Ohio	32,171	36,509	38,587
Jacob Ruppert			
New York, New York	32,054	47,900	52,705
G. Liebmann Sons			
Brooklyn, New York	32,000	41,013	41,963
Kleiner & Bros.			
Cincinnati, Ohio	30,041	41,051	38,569
Conrad Stein			
New York, New York	30,703	34,600	38,799

By May 1873-1874, production of the following firms had risen to place them among the first twenty: Henry Clausen, New York, New York (59,466 bbls.); Joseph Schlitz, Milwaukee, Wisconsin (54,432 bbls.); Valentin Blatz, Milwaukee, Wisconsin (45,148 bbls.); Lemp, St. Louis, Missouri (36,818 bbls.).

This is the period of truly great achievement by the two partners, but unfortunately no records exist to explain the basis for their success. Certainly youth and enthusiasm must have played a part; in 1869 the Captain was only thirty-three, and Schandein, twenty-nine. But youth alone could not have been the answer, as Valentin Blatz, whom they completely outdistanced, was also a young man. They had, in addition, charming personalities and great energy. Doubtless they often acted as their own salesmen, and their success may have been due to superiority in this branch of the business.

Pabst's imagination, optimism, and good salesmanship held in check by a regard for economy fitted him well for the situation. From the very beginning, his personality overshadowed that of the more retiring Schandein, and his judgment ruled the firm. His experience in transportation must have made it easy for him to think in terms of national distribution. The fact that he was a well-known figure in Chicago as well as in Milwaukee may have been of great importance. One can readily picture the big, genial Captain persuading the saloon proprietors who catered to the steamship trade that they should carry his beer. But backing up these immediate advantages was his good business judgment, his ability to hire the right people, and his willingness to invest heavily in expansion.

The brewery grew mightily to meet the new demand. From 1857 to 1864 it was little altered as sales had not maintained the level of the earlier year. During this period an old fermentation and storage building stood at the corner of Ninth and Chestnut Streets, extending about half way along the block toward Winnebago. Adjoining this was the new two-story brewhouse completed in 1857 with the statue of Gambrinus at the peak of the south end of the roof.[32] The home that Phillip Best built for himself in 1863 stood on the east side of Ninth Street.[33] By 1869

<hr/>

[32] This and the ensuing descriptions have been arrived at from pictures of the brewery.

[33] *Banner und Volksfreund*, Nov. 29, 1863.

the once proud brewhouse had been pushed into the background by new two- and three-story buildings along Chestnut Street that provided the additional fermenting, storage, and racking capacity needed for a brewery of some 30,000- to 50,000-barrel capacity. By 1872 the brewery occupied the entire block between Ninth, Tenth, Chestnut, and Winnebago Streets. The old brewhouse had now been altered and merged with the newer buildings, and Gambrinus, in order to be seen from the street, had been moved down to the top of an archway over the entrance to the loading yard on Chestnut Street.

MELMS'S SOUTH SIDE

The most important single addition of the period, however, from the standpoint of capacity and competitive position came not from additional building but from the purchase of Melms's large and up-to-date brewery. Charles T. Melms, the former leader of the Milwaukee brewing industry and more recently the third largest producer, died in 1869 leaving no heirs who wanted to run the brewery. The chance to buy this property presented the most important opportunity in the early history of Milwaukee brewing. Best and Company was beginning to forge ahead of its two nearest rivals. If either of them had acquired the Melms property, they might have become, for a time at least, the largest brewers in the city. On the other hand, Melms would cost close to $100,000, and Pabst and Schandein, in spite of handsome profits, had already made large investments in buying out Phillip Best and greatly expanding their plant. It may very well be that their bold decision to buy Melms, and their successful raising of the money to negotiate the purchase, was the most important single factor in their early dominance, not only in Milwaukee but also in the whole Middle West. Similarly, decisions to buy Falk, Jung and Borchert of Milwaukee, in 1892, to merge with Premier Malt Products Company of Peoria and Chicago, in 1932, and to buy the Hoffman Beverage Company of Newark, in 1945, may have largely accounted for the continuing leadership of Pabst in the nation.

Compared with its two historic rivals, Anheuser-Busch and
Schlitz, Pabst grew more through the absorption of other firms
than through the continual expansion of a single brewing
property.

There were some complications in the Melms deal. For
while Schandein and Pabst were trying to make up their minds
about the purchase, and to arrange the financing of it, Melms's
brewery was quickly and shrewdly bought for approximately
$80,000 from the estate by Melms's widow's brother-in-law,
Jacob Frey, of Fond du Lac.[34] Frey was really acting for Mrs.
Melms in an effort to rescue something from the numerous
creditors of the estate. The intimacy of the Best and Melms
families may have provided Frey with the advance knowledge
of Pabst's and Schandein's intentions, necessary for the success
of his action. On November 1, 1870, the partners purchased the
Melms brewery from Frey for $95,000.[35]

In acquiring this plant, Best and Company became the owners of what is generally conceded to have been the oldest beer
brewery in Milwaukee. It had been started in 1841 by a German
named Reuthlisberger, and located on the southeast corner of
Virginia and Hanover Streets in the old Walker's Point area on
the south bank of the Menomonee River. The property passed
through the hands of John B. Meyer and was bought by Franz
Neukirch with whom Melms formed a partnership. After Neukirch's withdrawal, Melms, in the latter fifties, made it one of
the leading breweries.[36] It was also one of the best equipped for
both manufacture and transportation. Sidings of the Chicago
and North Western and the Chicago, Milwaukee, St. Paul Railroads ran into the buildings, and a steamship dock stretched
along the Menomonee River. After this purchase Best and Company was in somewhat the same position in relation to local
competition as the Standard Oil Company was beginning to
occupy in Cleveland. They could outdo any competitor in get-

[34] *Sentinel*, May 18, 1870. See also *Melms et al.* v. *The Pabst Brewing Co.*, 93 Wis.
140 (1896), a suit regarding the inclusion of Melms's homestead in the sale.
[35] *Sentinel*, Nov. 11, 1870. See also note 34.
[36] "Wisconsin Census" [1860].

ting the greatest economies of mass production, and they could bring the heaviest pressure upon the railroads for reasonable rates.

Emil Schandein, establishing himself in Melms's former house, took direct charge of the new plant, which was christened the South Side; while the Captain built a home on the hill by the old brewery which had already come to be known as the Empire.[37]

ADVERTISING

The markets adjacent to Milwaukee which the brewers were exploiting at this time did not seem to justify national advertising. Large firms in other lines of business were in the same situation, only a handful of them sold to truly national markets. Hence, few national advertising mediums had been developed. There were no slick-paper magazines with great national circulations, no motorists to read country billboards. There was no syndicated newspaper advertising. Newspapers still were local, small, and highly competitive, so that advertising in any *one* would reach only a limited public. National religious weeklies, the best medium for many products, were generally closed to beer. Thus, in spite of their imagination as promotors, both Best and Pabst confined their selling efforts largely to personal promotion and notices in the local Milwaukee papers.

During the depression, after 1857, direct newspaper advertising by the brewers appears to have been abandoned altogether, but saloon notices in the *Banner und Volksfreund* increased in volume. The following are some samples of this kind of advertising from the summer of 1859.

Today and every day hereafter
big lunch
in
Best's Hall at Market Place.
GRASSMAN & ORTH.

[37] The name "Empire" was applied to the Best brewery in the *Milwaukee Directory* [1851], p. 45.

Low-priced Lager Beer!—
at the Source
and every morning free lunch!
3 cents per Seidel!
from now on at
Best's Beer Hall at Market Place.

GRASSMAN & ORTH.

For the Information of Everybody!
Beginning today, Thursday, August 18:
Lager beer of Best & Company,
The beer that beats them all,
2 glasses for 5 cents!
Morning Lunch.
Evenings we invite you to enjoy humorous
entertainment with piano accompaniment.

A. C. KUHN.

New arrangement in Best's Hall at Market Place. In order that, despite the current hard times, German "Gemuethlichkeit" shall not want for lack of good, low-priced drink in Milwaukee, we have imported rhenish chopin and half-chopin glasses and established a chopin-business.[38]

GRASSMAN & ORTH.

The same type appeared in the *Banner* the following season:

The Old "Bock" in Best's Hall on Market Street will be let loose once again tomorrow, Monday, February 20, 1860. In order to make his butting less painful and at the same time provide an appropriate remedy, we furnish good things to eat, which medicine may be had without cost. A "Bock-Butt" as always 3 cents.

Inasmuch as this "Bock" has been well-trained by Mr. Best and is capable of excellent performance, we have reason to look for a large attendance at this first appearance of the season of 1860.

FRIEDRICH HEINEMANN.

[38] Advertisements from *Banner und Volksfreund,* July 2, Aug. 3 and 18, 1859. A "chopin" (schoppen-glas in German) is a drinking glass with a capacity of nearly a pint of liquid, used mostly for beer drinking.

Next Wednesday May 16
We'll serve you Phillip Best's Bock Beer Brew!
Together with something good to chew!
And from Thursday on there will be Lager Beer.

Nothing better you will find in this locality,
So I say it very simply without flattery:
Come my friends, on Wednesday, to my splendid Bock-fest here.
And thereafter come always for freshest Lager Beer!

JOHN SCHAUSS
Custom House Saloon in Young's Block.[39]

The increasing importance of brewing from 1864 on and the support given to local papers by saloon advertising led to the kind of news notes by local editors that represent one of the earliest forms of public relations. The *Sentinel,* for example, published a front page article on May 19, 1864, headed "The Catacombs of Milwaukee" that began:

We recently spent an hour in the Mammoth Cave connected with the brewery of General Phillip Best, on 9th Street near Winnebago. The party consisted of some half dozen persons, Mr. Pabst, a son-in-law of General Best and formerly a lake captain, acting as cicerons.

Festivals and other special events often furnished the occasion for both advertising and subsequent news articles. The presentation of a cask of beer to the Sängerbund, in 1868, led to the following "good-will" note in the *Sentinel,* June 29, 1868:

THE MONSTER BEER CASK

Messrs. Pabst & Schoenstein [*sic*] who presented the huge cask of Best & Company's celebrated beer (from which more than 8000 glasses were drawn) to the Northwestern Saengerbund, deserves something more than a passing notice in connection with the fact. These gentlemen are sons-in-law and partners of General Phillip Best, and carry on the business of the brewery in the absence of General Best himself, who has been in Europe during the past year

39 *Banner und Volksfreund,* Feb. 19 and May 15, 1860.

with part of his family. Captain Pabst was formerly the commander
of the Comet, and afterwards of the ill-fated Seabird, and is well
known in all our lake ports as a man of unquestionable honor and
of attractive social qualities. Mr. Schoenstein [sic] is too favorably
known in the city already to make an item in regard to him, a
novelty to our readers. The firm of Best & Company began in this
city by manufacturing one barrel of beer per week, nearly thirty
years ago, and now makes 2,500 per month, having gained national
reputation for the excellent qualities of their manufacture.

In the summer of 1870, the summer being the period of heaviest beer drinking, the leading brewers of Milwaukee hit upon
a new scheme for industry advertising.

A Beer Fair is the latest enterprise in this city. Mr. Paul Bechtner, of
the Rink, will open the entertainment by a grand procession tomorrow morning. Every brewer will occupy a tap stand in the Rink, and
every visitor is called upon to vote for the beer "that liked him best"
on leaving the fair. At the close the brewer receiving the largest
number of votes will receive a massive gold medal, and those less
fortunate, silver ones of value in proportion to their rank in the
popular estimation. Vot a beeples! [40]

Best and Blatz received the first gold medals.

Extra large shipments of beer to Chicago or other outside
points were also used for advertising by having all twenty-odd
brewery wagons line up and carry the thousand or more kegs
to the shipping depot in a parade.[41]

MAINTAINING PRICES

In spite of the keen rivalry among brewers, the small number of competitors in each local market and the fact that most
of them depended largely on this market worked for price
maintenance. Price maintenance was encouraged also by the
local brewers associations that had been organized in key cities
since 1862. Thus the war of attrition that reduced the seventeen

40 *Sentinel*, June 22 and 28, 1870.
41 *Sentinel*, May 5, 1873.

breweries listed in Milwaukee in 1865 to ten by 1872, notwith-
standing the general prosperity, was fought on other fronts than
that of advertised price.[42] As we will see in more detail in Chapter VI, the gain or loss of markets depended on the "placing"
of draught beer in saloons or other retail outlets. Success in this
contest could be furthered by secret discounts and the spending of money by salesmen, but the reputation of the beer with
customers and the local popularity of the brewer were of greatest importance.[43] That is, there was undercover price warfare,
expressed in departures from the price agreed upon at the Brewers' Association meetings, but these cuts were limited by the fact
that they could be quickly detected by competitors, and that
factors other than price might be of greater importance to customers. If a man wanted Best's beer he would pay his nickel
for fourteen in preference to sixteen ounces of an inferior
product.

The first increase in price during the Civil War, from $5.00 to
$7.00 per barrel, in 1862, was the result of federal taxation, but
from then on the forces of the great national inflation carried
the price of beer upward to $10 a barrel; and, in 1867, in the
face of a national downward price trend, the brewers were able
to ask $2.00 per barrel more and maintain that price tempo-
rarily.[44] But at this point the retailers feared diminishing returns and warned the manufacturers of the danger in a "Memorial" from a committee of the Milwaukee Saloonkeepers
Association.

. . . . As further proof that the price of $12 is too high, we bring the
following points to your attention:

We have to bear the burden of all the high government taxes upon
all the articles that we sell and of the increased license fees, without
any assistance from the producer or the consumer, and find no
means of making it up in our retail trade. . . . .

[42] *Directory* [1865], p. 289; [1872], p. 304.
[43] To the degree that customers demanded a certain beer because of its taste—
"product differentiation" had been achieved.
[44] *Sentinel,* Jan. 24, 1860, and Jan. 1, 1873.

The demands of and necessary participation in charitable enterprises come upon us more than upon any other class.

The amount of time required for our business is not comparable in any other business activity; while we must of necessity put in still more time in order to fulfill our obligations, we are also required to pay higher rents for our business quarters than any other business.

Further it is more difficult for us, than for you or other businesses, to circumvent the unreliable quality of our commodities, and therefore have to take all the consequences, without any compensation.

The unrestricted freedom in the measure of the barrel of beer works always to your advantage.

In reference to the stated conditions, as well as to the prices of the barley and hops used in the manufacture of beer, we urge and expect a reduction of $2 per barrel in the price of lager beer, and herewith propose $10 per barrel for the present season.[45]

The petition was politely denied and the $12 price maintained in Milwaukee until 1869, when it was dropped to the $10 level and held there until the panic of 1873.[46]

INCORPORATION

Continuing high prices from 1866 to 1873, at a time when the cost of materials was declining, must have produced large profits. Best and Company, which could have been worth little more than $100,000 in 1866, was valued at $600,000 by the spring of 1873, and this growth had come from reinvested earnings.[47] Such a large firm could benefit from the advantages offered by incorporation.

Incorporation would not only provide a self-perpetuating organization that would not be disrupted by the death of either partner, but it would also permit the inclusion of two of the

[45] "Memorial" in company archives, translated from the German.

[46] *Sentinel*, July 29, 1870, and Jan. 1, 1873.

[47] As noted in the Preface, p. vii, the company records are fairly complete in the period 1873-1919. Therefore, direct footnote citations will not be made hereafter to material that is in its proper and obvious place in the company archives. See list of records in Bibliography, pp. 407-11.

young Bests as owners of a few shares. Charles, the able son of Phillip's brother of that name, was keeping the firm's accounts, and Henry, Phillip's only son, was now old enough to work. The same situation could be foreseen when the Captain's two sons grew up.

Other factors may also have influenced the decision to incorporate. As the company did a large interstate business and might unknowingly infringe upon state laws there was greater personal protection for the owners in having responsibility assumed by a legal entity. E. Anheuser and Joseph Schlitz both found it desirable to incorporate at about this same time. Possibly also a corporate title added dignity and importance to a big concern in a business where most production was by small proprietorships.

On March 13, 1873, therefore, the Phillip Best Brewing Company was chartered in Wisconsin. Capital was set at $300,000, represented by three hundred $1,000 shares. A surplus of $300,-000 was entered on the books to cover the value above capitalization, of plant and of inventories. The stock was initially divided as follows: Pabst, 142 shares; Schandein, 132 shares; Charles Best, 1 share; and treasury stock, 25 shares, with provision to sell stock to Henry Best when he reached twenty-one years of age. Pabst, the president, Schandein, the vice-president, and Charles Best, the secretary, were the sole directors. In twenty-nine years the little wooden brewery on Chestnut Street Hill had grown to be one of the large manufacturing enterprises of the United States.

THE NEW LEADERS AND THE CITY

Neither the Captain nor Emil Schandein could expect immediately to assume the German community leadership enjoyed by General Best, but both took an active part in outside affairs from the start. For business reasons, if for no other, it was important for a brewer to be a well-known figure. Success in the local market required liberality on his part, not only in the

form of loans to saloons, but also in gifts to various social organizations and needy individuals. The sales of the beer depended to a considerable extent on the popularity and prestige
of its producer. The fact that Pabst and Schandein were both
generous men who liked to give time and money for local welfare played an important part in their phenomenal success. The
Captain, for example, established a park with a rifle range for
the Milwaukee Sharpshooters Club, and then in 1873 gave his
holdings to the club.[48] It was said that he gave away as much
as a thousand dollars a year in small personal gifts. Often he
would make a special trip to someone's house to see what was
needed, so that his gift would show true consideration.

While he had no political ambitions, Pabst took an active role
in civic affairs. In 1865 he and Blatz, his chief competitor, were
made members of the chamber of commerce. Melms, the first
brewer in that predominantly Yankee organization, had only
been elected in 1861.[49] Starting in 1871 Pabst served a six-year
term as a city water commissioner.[50]

These early distinctions were due not only to the ability of
the young beer "King" but also to the gradual acceptance of the
importance of brewing itself by Milwaukeeans. The period
from the end of the war to the panic of 1873 was one of breath-
taking growth in the city. The manufacture of iron products,
long a leading activity, was given new impetus by the establishment of Edward P. Allis' Reliance Iron Works about the beginning of the war, and those of the Milwaukee Iron Company, later part of Illinois Steel, in 1866. But wheat selling was
the greatest business of the postwar period. These were the
years when Milwaukee was the world's largest primary wheat
market. In 1873, 28,000,000 bushels were sold on the exchange,
and 25,000,000 of them shipped out. In this tremendous upsurge
of business, brewing no more than held its own, but the fact

[48] *Sentinel,* Jan. 20, 1873.
[49] See membership list, Chamber of Commerce, *Annual Statement* [1861, 1865].
[50] *Sentinel,* Mar. 13, 1871; *Free Press,* Jan. 8, 1904 (scrapbook clipping).

that it did so and became "big business" along with the other leaders forced a new measure of respect from the non-German community. Furthermore, Milwaukee was becoming conscious of her greatness, and beer more than any other product was spreading her reputation.

CHAPTER IV

THE CAPTAIN RUNS THE COMPANY

In the twenty years after 1873, the name of Milwaukee became more and more associated with beer, and no brew was more responsible for this than Best's—or, as should now be said, Pabst's. Actually the name of the company was not changed until March 18, 1889, following the death of Captain Pabst's partner, Emil Schandein. By then, the brewing world and a large part of the beer-drinking public had long associated Best beer with the colorful Captain and the change of name was not much more than a formality. It had the advantage of giving an incentive to the Captain's two sons to whom he planned eventually to leave control. Since the Captain was the majority stockholder and administrative head of the company even while the name was Best, it seems simplest to refer to the company from this chapter onward, save in quotations or direct references to contemporaneous accounts, as the Pabst Brewing Company.

But much more than a change of name happened to the company in the two decades ending in 1893. By that year the company had grown as big as it was to be until after the repeal of prohibition forty years later. Its administrative and productive organizations were set; the general policies of emphasis on quality and wide distribution, that continue to guide the company even today, were established. In a word, in the twenty years between 1873 and 1893, the Pabst Company came of age. It is worth while, therefore, to examine the history of those years in unusual detail. To this history the next four chapters are devoted. In turn they deal with management, methods of production, competition for markets, and sales organization.

THE NATIONAL SHIPPERS

Naturally, Pabst management in these formative years, like the managements of other large corporations, was subject to conditions outside its own business and, indeed, outside its control. These external conditions are worth looking into at the start. Important among them was a 50 per cent increase in the population of the United States. This meant a lot of new beer drinkers. Since beer drinking was largely an urban habit, even more significant than the over-all growth in population between 1873 and 1893 was the doubling of the number of people in cities of over 8,000. More significant still was the fact that a great number of these new people were Germans who arrived in America in ever increasing numbers after 1880. Germans naturally turned to beer. But even among non-Germans in booming American cities, the tendency to drink beer instead of whisky was strengthened by two factors. One was the imposition of internal revenue taxes on whisky after 1862, which made whisky at two cents a shot a thing of the past. The second was the rise of industrialism. A factory worker could not generally drink hard liquor during the day and hold his job, but a glass or two of beer would not impair his efficiency, so nickel beer came increasingly to be the drink of the city man. The spread of central heating and the increasingly sedentary character of city life may have re-enforced these more obvious factors leading to a demand for lighter beverages.

The net result of all the changes in these years was an increase in beer and ale consumption of over 250 per cent. But huge as was the national rate of growth, it was far surpassed by the increase in the business of the big Western shippers who applied good managerial ability to a naturally favorable situation. According to rough but fairly reliable estimates for 1872, the firms that in the next twenty years were to be the four most important Western shippers—Best, Schlitz, and Blatz of Milwaukee, and Anheuser of St. Louis—produced in that year a total of 190,000 barrels or 2.4 per cent of the national total.[1] In 1893 these same four brewers produced some 2,800,000 barrels or 8.8 per cent of the national total.[2] In 1872 Best's share was 94,000;

---

[1] *American Brewer*, V, No. 6 (Jan. 1, 1874). 118-19.
[2] Sundry Papers Scrapbook.

in 1893 Pabst's was 1,095,585 barrels. Compared with the 250 per cent increase in total national sales, Pabst showed an increase in its own of over 1,000 per cent. (See table, p. 87.)

This tremendous growth coming on top of an 800 per cent increase in Best sales from 1865 to 1873 kept Pabst ahead of all competitors. Even so, others grew even faster than did Pabst. Of the four great shippers, Anheuser made the largest gain. In 1872 it was a small brewery with a production of perhaps 25,000 barrels; by 1893 it was second only to Pabst with a production of over 700,000. This company grew fastest after E. Anheuser's death in 1880, when control passed into the hands of his very able son-in-law, Adolphus Busch. Meanwhile, Pabst's other competitors were also doing well. In 1876, after the founder's death, the enterprising Uihlein brothers acquired control and expanded the business of the Joseph Schlitz Brewing Company. Valentin Blatz and his energetic sons also steadily expanded their brewery, until it became, in 1891, the major part of a British financed brewing "trust" called the Milwaukee and Chicago Breweries, Limited.

These four great companies, Pabst, Anheuser, Schlitz, and Blatz, together with Christian Moerlein of Cincinnati and W. J. Lemp of St. Louis, competed actively for the national market. In the principal Eastern cities, there were also big brewers such as George Ehret in New York, Bergner & Engel in Philadelphia, and P. Ballantine & Sons in Newark, the latter making ale, all of whom sold over 100,000 barrels in the mid-depression year of 1877. In their own areas these companies far outsold the big Western shippers, but none of them specialized in nationwide business. Their products seldom appeared outside the Eastern and southeastern states, and unlike the big Western shippers, the local brewers generally emphasized low price rather than quality. In the West, also, there were large local brewers such as Conrad Seipp and Downer & Bemis of Chicago, and Windisch, Muhlhauser and George Weber of Cincinnati. None of them, however, could match the growth of the big shippers.

LARGEST BREWERS IN 1877 [3]

	Annual Production in Barrels
George Ehret, New York, New York	138,449
Ph. Best, Milwaukee, Wisconsin	121,634
Bergner & Engel, Philadelphia, Pennsylvania	119,807
P. Ballantine & Sons, Newark, New Jersey	107,592
Conrad Seipp, Chicago, Illinois	95,167
H. Clausen & Son, New York, New York	90,642
Flanagan & Wallace, New York, New York *	88,677
Jacob Ruppert, New York, New York	84,432
Beadleston & Woerz, New York, New York	79,658
J. Schlitz Brewing Company, Milwaukee, Wisconsin	79,538
Wm. Massey & Co., Philadelphia, Pennsylvania *	75,193
Albany Brewing Co., Albany, New York *	72,723
Christian Moerlein, Cincinnati, Ohio	72,588
Frank Jones, Portsmouth, New Hampshire *	71,471
Reuter & Alley, Boston, Massachusetts	67,121
Clausen & Price, New York, New York *	64,896
Boston Beer Co., Boston, Massachusetts *	62,881
Yuengling & Co., New York, New York	62,740
W. J. Lemp, St. Louis, Missouri	61,229
Windisch, Muhlhauser & Bro., Cincinnati, Ohio	59,475
Louis Bergdoll, Philadelphia, Pennsylvania	57,735
Bernheimer & Schmid, New York, New York	54,471
Taylor & Son, Albany, New York	53,453
George Weber, Cincinnati, Ohio	52,894
Downer & Bemis, Chicago, Illinois	51,140
John Greenway, Syracuse, New York	50,913
Conrad Stein, New York, New York	50,000
Eckert & Winter, New York, New York	47,922
V. Blatz, Milwaukee, Wisconsin	47,663
Tracey & Russell, New York, New York *	47,391
Elias & Betz, New York, New York	46,969
E. Anheuser & Company's Brewing Association, St. Louis, Missouri	44,961
F. & M. Schaefer, New York, New York	44,895

* According to *Tovey's Brewers' Directory* [1882], these firms produced ale only. In 1877, P. Ballantine & Sons produced ale only. *One Hundred Years of Brewing*, p. 189; also see *American Brewers' Gazette*, Apr. 15, 1878, p. 55.

[3] List from *Brewers Hand Book* [1877], as listed in *One Hundred Years of Brewing*, p. 612.

Largest Brewers in 1895[4]

	Production in Barrels
Pabst Brewing Co., Milwaukee, Wisconsin	900,000-1,000,000
Anheuser-Busch Brewing Assn., St. Louis, Missouri	700,000- 800,000
Joseph Schlitz Brewing Co., Milwaukee, Wisconsin	600,000- 700,000
George Ehret, New York, New York	500,000- 600,000
Ballantine & Co., Newark, New Jersey	500,000- 600,000
Bernheimer & Schmid, New York, New York	400,000- 500,000
Val. Blatz Brewing Co., Milwaukee, Wisconsin	350,000- 400,000
Wm. J. Lemp Brewing Co., St. Louis, Missouri	300,000- 350,000
Conrad Seipp Brewing Co., Chicago, Illinois	250,000- 300,000
Frank Jones Brewing Co., Portsmouth, New Hampshire	250,000- 300,000
Peter Doelger, New York, New York	250,000- 300,000
Ruppert, New York, New York	250,000- 300,000
James Everard, New York, New York	250,000- 300,000
Christian Moerlein Brewing Co., Cincinnati, Ohio	250,000- 300,000
Bergner & Engel, Philadelphia, Pennsylvania	250,000- 300,000
Bartholomay Brewing Co., Rochester, New York	250,000- 300,000

DID LOCATION AID THE SHIPPERS?

As late as 1877, as the above table shows, many breweries in other parts of the country were as large or larger than the Milwaukee and St. Louis shippers. How and why, then, in the next fifteen years did the Western group forge ahead of all competitors? More particularly how and why did Pabst grow to be, by 1893, nearly 50 per cent larger than its nearest rival?

Many factors may be considered as possible answers to these questions. The factor of advantageous location is a logical one with which to start an analysis. Economic theory lists among locational advantages, low transportation costs for raw materials, fuel, and finished products, a supply of cheap and well-trained labor, and access to markets. Were there such advantages working in favor of big Milwaukee breweries in the way that the Cleveland location aided Standard Oil?

In many industries, nearness to raw materials has been most

---

[4] *Brewers' Guide for the United States, Canada and Mexico* [1896], pp. 17, 85.

important in favoring a particular location, but this seems to have counted for relatively little in the brewing business. Barley, the chief bulk commodity used in beer manufacture was not grown in sufficient quantity in any of the Middle Western states to meet the demands of the largest brewers. They used the local product, but they also bought barley in California and Canada. Practically all brewers did this, and the shipping cost on such barley did not vary substantially between Milwaukee, St. Louis, and other smaller Middle Western beer centers. Hops, the other raw material in beermaking, were used in such small quantities that transportation costs were unimportant. The makers of fine beer bought their hops on the basis of quality, and although hops were grown in Wisconsin and New York State, a certain percentage was regularly purchased in Bohemia and other German markets. Corn and rice were also experimented with during these decades as adjuncts to barley malt, but as corn was present everywhere in the North, and rice was grown nowhere in this area, they gave no detectable advantage to the Milwaukee and St. Louis locations.

In the days when even Pabst used wooden kegs, cooperage was an important annual expense. Besides the full 31-gallon barrels, for the convenience of smaller customers the brewers had to ship in half barrels, quarters, sixths, and eighths.

TOTAL BARRELS PURCHASED OR MANUFACTURED BY PABST [5]

Year	Whole	Half	Quarter	Eighth
1884	572	4,068	9,461	20,216
1885	304	3,815	5,917	22,216
1886	338	7,336	10,208	20,174
1887	86	8,192	10,633	26,496
1888	463	4,054	13,846	21,538
1889	1,999	13,683	21,633	29,531
1890	2,328	13,933	53,811	39,113
1891	1,026	16,034	51,097	47,111
1892	6,919	17,201	46,558	45,066
1893	3,049	24,715	19,654	45,396

[5] Annual Statement of Affairs, Books A and B.

By 1890 full-sized barrels cost about $2.75.[6] Smaller ones, of course, cost less, with eighths at around 80 cents. All these "packages," as they were called, were continually lost, broken, or worn out in transit. Besides, they needed frequent repitching in order to keep the beer from coming in contact with the wood. One source of loss is shown in the following letter written in 1878 by Captain Pabst to a brewer in St. Louis.

Yours of 24th August received and contents duly noted. With reference to the exchange of kegs let me assure you that we are always ready to make needed arrangements with you or any other brewer. Furthermore let me emphasize that it has always been the case with us that we always promptly shipped "strange" kegs to their respective owners. Our coopers have *strict orders* not to rebrand strange kegs, although we have on occasion, when we were hard pressed, made use of such kegs, but returned them at the earliest opportunity. I readily believe that you ran short of hoops during the flood, and do not hold it against you that you utilized "strange" kegs, yet I cannot condone your practice of rebranding them.

I remarked the other time that you may know nothing about it and yet I must assume that you have rebranded a considerable number (for we have found quite a few of them carrying your name), therefore I wish to request that you find out from your coopers the approximate number they rebranded and return to us the same or an equivalent number. Don't you think that's right? I give you my word of honor that we never branded kegs when we knew where they belonged.[7]

On cooperage costs, Milwaukee brewers did have a noticeable advantage. The near-by Wisconsin lumber industry supplied barrel makers with low-cost staves, and the Milwaukee barrel makers themselves paid appreciably less for labor than their competitors in Chicago or the East. A report of the chamber of commerce for 1871 rated Milwaukee wages 15 per cent below those of Chicago, and an article in the *Daily Review* for 1887

[6] *Milwaukee Daily News,* Aug. 7, 1891.
[7] Pabst to Lemp, Sept. 5, 1878. Translated from the German.

placed the Milwaukee price for half barrels at $1.25 in comparison with $1.75 in Chicago, $1.80 in St. Louis, and $1.60 in New York.[8]

This apparent advantage, however, was not as great as it may seem. For in the early nineties, Pabst and Schlitz grew so rapidly that Milwaukee coopers alone could no longer supply their needs. Both companies had to look elsewhere for barrels. To meet the situation they took a bold step. Between them Pabst and Schlitz set up their own Delta Cooperage Company with Fred Pabst as president and August Uihlein as vice-president. This company soon invested $151,418.92 in 41,879.82 acres of oak timber land in Tallahatchie County, Mississippi.[9] By 1893 Pabst was manufacturing 85 per cent of its full barrels and 25 per cent of its smaller sizes. Still, no saving connected with cooperage could really give a critical competitive advantage. At best, the difference brought about in the cost of beer per barrel could only be two or three cents.

Coal was another important material in beermaking. But coal did not vary greatly in price in the Western brewing centers, and the effect of existing differences was too small to be reflected in the price of beer.

This leaves ice and water as the only other bulky materials used in brewing. Ice was the one such material in which the Milwaukee brewers enjoyed a considerable advantage in transportation costs. The long, cold Milwaukee winters and the small lakes in near-by Wisconsin provided a natural ice supply superior to that of any other big brewing center. Ice was consumed in enormous quantities. The Pabst icehouse at Pewaukee Lake, for example, covered 22,500 square feet.[10] Ice was used for cooling the beer at the brewery, a process which early in the eighties cost Pabst around ten cents a barrel. Ice was also used to refrigerate freight cars for Southern shipments, and in warm weather this cost even more than 10 cents a barrel. The Mil-

8 Chamber of Commerce, *Annual Statement* [1871], p. 15; *Daily Review,* June 6, 1887.
9 Directors Record and Delta Cooperage papers.
10 Lorraine Culver Redfield, *The Story of Pewaukee, 1836-1936,* p. 18.

waukee advantage often went beyond mere price considerations. Toward the close of hot summers, Cincinnati and St. Louis shippers occasionally ran so low on ice for shipping purposes that orders had to be held back. In March 1878, for example, J. S. Pierce, manager of Pabst's Chicago branch, wrote after surveying the company's competitors' situation in the Southern trade, "But few of them are supplied with ice, and we are perfectly safe in holding full prices South this summer." [11]

Artificial refrigeration in the early eighties eased the internal cooling problems of the more southerly breweries but nothing in this period replaced natural ice in shipping.

There was once a popular notion that the quality of the local water gave brewing advantages to certain areas. But this is viewed today as an old wives' tale. In the days before city water systems, brewers had to use well water. Such water, regardless of locality, was usually too hard for good brewing, and as soon as lake water became available in Milwaukee, about 1873, Pabst began to use it in beer.[12] Lake Michigan water is well suited for beer manufacturing, but chemists at present find it no better suited than the water available to Pabst's competitors. Chemists point out that water, from sources as diverse as New York's Ashokan Lake, Lake Michigan, and the muddy Missouri River, makes good beer when correctly purified.

It seems clear, then, that of all the materials that may have given one brewing region certain advantages over others, ice alone seems to have been an important factor—one that clearly worked to the advantage of Milwaukee. All other locational factors affecting raw materials seem to have been minor or else about equally distributed among a number of cities. The same may be said of experienced labor supply. Labor came almost exclusively from the large German population which provided workers skilled in beermaking and traditionally attached to the

[11] Pierce to Best Brewing Co., Mar. 27, 1878.

[12] Water works were completed in the fall of 1873 by Board of Water Commissioners of which Captain Pabst was a member. W. J. Anderson and Julius Bleyer, *Milwaukee's Great Industries*, p. 51.

industry. Such workers were plentiful in St. Louis, Cincinnati, Chicago, and New York, as well as in Milwaukee and other cities.

Likewise, Milwaukee does not seem to have had any advantage over other Midwestern cities in nearness to markets. Actually Chicago and Cincinnati were nearer to the geographical center of the United States population, whereas St. Louis was about as far away as Milwaukee. The Middle Western brewers as a group may have enjoyed a shipping advantage over Eastern brewers since there was less local competition to the west of the United States population center than to the east of it. But among the Western group, Milwaukee and Pabst seem to have had no special shipping advantages.

The locational advantages of Milwaukee appear, therefore, to be those of slightly cheaper ice and labor. Taken together, they fail to provide a sufficient explanation of the success of Milwaukee as a shipping center as against the other principal brewing cities.

But one advantage not ordinarily thought of as locational may have been the relatively small size of Milwaukee. Each of its rival centers had a much larger local population to consume the brewery production. Lack of a large local market, while other factors favored production, may have led the big Milwaukee brewers to push shipping with a greater vigor than their competitors elsewhere.

POPULATION AND BEER PRODUCTION, CHIEF BREWING CENTERS

City	Population 1870	Population 1880	Production in Barrels 1880 [13]
New York, New York *	1,478,103	1,911,698	2,987,811
Philadelphia, Pennsylvania	674,022	847,170	765,844
Chicago, Illinois	298,977	503,185	458,894
St. Louis, Missouri	310,864	350,518	627,275
Cincinnati, Ohio	216,239	255,139	584,431
Milwaukee, Wisconsin	71,440	115,587	577,992

* As of present city limits.

[13] *Tovey's Brewers' Directory* [1881], p. 12. Production figures for these cities in 1870 are not obtainable.

The nearness and size of the Chicago market was a particularly important incentive of this sort, and once the Milwaukeeans made railroad and selling arrangements with Chicago, it was easy to expand from there into neighboring markets.

ADVANTAGES OF A FAMILY COMPANY

The foregoing considerations may account for the eventual sales leadership of Milwaukee, but other factors must be analyzed to account for the continued leadership of Pabst among Milwaukee's own fiercely competitive firms.

The large American brewing companies, prior to the entrance of British capital into the field in the late eighties, were closely held corporations with stock owned by one or two families, and control vested in only two or three executives. In the Phillip Best Brewing Company, for instance, there were only three original stockholders, who at the same time were president, vice-president, and secretary as well as all the directors of the company. Management was strictly a family affair, and problems actually could be settled at the family dinner table.

This situation could have been a source of weakness rather than strength; many breweries undoubtedly languished or failed because inefficient relatives were kept in power for "dynastic" reasons. The Best and Pabst families, however, generally supplied good managers, and the company prospered. The only difficulty arising from family management in the period 1873 to 1892 was a minor one that was satisfactorily adjusted. Henry Best, Phillip's son, received 23 shares of stock on his twenty-first birthday in 1874, in return for the deed to the real estate on which the brewery buildings stood. These shares gave Henry the "balance of power" between Pabst and Schandein, a situation that apparently irked the Captain. In the spring of 1876, the latter served notice that he would sell his 143 shares at their "actual value" within three months. This ultimatum apparently led to a compromise whereby Henry sold 22 of his 23 shares equally to the two senior executives for the $44,000 he had paid

two years earlier. This was $1,500 a share below book value at
this time, but probably a good enough bargain considering the
opportunities for a man with cash at the depth of the severe
depression. The Captain with 154 shares was now in complete
control of the company, a position he never relinquished up to
his death in 1904. Emil Schandein had 141 shares, Charles Best,
4, and Henry Best, 1. Except for the inheritance of Schandein's
shares by his widow in 1889, and the purchase of a few more
shares from Pabst and Schandein by Charles Best, no change in
stockholding took place during the next fourteen years.

The smooth functioning of management during these years
depended largely upon the relations between Schandein and
Pabst. Emil Schandein was an efficient company officer almost
in spite of himself. Left alone, he would never have chosen
brewing as a career. He would have been much better pleased
to have been a botanist and to have spent his life in scholarly
research. But having married Phillip Best's daughter, Lisette,
he had, in effect, become wedded to brewing as well. The fact
that he had to devote himself completely to the brewing business in order to keep up with the affairs of a mushrooming company, of which he was vice-president and one of only three officers, often made him unhappy. But this did not prevent him
from being an effective executive. He enjoyed the prestige and
power that accrued to him with marvelous speed; and he was
of value to the organization as an intelligent man who understood technology, as an amateur biologist who could expertly
appraise barley, and as a cultured genial representative of the
company with more "polish" than the lusty Captain. Schandein
accepted the wise policy, however, of following the Captain's
lead in business affairs until ill-health led to his virtual withdrawal from active management about a year before his death
in Germany in 1888.

Emil Schandein's death, besides leading to the company's
change of name, led also to the removal of two clauses from
the company charter which strengthened Captain Pabst's al-

ready dominant position as the real head of the concern. The deleted articles read:

And no act outside of the ordinary business of the corporation shall be performed by either the President or the Vice-President, without the consent of the other.

No act of the Board of Directors shall be of any validity if disapproved by the President or Vice-President, such disapproval shall be in writing and filed with the Secretary and by him entered in the Minutes.

These clauses obviously were not suited to a company where the vice-president might cease to be a principal owner. Hereafter the president could make decisions, backed by his majority control of the stock, without fear of veto.

Emil Schandein's post as company vice-president was filled by his widow, Lisette, who, until her departure for extended travel in Europe after 1894, was probably the only woman vice-president of a large brewing company. Schandein's death was followed in January 1890 by the resignation, because of ill-health, of the company secretary, Charles Best. Here, again, the Captain had a chance to strengthen his own position. He installed as the new secretary his oldest son, Gustav. Since the latter was still completing his education by studies and travel in Europe, the Captain appointed Charles W. Henning, who had worked his way up in the accounting end of the business under Charles Best, as assistant secretary. He was the first non-relative to become an officer since the founding of the company. Gustav Pabst and J. F. Theurer, the superintendent of brewing, were given a few shares of stock in 1889, and the Captain's young son, Frederick, Jr., and Henning received some shares in 1892. In this year the family character of the company was temporarily altered by Pabst's second major expansion through the acquisition of a competitor. Fires in the Milwaukee brewery of Falk, Jung and Borchert in 1889 and 1891 so upset their operations that the Captain was able to buy this company's equipment and good will for about half a million dollars worth of Pabst Brewing Company stock. Falk, Jung and Borchert, before the fires, had had a business of 200,000 barrels a year. The purchase in the fall of 1892, which transferred to Pabst what was left of this trade, was one of the main reasons for the 180,000 barrel increase in Pabst's sales in 1893. The problems resulting from the entrance of Ernest Borchert and Frank R. Falk into the Pabst management early in 1893, as vice-president and treasurer respectively, belong to a later period. For the time, the company continued to function smoothly under its one-man leadership.

Andrew Carnegie once boasted that by working in a partnership he could outmaneuver slower corporations with their need for formal meetings and much discussed decisions. But Carnegie could not have been thinking of corporations like the Captain's. Large sums were often spent by Pabst, and big contracts were let well in advance of formal approval, since ratification at subsequent board meetings was a foregone conclusion. Nobody doing business with the Captain doubted for a moment the validity of his word or signature, corporation or no corporation. As a result, incorporation and growth produced no bureaucratic redtape to handicap Pabst in competition with smaller partnerships.

FINANCIAL FREEDOM

Indeed, the handicaps, such as they were, were on the other side. Pabst had gained all the advantages of corporateness without sacrificing any of the appreciable advantages of small, family-type organizations. One of these advantages was that ownership and management were in the same hands. This meant that no Pabst stockholders required steady dividends in order to live; that all the stockholders could actually live from their managerial salaries. Thus, profits could be used for expansion to as great a degree as might seem desirable. The company could be built up solely by reinvestment of earnings.

The following table, showing big profits and small dividends, indicates how Pabst built up its net worth from about $600,000 in 1873 to nearly $12,000,000 in 1893, without ever selling any new securities or contracting any long-term indebtedness. In 1884 the company's capital was increased to $2,000,000; in 1889 to $4,000,000; and in 1892 to $10,000,000. In each case, this was done by distributing the accumulated surplus among the stockholders in additional $1,000 shares.

CONDENSED FINANCIAL STATEMENT, 1873-1893

Year	Net Profit	Dividends *	Capital	Surplus †
1873 ‡	$188,108	......	$300,000	$488,108
1874	17,559	......	300,000	517,500
1875 **	38,850	......	300,000	542,101
1876	182,614	$23,232	300,000	745,941
1877	147,071	......	300,000	865,545
1878	58,619	......	300,000	924,165
1879	175,643	20,377	300,000	1,099,812
1880	188,957	25,838	300,000	1,268,391
1881 ††	314,643	170,180	300,000	1,557,196
1882 ‡‡	310,400	19,728	300,000	1,597,416
1883	389,960	38,996	300,000	2,067,708
1884	396,951	59,273	2,000,000	666,036
1885	545,258	500,000	2,000,000	1,211,294
1886	502,599	300,000	2,000,000	1,213,893
1887	606,504	200,000	2,000,000	1,520,397
1888	571,291	200,000	2,000,000	1,891,688
1889	941,520	400,000	4,000,000	941,520
1890	1,560,254	200,000	4,000,000	2,101,774
1891	1,186,931	200,000	4,000,000	3,088,705
1892	1,132,380	......	4,000,000	6,001,269
1893	1,455,016	250,000	10,000,000	1,456,285

* Dividends are recorded opposite the years from whose profits the sum was derived, although payment was usually made the first of the following year.
† Apparent discrepancy in the list comes from revaluation of the assets from time to time.
‡ Covers a 6-month-10-day period because of change of fiscal year.
** Covers an 8-month period because of change of fiscal year.
†† Covers a 13-month period because of change of fiscal year.
‡‡ Covers a 15-month period because of change of fiscal year.

Over the entire period 1873-1893, out of $10,911,130.96 in earnings, Pabst paid out $2,607,623.42 in dividends, but only $357,623.42 was distributed during the first twelve years. No records exist from which we may learn the reasoning of Pabst and Schandein in deciding between dividends and reinvestment. Probably they regarded investment in the brewery, not as a matter of choice to be governed by relative rates of profit as between the business and possible outside ventures, but rather as a duty which must always come first. They had unlimited confidence in their company, and investment in its needs was probably a matter of faith and loyalty as well as percentage returns.

The opportunities for the investment of capital in the brewery and in booming Milwaukee combined were so attractive that Pabst and Schandein were loath to keep any cash tied up in working capital. Even though interest rates ran 7 to 10 per cent, they depended for a large part of the necessary money for running the business on two local institutions, the Second Ward Savings Bank and the Wisconsin Marine and Fire Insurance Company. Their main reliance was the Second Ward Savings Bank started as the Second Ward Bank in 1856 chiefly to supply the credit needs of the brewers. It was reorganized and be came a member of the National Banking System in 1866. Valentin Blatz served as president from February 1, 1866, to his death in May 1894, and Frederick Pabst was a director from 1869 until his death in 1904.[14] By 1881 the bank's resources of over $2,500,000 made it the fourth largest national bank in Milwaukee, but it can readily be seen that the Phillip Best account with loans totaling over $360,000 at the end of the year was of primary importance in its portfolio. By 1892, the company's Second Ward loans were running as high as $1,000,000 during the busy spring season.[15]

During periods of financial difficulty, Pabst, Blatz, and Schlitz not only reduced their loans sharply but often helped the bank meet Eastern obligations by advancing their own company notes for New York discount. In return they received equal co-operation from the bank.[16] The Captain freely made overdrafts for

14 Bruce, *History of Milwaukee City and County,* I, 357.
15 See Appendix, p. 404, for table of bank loans.
16 For example, a Pabst note for $61,700 at 10 per cent, Sept. 1, 1871, was not repaid until June 9, 1875. Receipts and Voucher Book, 1869-86.

7

large amounts and allowed interest to accumulate, a practice that was customary in Great Britain and in some European countries, particularly in connection with foreign trade, but which had not become traditional in the United States. This practice seems to have been the subject of frequent debates between Charles Best, whose precise methodical mind was bothered by this lack of conventionality, and the Captain who found it a convenient way of conducting business. Without question, this complete freedom of financial operation in the hands of an able leader like Pabst was an important factor in the company's continued success.

EXPANSION AND THE BUSINESS CYCLE

The Captain probably made most use of his financial freedom in making decisions about plant expansion. Pabst sales expanded in twenty years from 100,000 to over 1,000,000 barrels. In one year, 1879, sales jumped as much as 26 per cent. Naturally, such leaps in demand severely taxed Pabst's plant. But so successful was the Captain in forecasting the market and providing for it that it appears that capacity and beer on hand were always great enough to meet demand within a reasonable time.

Both Pabst and national beer sales tended to follow fluctuations in the volume of business in general, except that instead of falling in depressions, the national sales merely leveled off, and Pabst continued to rise, although less steeply than usual (see table below). Beer, as a whole, was the poor man's drink, and the unemployment of depression periods reduced his ability to buy. But the Pabst market stood up unusually well under adversity, due probably to the fact that Pabst sold to the more prosperous class of beer drinkers.

Naturally, construction that could be planned well in advance should be undertaken in low-cost depression periods. The Captain seems to have tried to build on this basis, although, in view of the general lack of knowledge of the business cycle at this time, his record may have been due more to chance than to good management. Moreover, many of his most important expenditures were not motivated by opportunities for low-cost expansion but by accident or pressing current needs.

IMPROVEMENTS IN RELATION TO SALES, 1875-1893

Year	Money Voted for Brewery Improvements	Annual Sales in Barrels	Beer Brewed in Barrels	Total National Withdrawals in Barrels *
1873	......	100,028		8,910,824
1874	......	114,162		8,880,830
1875	$24,984	115,649	Figures	8,743,745
1876	63,500	120,951	not	9,159,676
1877	39,800	120,732	available	9,074,306
1878	11,700	156,041	from	9,473,361
1879	12,500	213,285	company	10,270,353
1880	105,000 †	272,477	records	12,346,077
1881	95,000	324,269		13,237,701
1882	366,900	371,302		15,680,678
1883	......	376,530		16,426,050
1884	......	378,519	375,983	17,573,723
1885	199,000	385,234	......	17,747,006
1886	210,000	440,423	436,438	19,157,613
1887	39,000	460,200	463,191	21,387,412
1888	40,000	500,216	505,638	22,829,203
1889	187,000	585,299	608,908	23,235,864
1890	32,000	700,232	772,779	25,494,798
1891	232,000	790,290	804,548	28,192,328
1892	......	908,346	871,788	29,431,498
1893	33,000	1,084,051	1,095,585	31,962,743

* Tax-paid beer for sale. See *Brewers' Almanac* [1946], p. 28.
† Money largely supplied by insurance payments.

The major accident was the fire of December 21, 1879, which completely destroyed the malthouse, the elevators, and the office building. But this was fully covered by insurance and involved no new cash outlay. The most pressing current need which made construction imperative was the doubling of sales between 1887 and 1892. This could not have been predicted with safety and indeed it was not. Had it been, new equipment would have been purchased in advance at lower costs. Moreover, as the brewery gradually grew to a capacity of 1,500,000 barrels by

1891, there were certain replacements, new machines, and enlargements that had to be made constantly whether prices were high or low. New icehouses, stables, platforms, and incidental buildings were constructed year after year as needs developed, and probably no normally endowed human being could have predicted these needs far in advance.

A glance at the table of expenditures above shows a great outlay for 1886, just before the big upswing began in 1887. But this was not simply for expansion purposes. It reflects the outlay attendant upon one of the most momentous decisions in Pabst history—the decision to close the South Side Brewery and to concentrate all brewing in an expanded plant at the Empire. This move, which entailed the construction of a new brewhouse at the Empire, was planned in the fall of 1885 in what appeared to be the bottom of a major depression, and, presumably, contracts were let for most of this work by December of that year, a month of comparatively low costs. Before the work was completed, however, prosperity had returned, and wages advanced so that it is impossible to tell to what extent the company was able to take advantage of depression rates.

But, regardless of actual building costs at the Empire, the closing of the South Side Brewery had far-reaching effects on the history of the company that could not have been foreseen clearly in 1885. It also had other more immediate effects that the Captain perhaps should have evaluated more carefully at the time. He saw, to be sure, that operating two breweries required two sets of brewmasters, foremen, and certain other workers. Moreover, with Schandein's health failing, it seemed only a matter of time before an additional manager would also be required. These considerations influenced the Captain greatly. Presenting this momentous question to the board, he is reported in the minutes to have said,

that he was now prepared to show that all of the work of manufacturing could be done at the Empire Brewery, by making certain changes and alterations, which could be made at a comparatively small expense and would thus render the whole South Side Brewery superfluous.

He stated that it was well known that in common with all great commodities of trade, the selling prices of beer had been greatly reduced during the past few years and showed a tendency for a further reduction, and that with increasing competition he thought it would soon become an absolute necessity to economize and reduce the manufacturing and operating expenses of the company, in order to net to the stockholders a fair return of interest on the capital invested; that he had been consulting with the superintendent of brewing, the foremen and architect of the company and found that by making the changes and alterations above referred to and which he explained in full through the meetings and making them at once, the Empire Brewery could be in shape by about May 1st next, to manufacture at least 400,000 barrels of beer per annum, which was equal to the present annual capacity of both the Empire and South Side Breweries, and that then the South Side Brewery could be suspended and the property disposed of or used for some other purposes.

The President further stated that he had requested the Secretary to figure up how much money could be saved annually, provided all the beer was manufactured at Empire Brewery and that upon careful investigation, it was found that an annual saving of $40,000 to $50,000 could be achieved; that the changes necessary to give the Empire Brewery the full capacity of both present breweries would not cost more than $50,000 which was only $5,000 or 10,000 more than what would be saved in one year alone after the making of the proposed changes, and he would strongly recommend the immediate adoption of the plan.

He further added that if immediate action was taken and the work properly pushed all the changes could be completed by May 1st next and the South Side Brewery could then be converted into a Malt House for a malting and storage company, for instance, and the dock property disposed of to good advantage, or the whole property could be sold or whatever a disposal might seem best for the interest of the stockholders. He further stated that he had given the matter of

disposing of the South Side property considerable thought and attention and was of the firm opinion that the whole property could be
sold at an advantageous figure at an early date.[17]

The Captain's arguments apparently were not only convincing to him but also to the board. He failed to state, however,
that shipping costs were less at the South Side because of the
railroad sidings and steamship docks there, which eliminated
any need for costly trucking. Perhaps the Captain had not sufficiently considered it. Besides this, all the bottling equipment
was there. To be sure, the Empire stood on the books at over
$700,000 more than the South Side. But, since the new improve-
ments entailed in the end an expense of almost $300,000, rather
than the $50,000 estimated at the meeting of December 1, this
same amount spent on the South Side would have gone a long
way toward shifting operations to that center; and the Empire
might have been progressively abandoned without sacrificing
a large amount of new equipment. Hindsight shows that this
would have been far the wiser policy. The whole problem was
one of balancing immediate capital losses against long-run economy, and the Captain seems to have decided not to take the
loss. But if the business were to outgrow either brewery, as it
soon did, and to become more dependent upon shipping and
bottling, which also proved to be the case, a strong argument
could have been made for the South Side as against the Empire.

These arguments undoubtedly were considered in the meeting, and we can only guess why they lacked force. Perhaps the
problem of disposing of the real estate of the Empire and acquiring more land around the South Side appeared difficult.
Or possibly the fact that sales had not advanced to any great extent since 1882 led all three officers to feel that the period of
great sales expansion was nearing its close, and that with a
400,000 barrel capacity at the Empire, the company could stabilize on that basis. Conscious or unconscious sentiment for the

17 Directors Record, Dec. 1, 1885.

"Hill" and the old brewery in which they had all started work, and around which most of the family traditions lay, may also have had its effect.

THE CAPTAIN AND HIS STAFF

While the Captain may have made some mistakes in long-range policy, he had rare gifts as an operating and marketing executive. A leading New York brewer said: "He is one of the greatest minds in organizing and systematizing details, so as to secure the best results in economy of time and labor, and of thus increasing profits." [18] He possessed the combination of easy informality and rigorous control that makes for high morale. He was a fine plant manager as well as an imaginative planner. "He knew the different bottling machines," said the head of that department, "as well as the men who operated them." [19] Whereas Carnegie commanded respect as the "Scotch Devil" for his quick understanding and boundless energy, he was not liked by the men. The same could be said of John D. Rockefeller, John Wanamaker, and many of the other outstanding business leaders of the period. They ruled by drive and ability, but, unlike Pabst, could not meet the ordinary workmen on a basis of mutual understanding and sympathy. It was this side of the Captain's personality, according to the accounts of old-timers, that had a great deal to do with establishing the personal loyalty of office, selling, and brewing employees. As Henry Stark said later, "He treated his employees as if they were men and while he always met them on familiar terms his manner was such that his dignity as head of Milwaukee's largest institution was upheld and he commanded the respect of every man and woman in his employ." [20] It must also be remembered that few men of other than German birth or parentage were brought

[18] *Sentinel*, July 31, 1892.
[19] *Sentinel*, Jan. 2, 1904.
[20] *Sentinel*, Jan. 2, 1904.

into the home office, which helped to provide a certain cama-
raderie among the staff and to make them proud of the Captain
as a fine example of German leadership in an American city.

Like most of the other great pioneers, the Captain was a
prodigious worker. Fred Pabst, looking back to the eighties,
says:

The picture I have of the good old days is one of work and more
work. I remember very well how my father on many occasions left
for the brewery before breakfast early in the morning. He went
through the malthouse, brewhouse and cellars and then came home
for a hurried breakfast, after which he went back to the brewery
again and spent his time in the office or brewery until twelve o'clock.
Often he brought business friends home to luncheon and without
any relaxation returned to the brewery, where he worked until six
o'clock at night.[21]

During these long hours the Captain kept his hand on every
activity of the business, but, at the same time, wisely delegated
authority to men on the spot. The following letter to a traveling
representative is a good sample of the Captain's judicious handling of subordinates.

We received both of your favors dated St. Joseph, August 2nd inst.
and have carefully perused the same and must acknowledge there is
a great deal of truth in what you say. Ever since I held a responsible
position in younger days steamboating, I was always told to go ahead
and use my own judgment. I felt the responsibility of my action and
of course always used my best judgment and luckily generally came
out on the right side up. I have followed up this principle since I
have been in the brewing business and when we send anybody on
the road I calculate that that body shall use his own judgment to a
great extent. If that body is not the right man, a general as you
may call him, and his judgment is not good we should not keep him
and put some one else in his place. Sometimes you may find persons
hard headed and they think their way is the only way to heaven and
although they use good judgment generally they get out of the hack

[21] *Blue Ribbon News,* June 1936, p. 3.

now and then. For instance had we followed your Washington advice we would have been $2,000 out. Your New York business was not at all satisfactory. You were instructed to look into contracts and cancel all the contracts you possibly could. What did you do? You advised us to keep on. We sent a man to New York and in less than a week he had cancelled every contract in existence. Now your St. Joseph matter. I told you when you went there we did *not* want to buy that stock unless it was perfectly safe for us to do so, then you telegraphed for $13,000.00 without a word of explanation although you had had plenty of time to give us the particulars. All these transactions if they don't quite shake the confidence in the general, they set me thinking. For fear the general might get on the wrong side of the battle I want you to take this as it is given here. I talk to you openly and above board. You cannot complain of not having had authority enough whenever you want. We always let you have your way as far as possible. And so much as anyone can be reasonable. Now when you come back I will talk the matter over with you. Now be sure and look into the outstandings and again call Mr. Worst's attention to the same. We must under no circumstances let our accounts run up and make bad debts.[22]

In common with the practice in other companies, Pabst's clerical staff was expected to share the long hours of the chief executives and the laborers. Six days a week, office work began at eight in the morning and continued until six at night, with an hour off for lunch. In the summer rush, some overtime work was expected without extra pay. But good profits, rapid expansion, and relatively small management costs compared with other expenses in brewing allowed the company to give good workers continual raises in pay. Office salaries went up even in the depression of the 1870's as the company grew larger and each job came to be more responsible. The workers in this period benefited doubly, for, as their money income increased, living expenses tended generally downward.

[22] Pabst to F. E. Schmidt, Aug. 9, 1888.

Highest Salaries Paid Monthly [23]
(Exclusive of Officers of the Company)

1877		1885		1892	
Number of Employees	Amount	Number of Employees	Amount	Number of Employees	Amount
1	$333.34	2	$416.33	1	$833.33
1	250.00	1	250.00	3	416.66
1	150.00	3	200.00	1	300.00
2	125.00	1	191.56	3	291.66
2	83.34	2	175.00	7	250.00
3	75.00	1	166.66	4	208.33
1	60.00	2	150.00	2	200.00

Starting around 1881 Pabst frequently paid Christmas bonuses of $500 to $1,000, which were accompanied by personal notes of appreciation from the Captain like the following:

Mein Lieber Stark!

I enclose you our check for $500.00 in consideration and appreciation of your services. Hoping that the friendly relations that now exist may always remain and my best wishes for you and your family, I remain truly yours

FRED PABST.

Even though the form of the letter was fairly standardized, the men knew the Captain and knew that he meant what he said.

As long as the two chief proprietors owned most of the company's stock, they followed the rather common practice of taking their extra returns in dividends rather than salary. When, in 1891, the stockholders became more numerous, the Captain put his own salary at a more realistic level. Since Secretary Charles Best, Jr., was never a large enough stockholder to live on his dividends, his salary was based from the start on the estimated value of his services.

Monthly Salaries of Officers of the Company

	1877	1881	1889	1893
President	$208.33	$208.33	$208.33	$1,000.00
Vice-President	208.33	208.33	208.33	300.00
Secretary	250.00	416.66	833.33	416.66

[23] For detailed information on office staff in 1880, see Appendix E, p. 403.

EARLY ACCOUNTING

Charles Best's task of keeping the company's accounts was, of course, of great importance. Good cost accounting, even before the word was known in America, was a significant factor in Rockefeller's success. Can the same be said of Pabst's success during Charles Best's regime as head of the bookkeeping department? Did he develop methods that quickly revealed waste and inefficiency, and did these methods lead to innovations in plant organization? These questions can be answered in the affirmative, but not all at once.

While Charles Best had the concept of unit costs firmly in mind from the start, he was very young when he first assumed charge of bookkeeping, and, moreover, he was recording the transactions of a brewery of unprecedented size. He had previously been the head bookkeeper of a Chicago importing house, but he had much to learn from experience about brewery accounts.[24] From 1873 on he kept labor costs per barrel, for example, but he had not yet distinguished between managerial and operating labor, so that it would have been hard to have used his cost figure as a check on inefficiency at any given point. Barley and hops used per barrel were noted on a quantity basis throughout the period, but diminution of these costs came from changed methods of brewing rather than a drive for economy.

Charles Best's accounting practices seemed satisfactory enough until the close of 1884 when the depression may have led management to reconsider the company's whole production and control setup. An additional incentive to improving cost information at this time was the Captain's idea of shutting down the South Side Brewery and concentrating all operations at the Empire. Only from more detailed analyses than had been made in the past could the directors evaluate the two breweries from an operating standpoint and decide just how each one stood.

---

[24] His previous positions were: clerk and delivery boy in a retail grocery store, general utility boy and assistant clerk in a Chicago importing house, stock clerk and assistant bookkeeper in the same house, and finally head bookkeeper. Andrew Jackson Aiken and Lewis A. Proctor, *Men of Progress, Wisconsin*, p. 728.

The need for such decisions has been one of the chief incentives for better accounting in many American businesses. At Pabst's the needs of the situation led to the introduction of accounts for total raw material, total operating, and depreciation costs per barrel at both breweries. Furthermore, an elaborate cost analysis of all branches of the business was appended to the annual statement for 1884. The modern cost accountant would undoubtedly say that few of the operations were broken down sufficiently to permit critical analyses of unit costs, but Charles Best's efforts probably compared favorably with the practices of the average American big business of this period.

Depreciation was one of the concepts about which Charles Best and most other early accountants were careless. As was the case in most American companies, Pabst only entered occasional depreciation charges, usually when book values appeared to be out of line with market values. From 1873 until 1878, Pabst's brewing properties were not depreciated at all, but, in the latter year, slashing reductions suddenly were made in order to take account of the sharp decline in prices during the depression. Valuation of the brewing properties, which had stood at $487,271.13, was reduced to $381,400, and the resulting loss of $105,871.13 was charged against surplus. Typically, for the period, this reduction was not made on the basis of age but rather on the basis of changed market value. The general theory seems to have been to charge all replacements and repairs to operating costs. This allowed the assumption that each part of the structure would be continuously renewed, and would thus retain its full market value. This approach to repairs and construction like Pabst's approach to depreciation in general was very widespread at the time. Even many railroads kept no depreciation account but simply entered replacements as operating expenses.

Starting in 1883, however, Charles Best appears to have swung over to more modern accounting methods. He began to depreciate properties at varying annual rates which depended upon periodic examinations. Such examinations no doubt revealed greater wear and tear on some properties than on others, and many items, added to the depreciation schedule for the first time, were depreciated heavily in the initial year. An old artesian well, for example, on being added to the schedule, was initially depreciated 50 per cent. A few categories, such as cooperage, appear to have been depreciated at very low rates, as, for example, 5 per cent in 1883 and 2.5 per cent in 1884. These rates did not cover cooperage wear and loss, but the difference was made up by adding replacements to replenish the stock without capitalizing the additions. By 1886 Charles Best began to total all depreciation charges to get a figure for depreciation per barrel produced at both the South Side and Empire Breweries. He also got a figure representing general annual depreciation on all properties associated with the brewing business, including branches and other out-of-town properties.

Improved cost accounting does not seem to have caused any real change in Pabst's manufacturing methods, save, ironically enough, the now questionable abandonment of the South Side Brewery. Some changes in methods, to be sure, were made in this period, but it is difficult to attribute them to cost accounting. Raw grains were used to replace partially the more costly malt, and machinery replaced more and more hand operations, but the obvious savings from these changes did not have to be pointed up by cost accounting. An exception may be made in the case of ice machinery.

The actual money saving that would result from the introduction of the Boyle machine after 1879 was so uncertain that Charles Best made a detailed analysis of the costs of artificial refrigeration. The analysis from the standpoint of direct expense actually came out against the use of ice machinery, but the machinery was used more and more extensively, however, because it made possible appreciable savings in space and better control over temperature. The cost analysis in this instance, made in 1883, follows: [25]

[25] Annual Statement of Affairs, Book A, as stated.

Ice Machinery Expenses

Maintenance	$26,307.35
Repairs	5,185.12
Actual expense	31,492.47
10% wear and tear on whole system	9,804.39
Total	$41,296.86

Cost of Natural Ice for Cooling an Equal Amount of Beer

Cost of ice, based on four-year average	$29,986.47
Ten men for handling ice	2,700.00
Total	$32,686.47

THE ECONOMIES OF LARGE-SCALE PRODUCTION

From analogy with other industries, it would seem that economies of large-scale production should have accrued to Pabst simply from having gained an initial head start in the brewing business and then exploiting it. If this were true it would explain how the company maintained its leadership, once having acquired it. But if such economies were the principal secret of Pabst's continued success, its costs per barrel should have declined sharply as volume increased. This does not seem to have happened, and for good reasons. Unlike big purchases of manufactured goods, there is no economy in large-scale buying of agricultural products. Indeed, if anything, the effect of large purchases is to raise rather than lower such prices. Naturally this applies to barley and hops, the major raw materials in beer, and thus one of the major costs of production.

Raw-material costs, then, cannot be expected in the case of brewing to vary on the basis of volume, or to give any noticeable advantage to the biggest company. Nor is there any apparent advantage in transportation costs. Considerably smaller companies than Pabst could transport raw materials to their plants in carload lots; and as railroad rates on staple grains were not subject to large alterations, probably no company, however large, could have saved much on these transportation costs.

The problem of labor costs and general manufacturing expenses are not so easily disposed of, but, here again, it is difficult to find any particular advantage for the largest producer. The improvements in Pabst's accounting methods help a little in attempting to track down the elements of comparative labor costs and manufacturing expenses, and, while there can be no hard and fast conclusion, it is possible to get a rough general picture. The operating costs of the Empire and South Side Breweries would seem to offer an excellent basis for the comparison of expenses at different levels of production. During the fourteen years from 1873 until the closing of the South Side in 1886, the Empire produced from two to three and a half times as much beer as its sister plant—a difference comparable to that between a brewery like Pabst producing for the national market and the volume of a good-sized local competitor. How did this difference affect labor costs? From the following table the difference appears to be moderate in comparison with the total cost of making beer.

LABOR AND PRODUCTION AT EMPIRE AND SOUTH SIDE [26]

Year	NUMBER OF EMPLOYEES		SALES * IN 000's BARRELS		LABOR COSTS PER BARREL	
	Empire	South Side	Empire	South Side	Empire	South Side
1873 †	Figures not available	Figures not available	68	31	$1.07	$1.02
1874			78	37	0.995	0.9875
1875 ‡			52	25	1.015	0.98
1876			83	38	0.935	0.96
1877			85	35	0.84	0.85
1878	138	49	101	40	0.829	0.836
1879	143	58	136	55	0.743	0.76
1880	160	75	192	73	0.60	0.698
1881 **	235	102	241	97	0.645	0.595
1882 ††	355	79	340	104	0.623	0.66
1883	315	83	285	81	0.63	0.703
1884	346	88	298	80	0.603	0.708
1885	349	98	295	91	0.397	0.505

* Production figures not available, but the records of later years indicate a close correlation.
† Covers a 6-month-10-day period because of change of fiscal year.
‡ Covers an 8-month period because of change of fiscal year.
** Covers a 13-month period because of change of fiscal year.
†† Covers a 15-month period because of change of fiscal year.

[26] Figures exactly as given in Annual Statement of Affairs, Book A.

These figures are not entirely satisfactory because various amounts of malting and repair labor as well as managerial salaries at both breweries were included. But the downward trend at both plants was probably due more to improvements in technology and better organization of work than to increased volume. Similarly in the period from 1887 to 1893, when Empire production doubled, improvements in technology and lack of comparative figures for other firms prevent our isolating the gain due solely to larger scale operations. Output per worker went up at Pabst from 1,172 barrels annually in 1887 to 1,590 in 1893—a gain of 34 per cent—and total wage and salary costs per barrel declined 13.3 per cent, but smaller breweries may also have had similar gains.

Even a possible 10 or 15 per cent saving in operating costs per barrel, due to larger production, was too small in the case of a product like beer to drive out smaller competitors by price reductions. Transportation costs alone on the shipper's beer would absorb this advantage in most markets. The large producer found it far more advantageous to strive to maintain prices and to use the added margin for improving quality and pushing sales. In other words, a saving in production costs as against the smaller brewer allowed the big company to spend more money in building its market. Thus in 1887 Pabst spent only 57.7 cents a barrel for nonmanufacturing purposes, while by 1893, in spite of a slight decline in the general price level, the company was spending 87 cents.

Some reasons for Pabst's leadership have now become evident. The company in these years always had able executive leadership. Company morale was generally maintained among employees at all levels. More tangible, though certainly no more important in explaining Pabst's success, were wise additions to productive capacity and improvements in the brewing process. Both made possible an added margin for selling expenditures. The wise use of this margin increased sales and further reduced the cost of beer. The whole process allowed Pabst to keep its plant and its methods always up to date—indeed, a little ahead of most other brewers. How this, in turn, affected the company's success, we will examine next.

CHAPTER V

BREWING BECOMES MORE SCIENTIFIC

Two developments made the period from 1873 to 1893 the greatest, technologically speaking, in the thousands of years of brewing history. The first was the rapid introduction of new machinery. The second was the extension and application of scientific knowledge. New machinery ended hand labor in many processes and thus greatly increased productivity. It also provided apparatus much more susceptible to exact control. The new contributions of pure science helped greatly in solving the industry-old problem of how to produce a beer that would always look the same, smell the same, and taste the same when produced from the same materials.

By using new scientific theory and by installing new machinery, Pabst easily kept abreast of the best practices in the industry. As the industry's largest company, it naturally was not in a position to experiment with untried devices in its mass-production line. But, as soon as new processes proved their value, Pabst adopted them. The inventions of Pabst's own brilliant brewmaster, J. F. Theurer, contributed substantially to the development of more uniform beer.

IMPROVED MECHANISMS

The earliest technological improvements in this period were in malting where fundamental changes were made between 1875 and 1890. These changes corrected three major difficulties: uneven steeping and germination of the barley; unwanted germination in the drying kiln; uneven drying. Other inventions during this period made it possible to malt during the summer by the use of artificially chilled and dampened air.

These improvements were not adopted immediately by Pabst. But before building the new malthouse after the fire of 1879, Emil Schandein made a tour of the country's larger breweries to examine malting methods. As a result of his trip, Pabst installed new-style steep tanks for barley that could be emptied quickly and evenly so that the bottom of the mass of grain would not be soaked longer than the top. Schandein also found and Pabst installed new steel-wire kiln floors that helped to ensure uniform heating and drying of the barley. The inventions that were to affect the germinating process had not yet proved their worth in this country by 1879. Two years later, the Galland pneumatic system was patented.[1] Its first tests were not altogether satisfactory, however, and floor malting was therefore continued for a time. This old method, by which the wet barley from the steep tanks is spread evenly about two or three feet thick over a concrete floor in a cool room and turned from time to time by hand shoveling, is still preferred by some maltsters. In large breweries in Germany the practice was continued well into the present century This method is very slow and laborious, however, and improvement was badly needed. The first practical improvement came in 1885 with the successful installation of the Saladin pneumatic malting system in the malthouse of the L. C. Huck Malting Company in Chicago. This immediately attracted the attention of near-by brewers and maltsters, including, of course, Captain Pabst. After inspecting the system carefully, the Captain entered into correspondence in 1889 with the Saladin Pneumatic Malting Construction Company of Chicago and arranged for a partial installation which they described to him as follows:

I herewith submit to you project plans with estimates for arranging the two lower stories of your present large malt house for the Saladin Pneumatic System of Malting, providing therein 16 compartments, each 10 feet, 1 inch in width by 52 feet in length, with a height between perforated compartment floors and rack-bar rails 3 feet, 11½ inches, which is the maximum height prescribed by Mr. Saladin.

[1] Except where otherwise noted, all the general details concerning the scientific and technical improvements in brewing during this period are supported by the authoritative discussion in *One Hundred Years of Brewing*.

With this height upon each square foot will be loaded 1⅛ bushels of barley for germinating, which will be 589 bushels in each compartment, giving a yearly, 343 days, capacity of 16 compartments with 5 days for germinating, 646,486 bushels and with 6 days for germinating 538,738 bushels which latter period I would recommend.

The six remaining floors of your present malt-house would still have a capacity of 63,750 bushels per month for making malt by the old system, to which the pneumatic system will add 46,880 bushels per month, or future entire capacity of the house 110,630 bushels per month, which for each day will be 3,687 bushels of malt.

Your two malt kilns each with four floors 53 feet by 38 feet have an entire surface of 16,112 square feet, which I believe will be sufficient for the entire germinating capacity, particularly since the pneumatic green malt will be withered previous to transferring upon the kiln floors.

The steeped barley will be conducted into the germinating compartments from the present steep tanks in the attic together with the steep water through two 3 inch pipes placed downward along the posts and thence through branch pipes under the ceiling of the germinating room to be trimmed into the compartments by means of rubber hose, when the steep water will strain through the perforated compartment floors, escaping into the sewers.

The unloading from the compartments will be done by means of a power scraper into conveyors below the germinating floor, that will carry the withered green malt to either elevator leg, for which purpose the transverse conveyor will be geared to be rotated in either direction.

The power required will be:

8 Sturtevant Fans, each 19,100 cubic feet capacity per minute requiring 4 6-10 horse power........	40 horse power
8 Echangeurs, each 2 horse power................	16 " "
3 Malt Turning Machines, each 3 h.p.............	9 " "
Scraper, Conveyor and Transmissions............	10 " "
	75 horse power

I have prepared two plans, one with pressure fans on compartment floor, and the other one with all the fans in basement, which latter arrangement I would recommend.[2]

The total cost was set at $79,992.

This first installation was completed in 1891, and was so successful that in the next decade compartment malting was introduced on all floors of the Pabst malthouse.

Uniformity in the machine-made malt was soon supplemented by uniformity in the malt mash. This was achieved by replacing the old decoction method of mashing (described in Chapter II), with its tedious hand operations and need for additional vessels for boiling, with the upward infusion process. In this process mashing is started at a fairly low temperature—around 120 or 130 degrees F.—which is gradually raised to about 160 or 170 degrees F., by the infusion of hotter and hotter liquid. As the infusions are pumped mechanically into the mashing tubs, hand labor is altogether eliminated.

The use of steam heat for warming the mashing water, and for boiling the wort, made possible a uniformity and control of temperature which had been impossible in the days of direct cooking over a fire. The advantages of such exact temperature controls in organic chemical operations cannot be overemphasized. In a complex mixture, such as beer wort, a 20 degree change in temperature may lead to interaction between the various elements and compounds that will change the character of the resulting liquor. This was one of the continual problems of early brewing days. Now it was solved.

The use of steam-driven machinery to stir the mash in the tuns ensured additional uniformity in the brew by making it easy to regulate the mixing of the malt with the warm water. This also lessened the danger of pasty masses of flour forming in the mash that prevented the conversion of the imprisoned starch into sugar. Consequently, it led to a more uniform wort from a given quantity of malt. The wort in the brew kettles was

[2] H. Lotz, Saladin Malting Construction Co., to Pabst Brewing Co., Jan. 3, 1890.

also stirred by steam-driven paddles or revolving steam coils that provided heat as well. This constant motion not only prevented explosive bubbling, but also mixed the hops in more evenly.

One of the most serious causes of infection in beer, leading to unpleasant taste and murky appearance, was the practice of kraeusening. As explained in Chapter II, in this process, young, actively fermenting beer, full of yeast particles and other unstable organic substances, was introduced into the finished product in order to provide fresh carbonation. When Theurer arrived at Pabst as superintendent of brewing in 1884, he began to study the possibilities of carbonating by some other method. Before the end of the decade he had developed a system of collecting carbon dioxide that was given off in great quantities during primary fermentation, clearing it of impurities and readding it under pressure to the finished beer.

Theurer's elimination of the old-style chip casks, where the beer had been clarified by the settling of the solid particles on oak chips, through the use of filters, was almost as important as his pioneering in direct carbonation. In the old days no filters were fine enough to remove the minute particles of albuminoids and other solid matter that adhered to the oak chips in the final storage tanks. But "fining," or clarifying, by use of chips was at best an incomplete process and needed a continuous cleaning out of dirty chips, and a supplying of new ones. The introduction in 1887 of the new Stockheim filters, developed in Germany, was the first step in eliminating this second great cause of unreliable beer.

The importance of these changes was attested by the famous German brewing scientist, Dr. M. Delbrück, when he visited the Pabst brewery some years later.

I saw it here, the entire brewery was based upon the carbonating process. . . . . In the simplest manner the beer was supplied with that which under the old systems had to be done by treatment lasting for weeks and by kraeusening in the chip casks.[3]

[3] *American Brewers' Review*, VII, No. 40 (Apr. 5, 1894), 608.

One of the economies of brewing resulted from the opportunity to sell as cattle feed the spent grains from the mashing tuns. Until 1890, however, this spent grain was handled and shipped in a wet condition. Tons of water, with the small weight of useful feed, went along. This made transportation costs very high. About 1890, Pabst therefore started drying the feed in advance by installing ten mechanical driers with a combined capacity of 100 tons of wet grain per day.[4] This resulted in an appreciable saving.

Artificial refrigeration as a labor-saving device of this period ranked with mechanized pneumatic malting. It displaced dozens of ice cutters and handlers, just as the Saladin process did away with turners or shovelers on the malting floor. Artificial refrigeration, however, was more important for other reasons than the saving of labor: it allowed far more exact temperature control in the fermenting and storage rooms; it saved the very large amount of space necessary for ice storage and ice packing; it eliminated the deep cellars used for cool storage, and thus permitted brewing completely above the ground. This made for more efficient architecture. Now, more nearly horizontal production lines were possible. Storage tanks no longer had to be many stories below ground, so that containers no longer had to be filled at low levels or the finished beer no longer needed to be pumped to the surface. The better ventilation possible for the outside rooms in above-ground buildings also made for healthier working conditions.

Artificial refrigeration, however, was a mixed blessing to Pabst. Milwaukee, as we have noted, was far better supplied with natural ice than most brewing centers, and Pabst had icehouses for stocking large quantities in branch centers, so that artificial refrigeration lessened an important competitive advantage. This may help to explain the Captain's tardiness in installing artificial refrigeration. Beginning in 1875, several types

[4] *Western Brewer*, XX, No. 1 (Jan. 15, 1895), 95. See also United States Brewers' Association, *Report of Convention Proceedings* [1891], p. 50.

of refrigerating machines were installed in more southerly breweries, but only after long consideration of the reports of their use did the Captain decide that the Boyle type was the best. As Ferdinand Heim, a brewer of Kansas City who had installed a Boyle machine in 1878, wrote:

Our system . . . . in fact, was one of the first really successful ice machines to be installed in any brewery in the United States. We had visitors from all over the country from the larger breweries and packing houses.[5]

A Boyle machine of 150-ton refrigerating capacity, run by a 40 horsepower steam engine, was bought by Pabst for $12,500 on October 16, 1879, and installed early the following year. This one machine could displace only a part of the ice usually required, and, hence, its operation was carefully compared with the systems in use in other breweries before more machines were added. Schandein, for example, while studying refrigeration in eastern establishments in the spring of 1880, wrote:

With regard to the ice machine I couldn't learn anything beyond my report to you from Hoboken. So far the Cook system seems to be the best for it serves its purpose and keeps the cellars as dry as a room. With Portner's improvements it can't be surpassed. I've also seen Rankin's machine at Ruppert's, but it wasn't working at the moment, the pipes freeze, burst, etc., and it was regarded as an expensive humbug in which Ruppert has by now experimented away many thousands of dollars. Ringler in New York is now installing a machine which was made in Nordhausen, Germany.[6]

But the Boyle equipment stood the test and an additional $65,000 worth of Boyle machinery was purchased in the summer of 1881. By the end of 1886, the company owned the following ice machinery: [7]

3 Boyle machines of 150 tons refrigerating power
1 Boyle machine of 25 tons refrigerating power

[5] *One Hundred Years of Brewing*, p. 127.
[6] Schandein to Pabst, Mar. 30, 1880. Translated from the German.
[7] These figures and those immediately following are from the Annual Statement of Affairs, Book A.

1 De La Vergne machine of 75 tons refrigerating power
1 Weisel machine of 120 tons refrigerating power

The next year the purchase of natural ice dropped to a nominal figure, and ceased entirely after 1888.

While Charles Best did not find that the earliest ice machines saved any money on cooling alone, such machines made it possible to eliminate the very costly fermenting and storage houses where natural ice had been used. An old-fashioned fermenting room needed 20 feet of solid ice above the tanks which meant a pressure on the ceiling of 1,150 pounds per square foot. In the days of wooden construction, to build such a ceiling with as much as a 20-foot span was an engineering problem. In 1883 Best noted how the new machines also made possible the much more economical utilization of space.

We store 122,604 barrels of beer in the rooms cooled by the ice machines of which quantity we store 34,565 barrels in the rooms formerly filled with ice.

In 1891, a 300-ton capacity De La Vergne ice machine was added. This is still in the engine room in Milwaukee and was in active service until 1937. As better machines were developed, the cost of cooling each barrel was reduced below the cost of natural ice.

EXPENSES FOR NATURAL AND MACHINE-MADE ICE

Year	Production in Barrels	Natural Ice Expenses	Ice Machine Expenses (including depreciation)
1884	375,983	$10,811.13	$33,468
1885	385,234 *	14,312.79	28,052
1886	436,438	14,135.15	39,505
1887	463,181	527.56	44,162
1888	505,638	9.90	43,263
1889	608,908	none	43,919
1890	772,779	none	49,866
1891	804,548	none	64,366
1892	871,788	none	55,691

* Figures for 1885 are sales figures.

The ice machines also made possible another economy. They permitted operations at lower temperatures than natural ice could effect. This meant less foaming while storage tanks and containers were being filled. A new nozzle for use in filling the containers also reduced foaming waste. The result was that shrinkage in the volume of beer between storage tank and shipping container dropped from 22.18 per cent in 1886 to 10 per cent in 1889.[8]

The installation of electric dynamos and incandescent lights, supplied by the Western Edison Light Company, led to safer and better lighting.

THE CONTRIBUTIONS OF PURE SCIENCE

While practical men were introducing machinery that made beer cheaper and more reliable, laboratory scientists, often with no interest in brewing as such, were developing knowledge of great importance to brewers. This was particularly true of fermentation, understanding of which was greatly advanced between 1860 and 1890 by Pasteur in France and Hansen in Denmark. Before them, the Frenchman Cagniard de La Tour, in 1837, and the Germans, Knetzing and Turpin, in 1838, had pointed out that yeast was a vegetable organism that caused fermentation of the beer wort through its own development. But the further pursuit of their theories was hindered by the opposition of the great German chemist Liebig who developed a completely untenable theory that fermentation was due to motion set up in the liquid by some substance decomposing. This idea, backed up by Liebig's eminence, stood across the path of research on the bacterial or germ theory for the next twenty years.

In 1857, however, some irregularities in fermentation in a near-by distillery called Louis Pasteur to the study of yeast. Three years of inquiry resulted in a book, published in 1860, in which Pasteur demonstrated that yeast was not only a living organism but that the natural changes in this organism were re-

[8] Annual Statement of Affairs, Book A.

sponsible for the products of alcoholic fermentation. Pasteur showed that fermentation came from activity in the yeast cells themselves; he proved that, given free oxygen, yeast grew as a fungus, but, when denied oxygen, it acted as a ferment. Five years later in his *Etude sur le Vin,* he made perhaps his most important contribution to practical brewing by proving that heating the liquid containing the yeast to a temperature slightly under boiling—that is, "pasteurizing" the liquid—would stop the action of microorganisms, and, by so doing, would prevent both further fermentation and spoilage.

In the 1870's, Pasteur turned his attention to beer as the best medium for the continuation of his experiments, and thus he developed the theoretical basis for modern fermenting practice. As the wort came from the brew kettle, after boiling, it was free from bacteria or other microorganisms. If it were now exposed only to purified air, and the pitching yeast were also free from undesirable organisms, the results would be predictable. In his emphasis on the need for pure yeast, he did not mean yeast of a single variety but, rather, a yeast free from bacteria and other small organisms called micoderma, as well as certain harmful varieties of the yeast fungus.

These researches in beer led directly to Pasteur's *Etudes sur la Bière* in 1876, his theory of infectious disease, published in 1877, and his discussion of virus and vaccines, published in 1880.

It remained, however, for the Danish chemist, E. C. Hansen, working in the research laboratory of the Jacobsen Brewery at Alt Carlsberg near Copenhagen, to develop after 1878 the theory of "pure" yeast.[9] Hansen discovered that certain varieties of yeast hurt the flavor and appearance of beer, and that these harmful varieties could be eliminated by propagating a pure yeast from a single cell of a type favorable to beer. In 1883, Hansen successfully introduced such pure yeast into the practical operations of the Jacobsen Brewery, and published the results of his experiments in German the following year.

[9] Hansen, *Practical Studies in Fermentation,* passim.

Hansen's book was not translated into English until 1896, but the Milwaukee brewers learned of his work with extraordinary rapidity. Not only was pure yeast culture introduced at the Pabst brewery in 1887, but a research chemist was added to the staff to supervise brewing operations.

Pure science also aided the brewers through its contributions to the development of artificial refrigeration. The Carré ice machines, from which stemmed all later types, were based on the principles established by Faraday that certain gases could be liquified under pressure, and that the expansion and evaporation attendant upon the removal of the pressure would produce intense cold. Carré's chief contribution was to make Faraday's principles commercially available by the use of aqua ammoniae as the refrigerating gas. In 1860 Carré patented the first direct ancestor of the brewery ice machines of the next decade.

TOWARD A SCIENCE OF BREWING

The successful application of the methods of science to practical brewing problems opened up areas for new research and systematic teaching. Both research and teaching were expanded rapidly throughout the Western world by brewing schools, brewers associations, research institutes, and trade publications. To be sure, the art of brewing had been taught on a systematic basis in centers such as Munich, Vienna, and Prague since the 1830's or 1840's, but specialized brewing schools do not seem to have spread widely, even in Germany, before the scientific advances that occurred in the sixties. The school established in 1861 at Worms, the largest city near the birthplace of the Bests, was certainly one of the earliest of the new group. Graduates of such European schools soon appeared in the United States and set up their own courses of instruction. But the initial attempt to combine instruction with new research was the establishment of the First Scientific Station for the Art of Brewing by Anton Schwarz in New York in 1880.[10] This was followed in 1886 by

[10] Incorporated as the Schwarz Laboratories in 1922.

the Wahl-Henius Institute in Chicago, and the National Brewers Academy and Consulting Bureau in New York in 1888.[11] The annual meetings of the national and state brewers associations also served as forums for the exchange of the new knowledge. Five trade periodicals started in New York and Chicago between the late sixties and early eighties: *Der Amerikanische Bierbrauer* ["The American Brewer"] put out by A. Schwarz of New York in 1868; *The American Brewers' Gazette* by John Flintoff of New York in 1871; *The German and American Brewers Journal* by John Tovey of New York in 1876; *The Western Brewer* by J. M. Wing and Company of Chicago in 1876; and *Der Brauer und Mälzer* by Eugene Sittig of Chicago in 1881.[12] These monthly magazines, distributing news in English and German, spread political, scientific, and mechanical information of interest to brewers.

As early as December of 1881, the officers of Pabst were aware of the value of a trained chemist. Thus Charles Best wrote to Dr. A. H. Bauer, a German scientist in New York, asking that he recommend someone whom he thought suitable.[13] Bauer apparently could not find the right man, and it was not until 1886 that a German doctor of philosophy in chemistry, Otto Mittenzwey, was added to the staff at the Empire. Mittenzwey was probably among the first thoroughly trained scientists to enter the employ of an American brewery. Systematic testing and the application of the latest European learning now began to replace reliance on traditional panaceas, uncontrolled experiments, and rumors as to competitors' practices. In November of 1892, Dr. Paul Fischer, formerly assistant to Professor M. Delbrück of the Experimental Brewing Center in Berlin, succeeded Mittenzwey, who left to marry the daughter of a brewer in Troy, New York.[14] Dr. Alfred J. Schedler, in turn, replaced

11 Thomann, *Documentary History,* pp. 77-78.
12 *One Hundred Years of Brewing,* p. 149.
13 Letter, Dec. 17, 1881.
14 *Western Brewer,* XX, No. 1 (Jan. 15, 1895), 126. Interview with A. J. Schedler, Pabst Brewing Co.

Fischer as chief of the laboratory, in 1902, and was still the chief brewery technologist for Pabst in 1946. In his long career, he achieved many important improvements in technical processing. As a result, from the time of Mittenzwey and Fischer to the present day, Pabst has been a leader in the use of the laboratory as an aid to brewing.

FROM THEORY TO PRACTICE

The spread of knowledge and its adoption in commerce is a slow process. In spite of the gradual increase in brewing knowledge after 1870, the problems of the big national breweries grew steadily more numerous and the brewmasters had a harder time solving them than ever before or since. One of the great needs was for beer that could stand long-distance shipping in both kegs and bottles, and yet meet the uncompromising American demand for beer with certain definite qualities of color, clarity, and taste. The difficulties in producing such a beer harassed brewmasters for many years before they solved the problems involved by a mixture of scientific findings and practical experience. Meanwhile, brewmasters succeeded or failed, almost by chance, and in most of the big breweries changes were frequent.

The cures for uneven brews, even when known in theory, often took years to translate into practice, partly because of lack of the laboratory staff necessary to check all operations, and partly because some remedies required new types of machinery. Pasteurization, for example, as a guard against the growth and development of organisms, was known to scientists by 1880, but pasteurizing machinery was only developed at the end of the decade. Similarly, extreme chilling to precipitate all substances that might later make the beer cloudy when cold and the elimination of such precipitates through filtering were both recognized as theoretically desirable long before the mechanical developments that made them possible were perfected in the 1890's. The same lag between knowledge and commercial machinery retarded the use of constant pressure racking—that is, the filling of the barrels under constant pressure.

The lack of proper machinery, and hence the inability to control operations precisely at all points, meant that beer was produced under almost constantly changing conditions. Naturally, a good brewmaster able to adjust to such conditions was an important factor during these years in the continuing success of any big brewing company. At Pabst until the abandonment of the South Side in 1886, the situation was complicated further by having two breweries whose product had to be made as uniform as possible. The Captain fortunately appears to have had the ability generally to select able brewmasters, or to replace quickly those in whom he was mistaken.

The first Pabst brewmaster of whom we have official record, originally called foreman and later superintendent of brewing, was Philipp Jung who came as assistant foreman in February 1873. He was typical of the German experts who were flocking to America. In 1859, at the age of fourteen, Jung had become an apprentice in his grandfather's brewery in the Rhineland, and, after five years of training, he moved on to breweries at Frankfurt and Mainz. Coming to America in 1870, he soon became foreman with the Cincinnati firm of Foss, Schneider, and Brenner which he left to join Pabst.[15] At the end of six months, he was made foreman of brewing, and proceeded during the next six years to direct brewing so skillfully that the directors had few worries on this score. But Jung had business ambitions of his own and, at the end of 1879, he left Pabst to form a partnership with Ernest Borchert that was to grow into the brewing firm of Falk, Jung and Borchert. When Pabst bought out this firm, in 1892, Jung again withdrew in order to continue in business for himself.[16]

The years from 1879 to 1884 were a period of great business success, and also of continual brewing worries for Pabst. Neither

[15] *Germania,* July 10, 1911. [Clipping in the possession of Mr. Ernest Jung, Milwaukee, Wis.]

[16] *One Hundred Years of Brewing,* p. 335.

Adam Klinkert, who served as successor to Jung for one year, nor August Olinger, whose term as superintendent ran through 1881 and part of 1882, was able to cope with the changing conditions in American taste. Due partly to the hot summer climate of most of the United States, and to the desire to drink rapidly, most Americans wanted a lighter, drier beer than was made in Europe or had first been made in this country. While the desire for lightness in body, therefore, was a reasonable outgrowth of American conditions, the parallel demand for lightness in color, luster, and absolute clarity was based on purely aesthetic considerations that had no influence on the taste of the beer. A series of letters from John S. Pierce, the Chicago manager, to the Captain in the spring of 1880 emphasized the absolute necessity of lightness in color. "Can't you give us a paler, purer beer?" [17] he wrote in March. Then a few days later, "Our reputation in Chicago will certainly suffer if we don't get a different beer"; [18] and a little later, "Our customer Shaughnessy out on Graceland Road, sent us word that he could not use our beer any longer, it being so dark." [19]

To the brewmaster's troubles, arising from American taste, were added other difficulties. For the first time, in these middle years, Pabst salesmen were invading distant territories armed with the sales argument that although their beer cost more it was worth it. They were naturally quick to blame any lack of sales success on the failure of the production staff to provide them with proper beer. Naturally, the brewmaster usually had to bear the brunt of these criticisms whether or not he was truly at fault. In the Pierce complaints of 1880, based on lack of proper color and clarity, William Gruber, assistant superintendent in charge of brewing at the South Side, had to take the blame, as he had brewed the dark-colored beer while Superintendent Olinger had been personally supervising the brewing

[17] Letter, Mar. 11, 1880.
[18] Letter, Mar. 20, 1880.
[19] Letter, Apr. 4, 1880.

of proper colored shipping beer at the Empire. The Captain sent Gruber a memorandum on the back of Pierce's letter which must have been typical of many such messages from chief executives to the brewmasters in the 1880's.

This is the kind of letter we generally receive from Chicago. There is no doubt in my mind if that kind of beer keeps on, we will lose a great deal of trade which had cost us a great deal of trouble and money to get. It seems to me that we should not be subject to such unnecessary trouble if the brewing or manufacturing of beer has the necessary attention.

We surely furnish everything necessary to make good beer and I can only look at this as either carelessness or not the necessary knowledge of the business.

I write you this in a friendly way, at the same time I want to be understood that we *cannot afford* to have anything of this kind repeated, and expect that you will try your utmost, and work in harmony with Olinger in order to get over this trouble as soon as possible.[20]

The growth of bottled-beer sales and the expansion of the shipping market created still more problems for the brewmaster. Not only must American beer have new degrees of lightness, sparkle, and luster, but it must be able to retain its qualities for long periods under adverse conditions. In the old days, beer was kept unmoved in cool storage cellars until a few hours or, at the most, a few days before it was drunk. But beer in bottles, after being bumped around in freight cars and on wagons, might stand for weeks on the shelves of a warm, brightly lighted room before being sold, and might even then be stored in private homes for indefinite periods. Keg beer might have to make fifteen-hundred mile journeys, lasting for a week or more, in temperatures from forty below zero to a hundred or more above. None of the beers in the United States

---

[20] Memorandum on letter, Pierce to Pabst, Mar. 20, 1880.

9

or abroad in the early nineteenth century, if brewed for moderate alcoholic content, would have stood such treatment.

In April of 1882, John Metzler succeeded Olinger as superintendent of brewing and began what turned out to be a full decade of experimentation with new ingredients. Metzler, who had been connected with the brewing academy at Coblenz before coming to Pabst, brought the most up-to-date German knowledge to bear upon his twofold problem of producing a fine light-colored, light-bodied beer that would have stability under adverse conditions.[21]

There were two possible ways of achieving lighter color and lighter body: (1) more careful malting, and (2) the use of other grains besides barley. Malt is often called "the soul of the beer." It is the substance that gives the basic flavor to the wort and the bodily character to the finished product. The buying of good barley at reasonable prices on the primary grain market was one of the first requisites of successful brewing. No one market could supply the amount of carefully selected barley needed by the large American brewers. The Middle West, the Far West, and Canada were regularly stripped of their best crops, and often recourse was had to European countries. In 1873, for example, 180,000 bushels were bought by Pabst from Italy, and shipped westward from New York in 440 carloads.[22] American farmers gradually responded to this demand, however, and increased their barley acreage so that as time went on, the dependence of American brewers on foreign imports diminished. By 1887, for example, Pabst used 625,863 bushels of home-grown Western barley, 77,940 bushels of California barley, and only 14,853 bushels of Canadian imports.[23] Emil Schandein with his botanical knowledge became an expert barley buyer and trained able assistants. There seems no question but

[21] *American Brewer*, XXXV, No. 1 (Jan. 1902), 746.

[22] *Sentinel*, Dec. 1, 1873.

[23] Best Brewing Co., per Charles Best, to W. J. Jackson, secretary, Chamber of Commerce, Jan. 23, 1888.

that Pabst was being supplied with the best malting barley obtainable.

The treatment of the barley at the Pabst malthouse under the able management of Oscar Mueller seems to have been highly satisfactory. As the Captain so often emphasized, Metzler had the finest materials to work with; but, did he have the proper ones, did success under the new conditions demand new ingredients?

In the late sixties it was discovered that the starch in rice or corn meal could be converted to sugar by the excess diastase in barley malt if these grains were boiled before being introduced into the mashing tun. Both grains would produce a lighter bodied and a lighter colored beer than was possible with pure barley. The question confronting brewmasters was how much of these grains could be used without substantially lessening the fine flavor produced by the barley malt. From the early seventies on, brewmasters experimented cautiously to develop new formulas for beer based on these new grains. As German brewers had already used rice, which was cheap in Germany whereas corn was a relatively high-priced import, rice was the first grain tried in the United States; but further experimentation soon revealed that American corn was, at least, equally good.

Philipp Jung started using small quantities of rice in 1874,[24] and rapidly increased the annual amount from 81,000 to 867,000 pounds by 1877, but it would have taken a rare connoisseur, even in the latter year, to detect the seventeenth part of rice amid the barley. In 1878, Jung shifted from rice to about an equal amount of corn meal. There has never been any agreement to this day regarding which is the best subsidiary grain. The great majority of brewers, including Pabst, now favor corn, but some others, such as Anheuser-Busch, have continued to use rice.

Klinkert cut the use of corn drastically, which may have ac-

[24] Letter, Pabst to Schandein, Feb. 2, 1874.

counted for a slight darkening of some of the brews, and while Olinger increased the amount, he also used meal cautiously. But Metzler, a man made confident by his scientific knowledge and spurred on by criticisms coming in from the sales force, returned to the more vigorous experiments of Jung. Switching back to rice, he increased the amount to more than a fifteenth part of the weight of the malt in the brew during his first season. The next year he raised the ratio to one pound of rice to eleven of malt. But even at this level, careful malting and brewing were more important than the use of rice in securing a light-bodied and a light-colored product.[25]

Metzler's other problem, that of maintaining stability of taste and appearance under adverse conditions, presented great difficulties at this stage in the science of brewing. The most important single cause of instability was probably the process of kraeusening. This, as we have seen, introduced elements of extreme instability, particularly before the development of pure culture yeasts. That is, an active fermentation was deliberately introduced for the purpose of carbonation, and it is not surprising that occasionally it took the wrong turn and produced a cloudy precipitation or colloidal suspension. The simple cures for these problems, direct pressure carbonation and constant pressure racking and bottling, it must be remembered, were not known in 1882, and John Metzler had to deal with these difficulties with the methods he had at hand.

Metzler's most likely solutions seemed to be: improved fining to eliminate all suspended particles at the start, preservatives to prevent subsequent chemical reaction in the beer that might produce cloudiness, and improved methods of kraeusening, racking, and bottling. He started by introducing isinglass into the fining process to catch all suspended particles in a colloidal jelly that would settle out leaving the beer comparatively clear. In the end he had added a dozen substances that he hoped

---

[25] Materials used in brewing with prices are reported in Annual Statement of Affairs, Books A and B, for the years 1873-1901.

would improve the shipping qualities of the beer. These included various absorbing agents such as Irish moss and bone black; preservatives like sulphite of soda, salicylic acid, and even sugar in various forms. He also used sugar to ensure a higher carbonation by creating a beneficent afterfermentation.

Metzler's new ingredients contained nothing harmful to the drinker and, by and large, they accomplished their purposes. Occasionally, however, they produced unforeseen qualities in the beer. Emil Schandein who did much traveling, both for the company and for his own health, wrote frequent letters to the Captain reporting upon the condition of their own and competitors' beers in distant markets. From New York, for example, he wrote, "I find our beer good . . . . ———— beer has a sharp prickling taste, yet not very unpleasant." [26] While Pabst suffered occasionally from brews that did not fit the public's tastes, the company according to Schandein's reports appears to have had less trouble than its chief competitors. Thus Schandein writes from Hot Springs, Arkansas: "I find the beers generally not very good. Joe and Riebsame go out on investigations and report faithfully. They found ———— sour, as well as ————'s ———— in pints thick as lime brew." [27] A few weeks later Schandein found his own beer excellent. "All who drank it gave the best testimony thereof. Without flattering ourselves I can say that it is the best beer I have tasted since I left Milwaukee." [28]

Metzler's ability was proved by his later success as brewmaster with the large Brand Brewing Company of Chicago,[29] but during his stay at Pabst he was harassed by family troubles that took his attention away from his work. Early in 1884, Charles Best appealed to Anton Schwarz in New York for a candidate for the position of superintendent, and he recommended J. F. Theurer who succeeded Metzler in April of 1884.[30]

[26] Letter, Mar. 30, 1880. Translated from the German. Blank indicates name of competitor.
[27] Letter, Feb. 27, 1881. Translated from the German. Blanks indicate names of competitors.
[28] Letter, Mar. 7, 1881. Translated from the German.
[29] *American Brewer*, XXXV, No. 1 (Jan. 1902), 746.
[30] Best to A. Schwarz, Feb. 7, 1884.

"Fritz" Theurer was one of the great figures in the history of brewing and of the Pabst organization. In him the company acquired not only an excellent brewmaster trained at the Berlin Brewing College,[31] but also a gifted inventor whose works were to alter the basic processes in the industry. In the course of the next twenty years, he invented filters, yeast pitching machines, a barley washer, beer coolers, air purifiers, a special hopping process, and, most important of all, a system of direct carbonation for both keg and bottled beer.

While Theurer ultimately eliminated the need for kraeusening, at first he could only continue Metzler's experiments. His major initial change was to use both corn and rice in larger amounts than previously. As time went on, he decreased the quantity of rice and increased that of corn until, by 1893, the former was abandoned, and the standard beer was made up of about one part corn meal to two parts malt by weight.

There were still some lovers of fine beer who preferred the old-style German product, and for these, several thousand barrels of pure malt beers, amounting to about a tenth of the total production, were brewed. The cost of materials for these brands due to the larger percentage of malt, and the use of more imported hops, ran as high as 80 to 100 per cent more than for the standard product which up to 1891 was called Export Lager, and after that, Pilsener. Yet the great majority of Americans preferred this latter, cheaper type.

No matter how Theurer adjusted the formulas of his brews during this period, they were uniformly successful. Complaints practically ceased, and the officers felt that their beer was the best in the nation. The Pabst representative in Pittsburgh wrote in 1885.

I can at present go around with smiling face and head erect and tell everyone our beer cannot be equalled by any other, because it is a fact. I had several calls lately from people in the trade asking for

[31] American Brewers' Review, XVI, No. 4 (Oct. 20, 1902), 194; also see Western Brewer, XX, No. 1 (Jan. 15, 1895), 125.

our beer because they found it so good. I don't think I err when I say that a little additional expense in the production will be more than repaid in the saving of expenses in selling, or to put it in other words, the greatest economy lies in the production of an A-1 article.[32]

BEER IN BOTTLES

In the long view of the history of brewing, the introduction of large-scale bottling for shipping purposes may well have been the most important development in the industry. Ale, and even beer to be sure, had been bottled for centuries, but the old bottled ale was either nonsparkling and with a consistency more like thick wine and equally durable, or else the bottles had been prepared only for immediate consumption near by. Prior to the latter nineteenth century, no one had ever sucessfully bottled sparkling lager. The success of such a venture depended not only on producing a stable beer adequately corked, but also on the development of a means of transportation that would promise a profit from wide distribution. From this standpoint, bottled lager beer was a by-product of the railroads, and the beginning of its nationwide sales followed closely upon the completion of a railroad network.

Although at the present time bottled or canned beer is much the largest part of the business of the shipping brewers, it scarcely outgrew its infancy prior to 1893, by which time it had come to represent about 10 per cent of Pabst sales. Pabst started bottling lager beer at the South Side in 1875, but the bottling department soon brought so many new problems that in the very next year the company decided to turn this small and troublesome department over to the firm of Stamm and Meyer who operated in a small one-story building at the South Side.

When Fred E. Meyer died in 1880, Stamm was unable to carry on the bottling business alone, and a deal was made whereby Pabst purchased Meyer's interest from his estate for $22,320.24, and paid G. T. Stamm $27,000 for his share. Pabst

32 E. Schmitt to Pabst, Apr. 23, 1885.

also promised Stamm one third of the profits of their bottling department to January 1, 1883.

PABST BOTTLED-BEER STATISTICS, 1881-1893

Year	Number of Barrels Bottled	Labor Cost per Barrel	Total Cost per Barrel for Bottling	Profits per Barrel
1881	14,095	...	...	$1.25
1882	23,865	...	...	0.13
1883	24,750	...	...	loss
1884	25,422	...	...	0.33
1885	38,200	$1.06	$3.29	0.52
1886	56,321	1.15	3.39	0.62
1887	59,846	1.46	4.37	0.47
1888	68,450	1.57	4.39	1.67
1889	76,753	1.45	4.02	1.81
1890	101,069	1.36	3.75	2.21
1891	98,848	1.32	3.82	2.37
1892	109,758	1.24	3.58	2.64
1893	107,959	1.34	3.92	1.83

Bottling at this time was largely a hand-labor job, and the $49,320.44 paid to Stamm and Meyer for their equipment, contracts, and good will shows the low cost of starting such a department. Washed bottles were filled by hand with a rubber hose attached to an ordinary keg, then a cork was inserted into the foaming neck of the bottle, driven in by a simple pressing machine, and wired on by hand. A hand glued label and a tinfoil wrapper on the neck made the bottle ready for its heavy wooden case without benefit of pasteurization.[33] The cases, just as at the present time, were made up of either 12 quart or 24 pint bottles, but it is interesting to note that in those days the quarts outsold the pints.

During this somewhat sloppy bottling process, the chances were considerable that the beer would be infected by bacteria from the air. It is thus not surprising that the early bottled beer caused the brewmasters more trouble than they had ever had before. Added to their hazards was the fact that much of the

[33] *Northwestern Trade Bulletin*, I, No. 15 (Aug. 21, 1879). Clipping at office of the *Milwaukee Journal*.

bottled beer that Pabst sold at distant points was not bottled at the South Side, but was shipped in kegs and bottled by local agents, whose methods might not even be up to those of Stamm and Meyer. Charles Best, for example, writes back from Baltimore at the time of the convention of the United States Brewers' Association that Best's local agent there was having difficulty.

Another complaint which he makes is of a more serious nature and that is the quality of our bottled beer. I drank some of the last carload, just bottled this morning and found it very bright and clear, but with a strong, hard taste, touching almost a sourish taste. Kalling, however, seemed to be satisfied with this but complained that it would turn cloudy with a very heavy sediment in about 6 to 7 days after being bottled.

I could not account for this but assured him that we would send him our very best hereafter, etc.

Please speak to Philipp Jung about this and see that always good heavy stock is sent down here.[34]

As the demand for bottled beer grew, more and more attention was paid to its problems. The result was that during the eighties and early nineties bottling steadily became more mechanized. The first great improvement came in 1884, when the Goulding bottle-washing machines were introduced. On these machines each bottle was placed over a spindle surrounded with corrugated rubber brushes that rotated at 3,000 revolutions per minute. Bottle cleaning was further improved a few years later by the Birkholz-Theurer soak tanks, each one capable of soaking 125,000 used bottles overnight in a hot soda solution.[35] Filling machines, made by the Vilter Manufacturing Company of Milwaukee, superseded the rubber hose, and thus checked wastage through foaming. And a machine, from the Bottler's Specialty Company of Rochester, corked, capped, and wired bottles in one operation.[36] The final solution for bottle capping, however,

---

[34] Best to Pabst, June 4, 1878.
[35] *Western Brewer*, XX, No. 1 (Jan. 15, 1895), 106. Interview with Dr. A. J. Schedler.
[36] *Western Brewer*, XX, No. 1 (Jan. 15, 1895), 107.

was the Crown Cork and Seal Company's metal cap invented in 1892, but not fully perfected until after this period. Meanwhile, 1,500 different kinds of patent stoppers strove for supremacy.[37] Pabst, however, preferred to put its chief reliance on wired corks.

One of the most important steps in the bottling process was pasteurization to kill off growing organisms and thus stop spoilage. The problem here was to design a machine that would economically heat the bottles so gradually that they would not crack or blow their corks. This problem was solved in the 1880's by the development of tanks, in which long racks of bottles moved through separate compartments each with increasingly warm water until a temperature was reached sufficiently high and maintained long enough (140 degrees F. for 30 to 60 minutes) to destroy or retard the growth of organisms. The bottles then were cooled gradually, and passed on for inspection and labeling.

Another important improvement in the bottling was originated by Pabst around 1890.[38] Since the internal revenue law had no provision for bottled beer, it was necessary to barrel all beer solely for the purpose of affixing and canceling the $1.00 per barrel tax stamps. The Pabst Company, therefore, was filling about 75,000 barrels a year in the racking room simply to take them across the street to the bottling house where they were emptied. The company complained of this wasted effort to the local collector's office, but they were rebuffed by an unimaginative commissioner in Washington who after pointing out that no change could be made in the process without a revision in the law added: "Such a modification of the law as would permit the course indicated would not be regarded with favor by this office." [39] The Captain now decided to act for himself. Explaining the absurdity of the existing situation to Con-

[37] Frank Romer, *Reviewing American Brewing*, p. 34.
[38] *Daily News and Review*, Aug. 6, 1890; *Western Brewer*, XVIII, No. 1 (Jan. 15, 1893), 95; and XX, No. 1 (Jan. 15, 1895), 109-10.
[39] John W. Mason to Henry Fink, Jan. 30, 1890.

gressmen, he succeeded in getting the Internal Revenue Act altered by a law of June 18, 1890, so as to permit the construction of pipe lines from storage cellars to bottling houses.[40]

The Captain's efforts were largely inspired by the fact that Theurer and Richard Birkholz, a mechanical engineer employed by the Pabst Company about 1889, had invented a pipe line and bottling system that would guarantee the government against loss or fraud, and would greatly improve the mechanics of bottling. For this system, Pabst on March 4, 1891, completed a tunnel under Chestnut Street. In the tunnel were laid pipes one and one-quarter inches in diameter, of copper with block-tin lining. Parallel to them were laid refrigerating pipes to stabilize the tunnel's temperature in summer. Air pressure forced the beer through the pipes to twelve measuring tanks each of about 75 barrels capacity. These lay parallel with each other on the floor of a refrigerated room underneath the bottling machinery. The inlets and outlets of the measuring tanks were sealed and doubly locked with keys in possession of the internal revenue inspector. As the beer ran in through the unlocked inlet, a gauge on each tank showed the quantity; and after the inspector had closed and locked the inlet, it was possible to cancel stamps for the amount of beer registered in the tank. He then unlocked the outlet pipe, and the beer was forced by carbonic gas pressure to the filling machines. The carbonic gas used here was a by-product collected directly from the fermenting beer by the new Fischer-Theurer process. The gas was kept at a regulated pressure in the measuring tanks so that the beer entered the bottles with uniform force, resulting in uniform carbonation. The regulating device for this was a check valve that allowed the carbon dioxide, when it reached a pressure of over seven pounds, to escape into a low-pressure tank where it was collected, washed, and pumped back into high-pressure tanks that fed it, when needed, back to the measuring tanks.

Cheap, mechanized bottling was a great advantage to the big

[40] Act approved June 18, 1890. 51st Congress, 1st session, chap. 431, p. 161.

shippers, and bottled beer was soon to become their largest source of profits. But bottled beer meant wider distribution to many more buyers in distant cities and towns. Thus, improved technology placed a greater emphasis on marketing as the primary means of successful competition, and we must turn to this sphere to account satisfactorily for the continued success of the Pabst Brewing Company.

CHAPTER VI

WINNING A NATIONAL MARKET

CAREFUL selection of the finest materials and the adoption of the newest brewing processes made Pabst beer generally superior to that produced by some two thousand smaller brewers. But this superiority was not enough in itself to sell Pabst beer in large volume at prices that had to be somewhat higher than those charged by the local competitors. Advertising and salesmanship of a high order were required to give Pabst beer peculiar prestige in the mind of the buying public and to make the circled "B" (for Best) trade-mark a symbol of quality that marked with distinction the retailer and his customers. The other two Milwaukee shippers, Blatz and Schlitz, shared Pabst's problems, and, while still pushing their own products, all three joined in seeking national recognition of the peculiar excellence of Milwaukee beer. No other brewer, however, during the years from 1873 to 1893 handled the twin aims of boosting Milwaukee and his own product as successfully as Captain Pabst.

THE GENESIS OF MODERN ADVERTISING

In the late seventies, as sales moved upward, Pabst began systematic advertising in the Milwaukee newspapers and in Chicago's German-language press.

Starting in 1881, the company spread its advertising to local Wisconsin papers like the *Fond du Lac Democrat,* and to out-of-town agencies that placed copy in special publications such as the *Boston Journal of Commerce,* the *Washington Sentinel,* and the *National Illustrated Weekly.* There are no records explaining the selection of these agencies and mediums.

To supplement home-office advertising, Pabst's branches and agents also advertised in local papers, and secured occasional news articles. The news columns of the *Indianapolis Western*

ADVERTISING CONTRACTS [1]

(April 1879–May 1880)

Date	Medium	Price per Year	City
July 2, 1879	Freie Presse	$230	Chicago
August 3, 1879	Pravda und Vesternick	60	Chicago
June 4, 1879	Svornost	60	Chicago
July 1, 1879	Ill. Staatszeitung	230	Chicago
June 18, 1879	Volksfreund	100	Chicago
June 2, 1879	Svenska	24	Chicago
April 1, 1879	Eulenspeigel	20	Chicago
January 1, 1880	Beobachter	20	Chicago
May 1880	Banner und Volksfreund	100	Milwaukee
May 1880	Herold	100	Milwaukee
May 1880	Seebote	100	Milwaukee
May 1880	Arbeiterzeitung	100	Milwaukee
May 1880	Milwaukee Journal	...	Milwaukee
May 1880	Sentinel	100	Milwaukee
May 1880	Evening Wisconsin	100	Milwaukee
May 1880	Daily News	80	Milwaukee
May 1880	Daily Signal	...	Milwaukee
May 1880	Peck's Sun	100	Milwaukee
May 1880	Freiedenker	18	Milwaukee
May 1880	Ansiedler	60	Milwaukee
May 1880	Au	30	Milwaukee
May 1880	Milwaukee Chronicle	50	Milwaukee

Citizen in 1881, for example, boosted the company's new Indiana agent, Roter, Boughton and Company.

We found that although Milwaukee beer had only been introduced in this city a few months, that this firm only in their infancy as you might say, were shipping beer to all parts of the State and had increased their trade in two months from 100 dozen a week to nearly 1400 dozen per week, and was constantly increasing so much so that they were compelled to seek larger quarters.[2]

When Pabst's new, dark "Bavarian" and the more popular, light "Select," with a blue ribbon tied on each bottle, were in-

[1] See advertising memorandum contracts, 1879-1890. Names are reproduced as in memorandum contracts.
[2] *Indianapolis Western Citizen*, Aug. 14, 1881. Scrapbook clipping.

troduced in 1882, outlays for newspaper and periodical advertising jumped from $3,881.62 for the previous year to $6,793.03.
In 1884 the fortieth anniversary of the founding of the firm was
used as the occasion for newspaper notices and the distribution
of a large number of souvenirs. That year total costs for these
types of advertising were 125 per cent higher than the 1882
record. A news release of considerable length on the history of
the company was used by many papers and periodicals from
Duluth, Minnesota, to London, England.[3]

The product that increased Best or Pabst advertising outlays
most was, surprisingly, neither beer nor ale. It was a new product, "The Best Tonic," which was introduced in the late eighties
and vigorously promoted from the start. Here were developed
many of the techniques used later for beer promotion.

There were in the eighties several malt extracts on the drug
market. One group, of which Trommer's or Maltine were examples, consisted of thick syrups medicated with iron, quinine,
strychnine, or cod-liver oil. This type of tonic was taken by the
spoonful. Another group, like Hoff's or Wyeth's, was made up
merely of heavy-bodied, dark brews, like porter or stout, that
were consumed by the glass. A bottle a day was usually recommended for improving the digestion, adding weight, or increasing energy.

Captain Pabst saw in this second type of tonic the chance for
a self-supporting business that would advertise his beer.[4] In 1887,
therefore, he set up a specialty department to manufacture and
sell malt extract through a central sales office in New York
under the direction of F. Marquand, a metropolitan advertising
man. Marquand did not produce the results expected, nor was
he willing to save money by moving his headquarters to Milwaukee. At the end of June 1888, therefore, his services were
dispensed with, and the tonic was carried along by F. E.
Schmidt, the head of the specialty department in Milwaukee.

[3] Scrapbook clippings.
[4] Letter, A. Cressy Morrison to R. B. Cochran, Aug. 16, 1945.

Meanwhile, an unprecedented $91,787.50 had been spent on advertising, most of it during Marquand's administration. This was a tremendous sum for those days—one that is high-lighted by comparison with Sapolio, the then world-renowned soap for which only $70,000 had been appropriated in 1885.[5] Kountz Brothers of New York handled most of the expenditures for Pabst's Tonic campaign. Signs were used in the streetcars of New York, Philadelphia, and Boston, as well as on buildings and fences; and many small advertisements were run in newspapers and magazines. Although the directors were not pleased with the results, it must be noted that beer sales, which, after all, the Tonic was meant to strengthen, increased from 1888 to 1889 faster than in any previous year in the history of the company.

Pabst was fortunate in getting A. Cressy Morrison, a young man with many ideas, to take over the Tonic in 1889 at its new Empire Brewery headquarters. Morrison's job officially was confined to the specialty department, but since this department spent more than any other on most forms of advertising, Morrison really became an advertising manager for the company. He was more or less recognized as such since George Yenowine, editor of his own Milwaukee newspaper who had received a salary as Pabst's advertising manager, resigned his position at the end of March 1889.

Yenowine just before he resigned had started publishing small booklets for Pabst, about the size of a postal card, with twenty-five to fifty thin pages of riddles and jokes called "Secret" books. In one sense, these were merely a continuation of the souvenir booklets that the company had issued in 1877 and 1884. But these earlier books had been filled with information about and pictures of the brewery, whereas the new series was designed largely for amusement and contained little direct advertising. Morrison pushed these books and for the next decade they were issued at a rate of over 5,000,000 a year. *Untold Secrets, Wedding Secrets, Home Secrets, Baby Secrets,* and *Ominous*

[5] Frank Presbrey, *The History and Development of Advertising,* p. 394.

Secrets followed each other, all containing little stories about the value of the Best Tonic, as well as the advertisements for beer. *Ominous Secrets* was an attempt to collect and publish the world's superstitions; and the second page of several Secret books offered a series of prizes from five dollars to a hundred dollars for the best list of signs and omens not contained in the book. In addition to the Secret books, a fairy tale, *The Story the Malt Told,* written by Morrison, was widely distributed; and appropriate booklets were issued commemorating special Milwaukee occasions, such as the encampment of the Grand Army of the Republic and the national meeting of the Knights of Pythias. For the latter, the booklet, *A Story, Damon and Pythias,* was notable for its day in containing no advertising copy whatever beyond the Pabst trade-mark on the envelope and "Compliments of the Pabst Brewing Company" on the cover. In 1891 the catch phrase, "Milwaukee Beer Is Famous— Pabst Has Made It So," later used in newspaper and periodical advertising, first appeared in the booklets.

When the G.A.R. came to Milwaukee in 1889, the Captain's natural generosity and hospitality produced one of the greatest advertising coups of the period.[6] A grandstand had been erected along the lake front to command a view of a great fireworks display, and the entertainment committee, hard pressed for cash, planned to sell the seats at a dollar apiece. When this was proposed, according to a witness, the Captain got up and said: "I don't think we ought to invite these veterans to Milwaukee and then charge them a dollar to see the fireworks." To this a more money-minded member of the committee replied, "I suppose you'd be willing to pay the $12,000 we need yourself, Captain?" "Yes," he replied, "I'll buy them all if I can do as I please with them." When the committee agreed to that, the Captain said, "All right, the seats will be free but the veterans will be seated first, and others will have those that are left over."

[6] Interview with A. C. Morrison, May 16, 1945. See also *Daily News and Review,* Aug. 6, 1889.

10

To show their appreciation, the veterans paraded past the brewery, and doubtless many converts to Pabst beer were made among them. When the day of celebration and fireworks was over, the G.A.R. marched to saloons displaying competitors' signs and demanded Pabst beer, marching out again if it could not be produced.

"Well, Cressy," the Captain is reported to have said to Morrison, "I guess I'm a pretty good advertising man." "You've had the best advertising in the country," replied the latter, "but you're no advertising man. The reason you had such good results is that everyone knew you hadn't planned it at all; it was just your spontaneous generosity." [7]

The decision in 1889 to change the name of the company brought about an important stimulus to advertising activity. In general, the change was well received and given favorable publicity, save for a few local newspaper comments inspired by competitive interests. But it introduced an uncertain element into the selling situation. The public had to be taught the name Pabst as quickly as possible; and that meant additional advertising. The G.A.R. encampment in Milwaukee in the summer of 1889 was one of several favorable opportunities for publicizing the new name. Another was the fact that the company outsold its great competitor, Anheuser-Busch, for the first time in a couple of years, and could thereby resume its slogan, "The Largest Lager Beer Brewery in the World." [8] The awards won at the Buffalo Exposition in the fall of 1888, attended by more people than at any such meeting since the Centennial, were also used subsequently to emphasize the name of Best in Pabst publicity. The circled "B" trade-mark, associated in the public mind with Best beer, was retained, and the extensive advertising campaign for Pabst Malt Extract, subtitled "The Best Tonic," was counted on as a means of demonstrating the continuity. In this campaign, in addition to "general" or newspaper

[7] Interview with A. C. Morrison, May 16, 1945.
[8] Telegram, Adolphus Busch to Captain Pabst, Oct. 3, 1889.

and magazine advertising, vigorous "special" advertising was undertaken. This included fancy calendars, notices in railroad timetables and theater programs, and the distribution of souvenir cigar cases, matchboxes, memorandum pads, and New Year's cards, all with the name Pabst brightly displayed. While specialty department outlays were not up to the great expenditures of 1888, they, too, were kept at a relatively high level. "Signs and Views," indoor and outdoor signs and pictures given to retailers, were also more widely distributed to match the increase in branches, agents, and saloons carrying Pabst.

For the three years, 1891 to 1893 inclusive, which culminated in record-breaking sales in 1893, Pabst's total advertising expense probably was large even for a ten-million-dollar corporation selling in one of the most highly competitive markets. The largest single outlay in these years was in 1891, when the company spent $162,414.94. This was about 28 per cent more than in any preceding year, and was followed by a sales increase of 263,294 barrels, the most remarkable in the entire history of the company prior to 1933. The following year, management cut the advertising outlay almost 30 per cent and held it at about that level through 1893. Even so, that year was the best the company had ever had. Since we are dealing with an able management, these facts must warn us that there was good reason to attribute sales increases to factors other than advertising. Another indication of this is that advertising expenditures from 1884 to 1893, on an article costing about $4.00, increased only from 4 cents to 11 cents per barrel sold. Obviously, had management felt that there was a close correlation between this outlay and large sales, it would have been possible to increase advertising outlays very materially without any large increase in per-barrel costs.

All told for the three years, 1891-1893, Pabst's annual advertising outlay averaged $134,469.37 or a little over 2.5 per cent of the wholesale value of the product. The largest single annual item continued to be Signs and Views, $54,751.16; special advertising came next with $40,998.85; the specialty department for Tonic advertising averaged $25,292.84; and, finally, general advertising including all magazines and newspapers, except those used for the Tonic, was a weak fourth at $12,131.54.

ADVERTISING EXPENDITURES, 1878-1893 [9]

Year	General (Magazine-Newspaper)	Bottling Department	Specialty Department	Special Advertising	Signs and Views	Total
1878	$1,160 *	.....	.....	.....	$8,416	$9,576
1879	3,808	.....	.....	.....	6,849	10,657
1880	3,504	.....	.....	.....	5,059	8,563
1881	3,882	.....	.....	.....	20,367	24,249
1882	6,793	.....	.....	.....	9,678	16,471
1883	1,816	.....	.....	.....	10,888	12,704
1884	3,991	.....	.....	$11,229	15,799	31,019
1885	3,739	.....	.....	3,027	22,082	28,848
1886	2,611	$1,329	.....	5,120	26,992	36,052
1887	3,216	1,535	$650	3,736	22,719	31,856
1888	2,259	619	91,788	5,680	26,986	127,332
1889	10,933	5,007	18,484	3,816	45,718	83,958
1890	7,748	1,506	16,393	20,704	43,547	89,898
1891	14,054	2,372	35,387	49,310	61,291	162,414
1892	14,611	1,563	15,799	33,533	53,471	118,977
1893	7,729	50	24,692	40,054	49,492	122,017

* November and December only.

These figures show that Pabst placed no great faith in expensive magazine or newspaper advertising. Rather than to carry on a general national campaign without regard to locality, this type of advertising seems to have been used only to boost sales by keeping the good will of the Milwaukee press, or to back up the efforts of certain branches. None of the country's major magazines, except *Harper's,* and only a few big city newspapers outside of Milwaukee appear on a Pabst list made up for 1891 and 1892. Not until some years later did agencies like J. Walter Thompson and Lord and Thomas get Pabst to spend large sums on magazines and newspapers.

More important, perhaps, than periodical advertising was sales promotion by means of exhibits at fairs and expositions. American cities, proud of their nineteenth-century progress, were con-

[9] Advertising Account, General Ledgers. Prior to 1878, no general ledger account was kept for advertising.

stantly seeking to outdo one another with expositions modeled on those of the great cities of Europe. The committee that managed each fair tried to attract as many exhibitors as possible. The inducements were the advertising that accrued from the space used in the exhibition and the award of a medal or other certificate of merit. A company had to decide, therefore, whether the resulting publicity was worth the investment in space and equipment that was necessary to make it a contender for a gold medal. Captain Pabst favored an active policy in this respect, and Pabst was handsomely represented at the major latter nineteenth-century expositions. Most of the other big shippers felt the same way, so that brewing was usually well displayed and well rewarded at these fairs.

At the Centennial Exposition in Philadelphia in 1876, Pabst won a gold medal and the highest award for bottled beer. At the World's Fair in Paris, 1878, Pabst again won a medal.[10] During the eighties, Pabst won top awards at American fairs at Atlanta, New Orleans, and Buffalo.

The World's Columbian Exposition in Chicago in 1893 was the most important American fair of that period. Naturally there was keen rivalry among the three largest shippers, Pabst, Anheuser-Busch, and Schlitz, but Pabst came out a victor in most of the competitions. In the fair's agricultural building, Pabst displayed a thirteen-foot-square, gold-plated model of the Empire Brewery which is said to have attracted more attention than any other brewing display.[11] Pabst beer was cleverly "placed" in the eating places: it was not placed in expensive restaurants where the customer drank wine but was sold in the majority of the small stands and little restaurants where the ordinary beer-drinking visitors could afford to eat.

The final awards at the Chicago fair caused far more excitement than might be imagined today.[12] In addition to six special

[10] *American Brewers' Gazette,* XI, No. 8 (Nov. 15, 1878), 168.
[11] *Western Brewer,* XVIII, No. 8 (Aug. 15, 1893), 1779-80.
[12] For discussion of awards, see *The American Brewer,* XXVI, Nos. 11 and 12 (Nov. and Dec. 1893); *American Brewers' Review,* Sept. 28, Oct. 5, 12, 26, Nov. 2, 9, 23, 30, Dec. 21, 1893; Oct. 4 and July 19, 1894.

medals awarded to Anheuser-Busch, five to Pabst plus an honorable mention, and four to Schlitz, a jury was set up to give the highest award for beer. Trouble began over the personnel of the jury. Easterners complained that they had no representative on the jury and Westerners that the jurymen did not know beer. Both complained that the tally allowed twenty points out of a hundred for "commercial importance," a category that made little sense to those interested in the quality of the beer. The judges further confused things by making a preliminary finding in favor of Anheuser-Busch, but, on the basis of a revision of the chemical analyses, they swung to Pabst. Anheuser-Busch appealed to the Fair Commission which ruled on December 21, 1893, that no first prize should be awarded, and that the judges' point score was for their own guidance and should have been destroyed. Anheuser-Busch then threatened legal action against the World's Columbian Commission, and the judges temporarily altered their count to put Anheuser-Busch five eighths of a point ahead. At this point, Morrison persuaded the judges to stand by their original decision of 95% points for Pabst and 94⅔ points for Anheuser-Busch. This became final as the executive committee of the fair, in September 1894, refused to examine the matter further.

Just how much these victories at fairs and expositions raised sales between 1873 and 1893 cannot accurately be estimated. The awards were used as the theme in general advertising and Signs and Views, but, in any case, their effect must have been cumulative rather than immediate. Awards at two out of three major fairs were not reflected in any considerable increase in sales. The awards of 1876 and 1893 were followed in each case by business depression—the only decreases in Pabst sales during this period. Continuing depression in the following years made any subsequent effect impossible to detect. The Paris award of 1878 was followed by a record-breaking sales increase, but here again the upswing in business in the West was apparently the main cause.

"PLACING" THE BEER

Advertising and exhibiting were not the most expensive promotional items in pushing beer sales. More costly were the techniques of "placing" one's beer with retailers. Keg beer, which made up 85 to 90 per cent of the annual sales during this period, cannot be consumed commercially unless it is placed on draught beneath a suitably equipped bar. Sales, therefore, depend first on getting tavern-, saloon-, and hotelkeepers to take the beer. Ordinarily, saloonkeepers, unlike druggists, grocers, or dry-goods merchants who can crowd their shelves with many brands of similar articles, could afford to have only one or two brands of beer on draught, due to the cost of draught equipment and the perishable nature of beer in a tapped keg. Competition for outlets, therefore, was probably keener among brewers than among other businessmen, and it was here that brewers spent most of their promotional money.

Since sales increases rested partially on the number and type of drinking places that could be induced to dispense a given brand of beer, success depended on finding the answers to three questions: What led a proprietor to install a given brand of beer? What ensured the continued stocking of that brand? What led to pushing its sales over the bar? Completely satisfactory answers to these questions would require an analysis of the psychology of saloon proprietors and barkeepers as well as opinion polls of beer drinkers. A general knowledge of the men and the period, however, can lead to some fairly good guesses. We know from books on advertising in this period, for example, that local tradesmen had only limited faith in such promotion. It undoubtedly helped the traveler, agent, or branch salesman, in approaching a prospective customer, if he could argue that his beer would be backed up by newspaper advertising, that it had won awards at heavily attended expositions, and that attractive bar displays would be furnished. Favors such as match covers, memorandum pads, or calendars which could be distributed to the retailer's best customers also helped. Pabst's accounts, however, indicate that immediate inducements in one form or other, given by the agent or salesman to the saloon-keeper, were probably more convincing than anything else. These inducements usually took three forms: money spent at the bar by the salesman treating the bar's customers; discounts on the per-barrel price of beer; easy credit terms. These were three of the most powerful sales arguments used by all brewers, large or small, in placing draught beer.

The first of these, called "spendings" by the brewers and their accountants, were generally regarded by the brewers as one of the most unfortunate practices of the beer business. Yet any single brewer found it very difficult to break the custom. When the representative of the company whose beer was on draught came to get his order, whether he was a "peddlar" (the name given to the salesmen drivers of trucks) or an executive of the company, he was expected to spend a considerable sum at the bar treating the regular customers. This was an expensive way of attracting trade, not only because the products of other manufacturers had to be purchased, but also because the need for drinking with the customers in one establishment after another undermined the constitution and efficiency of the representative. Pabst's spendings for the sale of keg beer in Milwaukee between 1883 and 1893 show that this expense ranged from 23 cents to 43 cents per barrel sold. The amount on the Empire Brewery books reached as high as 92 cents a barrel, but this was due to listing discounts under spendings in certain years.

Though the brewing executives would have liked to end this practice, few tried to do so. William Merritt who represented Pabst at its new Kansas City branch in 1879 thought he had developed a system to do away with the evil when he wrote the Captain:

By dint of considerable firmness I have gotten a better price for our beer than I would have received if I had listened to the views of those who are really experienced in the business. I knew I could secure a large share of the trade in time and hold it at $9.00, in K. C., and stop all spendings but my own at a large number of the best dealers' places by getting the better class of saloonmen to agree that drivers should not drink while delivering owing to their being likely to get drunk and make a show of themselves as has been the case with one of Spenglers and one of Dicks men. I agree to allow these parties the money that would otherwise be spent in their places though the amount as I put it does not come to over half of what the drivers do spend. I allow the dealer 50¢ per barrel while the actual spendings come to nearer $1.00 per barrel. I have the dealer pay up regularly and after the first of each month I refund 50¢ for each barrel the party has paid for. By this means I have some hold on the dealer and I make sure to call on them once a month anyway myself as I pay the rebates personally and obtain the dealer's word to keep the matter private as between us only.[13]

But the "spendings" system was stronger than the man; Merritt did not make a success of the Kansas City branch and soon had to be replaced.

Less robust than the spendings system was the tradition that saloon proprietors were to receive presents of beer at Christmas time. This practice persisted for some years but was ended by agreement among the Milwaukee brewers in 1887.[14]

The brewers continued, however, to give competitive discounts and other allowances. When a proprietor took on a new beer, he usually had to drop some brand previously sold and therefore was in a position to ask for a discount from the stated price, as well as other compensations such as long-term credit and loans for new furnishings or remodeling. Similarly, when an agent of a competitor offered such inducements, the brewer already supplying the saloon or hotel had at least partially to meet such offers. Furthermore, the saloonkeeper who could sell a large steady volume expected some discount from the stated price, even if he did not change brands. Such discounts might run as high as 10 per cent, although more often they were 5 or

13 Letter, Aug. 20, 1879.
14 *Evening Wisconsin*, Dec. 23, 1887.

6 per cent. All brewers seemed to have been forced to grant
them on occasion, although they did not like the fact to be
known.

In general, decisions regarding spending, discounts, and other
allowances had to be made on the basis of information given
by fieldmen who knew local conditions. These men had to be
keen judges of honesty and ability among saloonkeepers, and
therefore they in turn had to be selected with great care. Charles
Best in commenting on a disappointing showing in the city of
Milwaukee in 1884 illustrates management difficulties in these
matters.

I deem it proper and fitting to call attention to the fact that we are
by no means as well represented in Milwaukee as we should be.
While other brewers in general show quite an increase in sales in
Milwaukee, our company shows but 40 barrels gain. The remarkable
small increase is due partly to the trouble we encountered during the
fore part of the year with the beer brewed by J. J. Metzler, the former
superintendent of brewing, partly to the fact that we have been
rather firm in prices, and less liberal in advancing money and chattels
for the purpose of starting new saloons than other brewers, and last
but by no means least, that we have not the proper representative in
our employ in Milwaukee, to advocate and propagate the sale of our
goods in an energetic and intelligent manner.[15]

That national ties and feelings also entered into the complex
business of marketing beer is illustrated in a letter from Pierce
in Chicago to the Captain in July of 1879:

We are getting along first rate with the Bohemians. Have not lost
Gep or any of them as yet. Of course they want a Bohemian agent,
but my experience in life is we don't always get what we want. It is
trouble enough to have to look after the Bohemian customers to say
nothing about an agent of that nationality. It is true that we got
three Italian customers from Schlitz, but not at a discount. Not one
cent off. We have a very good Italian customer on West Madison
Street. A few weeks since he sent for me, and when I went to see

15 Annual Statement of Affairs, Book A.

him, he said he could get me two or three good customers. All I had
to do is to allow him and them 10 per cent. I laughed at him, and
told him if I would give that or even 5 per cent, I could get all I
wanted without help. He said Schlitz would give that. I told him
that if Schlitz would give him that, and their beer suited him, I
would not blame him for leaving us, as I could give him nothing.
I expected to lose him, but, on the contrary, he stuck, and the others
came without solicitation. They even still have Schlitz signs out, and
I have not even called on them. It was no doubt a bulldozing operation with Schlitz and our customers, and the crop fell into our
hands. . . . . Dog eats Dog, I do not feel like complaining of our
business here, but it is hell on earth as usual.[16]

CONTROL THROUGH OWNERSHIP

The problem of getting good outlets for beer at reasonable
prices was such a persistent one that from the middle eighties
on, the brewers began more and more to buy their own saloons
and rent them out to operators who would carry the owner's
beer. Besides helping the brewers, this system helped meet the
high license fees that were enacted in many states at this time.
In some cases, the brewers also found it necessary to advance
money and furnishings in return for notes or chattel mortgages to enable operators to start business. These methods had
the great advantage of removing the pressure from spendings
and discounts, but they brought a host of new problems of their
own, concerned largely with planning and management of real
estate.

In 1880, Pabst began to invest small sums averaging about
$20,000 a year in properties in the Milwaukee area that might
be useful for retailing purposes. From 1887 on, as profits
mounted, larger sums were invested all over the country. In
1891, for example, Pabst invested $500,000 in property all the
way from Omaha to Boston. But greatest emphasis was still on
the home area. In his secretary's report to the board of directors
for 1892, Gustav Pabst pointed out the need for the company to

[16] Letter, July 3, 1879.

"husband its resources and retain, as far as possible, its earnings" to meet the demand for capital necessary to purchase real estate or advance money to customers for building purposes.

Between 1887 and 1893, Pabst spent about $1,400,000 for such land and buildings and $300,000 more for improvements. By the latter year the "general property" inventory of the company, which excluded brewery property, stood at $2,237,855.11 or about 20 per cent of the total book value of the business.

The true value of this type of investment depended upon wise and farsighted planning in the acquisition of such property.

The President stated, for example, that an offer had been made by Schwalbach to sell to the Company his property located at the Northwest corner of Galena and 10th Streets for $5,000 and that the property was very desirable for saloon purposes owing to its close proximity to the new Police Station to be erected on Galena Street between 9th and 10th Streets and that he would recommend the purchasing of the premises.[17]

A few months later, the Captain noted

that a valuable piece of property, adjoining the South Side Turner Hall and National Avenue, to the West had been offered to the company by one M. Reuter, who offered to sell it for $7,850 and as this property was desirable for saloon purposes, he would advise the Board to purchase the same.[18]

But the acquisition of real estate was not always entirely voluntary. If a customer did not like his landlord, or if he owned his saloon and wanted to sell it, he might coerce a brewer into buying the property by threatening to discontinue his beer. Other property was acquired through foreclosure of mortgages, where the occupying customer appeared so improvident and unlikely to succeed in business that the brewery had to protect itself.

The Captain appears to have been somewhat loath to rush

[17] Directors Record, Nov. 17, 1885.
[18] Directors Record, Jan. 12, 1886.

into this new type of competition. By 1887 Schlitz owned some fifty retail outlets in Milwaukee and an even larger number of vacant lots, whereas Pabst possessed less than a dozen outlets and only a few pieces of land.[19] Among the reasons for this slow expansion in Milwaukee may have been the Captain's desire for better than average quality in such outlets and his great interest in the national market. His approach to the problems of retail property ownership does not appear to have hurt Pabst sales prior to 1895. In the long run, however, his tendency to buy for prestige or advertising value may have been a decisive factor in loss of volume as compared to Pabst's two leading competitors.

Besides purchasing saloons outright, Pabst and others would help finance key dealers starting in business in new areas. Thus the Captain wrote to a traveler in St. Paul:

We would not be disinclined to render some assistance in the event that the right man were discovered, we are still of the same mind, and if you have somebody with the *right stuff* in him to manage a good saloon and also some money that he would risk by investment in that sort of business, then we would be willing to advance $500-$1,000 under suitable terms. We wouldn't be concerned about interest at all, but we ought to have some security for whatever amount we advance. Naturally, we don't want anything to do with a lease. We would be pleased to erect something on the order of what we talked about when I was there, but if we have a direct share in it, the thing wouldn't be advisable.[20]

After 1885, Pabst also invested small sums of money in saloon fixtures and furniture. By 1893, this account, depreciated by 50 per cent on the books, stood at $63,000. Property ownership, advances, and liens, however, could not eliminate spendings and discounts. No shipping brewer could afford to own more than a small fraction of the property occupied by

[19] "Real Estate Assessment Roll" [1887], Milwaukee Tax Commissioner's Office. The author wishes to thank Commissioner Thomas A. Byrne for making this survey possible.

[20] Pabst to Koenig, Jan. 9, 1890.

retailers selling his beer; and sharp competition among the big brewers, as well as between shipping brewers and local brewers, continued.[21]

PRICE COMPETITION

Price warfare, during the long-run decline in the wholesale prices of practically all commodities from 1865 to 1895, took the form, in most industries, of a struggle to maintain existing prices. Exceptions to this occurred in brewing in 1867 and in the spring of 1874, when unusually high prices for malt and hops led the brewers to attempt an increase in the price of beer. Both failed, however.[22] In 1873, $10 a barrel was a satisfactory wholesale price for Milwaukee beer sold to retail dealers in Milwaukee and Chicago. By 1893, Milwaukee brewers found it difficult to hold the price as high as $6.00. During temporary "beer wars" in several cities, barrels sold under $4.00, a price that did not even cover operating and transportation costs for the Milwaukee brewers.[23] In general, by the late eighties and early nineties the brewer was glad to net between $5.75 and $6.00 F.O.B. Milwaukee.

The Western shipping brewers, Pabst, Anheuser-Busch, Schlitz, Lemp, Moerlein, and Blatz, had varying relations to different local markets. In their own cities of Milwaukee, St. Louis, and Cincinnati, and in Chicago, they met the prices agreed on by the local brewers associations and, as indicated in the following letter from Leo Brigel of Cincinnati in 1880, they strove for uniformity of price in these markets:

Having been appointed by the Brewers Association of this city Chairman of a Committee to confer with you and others as to the advisability of advancing the price of Beer I take pleasure in addressing you on this very important subject which is certainly of

---

[21] Retail liquor outlets numbered 260,494 at the peak in 1906. *Brewers' Almanac* [1946], p. 9.

[22] *Sentinel*, Feb. 14, 16, 21, 23, 26, 1874. See p. 65 for 1867 price controversy.

[23] *Western Brewer*, XVIII, No. 1 (Jan. 15, 1893), 109; John E. George, *The Saloon Question in Chicago*, p. 73; *Daily News*, July 12, 1890.

great interest to you, considering the present cost of all material used in the manufacture and sale of Beer. I am satisfied that an advance of $1.00 per Barrel can be maintained, as you are aware that all other industries have formed combinations and have successfully maintained their prices. Should you consider the above favorable, we will meet you on any fair terms on points where we are in competition and for that purpose have selected a Committee to have an interview and agree upon all matters which may be of importance to our mutual interests. If you deem it advisable to call a meeting of Brewers of your city, St. Louis and Cinti [*sic*], please advise me and I will endeavor to have such called by you naming the time and place when it would suit your convenience to attend the same. A favorable and early reply will oblige.[24]

To this the Captain replied:

We have spoken to several of the Milwaukee brewers and find they are all in favor of raising the price of shipping beer by the first of May next, but we do not think that we will be able to raise the price here and in Chicago.

We will cooperate with you provided that some arrangement can be made by which all those that may join in the matter can be finally *bound to live up* to the agreement.[25]

But no such intercity agreement was achieved.

At more distant points such as New York, Philadelphia, Kansas City, or New Orleans, even though there were such big, well-equipped firms as Ehret of New York or Bergner & Engel of Philadelphia, the Western shippers tried to sell at a uniform price above that of the local competitors. This, however, was particularly difficult in New York and Philadelphia. In these cities there were too many brewers to make any type of price control really effective. As Schandein wrote to the Captain from New York in March of 1880: [26]

The various brewers sell at different prices and grant various percentage off, so that in fact beer is being sold in New York for as low

---

[24] Brigel to Best Brewing Co., Mar. 6, 1880.
[25] Letter, Mar. 10, 1880.
[26] Letter, Mar. 31, 1880. Translated from the German.

as $6.00 per barrel. . . . . The prices in Washington, Philadelphia, New York and Boston are:

	Washington	Philadelphia	New York	Boston
Schlitz	$10.00	$9.00	$9.00 & less	$9.50 & less
Bergner or local...	8.50	8.00	7.00-6.00	8.00
Junemann	9.00	8.00 (Clausen)	7.00	8.00 (Ehret)

The letter shows clearly that national sales depended more on quality than on price. Where local demand could be built up for extra quality, Milwaukee beer obviously could stand a price differential of $1.00 to $1.50. The retailer often recovered the difference by serving a smaller glass of the out-of-town beer for the standard price. In some cases, however, the costlier beer was carried for prestige and sold for less profit than the local product.

The bitterest warfare among the Western brewers took place in Chicago, where the big shippers of Milwaukee and St. Louis found their principal out-of-town market. Rivalry got so keen that in 1881 the Milwaukee and St. Louis shippers in self-defense joined the Chicago "selling pool," with market quotas based on the sales of May 1879 to May 1880.[27] This pool and all subsequent efforts to control the Chicago market failed, but new agreements were continually being drawn up only to be broken within a few months or a year. In the late eighties, British syndicates started combining the depressed Chicago breweries in an effort to stabilize competition and to produce the kind of profits earned in Milwaukee and St. Louis where prices were well maintained. The immediate effect, however, was a series of Chicago price wars from 1889 on, as the remaining small brewers battled the syndicates. The *Milwaukee Daily News* noted on July 12, 1890:

It will be remembered that all the large breweries in Chicago were purchased by an English syndicate some time ago. Since then the small breweries have been losing customers and trade until they now find it necessary to make a bold stand for their very existence.

---

[27] *Milwaukee Daily Journal*, May 20, 1886.

Prices were cut from $6.00 to $4.00 and even in some cases to $3.50 and $2.00 a barrel, to the detriment of Milwaukee brewers who shipped 325,000 barrels a year to this market. The *News* continued:

Thus far . . . . none of the Milwaukee brewers think the Chicago syndicate will try to invade Milwaukee, or that the price of beer at Chicago will affect this city, where beer is still sold at $8.00 a barrel, but they do not feel like taking part in the war at Chicago if it can be avoided.

The Chicago war or, rather, series of wars continued throughout the period under discussion. Early in 1892, the *Milwaukee Daily News* wrote optimistically of an impending settlement:

A movement is now on foot, said to be headed by the Anheuser-Busch Company of St. Louis, to bring about an agreement between all Indiana, Illinois, Ohio, Missouri, Wisconsin, and Kentucky brewers for the purpose of removing as far as possible the middle men and thus rid the business of one of the active agencies that serve to cut rates.

A number of the local brewers interviewed today said they knew nothing about the matter. The little local wars cut but a small figure with the large brewing firms of this city, which have established trades throughout the country and are not dependent upon any particular locality. The Pabst, Schlitz and Blatz plants have been greatly enlarged during the past year and they have a ready market for their entire outputs.[28]

Anheuser-Busch apparently failed to make any lasting arrangements, and the Milwaukee brewers were not in fact as independent of the situation as reported by the press. In his secretary's report of 1892, Gustav Pabst blamed the competitive situation for a reduction in profits.

The largest part of this decrease is attributable to the beer war in Chicago, where we were obliged to sell at $4.00 per barrel during the first nine months of the year, and also to a general reduction in prices in different, we might say all parts of the country where

[28] *Daily News*, Feb. 17, 1892. Scrapbook clipping.

11

in order to meet competition we were obliged to lower our prices or abandon the field to our competitors.

Prices are still tending downward, and we are called upon almost daily to grant reduction of from 20 to 30 cents per barrel, in some instances even as high as 50 cents per barrel, and the prospects for such earnings as have been made in years past are not the brightest.

Outside of the largest cities the shippers were able to manage price competition among themselves more satisfactorily. Without the aid of any theory of monopolistic competition, they all recognized clearly its practical mechanics. They knew that there were so few brewers selling a quality beer in the national market that price cutting by any one of them endangered the price level for all. In their efforts to minimize price competition among themselves, however, they had to be on the alert to keep retailers from playing off one big company against another. "The men we have to deal with," wrote Adolphus Busch to his "Dear Friend," the Captain, in 1881,

are greatly given to misrepresent facts, in order to purchase their supplies at lowest possible prices. I see with regret that you have credited such stories. Permit me to assure you, that we have never sold at less than $10.50 and $11.00, 2% off for cash, and any statements to the contrary, made to you, are not true. If you will be good enough to give me facts, I will produce proof to refute the allegations.

The prices of $9.50 and $10.00 are too low to leave the manufacturer a legitimate profit on his goods. Please see the colleagues of the Schlitz Brewing Company, and by a concerted action, and interchange of courtesies, tending to explode false reports, we could easily fix and hold the price of $10.25 and $10.75.

I have an understanding with Lemp, we refer all such reports made about one, to the other, and it is most surprising, what lies have come to light. I have no doubt of Mr. Lemp being willing to fully act in concert.

With kindest regards, and pressure of your hand.[29]

[29] Letter, Apr. 27, 1881.

Eight years later the same difficulties were still being fought, and the big Western brewers were beginning to think in terms of the need for closer organization. Busch wrote to the Captain:

Now you had better come down here, so that we can talk matters quietly over and on that occasion I hope also to be able to demonstrate to you that by the present way competition is running we are only hurting each other in a real foolish way. The traveling agents very often make false reports and try to get trade through misrepresentations and wrong statements; while they are out, they always endeavor to reduce prices and send such reports to their respective home offices as are generally not correct and only tend to bring forth a competition that helps to ruin the profits. Now a perfect understanding between your good self, Schlitz, Lemp and myself ought to be reached, matters regulated and I feel confident that each of the four concerns mentioned would then realize a profit of a half million or even a million more than they do now. All large manufacturing interests are now working in harmony, such as the iron interest, the glass interest, sugar interest, steel interest, etc., and only the brewers are behind as usual; instead of combining their efforts and thus securing their own interest, they are fighting each other and running the profits down, so that the pleasure of managing a brewery has been diminished a good deal.

Hoping to have the pleasure of soon seeing you here and with the Compliments of the Season to yourself and your family, I remain.[30]

THE TRUST MOVEMENT IN BREWING

Some months before Busch wrote this letter, several British financial groups became interested in forming American brewing "trusts" out of a number of medium and large firms. These plans were clearly in tune with the times. The example set by the Standard Oil Company in 1879, of forming a trust to hold the stock of many erstwhile competing companies was followed in 1884 by cottonseed-oil producers, in 1885 by linseed-oil producers, and in 1887 by distillers and sugar refiners. Why

[30] Letter, Jan. 3, 1889.

not, then, in brewing, where British capital might succeed in putting together one or more large combinations capable of controlling prices and production?

Some Americans seemed to know "why not." Apparently they hoped to forestall the British. "The brewers of this country," said Vice-President Merkel of the Kraus Merkel Malt Company, of Milwaukee,

cannot afford to permit the English syndicate to drive them out of the business they have built up, and they must organize for protection. . . . . The St. Louis Brewers have already formed an organization, but will join the national syndicate as soon as their fellow brewers throughout the country signify their willingness to come in.

It is the intention to form a gigantic stock company with a capital of $100,000,000 with which, virtually, to buy up every big brewery in the country.

We do not propose to be undersold by anybody nor will we attempt to crowd any one else out of the market by cutting prices below a living level. I don't think prices will be at all affected.[31]

The Americans accomplished nothing on their own account, however, and the British continued buying. In October 1889, three breweries in Indianapolis were acquired and, in February of the following year, two in Cincinnati. In St. Louis, the British syndicate acquired nearly all the breweries except Anheuser-Busch and Lemp.[32] The *Milwaukee Daily News* warned:

One by one the great English syndicate is gradually buying up all the breweries in the north and northwest that can be purchased. They have just closed negotiations by which the entire plant of the St. Louis brewer's association, consisting of 18 local breweries, has been purchased for $12,000,000. Only three breweries are still owned by local capitalists—the Lemp, Anheuser-Busch and Eberts. The terms on which the syndicate secures possession of the breweries is

[31] *Daily News and Review*, Sept. 14, 1889.
[32] *Daily News and Review*, Oct. 15, 1889, and Feb. 20, 1890.

a payment of $140 per share of 50,000 shares of $7,000,000 and the assumption of $5,000,000 indebtedness.

It appears to be the scheme of the syndicate to secure all the breweries possible, after which the public may expect a big beer war in which the syndicate will crush out all the individual brewers. The scheme by which the Standard Oil Company secured control of all the refineries and oil wells in Pennsylvania and Ohio will probably be re-enacted in this case, and those brewers who now refuse to sell, even at a fancy figure, will eventually be compelled to part with their holdings for considerably less than their plants are now actually worth. This same syndicate is also negotiating for the United Elevator Company, which controls ten elevators on both sides of the Mississippi. The option on the elevators expires in December and will be taken by the syndicate.[33]

But no syndicate which did not include most of the big shippers could wield great power over the market. The British knew this as well as anyone and, in the summer of 1888, a group of English financiers approached Captain Pabst through H. M. Bigelow of Minneapolis and D. Parrish of London. It is hard to tell whether the Captain was ever convinced that consolidation would be desirable, but he was interested enough to learn the terms offered by a number of English groups. Bigelow outlined the original London plan in more detail in a letter to Pabst and Best.

Your kind favor of the 22nd ult. was handed to me upon my return from Chicago a few days since. You will remember at the time you suggested a combination deal to include your Company, the "Schlitz" and "Blatz." Judge Davis cabled to his London friends asking if they would underwrite such a combination providing the arrangement could be made. They replied "Yes, if terms are reasonable on basis of income." It now appears as per Judge Davis' letter written since his return to London the £1,000,000 sterling was immediately subscribed with a promise to secure whatever additional sum might be necessary. I called upon Mr. Uihlein, the

[33] *Daily News and Review*, Nov. 11, 1889.

Chicago manager of the "Schlitz Company" and mentioned the subject. He was of the opinion expressed by yourselves that a gain of 50¢ per bbl. would result if the combination could be effected and looked upon the proposal with so much favor that he wished me to consult with his brother August. I knew, of course, that it would be useless to discuss the matter with him before obtaining your consent, and being made aware (almost by accident) of the position you took with the Chicago delegation regarding a "Trust," I concluded to leave the business untouched for the present at least. Still, knowing that so much can be said in favor of combining your three companies and thus remove the elements of a spirited competition throughout the entire country, and yet further being aware that the idea originated in your own brain, I feel that it is worth considering seriously in connection with the fact that our English friends are fully prepared to take it up. Your Senior would be pre-eminently fitted and would be selected as the head of the Company—for life if you consent. His associates could relieve him of all details so that the tax upon his mind and energies would probably be no greater than now. In case of sickness or death, Mr. Best would not be weighed down with cares and responsibilities as these could be divided with the other gentlemen connected with the management. The advantage of a world-wide advertisement incident to bringing the Company out in London would be second only to the "Guinness." I mentioned in a former letter the impetus given to that company, and increase of sales and profits of 30% within a year of the reorganization. Do not decide against this proposition hastily, but let it lie quietly in your desk rather than be discarded. The details of reaching a consummation I will volunteer to look after. The basis for present owners consent should be two-fold-1st character and condition of property and amount of live assets to be delivered and 2d the average income of past three years. The capitalization would be based on the latter but in my opinion your Company would be entitled to a larger per cent than the ratio of earnings, because of the superiority of your plant. If this commends itself and you choose to sound Messrs. "Blatz" and "Uihlein" and they are ready to entertain such a deal, you can avoid entirely the discussion of basis and details by stating that you will send for me, who will be able to present the English side, because of my familiarity with the subject. I do not assume this note in any spirit of egotism, but having already explained the thing to Mr. August Uihlein, and being assured of his confidence in me, I think that I could harmonize the views of all concerned without "giving away" the facts (profits) confided to me by either party and yet reach a basis mutually satisfactory to one and all.[34]

In the spring of 1889, both Pabst and Anheuser-Busch rejected an offer from Gibbs and Son of London. "I have been approached at least a half dozen times since I saw you," wrote the Captain to Alfred L. Cary in London, "but I will not sell. I had a cable from London on the same subject saying our brewery was offered there. It seems these Englishmen are crazy to get hold of these breweries but I will hold on a while longer." [35]

Later in the same year a new and specific plan was proposed through H. D. Faulkner of New York for a merger of Pabst, Schlitz, and Blatz.[36]

This proposal is based on the trade for the year ending May 1st, 1889, amounting for the three Breweries to 1,081,939 barrels, which taken at a net profit of $1.73 per barrel, equal $1,870,753 net profit per annum. . . . .

The Vendors to act as Managing Directors for a term of say five years on terms to be arranged.

The American Board of Management to be seven and include Captain Fred Pabst, Mr. A. Uehlein [sic], Mr. Val. Blatz, Mr. J. S. Mitchell, Mr. Nonmemaker [sic], Mr. John Black and Mr. H. D. Faulkner. The first three to be nominated by the sellers and the others to be nominated by the Company in London. It is suggested that Captain Pabst should take the Presidency and general management; Val. Blatz to be Treasurer, and ———— to be Vice President.

---

[34] Letter, Nov. 1888.
[35] Letter, Mar. 10, 1889.
[36] Original memorandum in company archives.

The purchase price of $16,500,000 it is proposed shall be apportioned as follows:—

Pabst (Best) Brewing Company.......................... 8,000,000
    Payable . . 3,200,000 in 5 per cent Debentures
            1,500,000 in shares (if necessary) at par
            3,300,000 in cash.

Joseph Schlitz Brewing Company...................... 5,500,000
    Payable . . 2,200,000 in 5 per cent Debentures
            1,200,000 in shares (if necessary) at par
            2,100,000 in cash.

Val. Blatz Brewing Company.......................... 3,000,000
    Payable . . 1,100,000 in 5 per cent Debentures
          800,000 in shares (if necesesary) at par
          1,100,000 in cash.

$16,500,000

This proposed division of the purchase price is based on the trade of the breweries for the year ending May 1st, 1889, which amounted to 1,081,939 barrels.

The Pabst Brewery....................	525,050	Barrels
The Schlitz Brewery.................	362,660	"
The Blatz Brewery..................	194,229	"
	1,081,939	

The proportion of shares to be taken by each of the Vendors as part purchase money is only a provision that they shall take them in case the public should not apply for so large an amount as is anticipated, but should the capital be over subscribed by the public, the amount would be paid in cash, unless the Vendors desired to have that amount or more in shares.

It is probable that the shares would command a considerable premium shortly after the issue of the Company and therefore the Vendors may desire to have a larger amount in shares, but in any case this amount cannot exceed more than one third of the total amount of the Preference and Ordinary share capital.

The Vendors must take the whole of the Debentures.

As the book value of the Pabst Brewing Company was just under $5,000,000 at the end of 1889, the price offered, contingent on successful floatation of the securities, was attractive; but the Captain decided again to "hold on a while longer." He is reported to have said, "Sixteen million dollars is enough to make a man's hair stand on end—but I have been walking around this plant and I'm kind of proud of it. No you can't have it. I am going to stick to it and give Milwaukee the largest brewery in the world." [37] When approached in December by still another group acting through F. L. Underwood of New York, he replied: "For the present I will hang on to the goose that laid the golden egg." [38]

As the brewing business boomed so did the financial ideas of the Underwood group. They wanted the Captain to arrange personally the acquisition of all the other Milwaukee breweries and to bring them into a $30,000,000 corporation in which Pabst would be valued at $13,000,000. Perhaps the figure, quite typical of the unreal values placed on merged properties in the booming years of the American trust movement, seemed a little dubious to the Captain. The figure of $1.80 per-barrel profit on which the capitalizations were based was far out of line with the past history of brewing. At any rate, he turned the offer down.

The last offer to the Captain of which we have record, prior to the panic of 1893, came in March of 1891 from Lord Churchward through Robert R. Odell, a Minneapolis lawyer.

I am authorized to offer you for a limited space of time a sum and price for the property, which will show 12% dividends, be it 8 millions or 25 millions. . . . . This offer includes $25,000. per year

[37] *Sentinel,* Jan. 2, 1904.
[38] Pabst to F. L. Underwood, Jan. 6, 1890.

to yourself as President and 10 per cent on all excess of profits above
a dividend of 10 per cent to stockholders; also includes the salary to
be paid the Secretary, your son, Gustave [sic] G. Pabst. . . . . The
money is ready: telegraph me and Professor Ciprico and I will come
and close the deal.[39]

This last offer must have tempted the Captain greatly. On
the basis of the profits of 1890 and 1891, he could have secured
over $5,000,000 for his personal holdings, and still have retained
the active management of the business. The same flourishing
conditions in the American beer business, however, that made
the syndicates anxious to buy must have made the Captain cool
toward selling. The Pabst business had been increasing at the
rate of nearly 100,000 barrels a year since 1888, and, with the
steady increase in national sales, who could tell how big the
business might grow. Beyond all facts and figures was the Captain's pride in his own company and his desire to run it his own
way. The latter would undoubtedly be ended by a sale, even
though he might remain temporarily in charge.

Early in 1891, an Anglo-American syndicate, the Milwaukee and Chicago Breweries, Ltd., of Chicago, broke the ranks
of the big shippers by acquiring the Blatz brewery and elect-
ing Valentin Blatz president of the new company.[40] Most of
the $11,000,000 capital of this trust was probably held by
Englishmen.

However, the other big American brewers held out and the
twenty-four syndicates with a total capitalization of £18,934,000
that had by 1891 bought American breweries were left in the
unenviable position of having the strongest unified American
firms as their competitors.[41] Moreover, brewing offered much
greater difficulties than such business as oil refining, from the
standpoint of national integration—difficulties that the international financiers too easily brushed aside. The beer from each

[39] Letter, Mar. 29, 1891.
[40] Western Brewer, XVI, No. 3 (Mar. 15, 1891), 623.
[41] For a list of syndicates in 1891, see Appendix G, pp. 405-6.

brewery had a character of its own that could not be exactly duplicated elsewhere. The trusts had no single quality that won and held customers. The economies to be derived from further increase in the size of operating units would not be great in the case of the larger breweries. The amount of capital required to start a brewing business was too low, and the savings of large-scale production minus shipping costs too small, to keep out the little fellows. Local competitors, who enjoyed advantages in personal contacts, community sentiments, and cheapness of distribution, usually could retain enough of the market to limit expansion of facilities by the "trusts." The result was that the syndicates scored no great success, and competitive conditions in the industry remained much the same as before. Probably as important as any factor in the failure of the trust was the fact that the local firms of which it was composed lacked the salesmen, agents, and branches that the big shippers had built up over many years.

CHAPTER VII

A NATIONAL SALES ORGANIZATION

ALL the advantages of fine brewing, low costs, and clever advertising could have been wasted by a weak sales force. It was probably in selling more than in any other activity that the Captain and Schandein had to excel their competitors in order to obtain the world's largest lager-beer business. Schandein was himself a fine salesman and an excellent judge of men. He acted as a sort of traveling supervisor of the company's affairs while the Captain stayed home and attended to production. Yet the Captain never lost track of what each agent and employee was doing in the field.

In attempting to capture far-off markets, the shipper had to meet two types of expense not borne by local brewers: the round-trip transportation for full and empty barrels; and the expenses of either a regional traveler, a local agent, or a branch. The local brewer of course had some selling costs also, but his sales staff operated from the brewery itself. This avoided duplication of managerial functions and buildings as well as saving hotel and railroad bills. Where the local brewer had additional selling and delivery expenses as in country districts outside his city, he had accustomed retailers to paying 50 cents a barrel more than in the metropolitan area. This was a help to the big shipper as well, for he could either add the 50 cents to beer sold to the country retailers or benefit from the smaller difference in price between local and shipping beer.

TRANSPORTATION PROBLEMS

Shipping problems rated high among those that Pabst salesmen had to overcome. Beer is not only a heavy, bulky commodity in relation to its value, but the need for returning empty bottles and barrels makes transportation still more costly. It seems remarkable indeed that these handicaps were so far overcome that Pabst beer sold not only from coast to coast in the United States, but from one end of the world to the other.

Freight rates throughout this period were extremely variable, and were a matter of bargaining between the railroad and the shipper. As a general rule, the larger the shipper and the keener the railroad competition in different areas, the larger the deduction or "rebate" the railroad would grant from its published rate. That Captain Pabst was a good bargainer is shown by the complaint he received in August 1879 from the general-freight agent of the Chicago, Milwaukee, St. Paul Railroad:

The price proposed by you is unreasonably low, and is just about what we get for switching a car from our South Milwaukee to the North side of the Menomonee River.

Before answering you I have consulted with Mr. Gault, who states, that he considers your rate suggested too low to admit of its being agreed to by our Company. I shall be very glad to have you call and see us, but desire you to prepare your mind in order that you may take up the subject with a more enlightened appreciation of the cost of performing the work expected from our company.[1]

While we have no information on rates paid by competitors, in view of the Captain's ability and his persuasive manner it may be assumed that, as the largest brewer, he got the biggest rebates. The Chicago and Alton, for example, in 1879 entered into an arrangement whereby it delivered keg beer to Kansas City and picked up the empty kegs from way stations for a dollar a keg round trip, an arrangement that the Pabst manager thought was remarkably good.[2] The way railroad freight agents tended to favor the biggest customer is shown by Pierce in a letter from New Orleans in 1878:

I have had a good talk with Morey and succeeded in getting empties reduced if we ship by way of Chicago which we certainly should do in all cases. It is the best route avoiding our liability to lay over, viz., Centralia. Morey gives us a rate on empties, New Orleans to

[1] W. G. Swan to Pabst, Aug. 18, 1879.
[2] Charles E. Merritt to Best Brewing Co., Mar. 20, 1879.

Chicago 40¢ per hundred. Same from Vicksburg and from Memphis 35¢ sure, and he thinks 30¢. This will be quite a saving to us in the aggregate, I think we will succeed in getting rates advanced from St. Louis and Cincinatti [*sic*], as Morey assures me he will work for that end, as his line is deeply interested in giving us a fair show in this country.[8]

These rates were unusually low as shown by the Captain's marginal note on the above letter.

Mr. Wallber: Please note these rates and way of shipping. Notify our customers how to return empties hereafter.

In addition to the effect of competitive pressures, railroad freight rates also varied due to density of traffic. Whereas in 1884 it cost Pabst only fifteen cents to send a barrel of beer to St. Paul, and only eighteen and three-quarter cents to ship to Pittsburgh, it cost eighty cents to reach Eau Claire or Stevens Point, Wisconsin, and a dollar to Ashland on Lake Superior.

There were also many transportation problems not connected with the matter of railroad competition. The scarcity of refrigerator cars for Southern shipment at certain seasons of the year, for instance, was such a serious difficulty in the seventies and eighties that the Captain considered building some cars of his own. After correspondence with a Chicago agent representing the Pullman and other car-building companies, however, he abandoned the idea for the moment.

Shortage of cars was not the only problem of this sort. The minimum amount of ice required to protect a shipment from Milwaukee to the far South in the summer months had to be solved by experiments. The railroads, of course, always wanted as little ice used as possible. "Try and not overload the cars," wrote Horace Tucker, general-freight agent of the Illinois Central Railroad Company.

The present excess put into the cars at St. Louis and Cincinnati on all shipments to New Orleans will average about 900 lbs. ice and

[8] J. S. Pierce to Best Brewing Co., Apr. 22, 1878.

straw. Our New Orleans agent states that it carries the beer through in good condition. Their refrigerator cars are inferior to ours; and I would like to have you make a test, putting in only 2,000 lbs. excess instead of six, eight, or ten as has been the case the past thirty days. Will you not try and do it? [4]

As the letter books reveal no further railroad complaints on this score, the experiment probably succeeded.

Ice entered into shipping problems in still another way. The ordinary small-town retailer lacked storage facilities for extra barrels, so he only ordered the amount he would use within a week. This would not have been so bad if each dealer in a locality ended his week on the same day. This rarely happened. Thus, each dealer would order on a different day, so that even though their total orders might come to a carload or about ninety kegs, this could not be delivered at one time. Nevertheless, with freight rates on less than carload shipments practically prohibitive, the company had to ship the ninety kegs at once. To aid the retailers, the company, therefore, had to build and supply icehouses throughout the Middle West to hold each dealer's beer until he was ready for it. Pierce, the able Chicago manager, tried in 1878 to work out a "sailing day" plan for the Michigan Central Railroad territories which would have permitted carload shipments without company storage.

Now perhaps we can load a car every two weeks, if we can assure our customers the beer will keep that time, that is, for the winter, and in summer we can load one car per week. I think it will be necessary to send a man over the road to make arrangements to all order the same day, or days. This might serve as a starter, and if it works well, act as a lever to induce other roads to do the same thing after a time. [5]

Unfortunately, there is no evidence regarding how well he succeeded in keeping the customers on schedule.

To the shipping brewers' normal though troublesome trans-

[4] Letter, June 10, 1878.
[5] Pierce to Pabst, Nov. 13, 1878.

portation problems, one that plagued Pabst in particular can be added. This was the bother and cost of hauling beer from the brewery on the hill to the freight depot at the Milwaukee River. This expense cannot be determined accurately from the books, since this type of trucking was not separated from local delivery service. But it was high enough after the removal of bottling from the old South Side to the Empire in 1890 to set the Captain thinking about building a railroad spur from the tracks by the river to the Empire, a distance of about half a mile involving a rise of some fifty feet. At the beginning of 1891 a local consulting engineer, E. M. Spalding, submitted an estimate for an electrified line.

I think the best plan for extending the track is to branch off from the Court track at the South Side of Chestnut St., curving to right 90 West up the alley at North side of your bottling works to 10th St., thence curving across and 90 North along 10th St. to Cold Spring Ave. If you rightly comprehend the plan, you know the court track is at grade of Chestnut St. My plan is to keep on the surface along the alley above mentioned and along 10th St. This plan will be inexpensive and as you own both sides of 10th St. I think there will be no objection to your laying two tracks, from the West end of the alley along North side of bottling works to Cold Spring Ave. The tracks can be put on the West 25 ft. of the street. By cutting through the old school house the court track can be extended into the bottling works at the place where you now load into wagons.[6]

The cost was estimated at $198,134.30 including right of way, a 120 horsepower electric engine, and a 140 horsepower generator. The annual operating expense was estimated at $21,840 including 6 per cent interest on the investment and depreciation on a thirty-three-year basis. It was calculated that the electric engine could pull two fully loaded cars up the 6 per cent grade. There is no record regarding what difficulties, political or otherwise, prevented the carrying out of this project.

[6] Spalding to Pabst, Jan. 8, 1891.

TRAVELERS AND AGENTS

As expensive as was transportation, the direct cost of local selling was higher. A hard won rebate might save 15 cents a barrel to a city where peddlars' spendings per barrel ran to 50 cents. Only able branch and agency management could cut this expense. An important element in the Captain's success was his ability generally to choose the right men as travelers, agents, and branch managers, and quickly to rectify his occasional mistakes.

The Captain's wise selection of territories for sales efforts was another important factor in spreading the business. There were three approaches to a sales area: a centrally located branch with a salaried manager and staff; a wholesale agent who bought from the company and sold on his own account; the retailers and wholesalers of the area might be visited by a salaried traveler from either the home office or the nearest branch. In theory, the type of distribution depended upon the volume of business with branches naturally being set up where volume was greatest. In practice, however, the type of distribution also depended upon the availability of good agents and the ease with which an area might be visited by travelers. Philadelphia and New York, for example—among Pabst's best markets—were served by wholesale agents for many years, while small cities like Houghton, Michigan, and Stevens Point, Wisconsin, had branch offices.

The travelers from the home office might have become the key men in the selling efforts of the company had their territories not been taken over after 1878 by branch managers. As each manager took over traveling and selling in his own area, the territory left to the home office was steadily reduced so that there never was a large traveling staff. In 1876 there was one official home-office traveler, J. Billigheim, who was paid $175 a month. Emil Schandein also did much of the work of a traveler in connection with his many other duties. Charles Best describes the traveling organization in 1888.

Two traveling men were employed permanently during the year while two more were tried for a short period but they were discharged for incompetency. Occasional short trips which were made by Schoeffler, etc., are not mentioned here. S. Danzinger was employed on the road steadily. He traveled 350 days in Nebraska, Illinois, Michigan, Wyoming, Utah, Idaho, Oregon, California, Washington Territory, Montana, Minnesota, Indiana, Iowa, New York, Pennsylvania, and Kentucky, at an expense of $5,739.05 or $16.40 average per day. This is a high average for ordinary traveling, even in our line of business where it generally becomes the duty of the traveler when visiting a wholesale customer to also visit his retail trade, but allowance must be made for the fact that traveling in the far Western states and territories where large distances are to be gone over, is very expensive, consequently no great fault can be found with his expenses though they will also admit of an improvement. He has been talked to on this point. . . . . F. A. Mohrhardt was active on the road 333 days with an expense of $3,474.25 or $10.43 per day, which shows that Danzinger uses money too freely and must again be admonished in that respect. He (Mohrhardt) traveled almost exclusively in Texas and Arkansas. . . . . He makes a somewhat better showing in point of sales, than Danzinger, but his great fault is a habit of making promises to customers for which he had no authority, and a still greater fault that all his customers require an unusual heavy financial assistance, in the shape of cash loans, ice houses, ice machinery or large lines of credit. For all, or most of these financial advances security of some kind . . . . has been obtained, but it is doubtful in the mind of the subscriber, whether this security is of a desirable or reliable nature, and great care will have to be exercised in the handling of this trade in such a far off country, in order to prevent extra-ordinary heavy losses in the coming years.[7]

Mohrhardt was paid $150 per month, and Danzinger $125. In addition to these general travelers, J. S. Pierce, the former Chicago manager, now credit manager of the company, had half a dozen "collectors" traveling for him who acted as sales agents in the near-by territories. However, there was no official sales

---

[7] Annual Statement of Affairs, Book A.

manager. In fact, prior to 1893 there was very little effort at developing functional management. All lines of authority in sales as in other functions terminated with the Captain to whom branch managers and travelers reported directly.

Wholesale agents were generally selected by the travelers or traveling branch managers, although occasionally they seemed to have been personal friends of the Captain or someone else at the home office. Some of the considerations in selecting an agent are illustrated in this letter from Schandein written from New England in the course of his travels.

Yesterday I returned from Manchester and Edward Wagner, who sold 500 to 600 barrels last summer, will now take 200 bbls. of our beer. I offered it at $7.50 Milwaukee, please endeavor to obtain the most reasonable freight rates possible, preferably under 55¢ per 100. Now he sells only Ehret's bottled in Portsmouth. Inasmuch as he controls all the trade in these sections, having lived in Manchester 22 years and being a good businessman, he wants to be independent, and will take our beer, for with Ehret he is only sub-agent while the agency is in the hands of Jac. Wirth. He had already obtained small shipments from Speidel and tried it. He assures me that it was the best he ever had, not excepted much publicized ——— "pale but fine," which should be called "pale with a greenish veil." With this we would gain one of our best cards and would have the satisfaction of having not only crowded out our two biggest competitors, but also of having made them harmless. For Wagner doesn't change easily, having had Ehret's for 3 years, but this beer is not as good as it was, and he wants to maintain his trade with good beer. The rest in person.[8]

Sometimes a small, remote city presented unusual difficulties. Charles Best wrote to Joseph Billigheim at Ashland, Wisconsin:

Concerning a suitable agent I regret to have to say that we have found none and for the time being have no one in mind. We have thought the matter over carefully and have concluded that it would be an expensive proposition to send a stranger as agent to Ashland

---

[8] Schandein to Pabst, Mar. 30, 1880. Translated from the German. Blank indicates name of competitor.

and that we may even suffer a serious loss during the first six months. In view of these circumstances it would be best for us despite all that has happened to win Mr. Toepel as our agent in Ashland. Undoubtedly we would acquire in him a good, well-known and in Ashland well-liked agent and with him the Miller clientele and in this way drive our competitors out of the field. This is obviously a secret affair and for you a difficult task, but we are of the opinion that if you, Mr. Wilhelm, and a few of the other in-fluential saloonkeepers really get after him, he will come around. You can make it hot for him if you'll make him understand that otherwise we will give him colossal competition and that it would be a point of honor with us to crowd him out of his territory com-pletely. That as agent of the Phillip Best Brewing Company he would occupy an entirely different position, etc., etc.

Should he accept our agency, then we will grant him the same status that Miller now gives him and further give him a present of $100.00 (one Hundred dollars) in cash. Beyond that you might personally promise him a fine suit of clothes, or something of the sort (you understand)? Make a quick and good attempt by all possible means to win the man over, then also to bind him. . . . . If we can win Toepel and induce him to take over promptly, then that would be a master-stroke and immediately make us masters of the situation. And now go to it, Billigheim, and show us what you can accomplish.

Looking for good news presently.[9]

The home office had to supply each agent with beer at a price that would allow him to make a reasonable profit. The Cap-tain's personal supervision in these matters is shown in the following letter:

From Billigheim's letter of the 22nd we perceive that the opposition in the beer trade is very strong at the moment, and we want to do all that we can to make the business easier for you. Accordingly, we will bill beer to you at $7.50 per barrel and have taken steps to obtain a lower freight rate, hoping that thereby you may be enabled to hold your own with other competing agencies. We are much

[9] Letter, Oct. 22, 1883.

concerned about the New Orleans trade and are always ready to cooperate for the promotion of the business. We would very much like to learn your personal views about it, for we have so far not heard from you in person about the price of beer, etc. So let us hear from you.[10]

N. Steiner of Muskegon, Michigan, wrote the Captain about some of the problems that harassed local agents.

There isn't much to say about the beer business, everything depends upon what the Grand Rapids beer is like. Those brewers furnish beer any place at $8 per barrel, no matter how far away or what the freight costs. But I must sell your beer for $10 here because I have to pay the return freight on the empties and the express charges on the money people send to me in payment. You can readily see that there isn't much left for me. So far the outside customers followed the custom of taking Grand Rapids beer until it got bad, then they would take mine until the other improved. Then they would sell Grand Rapids beer as Milwaukee beer, keeping a few of our empty kegs around to show the customers and say: "See, there we've got Milwaukee beer." So you see how hard it is for me to say in advance how much I will sell. Sam Chumard says he wants to bottle your beer. Since May 1st last he bottled 84 barrels of beer. I can get only $9.50 per barrel from him, but I do it gladly because it involves few extra expenses. So you can see what the conditions are that I can't pay for the $50 license myself. If you will pay the license, however, then I will sell your beer.[11]

As shown in this letter a certain minimum volume of business was necessary to support an agent. The home office generally supplied the agent with a delivery wagon and a horse or a mule. "Wachenheim and Herman's mule is worn out," wrote Pierce concerning Vicksburg in 1878, "I advise that we buy a horse for them, they won't have a mule." [12] The agent usually had to provide a storage place for beer and, in the warmer regions, an icehouse as well. If sales volume became too small to support

[10] Pabst to "Dear Hugo," Jan. 28, 1878. Translated from the German.
[11] Letter, Apr. 17, 1878. Translated from the German.
[12] Pierce to Pabst, Apr. 19, 1878.

an agent, the company found it better to leave local promotion to travelers, and to ship beer from the nearest branch direct to the retailers. "I will go to Elgin Monday P.M.," wrote Pierce, when he was Chicago manager, "I had intended to do away with that agency soon as he got rid of the beer on hand. Think now, we better supply his customers from here, at some price that will hold them, say $7.50 if possible. We cannot afford to sell beer in Elgin at $8.00 and pay an agent besides." [13]

Mistakes inevitably were made in choosing agents. This set up the delicate problem of withdrawing the agency without creating local ill will. "I regret exceedingly," writes the Captain to an agent who has failed to produce results, "that we have found it necessary to dispense with your services, I believe you have given faithful service and done the best you could, but it is evident that Washington especially requires a man more familiar with American society and manner of doing business than you are." [14]

Even though it was not always done, it was advisable, when the sales through a certain city became large, to supersede an agency with a branch presided over by a salaried manager. The Captain explains in a letter to Theodor Krekel, a dealer in Memphis, how such a transition should take place. While he uses the terms agency and branch in a confusing fashion, the distinction was always clear on the company books.

We are convinced an agency in Memphis for the sale of our beer would be a paying proposition and are determined to establish the same and that as quickly as possible. It is not our good fortune to know you personally, but Mr. Billigheim assures us that you are in any case the right man to take this matter in hand.

If you think that you can sell half as much beer as Mr. Luehrmann, then we are prepared to make arrangements with you, and offer you a salary of $1500.00 per annum, and if through your efforts the

[13] Memorandum to Pabst on back of letter from Jacob Stricken, agent for Best Brewing Co., Chicago, June 7, 1878.
[14] Pabst to Augustus Von Barber, Mar. 5, 1890.

business grows and becomes profitable, we shall not fail to improve your position from the pecuniary standpoint.

Our general conditions and rules for the managers of our "Branch Offices & Depots" are a written agreement in which the respective agent binds himself to devote his undivided attention and energies to the business, and there are furthermore detailed explanations of the duties, as well as a bond given as surety for execution of same, besides the other usual formalities. One very important problem is that of an ice house. Can a suitable one be rented, or must one be built?

It would be best if you would make a detour to Milwaukee, in order to discuss the proposition thoroughly, and execute the necessary papers.[15]

Often it was a close question whether a salaried man or an agent working on a profit basis would function most effectively. Pierce writes:

. . . . from all I can calculate now . . . . if we had a good salaried man here, and kept all our present trade, and made *no bad debts* we could save about 50 cents per bbl. That it may be better to wait until winter, then fix our ice house and put our man in. I think we could retain Redwitz trade and goodwill, by letting him have his beer at cost price as he says he is sorry that he ever took hold of the wholesale business.[16]

THE BRANCHES

Pabst had had a branch office in Chicago since the early 1850's, but it was not until the end of the seventies that the company began a general policy of branch expansion.[17] The first step in the new policy was to divide the Chicago branch into a northern and a southern division. John S. Pierce was put in

---

[15] Letter, Jan. 4, 1886. Translated from the German.
[16] J. S. Pierce to Best Brewing Co., Apr. 22, 1878.
[17] The *Sentinel* of Sept. 12, 1854, quotes the *Chicago Journal* regarding the agency of a Milwaukee brewery at Randolph and Market Streets. Since this was the later address of Best and Co.'s Chicago branch, and Best was one of the first breweries to start shipping to Chicago, it seems reasonable to suppose that the article refers to the Best office.

charge of the North Branch, but had general supervision over both. It was not long before he became the most important traveling representative of the company. By 1883, Pabst's Chicago sales staff was almost as large as that in the home city. Only the secretary of the company and the chief brewmaster received as large a salary as Pierce.

SALARY LEDGER OF THE CHICAGO BRANCHES IN 1883 [18]

NORTH BRANCH		SOUTH BRANCH	
J. S. Pierce	$417	H. Eickstaedt	$125
H. Pabst	125	A. Eickstaedt	80
B. Franz	100	A. Schumacher	50
C. Fleischer	125	C. Ziegenhagen	100
B. Goerens	100	A. Patzke	100
J. Schmidt	70	F. Kucera	100
J. Knoll	100	Joe Pelzer	80
G. Locke	75	M. Busch	80
B. Steil	80	C. Seifert	60
G. Colbeck	80	C. Roenmile	75
P. Fisch	80	W. Metzger	50
H. McGovern	83	Jacob Haas	80
Wm. Zernie	80	P. Reiland	80
F. Boese	75		
C. Martin	65		
W. B. Pierce	75		
H. Juhnike	80		
A. Schrer	50		
L. Bartels	125		
W. Lucht	65		
C. Lembke	75		
H. Graf	83		
A. Buntrick	60		
Geo. Haas	100		

The establishment of branches accords roughly with Pabst's expanding sales area. The first group of branches, opened between 1879 and 1884, included Kansas City, Peoria, St. Paul, and Ashland, and marked the penetration of the northwest central area. Except for a Pittsburgh branch, opened in 1884, no branches outside this area were attempted until 1888. Then a

[18] Separate sheet attached to Salary Ledger.

more ambitious circle was drawn through Louisville, Washington, Baltimore, New York, Buffalo, and Duluth. In the case of the big metropolitan centers, the branches superseded agencies which had existed since the seventies.

BRANCHES [19]

Name	First Year of Operation	Name	First Year of Operation
Chicago, Illinois (divided)	1878	Grand Rapids, Michigan	1891
Kansas City, Missouri	1879	Louisville, Kentucky	1891
Peoria, Illinois	1881	Dallas, Texas	1891
St. Paul, Minnesota	1881	La Salle, Illinois	1892
Ashland, Wisconsin	1883	Brainerd, Minnesota	1892
Eau Claire, Wisconsin	1884	Indianapolis, Indiana	1892
Stevens Point, Wisconsin	1884	Antigo, Wisconsin	1892
Pittsburgh, Pennsylvania	1884	Chilton, Wisconsin	1892
Streator, Illinois	1886	Fond du Lac, Wisconsin	1892
Wausau, Wisconsin	1886	Oshkosh, Wisconsin	1892
Calumet, Michigan	1887	Superior, Wisconsin	1892
Houghton, Michigan	1887	Baltimore, Maryland	1893
Minneapolis, Minnesota	1888	Brazil, Indiana	1893
New York, New York	1888	Rochester, New York	1893
Washington, D.C.	1889	Menomonie, Wisconsin	1893
Galveston, Texas	1889	Kaukauna, Wisconsin	1893
Terre Haute, Indiana	1889	Oconto, Wisconsin	1893
Buffalo, New York	1890	Houston, Texas	1893
Duluth, Minnesota	1891	Pocahontas, Virginia	1893
Denison, Texas	1891	Peru, Indiana	1893

In the Pabst setup a branch could often operate at an apparent loss and still make money for the company. This was possible because beer was sold to the branches at an arbitrary price F.O.B. Milwaukee, and it was up to the branch manager to resell for as much as his particular market would bear. In the highly competitive big city markets, particularly in Chicago, this resale price often was too low to pay expenses and still meet the price the branch paid the home office. But even if the branch lost 50 cents a barrel, while the Milwaukee price allowed the brewery a profit of $1.00, the net gain to the company was 50

[19] Annual Statement of Affairs, Books A and B.

cents. In 1884, for example, the Chicago branch sold 101,505⅝ barrels that were charged to it at the rate of $6.25 per barrel delivered in Chicago, or $6.098 F.O.B. Milwaukee. The loss on Chicago branch operations that year was $48,446.91 or 47.7 cents per barrel, so that the net return to the brewery actually was only $5.621 per barrel. Still the beer cost an average of only $5.264 per barrel, so the company in the end netted 35.7 cents on each barrel sold in Chicago. This figure, to be sure, was well under the company's average profit in 1884 of approximately $1.05 per barrel; but the Chicago business built up volume as well as the popularity and reputation of the beer on which larger profits in other areas depended.

In general, Pabst's best profits came from country sales where there was little or no local competition, and particularly from country sales made from the home office where there was no cost for branch administration. Not only could the price be held at a dollar or more per barrel above the city price, but country spendings and discounts also were lower. The home-office country sales, running between 38 and 50 per cent of the company's total from 1883 through 1893, were the real backbone of company profits; a net of $1.50 to $2.00 a barrel on this beer made it possible to expand sales in low-profit, highly competitive areas. Home-office city sales were less reliably profitable, since high spendings and discounts often cut the net return to the brewery to the level of branch profits. The contrast in returns from highly competitive and less competitive areas is clearly shown in the following table.

New York returned $6.34 to the brewery, but this was due to the luxury market there rather than lack of competition. A barrel of beer sold in Houghton up on the northern peninsula of Michigan, for example, brought in about $1.50 more profit than one sold in Chicago or Pittsburgh.

Keenness of competition in branch areas also affected the important item of losses due to bad accounts. In Chicago and Minneapolis, for instance, where rivalry was intense, bad-debt losses would run high since saloonkeepers were in a position to demand large credits in return for carrying the beer. Occasionally, however, the failure of a big customer of one of the smaller branches would wipe out that branch's entire annual profits. A defalcation at Houghton, Michigan, in 1889, for example, produced a loss equal to $1.97 on each barrel sold by the branch that year. In both types of sales area, however, the limitation of losses depended largely on the judgment of the home office in choosing fieldmen, and the judgment of the latter in estimating local credit risks. It was easy to sell beer on credit to irresponsible customers, but hard to hold business on a cash basis.

PRICE OF BEER AND NET RETURN FROM BRANCHES IN 1886 [20]

Branch	Average Selling Price at the Place Designated	Net Proceeds to the Brewery
Minneapolis, Minnesota	$6.97	$3.93
Chicago, Illinois	6.07	4.71
Pittsburgh, Pennsylvania	7.93	4.82
Streator, Illinois	6.88	4.83
St. Paul, Minnesota	7.40	4.96
Peoria, Illinois	7.00	5.27
Stevens Point, Wisconsin	7.73	5.36
Wausau, Wisconsin	7.41	5.86
Kansas City, Missouri	8.03	5.52
Houghton, Michigan	8.93	6.31

MARKETING BOTTLED BEER

Bottled beer at this time was still a minor part of the business of the home office and its branches and did not receive much attention from the sales force. Some branches bought bottled beer from the home office, whereas others erected local bottling plants or sold keg beer to near-by bottlers. Where the branch was far enough away so that freight charges on full cases and returned empties would run high, it was usually cheaper to bottle locally. Sometimes, however, the market was so far away that it was cheaper to ship bottles. This was true, for instance,

[20] Annual Statement of Affairs, Book A.

SALES BY STATES IN 1888 [21]

| State | BOTTLED BEER | | KEG BEER |
	Casks *	Cases	Barrels
Alabama	606	....	....
Arkansas	75	299	935
California	1,175	....	3,595
Colorado	400	900	337
Dakota	590	9,971	3,267
District of Columbia	....	....	1,824
Florida	....	....	126
Georgia	1,105	....	....
Idaho	200	....	....
Illinois	2,100	28,476	172,898
Indiana	....	4,438	12,809
Iowa	2,972	18,028	14,062
Kansas	735	2,761	876
Kentucky	10	....	1,480
Louisiana	590	....	1,206
Massachusetts	37	7	10,248
Michigan	1	20,706	15,818
Minnesota	270	19,750	21,694
Mississippi	85	....	....
Missouri	13,511	54,899	26,440
Montana	522	21,161	4,974
Nebraska	1,424	18,781	21,791
New Jersey	....	....	5,714
New York	5,015	10,338	14,404
North Carolina	100	....	....
Ohio	57	5,124	4,649
Oregon	1,406	....	....
Pennsylvania	584	15,997	12,689
South Carolina	85	....	....
Tennessee	....	2,262	....
Texas	3,785	210	7,452
Utah	3,268	100	180
Washington Territory	274	5	838
Wisconsin	1	10,724	64,640
Wyoming	2,000	....	....

* A cask was a barrel containing six dozen pints or three dozen quarts packed in straw.

[21] Annual Statement of Affairs, Book A.

in the distant trans-Rocky Mountain area and in foreign areas. From these places it was too costly to return empty bottles or kegs and, since bottled beer could be priced to stand the loss better than keg, bottles were shipped and simply charged off. Where bottling was done by an independent company, the branch sold them keg beer for this purpose at slightly less than the price to retail dealers.

In 1882, when bottled-beer sales were still insignificant, the company, it will be remembered, began the practice of tying a piece of blue ribbon around the neck of each bottle of the extra-quality, light beer, called "Select." This was simply an experiment, but it proved to be one of the most important in the company's history. The beribboned brand was not officially named "Blue Ribbon" until the latter nineties, but from the start the name was often used by customers asking for Best's or Pabst's beer. By 1892, the brand and the bottle had become so popular that the company was buying over 300,000 yards of silk ribbon annually to tie by hand around the necks of the sloping-shouldered, white bottles. With Pabst's Blue Ribbon, bottled beer had arrived.

As Pabst's total sales soared upward after 1888, bottled beer more than kept the pace. By 1890, 101,069 barrels were bottled at a profit of $2.205 per barrel. From then on, until 1893, volume increased only slightly, but profits rose to $2.638 per barrel in 1892, or a rate of return of about two and one-half times as high as on keg beer.[22]

Although Pabst products had been sold abroad by special order since the 1860's, no sales machinery had been set up to increase this business until 1886, when bottled beer had become firmly established. Then R. F. Farnaris was appointed as special agent in New York to take charge of export sales. Farnaris had to be given power of attorney to represent the company in order to conduct the necessary dealings with the customhouse and other governmental agencies; and, as the business increased,

[22] For bottling department production, refer to p. 124.

he was made the head of an export sales department in 1888. But even this was not as important as it sounds. The company's entire export business at this time amounted to a little over a thousand barrels a year, with the Caribbean countries and Australia as the largest customers. This was less beer than would be sold by the smallest Michigan or Wisconsin branch. The home office still made no special effort to promote foreign business beyond allowing Farnaris a generous traveling account for covering the Caribbean area. In 1890 the Australian market, one of the most promising, was lost, according to the Pabst annual statement, "through circumstances beyond our control," which apparently referred to the change in Australian customs duties.[23] But the opening of a market in Cuba in 1892 more than compensated for the loss. China, mainly through the port of Shanghai, was a small but steady customer.

EXPORT BEER SALES [24]

| | 1888 | | | 1893 | |
Destination	Dozen Quarts	Dozen Pints	Barrels	Dozen Quarts	Dozen Pints
Mexico	1,416	5,060	....	.....	4,000
Canada	1,708	4,045	....	144	860
British Columbia	1,452	300	....	4,140	550
Hawaii	2,304	1,250	....	3,384	1,620
South America	976	2,296	....	.....	.....
Costa Rica	.....	2,000	....	.....	.....
Australia	5,712	4,550	....	308	504
China	300	1,575	....	300	1,575
New York Export Branch	4,122	44,930	....	630	7,016
Winnipeg	.....	.....	269½	2,160	150
Cuba	.....	.....	689	.....	18,730
Panama	1,056	4,250	....	900	3,500
British Honduras	.....	.....	....	1,530	1,450
Canary Islands	.....	.....	....	4,800	.....
Total	19,046	70,256	958½	18,296	39,955

Pabst's export trade, at this time, was more valuable than sales figures indicate. The point is that Pabst was one of the very few companies building an export business. Even the company's

---

[23] Royal Commission on Customs and Excise Tariffs, *Minutes of Evidence*, Vol. I, Div. I, Stimulants, p. 35.
[24] Annual Statement of Affairs, Books A and B.

small volume in 1888, for example, accounted for nearly 30 per cent of the total beer export of the United States.[25] Pabst continued to emphasize the export business right up to prohibition, building a world-wide reputation for its beer.

We have examined many reasons for Pabst's success in the period 1873-1893: flexible, efficient management; traditionally skilled labor; good and progressive technology; well-calculated plant expansion; successful acquisition of the business of two large competitors; aggressive sales promotion; and one other element which cannot easily be evaluated—the Captain's own personality. The small but significant margin of superiority that the Pabst Brewing Company held over its nearest competitors and that made Pabst the world's greatest lager-beer brewery in the later years of this period may well have depended on this final fact. A harassed Minneapolis agent wrote to the Captain in 1883, "You will pardon me for saying that your presence will do us more good, as well as your Minneapolis and St. Paul branches, than anything else can." [26]

[25] U.S.B.A., *Convention Proceedings* [1894], p. 77.
[26] E. H. Bowen, Minnesota Bottling Co., to Pabst, Dec. 20, 1883.

QUALITY AND PRESTIGE FIRST

In the two decades preceding the panic of 1893, the market for the products of the shipping brewers grew even faster than the total market for beer. In the next twenty years this trend was reversed. The national market continued to expand but the big shippers, as a group, were unable to hold their former share of it against the competition of local brewers. Domestic beer sales

PABST SALES AND DOMESTIC CONSUMPTION, 1893-1919 [1]

	Pabst Sales (Barrels)	Total U. S. Withdrawals * (Barrels)	Per Capita Consumption (Gallons)
1893	1,084,051	31,962,743	14.8
1894	1,003,487	30,834,674	14.0
1895	955,149	31,044,305	13.9
1896	867,435	33,139,141	14.5
1897	806,548	31,841,362	13.7
1898	794,606	36,682,838	15.5
1899	856,600	33,836,651	14.0
1900	863,973	36,381,035	14.8
1901	898,252	37,478,297	15.0
1902	889,347	47,449,750	18.6
1903	946,404	46,654,823	17.9
1904	904,134	48,208,132	18.1
1905	875,681	49,459,540	18.3
1906	1,014,699	54,651,637	19.8
1907	1,086,140	58,546,111	20.8
1908	933,269	58,747,680	20.5
1909	904,459	56,303,497	19.3
1910	1,021,711	59,485,117	20.0
1911	1,033,514	63,216,851	21.0
1912	942,165	62,108,633	20.3
1913	935,699	65,245,544	21.0
1914	876,190	66,105,445	21.0
1915	735,098	59,746,701	18.7
1916	827,597	58,583,781	18.1
1917	849,846	60,729,785	18.5
1918	694,013	50,174,796	15.1
1919	494,614	30,546,418	9.1

* Tax-paid beer for sale.

[1] *Brewers' Almanac* [1944], p. 56.

reached an all-time high of 66,105,445 gallons, or 21 gallons per capita, in 1914—113 per cent above 1893. In the same period, sales of the three big Milwaukee shipping brewers increased less than 26 per cent, whereas estimates of the St. Louis situation indicate that the two big shippers of that city, taken together, also fell behind the increase in the national market.[2]

The big shippers, as a group, failed to hold their position for many reasons. Increasing ownership of saloons by large local breweries left fewer independent retailers to handle shippers' brands. Similarly, the increase in bottling by small brewers cut into a field that in 1893 had been mainly occupied by the larger firms. Relatively higher freight rates and the virtual ending of rebating by the Elkins Antirebate Act of 1903 placed a further handicap on the out-of-town beer. Probably most important, however, was the fact that, particularly in the latter part of this period, the manufacturing and selling costs of all brewers increased more rapidly than prices. This hit the shipping brewers most severely, for it left less and less margin for the promotion necessary to hold the national market. During the years from 1894 to 1904, when beer prices actually rose as fast as costs, the three big Milwaukee shippers still had the margin required for national promotion and, while they were unable to hold their old share of the market, they still increased their sales 40 per cent as fast as those of the nation. During the next ten years, however, when costs mounted much more rapidly than prices, the shippers' sales rose less than 13 per cent as fast as the national figures.

As the nation's largest shipper in 1893, Pabst was most severely hit by these external factors. The company's position was made more difficult by the Captain's policies. Above all, the Captain was determined to maintain the quality of Pabst beer and the retail outlets that sold it, even if these policies, involv-

[2] Sundry Papers Scrapbook. It should be noted that Schlitz of the Milwaukee shippers did show an increase of 88 per cent but this still falls short of the national rate of 113 per cent. It appears that Anheuser-Busch production about kept up with the increase in national demand, but that Lemp production did not.

13

ing higher costs and fewer sellers, were bound to react unfavorably on volume. Continuation of the rapid increase in sales volume of earlier years in this period of widespread ownership of saloons by brewers would have required investment by Pabst in many cheap or second-rate properties, and, to this, both the Captain and Gustav Pabst were unalterably opposed.

The net effect of all this on Pabst was to produce a period of profitable stability in contrast to the preceding period of rapid growth. From 1894 to 1916, Pabst's annual sales fluctuated between 735,000 barrels and 1,086,000 barrels and, except for the relative depression in brewing caused by the advance of state and local prohibition after 1915, followed the general trend of the business cycle.

The net worth of the company also remained practically stable in this period, increasing from $11,106,781.96, in 1894, to $13,001,316.22, in 1916, in current dollars, or decreasing slightly in "real" dollars based on any of the standard estimates, which indicate about a 30 per cent decline in the purchasing power of money during these years. However, Pabst paid out in this period $10,048,720 in dividends, and there was never a year in which the company failed to show a substantial profit.

The owner of a single share of Pabst stock in 1894, who never invested additional money, received not only cash dividends averaging about 4.5 per cent a year on his original investment, but also by 1916, a 74.24 per cent increase in his claim on the company's net worth due to Pabst's policy of buying up its own outstanding stock. This was surely a satisfactory result in an industry of which an analyst wrote in 1913:

During the last twenty years the percentage of gross profit on manufacturing operations in general has greatly decreased.

No business has suffered more from this shrinkage than that of brewing, for while in other lines of manufacture selling prices can be adjusted to meet increased manufacturing cost, such adjustments seem almost hopeless in the brewing business. . . . .

Increase in running expenses, cost of materials, and bad debts have so reduced the margin of profit that it has become essential not only to have correct cost accounts, but to arrange the books so that the brewery managers may ascertain without delay the results of current operations.[3]

FINANCIAL STATISTICS

Year	Net Profits	Net Worth	Dividends
1894	$1,100,497	$11,106,782	$1,000,000
1895	1,019,492	11,126,274	1,000,000
1896	1,002,224	11,128,497	100,000
1897	862,088	11,890,585	1,000,000
1898	653,801	11,544,387	100,000
1899	829,090	12,381,584	200,000
1900	801,165	12,982,749	200,000
1901	706,566	13,489,314	. . . . . .
1902	718,042	14,132,264	100,000
1903	778,465	14,810,729	100,000
1904	724,756	14,986,749	187,850
1905	782,392	15,392,501	376,640
1906	1,114,743	11,408,527	285,420
1907	921,710	11,881,325	337,340
1908	521,372	12,017,058	376,640
1909	943,480	12,489,738	470,800
1910	1,093,090	12,939,708	643,120
1911	999,244	13,117,359	725,840
1912	548,995	12,929,847	725,840
1913	880,899	13,231,367	579,380
1914	555,189	13,388,636	397,920
1915	370,563	13,214,322	527,795
1916	705,429	13,001,316	614,135
1917	392,499	12,838,897	503,248
1918	271,472	12,464,496	598,744

A CHANGED COMPETITIVE POSITION

Promotion had been the keynote of Pabst policy in the great period of expansion; but in the early years of this later period of stability, the company's watchword became economy. While Pabst's chief competitors, according to outside guesses, had increased their direct promotional expenditures, Pabst itself reversed its course. All direct expenses attendant on the placing

[3] Frank Weldon Thornton, *Brewery Accounts*, Preface, p. v.

of beer, such as spendings, allowances, discounts, entertainment, and traveling expenses, were reduced from a level of $340,000 per year in 1894 to about $275,000 a year in the early 1900's. Direct advertising outlays were increased, but probably not to the extent of other similarly placed American companies either in brewing or other highly competitive lines. Exclusive of Signs and Views for saloon and restaurant use, Pabst's advertising outlays in 1892 and 1893, the last years before the depression, had averaged about $69,000 a year. From 1898 to 1901, the first years of the new boom period, they averaged $102,000. But the years between 1893 and 1901 covered the greatest development in the early history of American advertising; and, while Pabst's outlay of $72,525.27 in 1893, for instance, was a large one for that time, the advertising budget of $81,638.34 in 1901 probably was less than that of other similar companies.

Earlier, Pabst had found that in one of the most keenly competitive of all American businesses, where savings through increased volume of production were fairly small, a company could only remain the largest in the field by continuous, aggressive, risk-taking expenditure designed to increase volume. Now, however, it was apparently decided that further expenditures for volume alone would no longer pay off and would probably be made at the expense of profits. For this reason Pabst put its emphasis on quality and prestige. These were maintained; but volume was not and consequently Pabst's two largest competitors, Anheuser-Busch and Schlitz, surpassed it in sales, the former in the late nineties, the latter in 1902. Anheuser-Busch and Schlitz maintained their sales lead on Pabst up to the time of prohibition, but, between 1905 and 1918, Pabst sales did not fall further in relation to those of the two competitors. This was due partly to an extensive advertising campaign, inaugurated in 1903, that, at an average cost of $316,800 a year, succeeded in selling ever larger quantities of bottled beer.

Moreover, there were compensations in being third in the industry. Firms battling for first place are inclined to assume heavy promotional expense merely to win the coveted honor.

Pabst avoided this. When the Chicago representatives of Price, Waterhouse & Co. first examined the Pabst books in 1904, which marked the beginning of continuous professional auditing, they commented:

The average selling expenses are also materially less than in the case of the company last referred to [a large unnamed "shipping" competitor] and, after eliminating freight on shipments to branches, they compare favorably with the selling costs of Western breweries doing more of a local trade.

Manufacturing costs were also kept low in spite of high quality and slightly smaller output. The same auditor's report notes:

Compared with the costs of a Brewery supplying a barrelage and doing a business over a territory more nearly corresponding to your own, your manufacturing cost as a whole is considerably lower.

This new status did not dissatisfy Pabst's management. Indeed, it permitted the adoption of conservative policies that allowed the company to minimize risks and to husband resources, so that it was financially well prepared for the advent of prohibition.

CHANGING SOURCES OF PROFIT

From 1896 to 1915, mounting costs of all types, because of rising prices continually threatened profit margins. General wholesale prices advanced 50 per cent in this period and then shot up nearly 100 per cent more between 1915 and 1918. From a low point in 1896, when city keg beer was netting the brewery only $4.50 a barrel, to 1904, when proceeds were $5.71 a barrel, beer prices kept pace with or slightly outran the increase in costs. But from 1904 to 1915, the situation was reversed: proceeds per barrel or per bottle increased only 2 to 10 per cent, whereas manufacturing costs, based on wages and prices of materials used, went up nearly 20 per cent—ultimately squeezing out all profits in the case of country keg sales, which once had been the most profitable part of the business.

TRADING PROFITS, 1904-1918 [4]

	1904	1905	1906	1907	1908	1909	1910	1911
City keg*	$55,233	$51,302	$77,038	$95,009	$81,752	$136,400	$160,530	$131,299
Country keg	134,732	39,800	76,348	132,773	33,860	89,594	102,663	96,853
City bottled	28,952	33,300	44,450	38,931	41,235	47,918	58,357	53,596
Country bottled	354,511	346,775	597,799	469,107	351,177	364,191	438,116	469,621
Branches (except Chicago)	187,065	203,203	302,891	227,826	41,187	240,108	328,578	284,968
Chicago branch (loss)	*64,496†*	*84,476*	*90,747*	*131,248*	*108,177*	*76,118*	*100,131*	*113,338*
Tonic	74,386	62,377	79,626	52,331	24,631	19,260	26,099	30,582
Total above items	$770,383	$652,281	$1,087,405	$884,729	$465,665	$821,353	$1,014,212	$953,581
Total net profits	$724,756	$782,392	$1,114,743	$921,710	$512,372	$943,480	$1,093,090	$999,244

	1912	1913	1914	1915	1916	1917	1918
City keg	$115,895	$148,879	$142,609	$137,884	$171,505	$204,723	$254,274
Country keg	26,714	74,407	*10,787*	27,532	17,629	*8,659*	*50,582*
City bottled	34,505	31,397	33,837	21,805	35,992	39,677	61,341
Country bottled	319,750	294,585	220,816	133,029	155,282	82,908	150,207
Branches (except Chicago)	*20,396*	103,075	21,515	80,968	148,066	103,925	277,237
Chicago branch	*91,023*	27,867	24,490	32,396	33,368	42,963	26,990
Tonic	20,369	....					
Pablo	....						100,034
Total above items	$405,815	$680,210	$432,480	$216,614	$561,842	$257,687	$819,501
Total net profits	$548,995	$880,899	$555,189	$370,563	$705,429	$392,499	$271,472

* City and country keg and bottled refers to beer distributed directly from the brewery. City applies only to Milwaukee sales.
† Losses are italicized.

[4] Price, Waterhouse reports.

The relative stability of over-all profits concealed a number of wide variations in the sources of returns. Up to 1893, the net profit on bottled beer had never been more than 25 per cent of the company's total. By 1896, bottled beer returned 30 per cent and in 1898, a poor year for other profits, bottled beer produced over two thirds of the company's total net gain. From 1904 to 1912, bottling profits steadily accounted for at least half of the company's net profit. From 1912 on, however, the profits in bottled beer began a sharp decline that continued with some deviations up to 1917. The decrease was due to a severe loss of sales volume in bottled beer in 1912 which was not regained in subsequent years, and to a sharp increase in costs after 1915, because of the war boom.

From 1904 through 1911, beer bottled by the home office and branches had totaled from 7,600,000 to 10,100,000 dozen pints per year.[5] In 1912, a host of troubles hit the bottled-beer market. Almost half of the Pabst bottled-beer sales were of Blue Ribbon, the successor of the old Select, a special quality beer generally sold to dealers at 8⅓ cents a pint. In New York City, a number of the local brewers entered the bottled-beer market and far undersold the "shipping" beers. This cut Pabst sales in that area about 378,000 dozen small bottles during 1912. In the "cut-throat" Chicago market, the company decided against further selling at prices below cost, and some local bottlers thereupon stopped packaging Pabst beer. But the most serious losses, those that could not be regained by a turn of the market, were due to local prohibition. As a result of state laws and their interpretation, three Pabst outlets—at Jacksonville, Florida, Fort Worth, Texas, and Kansas City, Missouri—lost a trade of 673,214 dozen pints.[6] All of these factors cut Pabst's national volume from 8,500,000 dozen pints in 1911 to 6,750,000 by 1912, and to 5,250,000 by 1914. Henceforth the trend turned moderately upward, but increasing costs minimized the profits from the gains in sales.

[5] It was customary, for accounting purposes, to reduce quarts to equivalent pints.
[6] President's report to the Board of Directors, Directors Record, Jan. 26, 1914.

Partly offsetting this loss in the bottled products was a rise in Milwaukee beer sales and profits. Between 1894 and 1905, this branch of the business had declined to a low level in relation to other sources of revenue, but by 1915 it again became the chief producer of profits and the company was once again obeying the Captain's maxim that a good shipping business should be based upon leadership in the brewery's own local market.

Branch sales were more important than indicated by the table of profits. Throughout the period 1894 to 1916, about half the beer sold was marketed through branches but, due to competitive pressure and branch selling costs, this part of the business never produced more than about a quarter of the company's profit; and in 1908 and again in 1912, total branch operations resulted in small net losses. The branches, however, brought a fair average return on an investment in facilities that only reached $619,928.43 in 1916. Moreover, the branches supplied the added volume that lowered the cost of all production, and they carried roughly half the overhead on about $4,500,000 invested in brewery property. The major branch problems continued to be in Chicago. There, the cost of selling was high because of cutthroat competition, and the price received was no more able to cover the arbitrary price charged the branch by the home office than in earlier years. While Chicago sales helped to carry the home-office expenses, the branch itself showed an annual loss varying between $64,000 and $131,000.

PROBLEMS OF MANAGERIAL SUCCESSION

Complicating Pabst's sales and profit problems in the period after the panic of 1893 were a series of fundamental changes in management. Up to 1892, as we have seen, the company was a one-man organization with only two important stockholders and three additional holders of a few shares each. On February 15, 1893, as a part of the conditions of the purchase of Falk, Jung and Borchert (see p. 83), Ernest Borchert was elected second vice-president and Frank R. Falk, treasurer, of the Pabst Brewing Company.[7] Philipp Jung, however, went into the malting business for himself; and after the end of the three-year period of abstention specified in the sale contract of 1892, he returned to brewing by buying out the small Obermann plant and organizing the Jung Brewing Company.[8] While by 1910 he had built his business up to 100,000 barrels a year and ranked fifth among Milwaukee brewers, he never achieved the earlier success of Falk, Jung and Borchert.

The addition of Falk and Borchert as Pabst officers, together with Mrs. Lisette Schandein as first vice-president, C. W. Henning as secretary, and the Captain's sons, Gustav G. and Fred Pabst, Jr., as members of the board, created an executive setup drastically altered from that under which the company had grown up. Management was no longer a family affair. There were now twenty-two stockholders with which to deal, including a number of comparative strangers. Still further changes occurred during the year 1894 when Mrs. Schandein resigned in favor of Gustav G. Pabst, now twenty-eight years old; and Fred Pabst, Jr., only twenty-four, took on additional executive duties.

STOCKHOLDERS IN 1894

	Shares		Shares
Fred Pabst	5,158	L. W. Falk	88
Fred Pabst, trustee	43	Emma Carpenter	59
Mrs. Lisette Schandein	3,500	Fred Pabst, Jr	112
Henry Best	33	Gustav G. Pabst	112
Louisa Falk	105	J. F. Theurer	100
Otto H. Falk	59	C. W. Henning	10
Herman W. Falk	59	E. Borchert	274
Frank R. Falk	88	Oscar Mueller	20
Clarence R. Falk	59	Jacob Heyl	118
		Total	10,000

[7] In addition to the company records, see *Western Brewer*, XVII, No. 11 (Nov. 1892), 2497-98.

[8] *One Hundred Years of Brewing*, p. 335.

For the first time in the history of the company, it was necessary to work out a careful division of managerial functions. The general plan as it was to operate for the next six years was: [9]

Fred Pabst, President
Over-all co-ordination and direction

Gustav Pabst,	Ernest Borchert,
First Vice-President	Second Vice-President
Brewing operations, Machinery, and Architecture	Branches and Auditing

C. W. Henning, Secretary,	Frank R. Falk, Treasurer
Advertising, Export Sales,	Purchasing, Rents, City
Office Management	Bottled Beer Sales,
and Insurance	General Finance
	and Labor

Fred Pabst, Jr.
Traveling, Transportation, Agencies,
and City Keg Beer Sales

On the face of it, there may be some question concerning the efficiency of this particular division of functions, but we lack the data for properly informed comments. One thing was clear from the beginning—there were fundamental differences in personality and opinion among the executives that would require careful adjustment and, as time passed, changes seemed advisable. Borchert resigned in 1899, and was succeeded as second vice-president by Fred Pabst, Jr., and in October 1902, Frank R. Falk resigned, and Henning added the duties of treasurer to those of secretary. In the broad sense, the root of Pabst's managerial troubles in the nineties seems to have been one that has afflicted many companies: circumstances suddenly arising that require too many managerial changes within a short period. Considerable credit must be given, on the other hand, to the Captain and to the new managers who took office at the beginning of a period of national financial and business troubles for

[9] Chart prepared by A. Cressy Morrison. [In the possession of Mr. Morrison.]

weathering the depression about as well as their largest competitors.

From the latter nineties on, the Captain paid less and less attention to the details of the business. While he came to the office almost every day, when he was not traveling for his health, he left active management largely in the hands of Gustav, Fred, Jr., and Charles Henning. But whether he was in Germany or California, he thought continually of the affairs of the company that was to so great an extent his own creation. From Wiesbaden, for example, he wrote in 1901:

You ask me Gustav do I want more details of the business? I don't want little details. But I would like to know something about the Cuba Plant, how New York is doing, what are you doing in Chicago, are you building? I see by the papers you are. How is the Blue Ribbon doing and a good many things of importance that came up which I would like to hear something of. For instance, our Annual Statement; here is the 18th day of February, at *least* a month after your meeting and I haven't heard nor seen a particle of it. I call that negligence of our worthy Secretary. I think a great deal of Henning as you *know* but he must wake up. Things *must* be kept up, and we must be alive, or take a back seat, others will run away with us.[10]

Gustav Pabst had a personality in many respects like that of his father. He was a good mixer, a hail fellow well met, a man who made friends easily. The workers regarded him "Just the same like the Captain." The chief difference between them seems to have been that Gustav was "easier going" and more interested in the producing end of the business, whereas his father's interest had been spread evenly over the whole organization. From the time Theurer retired at the end of 1902, Gustav Pabst was in reality the brewmaster as well as the president. He was determined to brew beer equal or superior to the finest German products. He had a series of beer taps put in the laboratory where often he spent an hour in "blindfold tests," methodi-

[10] The Captain to Gustav and Fred Pabst, Jr., Feb. 18, 1901.

cally judging by small sips at intervals of ten or fifteen minutes the merits of brews whose origin was hidden from him until he had rendered his decision. When he became president in 1904, he went to Dr. Schedler, the chief chemist, and said, "I want to impress upon you to take great care that the quality of our products is at all times preserved, and if there is a possibility for any improvement, I want to know it." [11] Regularly the president passed on the hops that were being used, supervised the barley buying and grading, and, in short, saw to it personally that Pabst beer was the best that could be brewed.

After Borchert's retirement, Fred, Jr., took over control of the marketing end of the business, and it was natural that some of the minor antagonisms that almost always existed between the production and sales forces in breweries were represented in the attitudes of the two brothers. Fred, Jr., reserved, conscientious, and hard driving, was the antithesis of Gustav; as one old friend has expressed it, each inherited a different side of the Captain's complex personality.

During these years when "the boys" were running the business, subject to occasional mediation by the Captain, the formal meeting of the board of directors had the same lack of importance in policy formation as in the early history of the company. During 1901, the board met only seven times, in 1902, eight times, and in 1903, three times. (See Appendix A, p. 400, for names of directors.)

The death of the Captain on January 1, 1904, at the age of 68, and the election of Gustav as president on January 11 led to no functional change in management, but beneath the surface it made a great deal of difference. He had not only exercised ultimate control of company affairs, but Fred, Jr., had remained active in the business largely in response to his father's wishes. William O. Goodrich, who had married Marie Pabst, took the vacant place on the board, and Fred, Jr., continued as an officer only long enough to make sure that the organization was in

11 Interview with Dr. A. J. Schedler.

GUSTAV G. PABST

shape to function smoothly without his help. On May 9, 1905, he resigned from the vice-presidency to devote his time to scientific agriculture.

With one of the two principal stockholders outside of the executive ranks, the board of directors assumed a new importance in company affairs. Fred, Jr., attended meetings regularly, and methodically went over company matters. His desire for detailed information led to the setting up on August 8, 1905, of the following system for the relations of the board with the officers of the company.[12] At a directors' meeting to be held on the second Monday in January, the president and other officers were to be elected and their salaries fixed; the brewmaster, heads of different departments, and managers of principal branches were to be confirmed, and no change was to be made in their salaries without the approval of the board; deductions for depreciation were to be set; and appropriations made for advertising. At each monthly meeting of the board, financial statements and the following items were to be submitted: monthly cost sheets; complete statements from the books, private and general, including office pay roll, and monthly branch statements, stock books, contracts, expenditures, loans, and leases; and complaints by customers.[13] For the next fifteen years, Gustav, Fred, Jr., and W. O. Goodrich guided the over-all policies of the company through the board meetings. This arrangement worked successfully because of the ability of Goodrich and the ultimate willingness of the two brothers to compromise differing opinions.

Gustav's chief executives were "Charlie" Henning and Henry Stark who now filled the offices of vice-president, and secretary and treasurer. Both men had joined the company in the 1870's and had worked their way up, principally in the accounting end of the business. They were precise, carefully dressed men who arrived punctually at eight each morning. Of the two, Henning

12 Directors Record, Aug. 8, 1905.
13 This material was not reproduced in the Minutes, and some of the records themselves have been lost.

was more fond of the pleasures of life. He loved good cigars, liquor in moderation, and hunting trips with Gustav. Both men saw to it that none of the discipline of the Captain's days was relaxed; but, under their regime, department heads began to assume an importance they had not had when all lines of authority were held directly by the Captain. This better institutionalized management left Gustav free to travel and to represent the company in the battle against prohibition.

HIGHEST SALARIES PAID MONTHLY AT THE EMPIRE BREWERY

Officers of the Company

	1896	1903	1911	1915
President	$1,250.00	$2,083.33	$1,000.00	$2,500.00
First vice-president	500.00	1,000.00	833.33	833.33
Second vice-president	500.00	1,000.00	......	......
Secretary	500.00	666.66	666.66	833.33
Treasurer	500.00	......	......	......

Other Executives

1903		1915	
Number of Employees	Amount	Number of Employees	Amount
2	$416.66	1	$833.33
1	375.00	1	416.66
1	333.33	3	300.00
4	250.00	3	275.00
1	233.33	1	250.00
1	225.00	4	225.00
1	208.33	1	208.33
1	200.00	2	200.00

The few changes in management that occurred between 1905 and 1917 were minor adjustments in the interests of greater efficiency. In 1912, W. F. Schad was made assistant secretary; and on January 27, 1913, a management advisory committee was set up composed of the officers of the company, and Henry Danischefsky, head of the real-estate department, and Fred H. Squier, advertising manager. This group met once a week, and all the other department heads submitted to it such matters as needed to go before the board of directors. The only major

change came in January 1917 when Charles Henning retired
and Henry Danischefsky succeeded him as vice-president.

Management costs were low for a twelve- or thirteen-million-
dollar corporation. Department heads failed to develop into
functional vice-presidents, as in many other large companies,
and administrative salaries were held down.

These moderate rates were still added to by year-end bonuses
of $100 to $1,000, and apparently compared satisfactorily with
the salaries in other Milwaukee businesses.

FINANCING STOCK PURCHASES

On several occasions during this period, the company bought
out large stockholders. Philipp Jung's shares of Pabst stock were
all purchased by the company by 1894. Ernest Borchert who
originally held 274 one-thousand-dollar shares sold all but 24
to the company shortly before his retirement in 1899, and the
remaining block in April 1906. The Falk family's holdings
of nearly 500 shares were purchased by semiannual install-
ment payments of $11,550 from the time of Frank Falk's retire-
ment until 1910, plus a final lump-sum payment of $395,520.84
on January 1, 1911.

Up to 1906, these payments could be made from profits, but
the death of Mrs. Schandein the previous year, and the desire
of the directors to buy her stock from her heirs, required bond
financing. This was arranged with the Wisconsin National
Bank, which underwrote a $3,000,000 issue of 4 per cent first
mortgage gold bonds, callable at any time at $105. One hun-
dred and fifty thousand dollars worth of these bonds were to be
repaid on June 1 of each year. With the aid of these funds, 3,018
shares of Schandein stock were purchased by the Pabst treasury
at par, and on December 12, 1906, a stock dividend of 3,322
shares, including some of the Borchert and Falk stock, was distributed pro rata to the remaining stockholders.

The desire of the trustees for some of the daughters and
granddaughters of the Captain to sell part of their stock in 1910,

and the financial payment due on the Falk stock that year, led to a change in the financial structure of the company. Capitalization was increased on June 18, 1910, from $10,000,000 (represented, since 1892, by 10,000 shares of $1,000 par value common stock, and no preferred) to $12,000,000 (represented by new issues of 100,000 shares of $100 par value common, and 20,000 shares of $100 par value, 7 per cent, cumulative preferred). The latter was issued to holders of the common as a 20 per cent stock dividend, with an additional 5 per cent of common from treasury-held stock. The new class of stock had equal voting privilege with the common. The preferred stock was redeemable by the company at any time at $115 plus interest to date, and the company was not to increase its bonded indebtedness beyond $2,600,000. As the bonded indebtedness, amounting to $2,500,000 on June 15, 1910, was paid off, no new debt of a similar character could be incurred without the consent of the holders of two thirds of the preferred shares. The heirs desiring to sell now marketed several thousand shares of the preferred stock at 99 through Hallgarten and Company of New York City, the only public offering of stock in the history of the Pabst Company. About a quarter of the preferred stock was repurchased prior to 1919, and the remainder retired during the reorganization forced by prohibition.

INVESTMENT POLICIES

Some years before these readjustments of the financial structure, Pabst's investment policies were basically changed. From 1887 to 1900, heavy investments were made in hotel and saloon real estate. In 1893, as we have seen, the Pabst Company had $2,237,855.11, or about 20 per cent of its net worth, invested in such property. From 1894 through 1899, active real-estate buying was continued.

In relation to the sums invested, relatively few parcels were acquired. This concentration of funds in "prestige" properties in certain localities as against the buying of many small outlets

New Investments in Real Estate for Selling Purposes [14]

(Exclusive of Branch Properties)

Year	Amount	Year	Amount
1894	$535,897	1898	$344,773
1895	515,766	1899	654,010
1896	226,863	1900	134,691
1897	1,019,026	1901	101,882

was a cause of concern to Fred Pabst, Jr. Thus on June 9, 1894, he wrote to his father from Cripple Creek, Colorado:

I took in Denver quite thoroughly and I will on my return home talk over the advisability of investing in saloon property.

Schlitz seems to be investing all over and we must adopt the same policy in the good towns in order to keep our own.

On the eve of his becoming vice-president four years later, he was still urging a broader investment policy. From Galveston, Texas, he wrote:

It sometimes strikes me that the results of all such work [traveling and promotion] will not be realized. I am already in my mind quite confident that any proposition involving money investments will meet with strong disfavor or opposition. . . . . Our competitors are making great efforts and we shall be compelled to get into a livelier pace. I wish you could have taken this trip with me as you would concur with me as to the necessity of fortifying our position here and insist upon it under all circumstances.[15]

Possibly the company's purchase of 135 pieces of property in 1899, the largest number in any single year, was a special concession to Fred, Jr., in honor of his assumption of the vice-presidency on July 1, or else an emergency response to some situation not revealed in the records, as the directors had previously voted, in April of 1899, "to cease to purchase real estate except such as it is deemed absolutely necessary that we should own." [16]

[14] As listed in the Minutes of the Directors Record, 1894-1901.
[15] Fred, Jr., to the Captain, June 20, 1898.
[16] Directors Record, Apr. 11, 1899. Mr. Fred Pabst could not, in 1945, recall the exact circumstances.

14

But, in any case, the spirit of the board resolution ultimately prevailed. Aside from the inevitable purchase of a dozen or two saloon properties a year, either through foreclosure or to prevent their falling into the hands of competitors, 1899 marks the end of Pabst's large-scale real-estate expansion. The value of "outside" real estate rose gradually from just under $6,000,000 at the end of 1900 to a high of $6,677,000 in 1910, at which time the company owned 428 selling properties in 187 cities.[17] By 1916, the book value of this property, principally through write-offs for depreciation, receded to $6,299,062.58. At the peak of its property holding, Pabst owned nine large hotels or restaurants in New York, Chicago, Milwaukee, Minneapolis, and San Francisco.

Besides investing in saloon and hotel real estate and buildings, Pabst, like other brewers, had to continue the practice of advancing money to independent retailers for fixtures. In 1905, Price, Waterhouse noted that the Pabst advances for this purpose stood about 30 per cent higher than average. Milwaukee city-saloon fixtures were carried on the books at $92,278, and country fixtures at $237,000. The costs of competitive bidding for outlets through these advances were shown by the fact that Pabst had been forced, between 1901 and 1905, to invest $99,000 in country fixtures without any compensating gain in country sales.

From the standpoint of direct profits, all this real estate was a poor investment. As Price, Waterhouse commented:

While many of your investments will undoubtedly be in first-class properties which may reasonably be expected to appreciate rather than depreciate in value, many of them must have been acquired at high costs through protecting book debts, etc. and we would therefore suggest for your consideration the advisability of making an annual provision to cover probable losses on realization.

The accountants advised an annual deduction of 2 per cent.

---

[17] In addition to the company records, see letter of Gustav G. Pabst in *Commercial and Financial Chronicle,* XCI (July 2, 1910), 42.

Pabst's investment in large, handsome establishments undoubtedly spread the name of the company and thereby increased sales. But these establishments also offered more than usual difficulties from the standpoint of management. They put the company into the chain hotel and restaurant business without any specialized staff for this kind of enterprise. Such a business presents very difficult problems, requiring honest and exacting local managers to prevent stealing and graft by hotel and restaurant employees and a hundred and one little irregularities that so easily consume profits. On the average, these restaurants and hotels paid their way, but did not provide any large return on the capital investment and did not in themselves serve as very large outlets for beer.

Pabst's investment in saloons, on the other hand, helped to sell beer. But it was an expensive way to do it. Saloonkeepers were notoriously bad bookkeepers, and rents or mortgage interest on such properties were always uncertain quantities. Not until 1909 did Pabst's total net rents top a hundred thousand dollars, and in 1916, the best year of the whole period, the net return on rents was only $120,025.34 or about 2 per cent on the capital involved. Furthermore—as pointed out by Price, Waterhouse—saloons were generally property not likely to increase in value, since they were usually located outside of areas of real-estate improvement.

Still, without this far-flung property ownership, neither Pabst nor any other shipping brewery could have maintained itself. The whole investment had to be regarded as one of the costs of selling, aggregating a loss of normal return on capital of perhaps $250,000 or more a year.

PLANT IMPROVEMENTS

Pabst not only had to face a host of new sales and investment problems after 1893 but the management also had to deal with other problems that persisted from the earlier period. Very important among these was the need for better transportation between the brewery on the hill and the railroad down on the river edge. After the failure of Pabst's electric-railroad ideas of the early nineties, there were, as far as the records show, no further plans until about 1899 when there were trade reports that Pabst planned an "elevated-railroad" circuit, 340 feet long and 33 feet wide, connecting the brewery with the warehouse and depot at the foot of Chestnut Street at a cost of $40,000.[18] There is no company record of any action on this proposal. In 1903, the Milwaukee Electric Railroad and Light Company suggested an arrangement for running Pabst freight cars on their streetcar tracks. The proposed spur from the line in Winnebago Street, however, would have required a relocation of the bottle house; and both the Captain and Gustav decided the change was not worth while. The Captain said:

If we tried the plan, we would have to rebuild our entire plant. As we arrange matters now we can deposit every keg and box and bottle where it is needed, whereas if we tried to ship our things by the plan talked of we could not do this without a great deal of extra handling.[19]

As Gustav summed up the situation to a reporter in 1904 in terms applicable from that day to the present: "We have thought often about a change in our style of transportation, but so far no good proposition has been presented to us." [20]

Another continuing problem was the maintenance of a first-class plant. While it was not necessary during this period to increase brewing capacity, the replacement of obsolete buildings, continual improvements in bottling machinery, and the introduction of the much more efficient electric power led to numerous investments in new equipment.

A fire in the malthouse in 1901 provided the opportunity to use insurance funds for a partial rebuilding of the malthouse and the installation of Saladin pneumatic malting machinery

---

[18] *American Brewers' Review*, XII, No. 12 (June 20, 1899), 475.
[19] *Journal*, Aug. 12, 1904. Scrapbook clipping.
[20] *Journal*, Aug. 12, 1904. Scrapbook clipping.

on all floors. A new fireproof grain elevator of fourteen circular bins and six segmental bins, with a total capacity of 120,000 bushels, was built in 1902.[21] Aging of the buildings and the gradual accumulation of needs for improvement made the old fermenting house unsatisfactory. In 1911 and 1912, a new one, with closed fermenting tanks and a new control laboratory on the top floor, was erected. The new tanks increased the excess supply of carbon dioxide that, since 1895, had been sold in cylinders through the Liquid Carbonic Acid Manufacturing Company that served both Schlitz and Pabst.[22]

The most important improvement in bottling during this period was the installation of machinery, completed on October 19, 1906, for applying the patented cap of the Crown Cork and Seal Company. This type of cap, the one in use today, replaced an aluminum cup and gasket device, sunk and expanded in the bottle neck, a stopper both difficult to insert and to open and not reliably airtight. Corking, however, was continued as an extra protection on bottles destined for export overseas.

In 1906 and 1907, a new Blue Ribbon bottling house was begun but, in 1908, management decided to build an addition to the old house instead, in order to keep all bottling operations under one roof. As a result the present Milwaukee bottle house came into existence. In addition to the Crown Cork equipment, the company now installed glass-lined storage tanks, Meyer soaking machines for washing, and Goldman horizontal pasteurizers.[23] The total outlay of all these operations came to $265,000.

In 1908, the bottling line and other power machinery in the plant were electrified at a cost of $300,000. The only other major expenditure for bottling equipment prior to 1920 was $110,000

[21] The cost of these improvements is not available because of a gap in the financial records between 1901 and 1904.

[22] See contract dated Aug. 20, 1895.

[23] The increase in the number of dozen pints produced per barrel of beer from an average of 26.06 dozen in 1907 to 27.04 dozen in 1908 was attributed to the use of glass enameled tanks. Price, Waterhouse Report, Mar. 5, 1908, p. 17.

in 1914 for ten Loew Hydro-pressure soakers and automatic bottle washers. In 1915, the Chicago and Cleveland branch bottling plants were also equipped with Loew Hydro-pressure soakers.[24]

Steel kegs were already being experimented with in 1910; but, at that time, there seemed no solution to the problem of guarding against contact of the beer with the steel save that of inserting a glass or a porcelain lining, which made the keg expensive, fragile, and heavy. Consequently, when a new cooperage shop was needed in 1912, the company put up a modern plant for making and repairing wooden barrels at a cost of $150,000.

From 1914 on to 1918, exclusive of new motor trucks costing $134,000, the company spent less than $25,000, all told, on the home plant.

Pabst's retention of the Price, Waterhouse auditing service in 1904 led to a standardizing of the company's depreciation practices, which were somewhat irregular in the old days. Buildings were henceforth depreciated at 2 per cent annually, machinery at 2.5 per cent, shipping cooperage at 20 per cent, saloon fixtures at 25 per cent, icehouses at 20 per cent, and livestock and vehicles at 10 per cent. As complete prohibition became a possibility, more acutely realized by Gustav Pabst than by most other brewers, the company started to write off its plant at an abnormally rapid rate. The book value of $5,149,512 at the end of 1914 was reduced to $2,926,498.83 by 1918 to represent more realistically the worth of the brewery for other uses.

PLANT OPERATION

This period of relatively stabilized output affords an unusually good opportunity to examine the rhythm of production and employment in the brewery. The basic unit of production in the brewery operations was called a "sud." This designated a particular brew going through one of the six parallel lines of

---

[24] *American Brewers' Review*, XXIX, No. 6 (June 1915), 264.

mashing tuns and brew kettles. The volume of each sud varied
from about 250 to about 325 barrels, depending on the demand
for beer. There was a gradual tendency toward more uniform
year-round use of the equipment as time went on, but the effect
of a hot, thirsty summer, or a cold, wet one, on beer demand
could always upset the schedule.

	1894	1895	1896	1911	1912	1913
January	334	336	163	197	268	267
February	297	61	216	231	244	284
March	272	250	374	337	260	269
April	300	303	317	271	280	180
May	311	381	366	360	330	271
June	374	373	367	435	302	313
July	233	386	355	391	314	331
August	455	367	345	302	289	316
September	184	297	132	252	259	266
October	517	258	103	178	247	256
November	276	160	113	203	426	200
December	161	142	125	233	198	217

Brewhouse employment was even more stable than production. From 1907 to 1911, for example, brewhouse employees
ranged from twenty-three to twenty-seven in November and
December to twenty-eight to thirty-one at the peak of the season
in June or July. At the slack season, the men often worked only
five days a week, whereas at the peak of production they occasionally worked a few hours more than their usual eight-hour
day, six-day week.

Except in bottling and malting, there was even less seasonal
fluctuation in other departments than in the brewhouse. The
bottle-house staff of several hundred was made up mainly of
inexperienced young people who were let off in the winter. The
twenty-eight to thirty regular maltsters, however, were largely
transferred to the cooperage department during the summer
shutdown of their regular work. The lager cellars, washhouse,

[25] Sud Books.

204 THE PABST BREWING COMPANY

coopers' shop and yard, and the trucks employed the largest staffs, but there were a score of other occupations around the brewery that required the services of from one to one hundred and three men (see Appendix C, p. 402).

THE PROGRESS OF BREWING

No outstanding developments either to reduce cost or to improve quality occurred in the brewing process between 1893 and 1920. The Pabst Company continued to brew two major types of beer: a relatively small quantity of all-malt beer, comprising about 10 per cent or less of the annual production; and the rest, a beer having some maizone, a corn meal, mixed with the malt, a type that had ultimately survived the earlier experimentation with rice and corn in various forms.[26] The proportion of malt and maizone was varied slightly from time to time but, practically speaking, a standard basis for fine "American type" lager had been achieved and the age of experimentation in this matter was past.

Malting was given unusual attention by Pabst during this period. The barley was divided into three grades so that each type could be malted separately. Eight days were allowed for slow germination and some barley and malt were carried over from one season to the next to avoid the use of improperly aged grain at the beginning of the new season in September or October.

Before 1893, Pabst had already solved fairly well the problems of protecting beer against exposure to the temperature hazards of travel. Now this protection was steadily improved by advanced chilling, improved filters patented by Theurer, and direct-pressure carbonation. The last of these made it unnecessary any longer to use artificial preservatives in Pabst bottled beer. This made the Captain anxious for a pure-food law that would not only prohibit other brewers from adulterating their

---

[26] The precise formulas of Pabst beers, even in this period, are trade secrets that the company does not wish to have published.

beer with sulphite of soda, but would also go a long way in convincing the public that beer was a pure and a safe beverage. For the latter reason, the United States Brewers' Association and other brewing groups worked for many years toward such legislation. In 1899, the Captain appeared at a Congressional hearing to testify on adulteration of food products.[27]

First of all [said the chairman], you have been in business a long time, what do you say as to a national law?

Mr. Pabst: I think it would be a very good thing. I think it would be a very good thing [*sic*].

The Chairman: It would assist the honest manufacturer?

Mr. Pabst: Yes, sir.

The Chairman: And protect the consumer?

Mr. Pabst: Undoubtedly.

The Chairman: Tell the committee just what kind of beer you make, for instance.

Mr. Pabst: Well, we think we make the best beer in the world—we try to. We buy nothing but the very best of material and we have the best of talent, and we spare no expense in making as good as can be made. We do that in order, of course, to increase our trade and in order to give the public something they want. And we claim that we make as good a beer as is made in any part of the world.

The Chairman: Do you use any preservatives in beer?

Mr. Pabst: No, sir.

The Chairman: Glucose?

Mr. Pabst: No, sir.

The Chairman: Do you use any salicylic acid?

Mr. Pabst: No, sir, we do not.

[27] *Adulteration of Food Products,* Senate Committee on Manufacturers, Senate Report, No. 516, 56th Congress, 1st session (Feb. 28, 1900), pp. 311-12.

"The brewers are strongly in favor of the establishment of Federal standards of purity for all articles of food and drink," wrote the secretary of the United States Brewers' Association to Senator W. P. Hepburn, March 10, 1902.[28] Such a law was finally enacted in June 1906 "preventing the manufacture, sale or transportation of adulterated or misbranded or poisonous or deleterious foods, drugs, medicines, and liquors, and for regulating traffic therein." [29] The law did not go so far as leading brewers would have liked, but it was at least an answer to the whispering campaigns of Prohibitionists and others about the poisonous ingredients of beer; and it forced higher standards on some small brewers.

The effectiveness of the Pabst methods without use of preservatives was attested at the International Hygienic and Pure Foods Exposition at Antwerp in 1907. As reported in the *Sentinel* for September 8, 1907:

The jury's task was a severe one, the tests of each beer extending over a considerable time. Pabst "Blue Ribbon" beer along with all the others was for weeks alternately subjected to extreme degrees of heat and cold. Of all the beers so tested Pabst "Blue Ribbon" beer was the only one found upon examination to retain all the properties originally contained in the brew. It was finally determined that the "Blue Ribbon" beer took first place among all the other varieties submitted by American and European breweries. Consequently the highest possible honors for the Exposition were awarded.

The fact that an American beer took first place was all the more remarkable because American beer had to be transported a great distance, a factor that might ordinarily have been a decided handicap as against the European beers sent to Antwerp. Pabst beer was in transit from the brewery in Milwaukee something like four weeks, and it was a generally accepted theory that a beer was injured by long transportation. The Pabst beer

---

[28] *American Brewer*, XXXV, No. 7 (July 12, 1902), 1075.
[29] Act passed June 30, 1906, 59th Congress, 1st session, chap. 3915, p. 768.

was apparently unaffected. "Its durability and pureness were found upon examination to be without fault." [30]

Unfortunately for the superior position of Pabst, which had met the difficulty without need for any new processes, Leo Wallerstein in 1908 obtained a basic patent covering the use of proteolytic enzymes as a means of "chill-proofing" and stabilizing beer in advance of bottling. The brewing industry switched over to this procedure, in some cases without paying royalties to the inventor. The resulting patent litigation lasted until the First World War. Meanwhile, the problem of cloudy beer in cold weather ceased to harass the small bottler, and put him, in this respect, on the same competitive level with Pabst.

Although every possible means was employed by Pabst to ensure uniform flavor and aroma in the beer, this was still not altogether possible prior to 1900. In the late nineties, the growth of unwanted yeast organisms gave the plant difficulty with several brews, and the analysis of the situation by the laboratory led to the sending of Dr. Fischer abroad in 1901 to make a thorough study of European beers. After sampling every well-known beer in Europe, it is said, he secured, through the Joergensen Laboratory at Copenhagen, eleven pure-yeast cultures from the breweries whose products he thought the best. These cultures, brought back by Dr. Fischer, were tested in Milwaukee, and the one pronounced best has been in use by the company ever since.

The retirement of Fritz Theurer in 1902 symbolized the end of the experimental period in brewing. Yet if Theurer occasionally brewed uneven beer due to experiments, such as new methods of hopping or cooling, he is generally credited with doing more, in the long run, to stabilize the quality of beer than any other man of his generation. It was Theurer, the reader will remember, who invented the carbonation system for Pabst that "revolutionized American brewing"; it was his experimental work that led to the automatic bottle washer; it was he who

[30] *Sentinel,* Sept. 8, 1907. Scrapbook clipping.

built the first spray-type carbonators, as well as a host of other devices too numerous to mention. There was scarcely a part of the brewing process that had not been improved by some Theurer method or device.

Frederick Bock, his successor as superintendent, who along with Gustav Pabst presided over brewing as long as preprohibition beer was made, never had to contend with the old difficulties, but never had the thrill of making important changes in process. Largely relieved of brewing or technological worries, Bock turned his attention to the improvement of barley. With the help of the Department of Agriculture, which supplied new seed free, Wisconsin farmers experimented from 1905 to 1912 with the Gutekorn, Princess, Primus, Chevalier, and Svanhals types of two-row barleys and found that only the latter did well in Wisconsin. In 1913, the Pabst Company contracted with some five hundred farmers for the entire local Svanhals crop of about 150,000 bushels at five cents over the market price.[31] To encourage similar experimentation elsewhere, Gustav Pabst donated a $1,500 prize cup for the best barley to be awarded at the Land and Irrigation Exposition in New York, November 3-12, 1911.[32]

The steady development of laboratory control of production was an important contribution to beer manufacture in this period. In 1894, Dr. Alfred J. Schedler, born in New York City but educated at Karlsruhe, Freiberg, and Nuremberg, Germany, joined Dr. Fischer as assistant chemist. Two men, of course, were quite unable to make all the tests necessary for complete laboratory control. They made tests from time to time on samples from all stages of the brewing process, but not from each brew as is done today, and they were bound occasionally to be late in detecting trouble. After Dr. Fischer's retirement in 1902, Dr. Schedler worked alone for some time. Between 1905 and 1908, he acquired two assistants; and by 1913, two more assistants had been added to his staff; but the group was still too

[31] *Blue Ribbon News,* May 10, 1913, pp. 23-25.
[32] *American Brewer,* XLIV, No. 3 (Mar. 1, 1911), 136.

small for complete control through testing. Meanwhile, a pilot brewing plant had been set up in the new laboratory built in 1912, and experiments were again begun on beverages salable in dry areas.[33] In 1915, Pabst chemists developed a nonalcoholic cereal drink, called Pablo, that had some of the qualities of beer. It sold moderately well where real beer was prohibited, but lacked stability when stored for a month or longer in warm rooms. As a result, experimentation was continued that led directly to the near beers and the malt syrups of the prohibition period. Dr. Schedler and the laboratory were also to play a leading part in the planning of all of the new products of the prohibition era.

[33] J. F. Theurer had developed such a beverage in 1895 called Caramelized Extract of Malt. See Mock and Blum, *List of Patents of Non-Alcoholic Beverages,* p. 104.

CHAPTER IX

HOLDING A QUALITY MARKET

CAPTAIN PABST'S policy of establishing expensive retail outlets such as hotels and restaurants rested ultimately on the expectation that the association of Pabst beer with certain smart places would create a demand for it everywhere. The owner of a small saloon, he hoped, would regard the carrying of Pabst beer as a badge of standing and respectability, and travelers would be induced to patronize with confidence places that displayed the Pabst sign.

The Captain persisted in this policy even during the depression after 1893, and in the late nineties, he intensified his campaign to make the name Pabst synonymous with quality and distinction. He knew, of course, that the working classes would always be the most numerous customers, but he was anxious also to raise the social standing of beer through associating it with luxurious living. This could best be done by associating beer with the smartest restaurants in the big cities. Naturally, the greatest fame was to be won in New York, so the Captain made his strongest bid there. He had an additional reason to tie up with the best places in New York, for that was about the only way he could successfully invade the metropolitan market. New York's local brewers had a particularly tight grip on the saloon situation there—Ehret, alone, controlling 800 or 1,000 such outlets.[1] With "exclusives," places selling only Pabst, very difficult to acquire, the best way to impress the Pabst name on the independent retailers and the general public was through two or three outlets of real distinction. Even if they provided no great volume of sales, they would give the Pabst name a leading position; and, in addition to the local advantages, the importance of New York as a travel center made this a matter of national importance.

[1] Letter, Gustav Pabst to Captain Pabst, June 9, 1894.

The Captain with his usual vigor and perception struck at the very heart of the city. On the triangular plot facing Broadway, Seventh Avenue and 42d Street, the center of the new amusement section where the Times Building now stands, he arranged for the construction of a nine-story hotel by taking a long lease on the completed structure. This Pabst Hotel, for bachelors, was opened on November 11, 1899, under the management of James B. Regan, also proprietor of the famous Woodmansten Inn at Pelham Bay. The glass-enclosed ladies dining room on the second floor, with the cuisine presided over by Louis Mercier of Delmonico's, commanded a view of New York's busiest thoroughfares. The hotel took half-page advertisements in New York papers to announce its opening, and the papers co-operated with extensive news stories. William Hooker reports that the Captain "chose a live wire newspaper reporter to handle the press work while this campaign was going on, and that man was the late Curtis M. Treat, who perhaps did not miss visiting a single one of the saloons in New York. It was Treat's custom to mount a table or chair and invite the 'house' to have a couple of mugs of Pabst adding that 'the drinks are on Captain Pabst.' "[2] But the greatest publicity of all came three years later when, in order to build the original subway line, the Pabst Hotel was condemned and torn down. This was the first time in New York that a large steel skyscraper had been razed. Some of the newspapers attacked the policy of destroying such valuable new property and kept an argument going in the press that must have made Pabst a household word all over the metropolitan area.[3]

At Columbus Circle in December 1900, the Captain made a

[2] William F. Hooker, *Bill Hooker's Old-Time Milwaukee and Men Who Helped Make It Great,* p. 22.

[3] In addition to the company records, see *New York Journal,** June 25, 1899; *Caterer's Monthly,** Nov. 1899; *New York Herald,* Jan. 7, 1900; *New York American,** Sept. 21, 1902; *Chicago American,** Sept. 28, 1902; *American Brewer,* XXXV, No. 11 (Nov. 1902), 1360; *Pabst Brewing Co.* v. *Thorley,* 127 Fed. 439 (C. C. S. D. N. Y. 1904), 145 Fed. 117 (C. C. A. 2d 1906). [Starred (*) references are to scrapbook clippings.]

lease and a building arrangement on an even grander scale. A large restaurant and an adjoining theater were built on the block off the west side of the Circle between 58th and 59th Streets. The opening of the Grand Circle Restaurant in the south end of the building was timed closely with the opening on January 20, 1903, of *The Wizard of Oz* at the new Majestic Theater located in the north end; and once again everyone in New York was talking of the achievement of Captain Pabst.[4] Meanwhile, he had also invaded Coney Island and constructed a large pavilion called Pabst's Loop that was circled by all of the trolley cars carrying people to and from the city. This pavilion was wholly destroyed by fire in 1908 and not rebuilt, as its location had proved less advantageous than those nearer the ocean.[5] The greatest investment of all was Pabst Harlem at 125th Street near Eighth Avenue. When it was opened on September 22, 1900, after an expenditure of some $300,000, it was the largest restaurant in America, capable of feeding 1,400 people at one time. In those days it was thought that Riverside Drive and the upper West Side of New York might develop into the most fashionable section, and no expense was spared in the interior decoration of the Harlem, which included, on the wall of the main dining room, Ernest Berger's "Dedication of the Fountain," a painting valued at $20,000.[6]

Pabst made similar investments, though on a smaller scale, in other big cities. The Pabst Cafe in San Francisco at Powell and Ellis Streets, decorated with frescoes of medieval Germany, was the most famous German restaurant on the coast. The Union Hotel, at 117 Randolph Street, in the center of the Chicago business section, attracted attention by being one of the

---

[4] In addition to the company records, see *Theatre Magazine,* Mar. 1903, p. 60; Chicago *Inter-Ocean,** Feb. 15, 1901; *Chicago Chronicle,** Feb. 28, 1901; *New York Daily American,** Jan. 21, 1903; *American Brewer,* Feb. 1903, p. 91; *New York Herald,* Jan. 21, 1903. [Starred (*) references are to scrapbook clippings.]

[5] In addition to the company records, see *Wine and Spirit Gazette,* July 31, 1900. Scrapbook clipping.

[6] In addition to the company records, see *Commercial and Financial World,* Sept. 24, 1900; *Wine and Spirit Gazette,* Oct. 1900. Scrapbook clippings.

first hotels to have all rooms connected with the office by telephones. The *Milwaukee Sentinel* called Pabst's Kaiserhof in Minneapolis, an elaborate Gothic and Renaissance building with a colored glass roof, "The most genteel, the largest and most elegantly finished and furnished restaurant in the Northwest."[7] At Whitefish Bay on the shore of Lake Michigan above Milwaukee, the company maintained an elaborate summer resort with a hotel, pavilion, and landscaped park. In order to assure its prestige in the home community, the company, in 1906, built the exotic Gargoyle in Milwaukee at Third Street and Wisconsin Avenue, almost the exact center of the city. Again a blending of Gothic and Renaissance architecture was employed, featured by gnomes and gargoyles from which the restaurant took its name. The main dining room was two stories high, surrounded by a balcony, and topped by massive silver candelabra.[8]

ADVERTISING

This "famous place" policy was an oblique approach to sales and it naturally had to be supplemented by additional measures. Advertising, special promotion, discounts, and liberal spendings were valuable in connection with any beer sales policy, but they were particularly useful in supporting Pabst's plan of purchase for prestige where the outlets themselves were not counted on to supply the desired volume of business. That is, if the beer was to be marketed among independents on the basis of its reputation, it was likely to be in competition over the bar with one or more rivals, and both the barkeeper and the public had to be reminded continually of its merits.

In 1895 A. Cressy Morrison launched a three-year campaign for the beer and Tonic in *Harper's* weekly and other magazines based on the general idea that brewing began in Egypt, developed in Germany, and reached perfection in America. The

---

[7] *Sentinel,* Apr. 15, 1906.
[8] It is interesting to note that 1906 marked the beginning of a rapid rise in city sales, although it is obviously impossible to prove the direct effect of this "prestige" outlet.

15

copy was built around large pictures, Egyptian the first year, German the second, and American the third. *Advertising Experience,* in January 1898, hailed the campaign as an innovation.

These Pabst advertisements have been considered by experts the most distinctive of any that have appeared in the weekly and monthly publications. That this successful series of advertisements could not have been possible, had it not been for the fact that the Pabst Brewing Company had planned beforehand the three years' campaign in the advertising of their product, is only too true, and it seems strange that other advertisers do not make their space equally effective by laying out their plans in advance.

When A. Cressy Morrison resigned as advertising manager in 1897, he was succeeded by the man who had been his assistant for some two years—Joseph R. Kathrens. Kathrens was a former newspaper publisher who once had owned a Sioux City newspaper and had done publicity work in New York City.[9] While, during his career at Pabst, he was to initiate some nationally famous campaigns, he had at first to buck the management's policy of cutting down its previous level of magazine and newspaper advertising. Kathrens started at $175 a month and, naturally, was not regarded as an important senior department head of the company. Advertising managers were in a hard spot in all companies in the latter nineties. Advertising mediums and practices were growing at a rate that business executives could scarcely appreciate. Campaigns that appeared daring from the standpoint of a few years earlier might, in truth, be small scale and behind the times. Kathrens had to create executive confidence in himself before he could persuade management to embark on any extensive campaigns of his own devising.

During the period from 1898 to 1902, when little was done in the way of national periodical advertising, Pabst sought publicity by introducing new brands backed up by extensive souvenir distribution. Brewmaster Theurer appears to have been one

[9] *Sentinel,* May 11, 1902. Scrapbook clipping.

ADVERTISING EXPENDITURES, 1897-1902

(Exclusive of Signs and Views)

	1897	1898	1899	1900	1901	1902
General *	$ 2,247	$ 4,038	.....	.....	.....	.....
Special	292	3,267	$ 1,687	$ 1,906	$ 2,266	$ 6,152
Magazine	75,169	28,297	1,192	13,536	.....	7,600
Newspaper						
(national)	712	2,371	.....	.....	.....	.....
(local)	4,004	5,499	13,394	3,259	18,642	40,747
Contributions	.....	308	1,175	492	184	190
Novelties, souvenirs,						
and circulars	25,759	22,804	51,014	41,045	19,687	17,715
Posters and posting..	5,825	2,041	2,425	156	273	514
New York	50,277	6,400	3,016	2,026	900	.....
Milwaukee	.....	1,296	5,403	2,324	2,667	5,606
Cleveland	172	.....	.....	.....	.....	.....
New England	27	.....	.....	.....	.....	.....
Canadian	.....	2,810	2,125	168	.....	.....
Iowa	.....	610	.....	.....	.....	.....
Specialty dept.	4,534	3,735	.....	.....	.....	.....
Tonic						
Special	.....	.....	4,764	17,932	.....	.....
Newspaper	.....	.....	27,299	309	1,219	155
Booklets	.....	227	7,156	77	5,315	311
Window displays	17,430	4,641	8,133	160	5,577	18,889
Printed matter	23,645	9,367	9,901	271	282	1,490
Magazine	.....	.....	.....	.....	22,746	24,416
Express on advertising						
matter	.....	.....	2,481	1,250	1,880	1,512
Total	$210,093	$97,711	$141,165	$84,911	$81,638	$125,297

* It is not possible, from the existing records, to define all of these categories.

of the leading spirits back of this new brand campaign. While on a trip to Europe in 1896, he wrote to the Captain,

I am also of the opinion that we must come out with a new brand of beer and advertise it so strongly that people begin to talk about it. That beer must be planned carefully so we get the right kind. That is easier to discuss personally than to write about and I will think the matter over carefully.[10]

Brand changes were started with the introduction of Doppel Braeu (Double Brew), an all-malt Muenchner beer in 1896, but this was a high-priced beer with limited sales possibilities. A new, popular brand, Pabst "Century," was put on the market

[10] Letter, July 18, 1896. Translated from the German.

between 1899 and 1902, and pushed with considerable local and souvenir advertising. An autumn Bock season was also introduced in 1899. In 1902, "Red, White and Blue" beer, in tune with the nationalistic enthusiasm during Theodore Roosevelt's first term, replaced Century. Century and Red, White and Blue were very similar to the standard Bohemian which, both in kegs and bottled as Export, continued to be the mainstay of Pabst sales.

Kathrens thought up many novelties to aid the campaigns for the new brands, such as a St. Patrick's Day bottle with a shamrock in place of the usual trade-mark and the word "Pabst" in the middle of the shamrock.[11] Learning of the development of the present-day type of match book by the Diamond Match Company, he secured exclusive rights, in 1899, for beer advertising on their match books by giving Diamond their first ten-million-book order.[12]

SALES OF BRANDS

(In Barrels)

	1897	1898	1899	1900	1901
Bohemian	590,850	729,294	771,737	701,179	759,336
Bavarian	70	92	130	219	332
Select *	22,082	31,068	32,233	31,252	36,672
Hofbraeu	194				
Drawback	6,279	12,621	18,417	17,656	11,588
Export Lager	160,720				
Doppel Braeu	12,384	5,779	13,993	13,797	13,977
Blue Ribbon †	6,776	8,451	9,321	8,965	748
Malt Mead	866	1,744	1,190	995	796
Red, White & Blue			3,375	12,130	15,257
Century Braeu			532	71,993	39,002
Bock					13,454
Kloster Braeu					569
Tonic	6,327	5,557	5,672	5,787	6,511

* Carrying the Blue Ribbon label.
† Presumably Blue Ribbon Bock.

[11] Sentinel, Mar. 23, 1899.
[12] Sentinel, Aug. 20, 1899; Herbert Manchester, The Diamond Match Company, p. 67.

After 1902, however, promotion through a variety of new brands was given up. Henceforth, Pabst only made four beers: Bohemian, the standard beer, bottled under the label Export, Doppel Braeu, and Blue Ribbon, and, in the early spring, Bock. Advertising was now concentrated on Blue Ribbon in bottles, and this remained Pabst's featured beer up to 1919. There were two obvious reasons for this concentration: Blue Ribbon was a fine product that made an excellent standard bearer for a quality line, and bottled beer was the fast-growing source of profits in the shipping business.

In 1903, the period of low advertising outlays was abruptly ended by a national campaign for Blue Ribbon conducted through J. Walter Thompson, the agency that played an important part in building American magazine advertising. A blue silk ribbon, it will be remembered, had been used on the neck of Select bottles since 1882, but the words "Blue Ribbon" were not added to the Select label until the beginning of May in 1895, and the Pabst seal did not replace the word "Select" on the label until April 21, 1897. In January 1898, the Blue Ribbon label was adopted, and on March 27, 1900, a label with the words "Blue Ribbon" on it was registered as the trade-mark for Pabst lager beer.[13]

The Blue Ribbon campaign began in May 1903, with dignified, textual advertisements emphasizing purity, cleanliness, expensive malt, and delicate flavor. The advertisements appeared on alternate months in two lists of national periodicals. The short, simple statements about Blue Ribbon were similar to Kathrens' copy of the previous year of which the editor of *Advertising Experience* had written:

Pabst sticks to one style of ads in newspapers, as seen herewith, but we must say it is a very effective type ad and is worthy of the attention of a great many users of small space. . . . . It is as good as a whole page and yet it occupies only a little more than an eighth page double column.[14]

[13] Registration No. 34,379, dated Mar. 27, 1900.
[14] *Advertising Experience,* XIV, No. 6 (Apr. 1902), 22.

One list of magazines included *Collier's, Judge, Leslie's Weekly, Life, Puck, Town Topics,* and *Town and Country;* the other, *Ainslee's, Black Cat, Booklover's, Broadway, Harper's, Lippincott's, Metropolitan, Munsey's, National Outing, Popular Monthly, Recreation, Scribner's, Smart Set,* and *Strand.* Starting in September 1903, illustrations were used: a picture of the brewery in September; and a picture of two Blue Ribbon bottles on a table with a glass of beer and a plate of oysters on the half shell in November and December. This second picture—to become almost as famous in the history of early twentieth-century display advertising as the Victor Talking Machine Company's "His Master's Voice"—was acquired through the Gugler Lithographing Company of Milwaukee early in 1898. In color reproductions of this picture, the brilliant amber of the beer in the Blue Ribbon bottles and in the glass was contrasted with a rich, deep red background and the bluish-white oysters in the foreground; but, even in black and white, the design and content of the picture had an aesthetic and sensuous appeal unusual in this period of advertising.

In January 1904, a single revised list of magazines was drawn up, and advertisements were inserted monthly. The oyster picture was used first as a straight illustration, then as a kind of Pabst trade-mark. By August, for example, the advertisement used in the magazines was made up three identical copies of the oyster picture in a column with no text except "Pabst Blue Ribbon, the Beer of Quality."

A newspaper campaign was also started through J. Walter Thompson in April 1903 in over two hundred cities where Pabst had dealers or branches. The copy was similar to that first used in the magazines, and was generally inserted two or three times a week.

Meanwhile, 160,000 copies of the oyster picture on eight- by ten-inch cardboard folders, advertising aluminum bottle stoppers on the inside, an additional 100,000 pictures on similar size single cards, and 25,000 pictures on metal signs were distributed to dealers. Twenty-five thousand sixteen-sheet posters were put on billboards in two hundred and fifty cities in the summer of 1904.

Although the advertising helped the sale of bottled beer from the brewery, which increased from 2,180,860 dozen pints in 1901 to 3,244,887 dozen pints in 1905, it did not immediately boost keg sales. Management must have been satisfied with the situation, however, as Kathrens' salary was raised to $5,000 in 1904, and continuously larger sums were spent on his campaigns until the panic of 1907.

ADVERTISING EXPENDITURES, 1897-1919

(Exclusive of Signs and Views)

1897	$210,093	1909	$116,512
1898	97,711	1910	293,296
1899	141,165	1911	326,416
1900	84,911	1912	319,713
1901	81,638	1913	350,509
1902	125,297	1914	294,072
1903	229,830	1915	84,003
1904	209,200	1916	85,495
1905	220,615	1917	168,915
1906	242,924	1918	174,261
1907	313,504	1919	145,627
1908	109,108		

In January 1906, Kathrens resigned from Pabst to join the J. Walter Thompson agency.[15] Although his assistant, Fred H. Squier, took over, he was not given the title of advertising manager or the salary that would go with it for several years. The Pabst account was transferred for reasons unknown, in March 1906, to the Charles H. Fuller agency of Chicago which specialized in newspapers, but the following year it was returned to J. Walter Thompson.[16]

During the two years following the panic of 1907, the adver-

[15] *Daily News,* Mar. 6, 1906. Scrapbook clipping.
[16] *Fourth Estate,* Mar. 10, 1906 (scrapbook clipping); *Printers' Ink,* LXVIII, No. 9. (Feb. 27, 1907), 26.

tising appropriations were cut to less than half the usual sum; but, beginning in 1910, a new series of intensive Blue Ribbon campaigns were launched. The potential market for bottled beer to be drunk at home was immense, and, with the rise of manufacturing costs, it was becoming the only really profitable branch of the shipping business. The principal theme of the advertising efforts of these immediate prewar years was that it was "smart" to like beer. Motorists, substantial businessmen, and, finally, stylishly dressed women were pictured in magazine and newspaper advertisements in the act of enjoying Pabst Blue Ribbon. "Pabst has done about as much with half tone advertising as anybody in the country," noted the *Brewer and Maltster* in June 1914, "and their present campaign may be taken as about the most that can be done with this style of work." [17]

Tonic advertising had lagged for a number of years after Morrison's time, but the advance of the prohibition movement after 1912 led to new emphasis on the Tonic, in spite of a number of "dry-state" laws forbidding its sale in drugstores. "It is unusual," noted the editor of the Pabst *Blue Ribbon News* in 1914, "to pick up a magazine and not find our extract advertised in it." [18] A circular describing the Tonic was included in every case of beer delivered to homes, and a deluge of calendars, circulars, and similar "dealer helps" continued.

The depression that started in 1913, the advance of the prohibition movement, and the war all checked advertising activity. After 1914, budgets fell from about $300,000 annually to a third or half that sum.

Such is the history of the major national advertising efforts that must have made the Pabst name known to every regular reader of magazines. Meanwhile, all the older and lesser forms of sales promotion traditional to the beer business were vigorously pursued. Press releases were regularly given out to pub-

[17] *Brewer and Maltster*, XXXIII, No. 5 (June 15, 1914), 29.
[18] *Blue Ribbon News*, Apr. 4, 1914, p. 7.

licize new Pabst developments. The rebuilding of the malthouse in 1902, for example, was made the basis of an educational campaign on new methods of malting that was not only featured in Pabst advertising but led to extensive articles in the local newspapers, and in *Collier's*.[19] Christian Benkard, hired by the Captain to promote publicity in German periodicals, succeeded in placing in *Over Land and Sea* an article, entitled "The Largest Beer Brewery in the World." Benkard also saw to it that German papers carried notices of the Chicago World's Fair awards, which was doubly important because these "fatherland" papers were often copied by the American German-language press.[20]

Novelties, souvenirs, pamphlets, signs, and window displays were an important part of advertising expenditure. Blue Ribbon playing cards, calendars, matches, stationery, and fancy postal cards were distributed to dealers, either free or at a small charge. When there were a number of important openings, such as those in New York, the cost of such novelties might be over $50,000, but in most years it was about $25,000. The local agents or branch managers had to have literature to distribute to hotels, saloons, and store owners, featuring new developments, new brands, and other arguments for the superiority of Pabst. These sheets and pamphlets also helped to educate the saloonkeeper in regard to his business. Many varieties of signs were offered to the retailer, from small placards behind the bar, size about $6\frac{1}{2}$ by $13\frac{1}{2}$ inches, to muslin streamers 2 by 12 feet and an electric sign 2 feet, 8 inches by 8 feet. Framed pictures about 2 by $2\frac{1}{2}$ feet, generally featuring attractive girls or views of the brewery, but occasionally reproducing famous paintings, were available for interior decoration. By far the most famous of this series of pictures was the "Blue Ribbon and Oysters" so extensively used in the newspaper and magazine campaigns.

---

[19] *Collier's Weekly*, XXXV, No. 5 (Nov. 1, 1902), 16; *Sentinel*, Oct. 12, 1902; *Journal*, Oct. 13, 1902; *Daily News*, Oct. 13, 1902 (scrapbook clipping); *Evening Wisconsin*, Oct. 13, 1902 (scrapbook clipping).

[20] Benkard to the Captain, Jan. 30 and June 10, 1894. Translated from the German.

By 1914 the cost of Signs and Views reached over $58,000, and even in the remaining years of reduced advertising expenditures, it averaged about $25,000.

Starting in 1904, and for three years thereafter, a perfectly matched six-horse team of dapple-gray Percherons in gold ornamented harness, drawing a handsome navy-blue brewery wagon with red wheels, was exhibited at fairs and expositions. This was not only good publicity in itself in the days of a horse-loving public, but it also made it possible for Pabst to win prizes even at fairs where beer was not exhibited or where a local product was clearly destined to win the highest award for beer. At the St. Louis World's Fair in 1904, the team won ten firsts and attracted almost as much attention as the Pabst Jai Alai Cafe and Roof Garden. At the International Stock Exposition in the same year, it won six more firsts. In 1905, first prizes were won at the Iowa, Minnesota, and South Dakota state fairs. The team was shown in all large cities, and attracted attention en route through its special railroad car painted with a picture of the horses and the caption "Pabst Prize Team" in large letters.

Starting with Fox's and Loew's development of nickelodeons, or cheap motion-picture theaters, a new advertising medium was temporarily created. These theaters ran glass lantern slides carrying illustrated songs for audience singing, advertisements, and theater news. Squier entered this field by supplying both slides advertising Blue Ribbon and blank slides with the Blue Ribbon trade-mark at the bottom on which the proprietor could write theater news.

The Captain's maxim that a great brewery business must have its home market as a base was never forgotten by Pabst. A monster electric sign on the tower of the Empire building at Grand Avenue and West Water Street in the center of business and night life was put up in 1910 to remind Milwaukeeans of Pabst beer. It was 38 feet long and 22 feet high with Pabst Blue Ribbon in 3½ foot letters, and showed a finger pointing at a Blue

Ribbon bottle 18 feet high held by a gigantic hand. At night the lights flashed in such a way as to make the hand appear to move and the blue ribbon to wave.[21] A less pretentious local sign was the cause of some amusing competitive warfare, of which Fred Pabst, Jr., wrote:

We had a very conspicuous sign along the railroad tracks near Kenosha, a big trademark of Pabst, Milwaukee, with a hand pointing north in the direction of the plant. It was very striking and probably a little too showy for our chief competitors of those days, the Schlitz Brewing Company owned by the Uihlein Brothers, so they put a sign a few rods south of it reading, "Drink Schlitz Beer." Of course that was a kick in the shins for us.

A short time before this I had married a daughter of Mr. Uihlein and I felt I ought to watch my step and if we did strike back at it, it should be done in a very subtle way. I thought it was subtle to place a sign between the two reading, "If you can't get," which made the whole thing read, "Drink Schlitz Beer if you can't get Pabst." Probably my sense of what was subtle was rather elastic. At any rate Providence was right with us. We had a semi-hurricane and the Schlitz sign was blown down. It was never put up again. The storm helped them to withdraw gracefully.[22]

Besides ads to read and signs to see, Pabst engaged in all types of special activities to keep its name before the local people. The Pabst Theater, the St. Charles Hotel, the Pabst building at Wisconsin Avenue and East Water Street, and the Whitefish Bay resort, all started before 1900, were standing reminders to Milwaukeeans. In the summer of 1901, a Pabst coach line from Milwaukee to Waukesha Beach by way of Pewaukee offered the thrill of old-style stagecoach riding along a historic route. Pabst Park covering eight acres off North Third Street near the city line at the highest point in Milwaukee offered dancing, concerts, target shooting, and picnics.

[21] *Sentinel*, Dec. 1, 1910. Scrapbook clipping.
[22] *Blue Ribbon News*, June 1936, p. 3. See also *Sentinel*, June 14, 1899; *The Advertising Man*, June 1899 (scrapbook clipping).

In local activities both Kathrens and Squier found an enthusiastic backer in Gustav Pabst. In 1907, the company helped to buy an elephant, the Countess Heine, for the Milwaukee zoo. When she arrived, she was marched in a parade from the Milwaukee freight station to the brewery.

C. S. Wright, private secretary to Colonel Gustav Pabst appeared upon the scene. He carried a bale of hay. It was tied with blue ribbons. The Countess squealed shrilly. Keeper Bean received the gift and presented it to her. She ate the ribbons and scattered the hay in amiable benediction.

The crowd dispersed after Colonel Pabst said a few words. Down the brick paved yards it hustled until it reached the Sternewirt. It hastened within. Refreshments were served, ad lib.[23]

Conventions were always entertained in grand style by the big Milwaukee breweries. When the Travelers Protective Association met in Milwaukee in June 1908, for example, Pabst entertained the 2,000 delegates at a German luncheon with beer, cigars, and souvenirs.[24] The Milwaukee visits of presidents, governors, and other political, business, or artistic notables were made the occasions for parties at the brewery. Everyone, important or unimportant, was welcome to inspect the plant and partake of Pabst hospitality at the Sternewirt, and, over the years, many thousands were entertained. After seeing Pabst, the Reverend S. Reynolds Hole, Dean of Rochester Episcopal Cathedral, England, wrote in his book, *A Little Tour of America,* some four pages about the brewery, commencing:

But the most notable sight to be seen in Milwaukee is the brewery of Frederick Pabst. Imagine a dozen of the largest Lancashire factories collected and connected together, greatly improved as to architectural design and finish, and covering thirty four acres of ground. . . . .

One hundred men are employed in washing the barrels. The fire department is complete in all its details, and the firemen regularly

[23] *Sentinel,* Aug. 2, 1907. Scrapbook clipping.
[24] *Sentinel,* June 24, 1908. Scrapbook clipping.

drilled. Visitors are received daily, guides are provided and every part of the brewery is open to inspection.[25]

As more and more money was invested in building the reputation of Milwaukee beer in general, and Pabst Blue Ribbon in particular, it became necessary to defend both labels from fraudulent use. On September 17 and October 24, 1900, Pabst, Schlitz, and Blatz obtained identical Circuit Court injunctions from United States Chief Justice Melville W. Fuller against New York companies attempting to bottle local products under the label "Milwaukee Beer." [26] The companies jointly publicized the decree in a four-page circular to dealers and bottlers. This was neither the first nor the last of such actions, but eternal vigilance has prevented labeling abuses from existing for more than brief periods.

Some small brewers could not resist the temptation to gain from the great Pabst advertising campaigns by naming their products Blue Ribbon and adopting a similar label. Pabst won a United States Circuit Court decree in January 1905, enjoining firms from using the Blue Ribbon label in any form or using words having a similar sound; and damages were ultimately awarded the company for infringement of trade-mark rights.[27]

SPENDINGS AND ALLOWANCES

All the prestige and publicity that could be gained by ingenious advertising, however, would not weigh as heavily with some independent saloonkeepers as discounts and spendings. If relatively few saloon properties were to be owned outright, more trade had to be held by such cash inducements. In this area, the policy of depending more on quality and reputation than on

[25] S. R. Hole, pp. 197-99.
[26] In addition to the company records, see also *American Brewer*, XXXII, No. 6 (June 1899), 302, and XXXIV, No. 4 (Apr. 1901), 180-81.
[27] *Sentinel*, Jan. 31, 1905; *American Brewer*, XXVIII, No. 1 (Jan. 1905), 18; and Decree, *Pabst Brewing Company* v. *St. Joseph's Brewing Company*, U.S. Circuit Court, Western District of Missouri, Sept. 21, 1908, in Pabst records.

ownership and control does not appear to have been strongly supported. The Pabst management does not seem to have been willing to accept the fact that they needed to spend and allow more than their big competitors who had gone in for the ownership of more small properties.

From the standpoint of business ethics, rather than sales promotion, the policy of economy and strict dealing did Pabst great credit. Extra big discounts were essentially cutthroat competition, and spendings and easy credit were demoralizing to the whole trade. Saloonkeepers were taught that Pabst salesmen would not compete by these means to buy their patronage. On October 31, 1899, a general order was sent to branch managers reading:

Commencing from this date, no beer is to be presented, free of cost, or at reduced rates, to anyone, unless permission is first obtained, in each instance, from the Home Office. The practice of giving presents has reached such proportions, that it has developed into an abuse. Kindly comply strictly with this order.

The total of Pabst's spendings and discounts failed to keep pace with the rise of prices in general or beer in particular during a period of mounting competition. As noted earlier, when Price, Waterhouse representatives first examined the books in 1904, they were struck by the smallness of the Pabst selling costs. Perhaps this is a partial answer to Pabst's loss of leadership in sales volume.

From 1905 on, the emphasis in attracting business by discounts, rebates, and special allowances was shifted from "country" to "city" (Milwaukee) sales, with the result that, by 1914, Pabst appears to have regained its old position of leadership in the local market.

This experience in Milwaukee fortifies the theory that, at this stage of the brewing industry, the control of many saloon properties was a better way of increasing sales than by advertising expenditure. The number of retail outlets in Milwaukee licensed by Pabst was increased from under 250 in 1898, when local sales were on the downward trend, to nearly 400 in 1907, when sales were sharply rising.[28] At this time the Baker Law prohibited the granting of further saloon licenses until the city should reach 500,000 population; and as this did not happen before 1919, Pabst and Schlitz, which had followed a similar policy of extensive buying and licensing, were left in a very favorable position in the local keg-beer market. Miller, which had recently expanded to be the fourth largest Milwaukee brewery, also built itself a secure position in the home market in the same way.

SPECIAL SELLING EXPENSES

	Allowances and Discounts	Spendings	Total
1894	$249,857	$43,683	$293,540
1895	245,836	41,172	287,008
1896	255,224	43,035	298,259
1897	238,810	36,640	275,450
1898	198,041	35,927	233,968
1899	179,637	32,891	212,528
1900	175,757	29,754	205,511
1901	171,767	29,995	201,762
1902	156,786	31,073	187,869
1903	381,390 *	24,305	405,695 *
1904	356,037	24,909	380,946
1905	309,271	30,480	339,741
1906	368,580	34,173	402,753
1907	378,649	36,643	415,292
1908	353,226	30,154	383,380
1909	336,318	31,235	367,553
1910	360,669	33,874	394,543
1911	352,286	34,552	386,838
1912	348,845	31,375	380,220
1913	357,643	33,105	390,748
1914	393,430	30,766	424,196
1915	317,747	27,169	344,916
1916	400,781	28,485	429,266
1917	301,649	23,185	324,834
1918	273,718	18,535	292,253
1919	283,867	18,012	301,879

* From 1903-1919, figures include rebates in addition to allowances and discounts.

[28] *Sentinel*, Aug. 24 and 28, 1907. Scrapbook clippings.

In spite of Pabst's mighty efforts to push bottled beer, "city keg" was its most profitable market division after 1915 (see table, p. 186). In a sense, this illustrates the national difficulties of the shipping business. The increasingly tight control of retail outlets was making the business of one of the biggest shippers more local in character. Only the greatly increased use of bottled beer or laws preventing the ownership of saloons by breweries could alter this situation; and these developments did not occur until after 1933.

PRICE COMPETITION

Price maintenance in local markets was from first to last a major problem of the shipping brewers. In the period up to 1898, this took the form of trying to preserve the existing structure. From then on, the emphasis shifted to gaining adherence to price increases needed to cover higher costs. The situation was greatly complicated by the traditionally entrenched policy of special discounts and credits, which made it hard to ascertain the true price in any market. During 1903, for example, the price received by Pabst for a barrel of beer sold in Milwaukee varied from $7.19 to $9.51, and the cost of selling it from 49 cents to $2.26.

The severe depression from 1894 to 1897 put unusual pressure on the price structure and gave new life to the old Milwaukee Brewers' Association. This organization, not to be confused with the Chicago and Milwaukee Brewers' Association, now attempted to stabilize prices and saloon ownership in Milwaukee County.

But the shippers' problem could not be solved locally. "We feel it our duty to call your attention to the present state of the beer business in Duluth," wrote a local brewer to the Captain.

In December 1893, the price of beer was forced down by the agents of outside brewers from $8.00 to $7.00 per barrel and soon after it was agreed in writing by all agents to hold the price at $7.00 with a maximum spending of 40¢ per barrel. This agreement was almost immediately thereafter violated, and in many instances a discount was given of from 50 to 75¢ and even $1.00 per barrel, such discounts always being made secretly. Then rebates became more frequent and now the same state of affairs exists as in 1893. We have no positive proof in hand as we did at that time in the shape of checks for rebate made by agents or general agents, but we have the assurance from many saloonkeepers that these discounts are being given. The matter has gone so far that the agent of a certain Milwaukee brewery has gone to a certain customer of ours who handles nothing but our beer and offered to him a loan of $6,000.00 without interest *and* a discount of $1.00 per barrel and 25¢ on each case of beer.

The result of all this will surely be the reduction of the price of beer to $6.50 or even $6.00, a thing we all would be glad to avoid. Things may even go further than this and a general beer war may be brought upon us.

Now we call your attention to this as friends and hope you may find some way to remedy the existing state of affairs. We have always done our utmost to uphold the price of beer and do not desire to increase our sales at the expense of others. If we hold our percentage and hold prices, that is all we are looking for.

We would certainly be ready to enter into any reasonable agreement as we would certainly be the biggest losers in case of a war and as we have so far lived up to our promise we ought not to be made the victims of the fallacy of brewery agents.

We address this to you personally, feeling that you personally would be interested in assisting us to maintain a decent basis upon which to operate the beer business in our town.[29]

In December of the following year, Adolphus Busch observed to Charles W. Henning, "Our endeavor must be to do better in the future, to live more harmoniously and not try to secure our competitors' trade by unfair means." [30] And a few weeks later the Captain complained to one of his salesmen: "It seems curi-

[29] Percy S. Anneki to Pabst, May 9, 1896.
[30] Letter, Dec. 24, 1897.

16

ous to me that any little tea kettle fellow brewing maybe ten barrels a day should scare all the Chicago and Milwaukee brewers into a reduction in price. The price must be kept up." [31]

The next expedient tried was a Western Shipping Brewers' Association. In the spring of 1898, eleven brewers in Milwaukee, St. Louis, Minneapolis, Omaha, Kansas City, Quincy, and Cincinnati entered into an agreement on trade practices.[32] During the first few years of its existence, the association met once a month in Chicago; and, besides regulating direct competition for customers, they abolished the furnishing of expensive novelties, such as matchboxes, corkscrews, trays, and knives to wholesale and retail dealers. Such activities were now of questionable legality, but up to 1902 businessmen neither clearly understood nor were much bothered by the antitrust law.[33] The beginning of real enforcement of the law by Roosevelt's Attorney General, Philander C. Knox, led to a de-emphasis of the activities of the association. The *Milwaukee Journal* noted in January 1912, when the association offices were finally closed, that fear of retaliation by other shippers had, in any case, long since placed an effective check on the old cutthroat methods.

It operates in this manner: The Lemp Brewing Company, St. Louis, for example, might wish to take a certain carload customer who had appealed to the Lemp Brewing Company without solicitation. The Lemp Company might be able to net a fair return on the sale of product to the particular party, but desists from taking the customer because it knows from their daily business that the Blatz Brewing Company could retaliate, not to the extent of taking one carload customer, but six to eight, in some particularly strong Lemp field.

The fear therefore, that the large shipping brewers entertain for one another, actually operates more effectively than an agreement. The large brewers are today operating on a small margin of profit,

[31] Letter, Jan. 28, 1898, quoted in *Blue Ribbon News,* June 1936, p. 3.
[32] *American Brewer,* XXXV, No. 8 (Aug. 1902), 1170.
[33] Henry R. Seager and Charles A. Gulick, Jr., *Trust and Corporation Problems,* pp. 384-85.

in fact are not making more than the large packers which is approximately 6 per cent. The large packers of the country would not be in the throes of the law if they had adopted this theory as a working principle. In other words, the brewers don't interfere very much with one another's trade because it is decidedly unprofitable to do so.[34]

Changes in the federal tax because of the financing of the war with Spain introduced an upsetting factor into the price situation. On June 14, 1898, the tax was raised from $1.00 to $2.00 a barrel. This increase led to the establishment of many new state or local brewing associations that strove for effective co-operation in handling the tax situation.[35] It was reduced on June 30, 1901, to $1.60 and returned to the $1.00 level on July 1, 1902. The First World War produced similar changes. In order to increase government revenue in the depression that had been accentuated by the outbreak of the war in Europe, the tax was raised in October 1914 to $1.50 a barrel. On October 4, 1917, it was set at $3.00 and on February 25, 1919, at $6.00 where it remained until prohibition.

In June 1902, just prior to the tax reduction of that year, the Milwaukee Brewers' Association drew up a three-year agreement to prevent cutthroat solicitation of local business by levying "fines" on those acquiring new customers. But all the brewing associations together were unable in the long run to control price movements in most sections of this industry of some 1,500 competitors.

From 1904 until 1915, general price increases were impossible to maintain, with the result that, by 1914, profits on keg beer sent from the home office to agents or other nonbranch customers had nearly vanished.

---

[34] *Journal*, Jan. 4, 1912.
[35] See list, *American Brewer*, XXXV, No. 8 (Aug. 1902), 1167-70.

NEW EFFORTS AT CONSOLIDATION

Consolidation of all the big breweries by British capitalists offered a more reliable cure for the problems of competition than any number of associations based on nothing more substantial than "gentlemen's agreements." In the middle of 1894, it appeared that more of the local Chicago brewers might be brought together by a British syndicate acting through H. M. Bigelow of Minneapolis. The Captain supported the plan, and it was expected that a consolidation of the Milwaukee brewers would follow. The continually deepening depression and the impossibility of successfully marketing new securities were probably the chief factors preventing the carrying out of these projects.

With the return of prosperity in 1898, the financiers again began planning for brewing consolidation. By 1899, plans had been formulated in London to combine the large breweries, and the Captain journeyed to New York for a conference at which he was offered $14,000,000 cash, exclusive of the real estate. We have no further news on this offer, but, by the beginning of the following year, Alexander Konta, a promoter who had married a Lemp, was trying to organize a consolidation for a London group. He wrote Gustav on March 16, 1900:

There shall be no more promises, no more future possibilities, but facts are what I am after, and facts, to which you gentlemen are entitled—and so am I. It will not be simply to state that the deal will go through, that there can be no doubt about it—but we want to know, now, whether it will go through, how, when and where.[36]

But the deal never went through, perhaps due to the reluctance of Mr. Busch, whose rapidly growing sales put him in the key bargaining position that the Captain had enjoyed a decade earlier.

Encouraged by the close family ties between Pabst and Lemp, because of Gustav's marriage to Hilda Lemp, Konta never gave

[36] Letter, Mar. 16, 1900.

up hope of bringing about a consolidation of the "big four." In 1909, the Hirsch Syndicate, Ltd., of London provided Konta with the backing for a new attempt that came very close to succeeding. A detailed plan was drawn up by the syndicate for combining Pabst, Schlitz, Miller, Anheuser-Busch, and Lemp into one company whose securities would be listed on the London Stock Exchange. Konta submitted the following proposal to the Pabst Brewing Company:

Considering the growing difficulties the breweries of this country have to contend with, and the danger threatening their very existence, it would seem prudent to take decisive steps as soon as possible, to secure absolute harmony of action between the large shipping establishments, to reduce expenses in the management of the business, at both the manufacturing and selling end of it, and to enable the owners of such brewery properties, who may prefer to gradually withdraw from business, to dispose of their holdings.

For this purpose it is proposed to merge these large shipping breweries into one corporation upon the following basis.

The several brewing companies are to transfer their plants and properties to a new corporation, called for instance, the Union Breweries Company; such conveyance to include the complete brewery plants, all the real and personal property belonging thereto and necessary for the uninterrupted running of the same together with all the book accounts and bills receivable, also all property real and personal used for running branches and agencies, and the ice and beer storage houses throughout the country, also all leases, contracts, and all other assets excepting therefrom only the outside investment properties, with the proviso, however, that a proper written guarantee shall be given to the Union Breweries Company, that any and all beer sold in such investment properties shall be that of the said Union Breweries Company for a period of ten years.

The vendors are to receive in payment therefor five per cent bonds at par, to be issued by the said Union Breweries Company covering all its assets for the full value of such plants and properties, such value to be determined as hereinafter provided, and in addition thereto they shall receive common stock of said Union Breweries

Company in the amount of forty-five per cent of the amount of the bonds.

The value of each plant and properties shall be computed at the rate of seven times the average net profits made by the respective breweries for the years 1906, 1907, 1908, which net profits shall be determined under a uniform method of auditing for all parties hereto, with the proviso, that such profits shall not include any revenue derived from the outside investment properties reserved and excepted from the transfer.

The bonds are to run from five to forty years, and a sinking fund of 2½ per cent per annum upon the total amount of bond issued, is to be provided, for the purpose of retiring them serially every five years.

There shall be no other stocks or bonds issued by the said Union Breweries Company, excepting that there shall be kept in the treasury of the company an amount of common stock, equal to the amount of the outstanding bonds which stock shall be issued for the only purpose of exchanging the same bonds at par, at the option of the holder of such bonds.

This convertible feature of the bonds is expected to make them very desirable and sought for among the investing public, who will appreciate that these bonds underlie stock yielding about 15% dividends.

The following example will show that the net earnings are nearly three times the interest charges, and the dividends on the stock amount to 15 per cent after a sufficient reserve has been set aside for the redemption of the bonds at maturity.

Profit	$1,000,000	Bonds	$7,000,000
		Stock	3,150,000
Interest on Bonds	350,000	15 per cent on	
Sinking Fund 2½ per cent	175,000	$3,150,000	472,500
Available for dividends	475,000		
	$1,000,000		

This earning power of the stock would give it such high quotation in the market that the bonds would probably be in great demand.

Arrangements have been made to have both kinds of securities listed on the New York and London Stock Exchanges where under the now prevailing favorable conditions, and with the excellent financial connections already formed, a good market for them will be created.

There can be no question, that under a combined and concentrated management great economies and savings can be effected, that greater influence can be exerted upon the public generally, and in elevating the business and its saloon patrons; and that it secures to the owners of the properties an opportunity impossible under present circumstances, to diversify their investments, or to convert them altogether if they are so inclined.[37]

On May 3, 1909, Gustav Pabst wrote to Konta: "I have been authorized by our Board of Directors to inform you that we are already [sic] to enter into the proposed merger on the plans as outlined above." [38]

When once again the attempt failed, the syndicate approached the Pabst Brewing Company alone with a plan for public financing. "Based on approximate annual net earnings of about $1,200,000.00," wrote Theodore Gross for the Hirsch Syndicate, "I would suggest the reorganization of your company on the following lines:

$3,000,000, 5% Bonds, absorbing for interest, ... $150,000
$5,000,000, 7% Preferred Shares, absorbing for interest, ...   350,000
$5,000,000, Common Shares, 10% estimated dividends, ...   500,000
      leaving $200,000 for bond redemption and surplus.

We contemplate to make an international issue of all these securities in New York, London, Paris, Berlin, Amsterdam and Brussels, in our choice, to arrange to have them quoted on the respective Stock Exchanges and to make their value known to the investing public through our allied banks and bankers.

Knowing from the information furnished me by you the intrinsic value of the business, and basing the success of this issue on our vast

---

[37] Copy of letter in Directors Record, May 31, 1909.
[38] Directors Record, May 3, 1909.

experience in the placing of securities, I believe with average good earnings during the next two years, these shares will be quoted at the end of the period at a conservative estimate as follows: $120 for the Preferred Shares, $150 for the Common Shares. In making this estimate I assume that your business will continue its course of expansion as shown by the results of the last five years.

If we can show the European investor who now more than ever turns to the United States for the placing of his surplus funds a steadily growing business enterprise, your shares should soon be classed among the favorite industrial securities abroad.

We will organize an English "Advisory Board" to consist of at least three prominent men in London to represent your company abroad. Such Board to receive all statements as to earnings and development of the business, the same as the American Directors, to enable them to keep the foreign shareholders fully advised.

Concerning our ability "to place" securities, our facilities for the purpose are unsurpassed by any other firm in London. During the period of about three years we have placed in France alone shares to the amount of One Thousand Million Dollars (£200,000,000). This will give you an estimate of our prestige with the public as well as our own financial strength.

I expect that the firm of L. Hirsch & Company will be directly represented here by 1911 for the purpose of enlarging their scope in the United States. We contemplate to make a specialty of the issue of industrial securities and to give this branch of the business our fullest attention, expecting to be as successful with the placing of securities on this side as we now are in Europe.

In return for the services to be rendered to you, as well as the payment by us of all the expenses attached to the issue of the new company, we will charge you a commission of 5 per cent on the total amount of the securities to be issued; such commission to be received by us not in money but in the securities as issued, in bonds, preferred or common shares.[39]

Why this offer was refused, we do not know.

[39] Gross to Pabst Brewing Co., Dec. 21, 1909.

SELLING IN THE FIELD

The methods of distribution employed by Pabst continued to depend more on the availability of proper agents with storage facilities in local markets than on the size of the community. New Orleans, for example, was handled through an agency until 1908, and San Francisco and Los Angeles were always agencies, whereas Fort Worth, Texas, became a branch in 1897. If the company had to build a large icehouse and office as well as supplying horses and wagons, it often seemed best to establish a branch and exercise more effective control over the situation. A suitable local agent, however, in small or distant cities continued to be preferable to a branch setup because the company invested less money and took less risk, and the agent had local connections and the incentive of personal profit. Consequently, there were only forty to fifty branches in contrast to over five hundred agents in the Pabst sales organization at the turn of the century. But the branches, as a result of the large sales of such offices as Chicago and New York, sold more beer than the agencies.

Chicago continued to stand by itself among the branches. It was the outlet for about one third of the beer sold by branches or about 15 to 20 per cent of the company's total.

The New York branch did a fair, but unspectacular, business under the management of Charles F. Blancke from its creation in 1888 to the beginning of 1896. In this latter year, the Captain decided to do something about New York. The branch was incorporated as a separate subsidiary company, with Gustav Pabst as president and Charles Henning as secretary. Under an able, aggressive manager, Eugene Schleip, a major promotional campaign was undertaken. Fifty thousand dollars was spent on New York advertising in 1897; and from then until 1900, J. Walter Thompson, the company's advertising agent, served on the board of the subsidiary.[40] Car cards, posters, and many

---

[40] New York City, *Copartnership and Corporation Directories,* XLVI [1897-98], XLVII [1898-99], XLVIII [1899-1900].

238 THE PABST BREWING COMPANY

other mediums were used. One writer remembers that in Manhattan "every dead wall said: 'Milwaukee Beer Is Famous—Pabst Has Made It So.' " [41] Tall men, six feet four or more, were hired to go into every crowded saloon on the island, buy beer for the house, and talk up Pabst.[42] This whirlwind campaign was dropped at the end of the season and subsequent New York advertising was on a more moderate scale; but the name Pabst was kept before the metropolitan public by the building and the opening of the great Pabst hotels and restaurants. As a result, Pabst New York sales increased from 12,770 barrels in 1896 to 34,033 barrels in 1901. Meanwhile, a steady pressure was maintained to get all the leading hotels and restaurants to carry Pabst, until by 1913 the company had 125 outlets in New York City, some of which, as in the case of the cafe opened in the new Woolworth Building that year, were "exclusives," handling only Pabst.[43]

No such efforts were exerted to build up any of the other Pabst branches, as none of them had the national and worldwide advertising value of New York. Aside from Chicago and New York, Kansas City, St. Paul, Cincinnati, Cleveland, and Washington were the branches generally doing the largest volume of business.

The general trend from 1894 to 1914 was to discontinue branch relations in some of the smaller cities and to open branches in the larger ones. A general redistribution of the branches occurred between 1895 and 1900; six branches in small cities and two in large Texas cities were closed, and seventeen new ones opened, including branches in Cleveland, Denver, Omaha, Philadelphia, Fort Worth, Richmond, Newport News, Cincinnati, and Detroit.

The areas where neither agents nor branches existed continued to be covered by travelers attached to the home office.

[41] *Journal*, May 30, 1930.
[42] *Journal*, May 30, 1930.
[43] In addition to the company records, see *American Brewer*, XLIV, No. 9 (Sept. 1, 1911), 458.

HOME-OFFICE TRAVELING MEN IN 1902 * [44]

	Accounts
R. J. Mentzel, Wisconsin, Minnesota, South Dakota, Iowa, Minnesota, Michigan, South Dakota	19
C. T. Shewell, Illinois, Michigan, Indiana	23
A. F. Schaffer, Iowa	4
A. A. Goldsmith, Florida, Louisiana, Mississippi, Arkansas, Kentucky, Tennessee, Alabama	14
A. F. Luening, Montana, California, Washington, South Carolina, Montana	9
A. Steffens, Ohio, Illinois, Pennsylvania, West Virginia, New York, Rochester, Elmira, Binghamton, Oswego	13
R. Pause, Jr., Wyoming, Colorado	5

* Direct office sales not made through salesmen covered sixty accounts in seventeen states.

While these men reported on conditions in their territories and the advisability of establishing agencies or buying properties, it was necessary for one of the top executives of the company to follow up these suggestions by personal visits. Thus, some officer always had to spend a good deal of time traveling. Schandein and Pierce, as we have seen, did this in the early days and Fred Pabst, Jr., took over such work in the early nineties. The following letter to his father, in 1894, illustrates the kind of problem dealt with by traveling executives.

We have quite a number of customers in Southern California with good prospects of establishing more trade. I consider this territory quite important and although I dislike spending so much time away from the office at this time of the year I thought it well to look the situation over. The local breweries are working very hard but I can conscientiously say we are doing better than the other Eastern firms. Our beer enjoys a very good reputation.

Our deal with the Royal Eagle Distilleries Company will in my opinion be a good one. Mr. Rohrbacher formerly President of the U. S. Brewing Company is now President of the Distilling Company. He is financially good and the officers will all sign a bond

[44] Annual Report of Sales, made through traveling men and secured through offices by correspondence, 1902. Separate sheet inserted in Annual Statement of Affairs, Book B.

making themselves personally responsible. Messrs. Rapp and De-Barry will do the bottling and I anticipate a large business. Including beer shipped to other points in the vicinity of San Francisco our sales should reach fifteen and probably twenty cars a month. At any rate the parties are pushers and understand the business.

I visited the Peoples Palace formerly the Pabst Palace. They are doing an immense business and as everything turned out we made a mistake in not retaining it. Its [sic] financially a success and as an advertisement medium it would have been of great value to us. This again shows that our travelling men should have the authority to use their judgment in such cases of course after consulting with the home office. If they are lacking in judgment and incapable, they are of no use to us.

Mr. Gustav Walter, proprietor of the "Orpheum" wishes to borrow at 6 per cent $5,000.00 for one year with the privilege of borrowing $5,000.00 more for the same length of time if necessary. I have not had an opportunity to look into his responsibility but will do so on my return to Frisco. The place is now selling about 3 barrels San Francisco beer. They have no tables in the place but Mr. Walters promises to make a regular beer place should we make the loan. He proposes to advertise extensively. I noticed he is a heavy advertiser and good businessman. He could in this place double his sales. He wants the money for fixing up another place in which he will serve a regular bill of fare meal free of charge. Other places have variety shows, etc., as an attraction but they are getting quite numerous and a little out of date. Mr. Walter's scheme seems to be a winner and I think it well worth time to look into it carefully.

I would over-reach my authority in making this investment or loan rather and would like to be informed on receipt of this whether I can act according to our judgment in the premises.[45]

As branches and agents increased in number and large areas were cut off by state prohibition, the need for home-office travelers diminished until, by 1913, there were only four.

The promotion of sales efforts through company magazines

[45] Letter, July 25, 1894.

was spreading in the years just before the First World War, and Pabst decided to try the experiment. In May 1913, the *Blue Ribbon News* appeared, "Published in the interests of Pabst's Blue Ribbon Distributors, Branch Houses and Salesmen, to further the 'get together spirit.'"

An idea of the character of the magazine, under the able editorship of Squier, can be gained from the table of contents given below.[46]

	Page
Editorially	3
Pabst Exhibit at Porto Rico Fair	5
The Costly New Blue Ribbon Sign	6
Pabst Extract—A Money Maker for Distributors	8
The Pabst Hop Farm at Wauwatosa	9
Blue Ribbon Beer Wins Highest Award as World's Purest Beer	14
Famous Pabst Eating Places	
2. Pabst Harlem, New York City	20
Personal Gossip	27
Pabst Invades Egypt	28
A Good Local Advertising Scheme	29
Three New Pabst Advertisements	Covers

It was profusely illustrated with pictures of executives, salesmen, and agents, saloons and restaurants selling Pabst, and reproductions of company advertising material. The rise in interest about prohibition is shown by fourteen pages on this subject out of a total of thirty in the September 1914 issue. Early in 1915, for reasons unknown but probably connected with retrenchment during the depression, the magazine was discontinued and was not resumed until after the repeal of prohibition.

While Pabst sales efforts depended upon the arguments of quality and prestige rather than price, every effort was made in the distant markets to keep the latter as close as possible to that charged by the local brewers. It was hard to come within a dollar or so of meeting local keg prices after paying the price charged by the home office and still make a profit. In the field of bottled beer, throughout the country as a whole, there was

[46] *Blue Ribbon News*, July 1913, p. 3.

less local competition and more possible outlets so that profitable prices were more easily maintained.

PROFIT ON BRANCH BOTTLED AND KEG BEER [47]

Year	Branch Bottled Beer (Net Return per Barrel)	Branch Keg Beer (Net Return per Barrel)
1913...................	0.76	0.05 *
1914...................	0.51	0.17 *
1915...................	0.24	0.41 *
1916...................	0.84	0.01 *
1917...................	0.14	0.47 *
1918...................	0.14	0.28

* Represents loss.

Expense was saved by bottling at the larger or more distant branches as well as at the home brewery. In this way, locally bottled Bohemian or Export could be offered at prices substantially less than charged for the Milwaukee bottled and close to those charged for local products. In the early 1900's, for example, Ohio branches could sell bottled Bohemian to dealers at $1.00 for a case of two dozen small bottles, whereas, for the same beer bottled in Milwaukee, dealers were charged $2.25 for a case of three dozen. These prices did not include the charge for bottles and cases which was generally 3 cents each for small bottles, 4 cents for large, and 24 cents for the wooden case. Prices varied from one area to another, depending, in general, on transportation costs. In Kansas City in 1902, for example, Export sold for $2.28 for three-dozen small, and Blue Ribbon for $3.88. By 1904, prices for Blue Ribbon in cases of three-dozen small bottles ranged from $2.75 in the near-by Middle West to $3.00 in the Gulf states and the Far West. These prices allowed the retailer to make a fair profit on the Bohemian or Export at 10 cents and the Blue Ribbon at 15 cents a small bottle.

The general distribution of Pabst sales during this period is illustrated in the following table.

[47] Price, Waterhouse reports.

ESTIMATED AVERAGE BEER SALES BY AREA AND STATE, 1909-1913 [48]

Sales Area	State	Barrels
North		
	New Hampshire	2,561
	Massachusetts	11,668
	Rhode Island	285
	New York	93,756
	Pennsylvania	12,396
	Maryland	4,724
	Virginia	18,548
	West Virginia	3,421
	District of Columbia	9,792
	Total	157,151
South		
	South Carolina	285
	Georgia	7,969
	Florida	7,399
	Alabama	2,561
	Tennessee	1,423
	Mississippi	1,139
	Louisiana	5,841
	Arkansas	7,969
	Texas	44,398
	Total	78,984
Central		
	Michigan	33,933
	Ohio	56,637
	Kentucky	5,723
	Indiana	22,997
	Illinois	244,092
	Wisconsin	180,961
	Total	544,343

[48] Estimate made from company records by W. W. Heusner, Director, Market Research Dept., Pabst Sales Co., Chicago, Ill., Nov. 1945.

ESTIMATED AVERAGE BEER SALES BY AREA AND STATE, 1909-1913
—*Continued*

Sales Area State	Barrels
Midwest	
Minnesota	41,463
Iowa	16,222
Missouri	77,489
South Dakota	1,707
Nebraska	16,507
Montana	6,830
Wyoming	9,961
Colorado	4,282
Idaho	285
Utah	4,554
Total	179,300
Far West	
Washington	1,423
Oregon	569
Nevada	1,138
California	7,400
Total	10,530
TOTAL UNITED STATES (Domestic)	970,308

Branch production would have been a more drastic expedient than branch bottling for meeting local competition in distant areas, but it would have raised problems that the technicians of those days could not solve. When the Anheuser-Busch Brewing Association, in 1897, was reported to have bought all but two of the Texas breweries, and to be bargaining for the remaining one, the Captain simply noted: "No harm done if Busch does buy them." [49] Local production, however, sometimes had the advantage of giving the beer some of the standing of the local products in areas where "home market" feeling was strong. The mayor of Fort Worth wrote the Captain:

I want to congratulate you and your representatives on the enter-prise and public spirit manifested in getting your product on sale

[49] Memorandum on letter from Martin Carey to Pabst, Apr. 12, 1897.

on the grounds during our recent race meeting. I am, as you know, in favor of "Home Industry"—but I believe I am broad enough to give credit where credit is due.

Come down and see us and see if you cannot see it to your interest to make your beer here, instead of paying the freight so far.

Will give you a cordial welcome.[50]

But neither the Captain, Gustav, nor most of the other large shippers attempted to manufacture in more than one plant.

In order to avoid having certain states tax branches for the total assets of the Pabst Company and to gain other legal bene-fits, it was necessary to establish local corporations in place of direct control. Thus the Pabst Brewing Company of New York, W. D. Jones and Company, the Blue Ribbon Distributing Company, the Blue Ribbon Commercial Company, the Pabst Company of Omaha, and the Milwaukee Beer Company came into existence.

The last named organization has an especially interesting background, illustrating state efforts to milk "foreign" companies. From 1897 to 1901, Pabst engaged in a long legal battle with the state of Texas over the imposition of a special franchise tax on the capital stock of out-of-state corporations, which the company claimed was violating a previously issued ten-year license to do local business. Claiming a violation of its laws, the state retaliated by refusing to renew the Pabst license when it expired in 1901. This necessitated a series of changes in organization for the conduct of Texas business. The company first transferred the Texas property to the Captain who personally conducted the business until his death in 1904; then a Pabst beer agency was incorporated to hold the property. This was superseded on January 15, 1906, by the Milwaukee Beer Company with a hundred-thousand-dollar capital stock wholly owned by members of the Pabst organization. The Milwaukee Beer Company continued to do business under Texas license until prohibition.

[50] B. B. Paddock to Pabst, Oct. 18, 1897.

17

World-wide sales of Pabst beer were regarded, as in the earlier period, as an important part of Pabst prestige. Consequently, exports were accorded a sales importance far greater than their volume would seem to warrant. Latin America, Canada, and Asia continued to be the chief foreign markets. In Cuba a branch bottling house and depot costing some $60,000 was established at Havana in 1900. The Philippine campaigns, from 1898 to 1901, gave an opportunity to popularize Pabst in the islands. Through an agency at Manila, Pabst beer was distributed free to the military companies responsible for major victories.[51] Pabst beer was pushed in other Asiatic areas by its Manila agent through the souvenir distribution methods that were ruled out domestically by the Western Shipping Brewers' Association. The *China Gazette* noted on January 10, 1899:

Messrs. Mustad & Company, the agents for the famous Pabst Beer, have sent us an acceptable reminder of the grand scale upon which that nectar of Milwaukee is advertised—a dozen of beer, with six neat glasses, two corkscrews, a box of pocket matches, with some very interesting literature dealing with the virtues of Pabst. But this great beer is so well known that we should hardly think it needs such costly advertising, though needless to say we appreciate it vastly.[52]

In Shanghai and other large Chinese cities, Pabst was generally available. In 1903, for example, a million bottles were shipped to China in one consignment.[53]

The First World War opened additional markets such as Australia, which had previously bought English ale and German beer; and the Pabst agents, Teasdal and Littley of Sydney, set up subagencies in the leading cities.[54] But the Caribbean area was the largest steady export market. The following analysis for the typical year, 1909, will give an idea of the extent and distribution of exports.

[51] *American Brewer*, XXXII, No. 6 (June 1899), 323.
[52] Scrapbook clipping.
[53] *American Brewer*, XXXVI, No. 1 (Jan. 1903), 29.
[54] *Blue Ribbon News*, Jan. 1915, p. 12; see also *American Brewers' Review*, XXVIII, No. 11 (Nov. 1914), 520.

EXPORT SALES

(February 1909–January 1910)

	Dozen Small Bottles	Casks
Canada	34,956	...
Central America	6,528	...
Guatemala	4,934	...
British Honduras	4,672	...
El Salvador	1,312	...
Nicaragua	640	...
Costa Rica	512	...
Panama	37,480	215
Mexico	1,792	...
West Indies	916	...
Haiti	576	...
Jamaica	692	...
Barbados	224	...
British West Indies	256	...
Cuba	15,488	415
Puerto Rico	3,746	7,727
Trinidad	1,824	...
Bermuda	64	...
South America	1,888	...
Bolivia	672	...
Chile	576	...
Peru	5,280	...
Brazil	160	...
Argentina	33,764	...
Colombia	4,672	...
Dutch Guiana	214	4
British Guiana	384	...
Philippine Islands	64,528	...
Hawaii	...	35
China	2,048	...
Singapore	160	...
Australia	352	...
New Zealand	897	...
India	1,248	...
Europe	3,718	7
Turkey	128	...
Egypt	1,984	...
Mombasa	128	...
New York for transshipment	18,422	...
Total	257,835	8,409

According to the United States Brewers' Association Report, the Pabst volume was nearly one third of the total American export sales.[55]

This concludes the analysis of the strictly business aspects of Pabst before prohibition, and it also concludes the main section of our business history. Pabst activities from 1919 to 1932 were in new fields that concern the history of brewing only indirectly; and Pabst, since 1933, is too recent a story to permit full analysis. But, in addition to the productive and marketing activities of the earlier years, a business history must also try to analyze the company's relations with its workers, with its community, and with the government, even though the record of these relations is far from adequate.

[55] United States Brewers' Association reported total export of 635,361 dozen bottles, plus 246,525 gallons, from May 1, 1909, to May 1, 1910. *Yearbook* [1910], pp. 292-94, Tables B and C.

CHAPTER X

PABST IN MILWAUKEE

A large manufacturing company is necessarily an integral part of the whole social community in which it functions, and its history must tell some of this broader story too. More than any other cities in the world, American cities have been influenced in their development by the needs of business enterprise. Most American cities have a social core composed of a group of key business concerns, the people to whom these companies give a livelihood, and certain other auxiliary business organizations to care for the daily needs of the employees. The hours of work and the rates of pay of both manual and office workers, and the profits of these enterprises, determine the standard of living and the material welfare of the community. But the key enterprises not only furnish the economic basis of life, they also must provide in large part the intelligence and administrative ability for social, political, religious, intellectual, and artistic leadership in the community.

The general types of influence exerted by a large company in its community may be listed under six headings. (1) Opportunities provided for the training and stimulation of young executives, and for successful careers. (2) The effect on the living conditions of the mass of the company workers and their dependents, including creation of special educational, housing, or recreational facilities, provision for old age and sickness, and the general interest of the company in the "tone" of lower-class community life. (3) Community improvements resulting from improvement of the company's business facilities, and, conversely, benefits to the company and its business from independently initiated community developments. (4) Influence of the company or its leaders in politics and in the public expression of community opinions and ideals. (5) Encouragement given by the company or its leaders to social, educational, religious, and artistic projects not immediately connected with the business of the concern. (6) Participation by the company or its leaders in philanthropic and welfare activities not primarily connected with its own workers.

OPPORTUNITIES FOR YOUNG MEN

In relation to their capital and sales volume, neither Pabst nor other brewers of that day were large employers of office help or of minor executives. But while the office staff at the Empire was small, the spread of branch offices created some added opportunities for advancement. A number of young men who started as beginners in the Best Company in the period of rapid expansion rose to positions of some importance. Oscar Mueller who started in 1879 as a maltster became superintendent of malting; John S. Pierce, coming as a barley buyer in 1876, ended as general credit manager with charge of the two Chicago branches; Charles Henning and H. J. Stark, both starting in the middle 1870's as bookkeepers, rose to be officers of the company. A dozen others secured incomes that marked them as "business successes" and men of standing in the community.

As the Pabst Company scarcely altered its size between 1893 and 1919, the opportunities open to young executives were then limited mainly to replacing their superiors when the latter retired. One company policy, however, was particularly favorable to young Milwaukeeans: outsiders were seldom brought in at high salaries over the heads of the local staff. As a consequence, while opportunities for really high salaries were limited, the security of a Pabst executive job was attractive.

So was the security of most of the workmen employed in brewing and malting. Subject only to occasional layoffs in the winter, the brewhouse workers had steady jobs and many of them spent their entire working life with the company. The seasonal stoppage of malting in the summer did not lead to labor turnover, since the same employees were regularly rehired in the fall; and since the time off was regular and predictable, it was possible for them to fit other activities into this period. Often, as noted on page 251, they found work in other departments, such as the racking room or washhouse, which were busy meeting the heavy summer demand at the very time when the maltsters were idle. Surveying the employment figures over the years, it can be said that brewing produced a high degree of job stability for both executive and worker. Pabst sales, as we have seen, did not react violently to the business cycle, and the numbers employed varied less than the production.[1]

HOW THE WORKERS LIVED

Even when the working day was cut to ten hours after 1886, Pabst workers spent most of their waking hours in activities directly connected with their jobs. During those hours at the plant, it made little difference to them what they were paid; the main question was: how pleasant or interesting was the work. Up to 1886, brewery hours were long, running as high as seventy to eighty per week, but the work in most departments was unusually pleasant as compared with other industrial employment. The whole pace of brewing even today is necessarily moderate, for although the brew needs continuous supervision from raw grain to finished product, the process cannot be hurried. There was no deafening clatter of machinery or nerve-trying vibrations. Workers, outside of the bottling department, could take time off for a mug of beer without an assembly line getting ahead of them. The bottling department was partly an exception to these generalizations. Here, since the 1890's, there has been a moving assembly line, but it soon came to be so well mechanized that it needed supervision more than it needed precisely timed hand operations. The bottle house during the period before 1911 was largely staffed by boys and girls who

---

[1] Presumably, any prepared food or drink industry has higher stability than those manufacturing semidurable or "production" goods. See J. Parker Bursk, *Seasonal Variations in Employment in Manufacturing Industries.* See Appendixes C and D, p. 402, for Pabst employment figures.

either left the company when they grew older or were graduated to office work or other brewery positions. In contrast with other departments, therefore, the bottle house, during most of the period prior to 1919, did not furnish permanent positions for many employees and has to be distinguished from the general conditions of employment within the firm.

In malting and some stages of cooling, fermentation, and storage, workers were exposed to broad changes in temperature and humidity as they moved from one room to another, but there is no indication at Pabst that otherwise healthy workers have been made ill by these conditions. The Wisconsin factory inspectors noted in their first report on Best in 1887 that "unlike other breweries inspected the men here suffer little from steam. . . . . There is plenty of light in all departments of the establishment—something that cannot be said of other breweries." [2]

Brewery work was also relatively safe. In 1888, for example, when the state Bureau of Labor Statistics made a detailed accident report, the only case at Best's was that of a man who fell and broke an ankle. The company paid full wages and the doctor's bill.[3] This was undoubtedly an exceptional year, for while the Wisconsin Bureau stopped reporting individual brewery or even brewing industry accidents, a survey made by the United States Brewers' Association for the years 1909-1910 indicated that in the industry as a whole, one worker out of sixteen was injured each year.[4] The average time lost per accident at that time was 27.9 days. The rate had undoubtedly increased with a larger volume of bottling, as the breaking of bottles accounted for many minor injuries. But fatal accidents were so rare that none appear in the association's two-year analysis.

[2] *Biennial Report of the Bureau of Labor and Industrial Statistics of Wisconsin* [1886-87], p. 303.

[3] *Biennial Report of Labor Statistics* [1888-89], p. 70A.

[4] Edward B. Phelps, *A Summary of the Possibilities and Probable Cost of the Proposed Plan for Workmen's Compensation and Old-Age Pensions for American Brewery Workmen*, p. 9.

As early as 1893, the Pabst Company started an insurance plan for its steady employees. Members were assessed 25 to 40 cents a month, based on earnings, and the company contributed an equal amount. In case of death, the insured's family received funeral expenses and half the amount of his yearly wage. In the case of injury, expenses and half wages would be paid for one year.[5] Unfortunately, no records exist regarding the number of workers who took advantage of this opportunity.

Only a handful of American companies at this time made any provision for pensions to regular employees, and Pabst was not among them. This situation did not work as much hardship on old Pabst employees, however, as on the workers of companies employing thousands. The "personal" relation between boss and employee really existed under the Captain, Gustav, and later under Fred Pabst, Jr. They knew all the old, steady employees, and they personally looked after them in time of need.

Compensations for accidents were handled similarly. Regardless of insurance plans or the state law of 1911, each case came directly to the attention of top management, and was dealt with on its merits either by additional payments or work of some type that a sick or injured man could perform.

The company has always sought to control the amount of beer consumed by issuing only a limited number of checks, each good for a mug of beer. The workers, through their union, on the other hand, have generally asked for larger allotments. But the seriousness of the problem has been greatly exaggerated as a result of prohibition propaganda.

Workers' living conditions away from the job depend upon both the level of real wages and the opportunities afforded by the community. Milwaukee brewery workers were relatively fortunate in both respects. As will be seen in the next chapter, brewery wages from the 1870's on were high compared with those of equally skilled workers in other trades. In 1892 and

[5] *Biennial Report of Labor Statistics* [1893-94], p. 105A.

1893, the first two years after the beginning of the modern series of brewery union contracts, the average per capita wage in brewing was only exceeded by that of rolling mills among the ten leading industries of Milwaukee.[6] The city also offered good housing at prices within the reach of brewery labor.

From the earliest times in Milwaukee, married brewery workers appear to have been able to live in pleasant, one- or two-family houses with some land around them. While criticizing the lodgings and tenement houses in which many unskilled workers of other nationalities were forced to live, the Wisconsin State Bureau of Labor Statistics said of the typical German laborer's dwelling:

Each house has a small yard in front and a garden in the rear. . . . . These people are thrifty and industrious and seek as soon as possible to own the house and land which they occupy. . . . . The German desire for ownership and the Polish custom of inhabiting small frame houses is probably what has given Milwaukee the reputation of being a city of homes.[7]

Victor Berger, the famous Milwaukee Socialist leader, was always proud to show visitors the homes of the unionized German workers.[8] A sample has been taken of houses and apartments advertised for sale or rent in the *Milwaukee Sentinel* during the 1890's. The list, however, is not a satisfactory indication of price, as the cheaper homes were seldom advertised. The fact that a four-room cottage, for example, on Sixteenth Street near State Street (a "good address") could be bought at the top of the boom in 1892 for $1,900 would indicate lower prices for unadvertised property in less desirable locations. Furnished rooms were advertised for $4.00 per week with board, and $5.00 or more per month without board. Houses for rent started at $12 per month. A good eight-room-and-bath brick house in an excellent locality was offered at $18 a month in 1890. While this

---

[6] *Biennial Report of Labor Statistics* [1893-94], p. 112.
[7] *Biennial Report of Labor Statistics* [1905-06], p. 315, also illustration xix.
[8] Interview with Mrs. Frank Hursley, nee Doris Berger, Aug. 18, 1945.

latter would seem beyond the means of an ordinary workman (see p. 281 for wages), it could be brought within reach by subletting one or two rooms.[9]

The atmosphere of the German section of the city that stretched north and west of the Empire Brewery seemed more pleasant than that of the average American industrial center of the period. Wide, tree-lined streets, parks, beer gardens, and German festivals remain pleasant memories for the living members of the generations that worked from the late eighties to the beginning of prohibition.[10]

DEVELOPING MILWAUKEE

During her greatest years of expansion, particularly in the 1880's, Milwaukee grew through the reinvestment of local capital by companies and individuals such as Pabst and its owners. Their confidence in Milwaukee's future stemmed largely from the increase in population of from 115,587 in 1880 to 204,468 in 1890 which inspired hope that the city was to hold its position as a gateway to the northwest. German immigrants accounted for an appreciable part of this increase. Thousands of them, displaced by the advance of the industrial revolution in the fatherland, were attracted to the United States by its general prosperity. With this impetus from new population, all the established industries in Milwaukee went ahead at a breathless rate in these years; and to a large degree, the great wealth produced stayed in Milwaukee. In 1891 the "foreign capital" invested in Milwaukee was estimated at only 8½ per cent of the total.[11]

Milwaukee soon grew very conscious of its position as a Middle Western metropolis. Every year from 1881 until 1902, a Milwaukee industrial exposition was held in a great rambling

[9] *Sentinel,* Jan. 1, 1890, Feb. 5, 1892, Jan. 6, 1894, Jan. 1, 1899.

[10] The author is aware that these are not reliable criteria. The men interviewed were members of the Pabst Old Timers Club and a few journalists, all of whom may represent the more fortunate group.

[11] Anderson and Bleyer, p. x.

pseudo-Gothic building erected for that purpose on the block where the Auditorium now stands.[12] The organization behind these annual exhibits was headed by the principal businessmen of the city: John Plankinton, the leading Milwaukee packer, who was president, and Captain Pabst, who was the first vice-president and subsequently a director for many years.[13] In 1888 the old Merchants Association organized an "Association for the Advancement of Milwaukee" of which Gustav Pabst became secretary in 1891.[14] Probably no local group co-operated in the purposes of these organizations more vigorously than the brewers. The knowledge that brewing companies would provide royal entertainment lured conventions to Milwaukee, and made it one of the great convention cities of the country. The brewers, more than any other industrialists in Milwaukee at this time, were selling to a national retail market in which their very business depended, as we have seen, upon making the name of Milwaukee known. In the nineties, the two leading breweries adopted slogans typifying this effort: "Milwaukee Beer Is Famous—Pabst Has Made It So," and "Schlitz, the Beer that Made Milwaukee Famous."

Milwaukee's growth was particularly favorable to the beer business. The 34,000 immigrants, who came to Milwaukee between 1880 and 1890, not only included a fine supply of brewery workmen but a small cityful of new German customers as well.[15] From 1879 to 1889, Milwaukee beer production increased almost threefold, and in the latter year it became Milwaukee's largest industry from the standpoint of value of product as well as capital investment.[16]

The leaders of Pabst reinforced the community pattern by

[12] This building burned June 14, 1905, and was superseded by the Auditorium. Bruce, *The Auditorium*, p. 5.

[13] *The City of Milwaukee Guide* [1886], p. 3.

[14] Anderson and Bleyer, pp. xiii, xix. See also Bayrd Still, "Milwaukee, 1870-1900," *Wisconsin Magazine of History*, XXIII (1939), 147-48; "Development of Milwaukee in the Early Metropolitan Period," *Wisconsin Magazine of History*, XXV (1942), 299.

[15] *United States Statistical Abstract* [1910], p. 61.

[16] *Sentinel*, Jan. 1, 1890.

investing their money at home. The profits of the company, as we have seen, were largely left in the business, and up to 1893 the firm invested most of its surplus in Milwaukee property. The Captain and Schandein also invested their growing personal fortunes in local ventures.

The Captain leased the Kirby House at 430 East Water Street, one of the best downtown hotels, in 1891 for ninety-nine years at $6,000 a year. In 1892 he erected the Pabst Building at a cost of about $750,000.[17] This was a thirteen-story skyscraper, then Milwaukee's tallest building, located at the corner of Wisconsin Avenue and East Water Street on the site of the first house on the east side of the Milwaukee River and almost the exact center of the downtown section.[18] At the same time, he set up the Pabst Heat, Light and Power Company which built a powerhouse on Broadway, between Mason and Wells Streets, to provide electricity for all the near-by Pabst buildings.

A number of outstanding real-estate investments were made by the Pabst Company. In 1888 the development of Whitefish Bay as a pleasure resort was begun by erecting a pavilion and a restaurant that raised the book value of the property to $150,000 by 1891. During the next twenty years, the company continually invested more money, making this one of the most popular amusement spots for Milwaukeeans. The St. Charles Hotel on East Water Street, near the City Hall, was bought and remodeled by the company in 1890, and its name was changed to the Pabst Hotel. In 1893, it resumed its old name and soon competed with the old Plankinton and new Pfister for the best patronage of the city. The company also bought the Stadt Theater on Third Street in 1889 and the Nunnemacher Opera House at Market Square, opposite the City Hall, in 1890. The latter was remodeled into a modern theater and cafe at a cost of over $200,000.

17 In addition to the company records, see *Journal*, Apr. 15, 1904.

18 A tablet was placed by Captain Pabst on the building in 1903, under the supervision of the Old Settlers' Club of Milwaukee County. Louise Phelps Kellogg, "Wisconsin Historical Landmarks," p. 68.

These real-estate activities made the Pabst Company during the 1890's the largest property owner in Milwaukee.[19] Its holdings were further increased in 1894 when the Captain sold it the power company and a number of smaller properties for some $500,000. The Pabst Company in turn sold the power plant two years later at a good profit. In 1897 the Captain also sold the Kirby House lease and the Pabst Building to the company. New local investments after the nineties were on a small scale except for the famous Gargoyle Restaurant on Grand Avenue [20] in 1906.

Meanwhile, the Captain personally became interested in two other important ventures. In the late eighties, according to his old friend, Julius Wechselberg,

Some of us who had property adjoining his out in Wauwatosa greatly desired to secure the building of an electric line to the property so it could be platted. We went to Captain Pabst and stated our wants, telling him that we wanted him to give us a liberal donation as a bonus to secure the road.[21]

The Captain apparently took up the idea with enthusiasm and in 1890 helped form the Milwaukee and Wauwatosa Motor Railway Company. At first the backers planned to run small steam trains over the route but, after the building of the Pabst power plant in 1892, an electric road was projected. From 1891 to 1896, the Captain was the principal stockholder of the company, but bad times and right-of-way problems delayed construction.

In the spring of 1896 when business prosperity was returning, New York interests, represented by William Nelson Cromwell of the firm of Sullivan and Cromwell, entered into an agreement to buy the motor railway company and the power plant and to merge them as a subsidiary of the Milwaukee Electric Railway and Light Company. Meanwhile, as the summer pro-

---

[19] *Sentinel,* May 16, 1897. Scrapbook clipping.
[20] Grand Avenue is now named Wisconsin Avenue.
[21] *Sentinel,* Jan. 2, 1904.

gressed, the Democratic presidential campaign of William Jennings Bryan, on a liberal platform calling for regulation of corporations and free coinage of silver, alarmed many businessmen. The "silver-tongued" orator, they feared, would align labor with farmers in an attack on American business, and investors sought to curtail all new commitments. Cromwell wrote to the Captain on July 22 proposing that they cancel their agreement of sale.[22] The Captain replied in a letter that showed his stature as a businessman, able to think beyond such passing excitements.

I most emphatically decline to consider your proposition to postpone the consummation of our deal until after the fall election. This is not because of any lack of faith on my part in the stability of our government or its financial affairs. This country is too large and too broad and the interests of its millions of citizens are too diverse to admit of any halt in the progress of our advancement by any one selfish faction, however numerous or strong. Be that as it may, the plain fact is that you have made a contract to purchase and I have made a contract of sale with respect to two valuable properties here in the city of Milwaukee; that I have gone on and made partial delivery to you and you have accepted same to such an extent that you are now operating the Wauwatosa road, have changed the rate of fares so that it cannot be restored, and have caused publicity to be given in this community of the whole transaction. Some details were lacking to complete the final adjustment in the matter of dollar and cents relating to the expense of heating and lighting of my buildings, but between gentlemen this affords no excuse, as it seems to me, for the summary postponement of this transaction in the manner proposed by your letter. I do not believe that the Milwaukee Directory of your company will feel that you are justified in the course described. They are gentlemen of high standing and their word passes at par in this community.[23]

The deal was consummated and the Captain withdrew from the traction field.

[22] Letter, July 22, 1896.
[23] Letter, July 28, 1896.

In 1892 he took the lead in organizing the Wisconsin National Bank with a capital of a million dollars and with offices on the second floor of the Pabst Building. In spite of the panic and depression of 1893, the bank immediately became one of the city's most important financial institutions with $4,533,-203.53 in resources by the end of its first year in business.[24] Its original officers were the team that had led the old Phillip Best Brewing Company to its great success: Captain Pabst as president and Charles Best as vice-president. Thus the brewing company entered the so-called age of "finance capitalism" in virtual control of its own banking connections. The bank remained the Captain's chief interest aside from the brewery and his farm. During his presidency, which lasted until his death in 1904, the Central National Bank was added by merger; and after the depression, the bank grew steadily in keeping with the good money and banking conditions in the years around the turn of the century.[25] Upon the Captain's death, the bank bought its building from the Pabst Company, but the company continued to place much of its business there; Gustav Pabst and W. O. Goodrich of the Pabst board were directors of the bank.

Aside from enterprises in which they could personally play an important part, neither Schandein nor the Captain accepted many directorships. Schandein was a director of the Northeastern Life Insurance Company for some four years, but this appears to have been his only "outside" connection of this type.[26] In the seventies the Captain became a director of the Milwaukee Mechanics Mutual Insurance Company and of the Second Ward Savings Bank, and held these offices until his death, refusing all other such invitations.[27] His only out-of-state activities, not connected with brewing, of which we have a record were the Pabst Mining Company and the Idanha Company for spring water, neither of which was of lasting importance.

[24] Copy of bank statement in company records.
[25] Jerome A. Watrous, *Memoirs of Milwaukee County*, I, 570.
[26] *United States Biographical Dictionary, Wisconsin Volume*, p. 432.
[27] *Sentinel*, Jan. 2, 1904.

Gustav Pabst, like his father, confined his active business connections, outside the brewing industry, to local companies. During the years before 1919, directorships in the Merchants and Marine Insurance Company and in the Allis-Chalmers Manufacturing Company, between 1913 and 1916, were his only business connections outside of the Wisconsin National Bank and its associated Wisconsin Trust Company.[28] Fred Pabst,[29] after his resignation from the vice-presidency in 1905, devoted himself to the affairs of the Milwaukee Refrigeration Transit Company, virtually a Pabst subsidiary, and to his large farm at Oconomowoc.

The development of farming and stock raising was a hobby that grew into an extensive business with the Pabsts. In the eighties the Captain bought a 225-acre farm out in Wauwatosa, some five miles west of the brewery, as a summer home. Each day in the warm seasons of the year he would drive in from the farm to the brewery behind a pair of chestnut-colored horses driven by John Duncan, a Negro, who served him for many years. This farm, "perched on top of a hill of steep ascent, embowered in grape vines," was, from 1885 on, the Captain's greatest interest aside from the brewing business.[30] Stimulated by his experience with the use of draft horses, he made a study of the work animals of the world, and came to the conclusion that French Percherons were the type best suited to the United States. Importing prize horses from France, he could boast, by the middle eighties, "I have succeeded in getting together a herd of mares that for quality and richness of breeding have no superior in the world." [31] Stud fees were made so low that the strain could rapidly be spread to provide the state with better work horses. For pleasure purposes he also had German coachers.

[28] Interview with Edwin Pabst, Aug. 23, 1945. See also *Sentinel*, Mar. 10, 1913.

[29] From this point on, Frederick Pabst, the Captain's son, will be called Fred Pabst, the name by which he is generally known.

[30] Anderson and Bleyer, p. 118.

[31] Anderson and Bleyer, p. 118.

18

The period from 1920 on, when Fred Pabst as president of the company became an active Milwaukee business leader, falls outside the scope of this chapter. During the years from 1905 to 1920 his main activities were horse breeding and scientific agriculture on his extensive farm. Fred Pabst developed an interest in farming even greater than his father's. When a young man, he started importing and breeding Hackneys and Percherons. He also bred hunters and trotters. After his father's death, as the town closed in around the old farm, Fred and his wife, Ida Uihlein Pabst, moved to Oconomowoc, thirty miles to the west, and established a farm that ultimately grew to over 1,400 acres. There he continued his interest in horse breeding and training. Heavy hunters became his particular specialty. Riding his own horses, he won many prizes and became a nationally known horseman. The First World War put a temporary end to these activities as he "felt that all time, money, and effort should be devoted to the needs of the nation, and he considered the luxury of breeding horses for pleasure use an affront to the suffering world." [32] At Oconomowoc he also developed an outstanding Holstein herd. The latter led him into the milk and cheese business. Long before prohibition, Pabst's Holstein Farms were turning out Swiss wheels and the ancestors of the cheese that was to become famous as Pabst-ett. The Oconomowoc property borders on a large lake, and Fred took up sailing with the same intensity and seriousness that he devoted to his business affairs. Among the boats with which he won many trophies, the "Comet II" achieved national fame.

Gustav Pabst acquired Hollyhock Farm, adjoining Fred Pabst's farm, as a summer home where he also raised purebred Holsteins. This herd which he sold intact in the middle 1920's has become nationally famous among stock raisers. His interests also were in the development of animal life. He brought English ring-necked pheasants, Hungarian partridge, and new varieties of quail to Wisconsin. Two Nubian lions were added

[32] Supplied by E. L. Morris from an interview with Fred Pabst.

to the Milwaukee zoo at his expense, and he was largely responsible for the zoo's acquisition of an elephant.[33] Gustav also bred and trained prize-winning dogs and horses for which he formed such strong personal attachments that his wife said that if she had to be reincarnated in some subhuman form, she would like to be one of Gustav's dogs. As would be expected of a man with these interests, he was a fine horseman, an excellent shot, and a great devotee of hunting and fishing.

Both Schandein and the Captain took active roles in community leadership. The former in 1880 founded the Milwaukee German Society, aimed especially at helping newly arrived immigrants to adjust themselves, and became its first president.[34] He also served as president and secretary of the local brewers' association. Although he never sought a political office, and discouraged a campaign by his friends to win him a gubernatorial nomination, he attended the National Democratic Convention of 1884 as delegate-at-large from Wisconsin.[35]

The Captain held minor offices of a nonpartisan type such as Second Ward alderman in the sixties, Water Commissioner in the seventies, and Commissioner of Public Debt from 1889 to 1892, but he declined to run for any elective office where campaigning was necessary.[36] In 1891 a movement to nominate him for governor raised the question of the Captain's political affiliations. One editor speculated that it was

. . . . a toss-up as to whether he is a Republican or a Democrat, but it is quite certain that he is not a Prohibitionist. Two gentlemen who know him well were discussing the subject a day or two ago, and one claimed positively that Captain Pabst was a Republican, while the other was equally certain that he was a Democrat, so a third gentleman very likely to know was appealed to.

[33] *Sentinel,* June 30, 1908, and Jan. 30, 1910. Scrapbook clippings.
[34] John Goadby Gregory, *History of Milwaukee, Wisconsin,* IV, 1060.
[35] *Sentinel,* July 23, 1888.
[36] *Journal,* Jan. 2, 1904. Scrapbook clipping.

"Captain Pabst is neither," said he, "he votes for the men he prefers, regardless of their politics. He voted for Garfield for president 8 years ago, and I understand that Cleveland received his vote 4 years ago. For whom he voted last fall nobody appears to know. Captain Pabst never attempted to control the votes of his men. . . . . On the whole Captain Pabst has been regarded as more of a Republican than a Democrat. The presumption, when Mayor Brown appointed him as a Commissioner of Public Debt to succeed the late Guido Pfister, was that it was a case of a Republican succeeding a Republican. I think Captain Pabst is not at all pleased with this talk of nominating him for governor. He has no taste for politics, and when the Democrats a couple of years ago seemed bent on nominating Emil Schandein, Captain Pabst strongly disapproved of the idea. He realized that the Democrats wanted to nominate his partner simply to 'tap his barrel.' " [37]

As P. V. Deuster, editor of the German-language *Seebote,* continued to propose the Captain's name as a candidate on the Democratic ticket, the Captain gave a public interview to settle the question saying that he was too old a man to be flattered by the mention of his name with so high an office, and that under no circumstances whatever would he be a candidate for any office.

"But if I were to be a candidate," added the Captain, "I would not be a German-American or Irish-American candidate, but a plain American. I am an American. I love the country of my adoption, and I only regret I could not have been born here—but I would not take any office if I could have it without an effort." [38]

By the middle nineties, the Captain was generally recognized as the leading German-born citizen of Milwaukee. Politicians sought his advice regarding appointments in both Wisconsin and Washington. His leadership in local Germanic affairs is

[37] Chicago *Inter-Ocean,* Sept. 10, 1889. Scrapbook clipping.
[38] Chicago *Inter-Ocean,* Sept. 10, 1889. Scrapbook clipping.

also shown by his election as chairman of the Milwaukee committee that welcomed Prince Henry of Prussia in 1902.[39]

Both Gustav and Fred Pabst continued the tradition of avoiding public office. While Gustav Pabst was made a colonel by Governor Peck for service on his staff from 1891 to 1895, his abiding interest was in talking politics rather than in participating. He loved to argue political issues with the farmers around his country place at Hollyhock Farm, and to exhort them to vote the "right" way, but he never ran for any office. As third vice-president, first vice-president, and finally president of the United States Brewers' Association in the critical half-dozen years before the prohibition amendment, Gustav was very much "in politics," but his only aim seems to have been that of protecting the brewing interests.

Gustav and Fred were active proponents of outdoor sports. They awarded trophies for athletic contests, automobile races, aero clubs, and horse shows. They took a leading part in organizing the first Milwaukee horse show in 1903, with Gustav as chairman of the committee. Fred also organized annual horse shows at Oconomowoc. Gustav early became interested in aviation and gave a balloon named the "Pabst" to the Aero Club.[40]

THE HEYDAY OF GERMAN MILWAUKEE

Beer, perhaps more than any other single product, had built the reputation and fashioned the social life of nineteenth-century Milwaukee. Brewing had led to the largest capital investment, had attracted the greatest number of visitors, and had given the city national and international fame. In all these activities, Captain Pabst was the recognized leader. Local societies honored him in return. The Wisconsin Academy of Science, Arts and Letters, the Wisconsin State Historical Society, and the Musical Society of Milwaukee elected the Captain to membership, and the latter made him its president.[41]

[39] *Sentinel*, Mar. 4, 1902. Scrapbook clipping.
[40] *Sentinel*, Mar. 10, 1907, July 7, 1908, Jan. 30, 1910; *Free Press*, Feb. 9, 1903. Scrapbook clippings.
[41] W.P.A., "Notes on Biography of Captain Pabst."

Up to the turn of the century, Milwaukee culture continued to have a strong German character with many of its customs built around the rites of beer drinking. Opera flourished with a twelve-week annual season from 1885 to 1893 under the direction of Paul Zabel at Schlitz Park.[42] The music was generally light, ranging from popular grand operas, such as *Martha,* to Gilbert and Sullivan; but the singers were always among the best from the Metropolitan and Emma Abbott Opera Companies. The old Stadt Theater group with its excellent stock company, which was started in 1884 to produce famous German plays, was moved in 1890 to the new Pabst Theater building where the patrons could quench their thirst during the intermissions at the handsome new Pabst bar. Another example of German culture, the Brewery Workers' Masked Ball, was the most interesting social event of the season from 1869 on, until Milwaukee's old customs were killed by prohibition and the war. The spectacle of thousands of masked dancers cavorting on the floor and drinking free beer while "society" watched from the balcony was one of the chief inspirations for Charles K. Harris' famous song, "After the Ball is Over."[43]

That the Captain's interest in German art and culture went beyond the commercial stage is indicated by his and Fred Pabst's contributions to a traveling library to bring German literature to the country folk in the environs of Milwaukee, and his assumption of Schandein's place in 1889 as a director of Luening's Conservatory of Music.[44]

By the middle nineties, the greatest days of the old culture were passing. New non-German immigrants were coming in large numbers. Within little more than a decade the relative decline of German habits and culture began to show itself in a change in the importance of brewing. While the other leading

[42] *Journal,* Apr. 7, 1933.

[43] *Sentinel,* Nov. 27, 1871. See also *Journal,* Apr. 7, 1933.

[44] Hense-Jensen and Bruncken, *Wisconsins Deutsch-Amerikaner,* II, 190. Letter, Irme Boos, secretary, Luening's Conservatory of Music, to Captain Pabst, Feb. 15, 1889.

Milwaukee industries continued to advance, the brewing industry ceased expanding after its record sale of 3,800,000 barrels in 1907. By 1914 the value of brewing products was about equaled by the total of all metal manufactures.[45]

Milwaukee was becoming a mature community, with fewer new adjustments to make and less pioneering to be done. With German immigration dropping sharply, the rate of growth in the city fell from a 77 per cent increase in the decade of the eighties to 40 per cent in the nineties, 31 per cent in the first decade of the new century, and 22 per cent in the following decade. The astute young Selig Perlman wrote in 1910 that 1893 marked the end of the German or "pre-American" period of Milwaukee society.[46] The afterglow of the sunset of the "German Athens" lingered on in institutions such as the Pabst Theater but, from the depression of the middle nineties, a new, less *gemuetlich,* less picturesque, and more typically American city began to emerge.

The Pabst Theater, owned by the company and conducted by the Stadt Theater group, remained as the home of one of the finest artistic contributions of the old culture. Under the direction of Leon Wachsner, who presided from the founding in 1884 until his death in 1909, the group opened at its new location with Goethe's *Egmont* on September 17, 1890.[47] In 1895 the theater burned, and the Captain, who was in Europe at the time, cabled to rebuild at once. By November 1895, the present building was completed. The director through a guarantee fund reaching $40,000 the first year, largely supplied by the Captain and Mrs. Schandein, was given free rein in getting stars of the German theater. The winter's bill was generally made up of a mixture of current and classic German comedies and dramas, often performed by special guest artists from Europe, with the season occasionally running to over a hundred performances. In the later years, particularly, plays were given in English.

[45] United States *Census of Manufacture* I [1914], 1654, 1663.
[46] Selig Perlman, "History of Socialism in Milwaukee, 1893-1910," MS.
[47] Souvenir booklet [1891]. See also *Evening Wisconsin,* Sept. 18, 1890.

Among the high lights were Leo Dittrichstein's translation of and appearance in *Are You a Mason?* and *White Horse Tavern,* and Richard Mansfield's starring in *Old Heidelberg.*[48]

Direction was continued by Wachsner's widow until 1913 and then by Ferdinand Welb until the First World War ended the company. Due to the continued interest and financial support of Mr. and Mrs. Fred Pabst, the Pabst Theater continued its activities after the war, but without a local stock company. The Chicago Symphony came to perform one night a week during the season; and ballets, road shows, and other orchestras came to the theater on many other nights. Mr. and Mrs. Pabst poured "tens of thousands" of dollars into the theater during the depression of the thirties so that Milwaukee would not be without a place to house music and drama. The German-language theater, however, together with several other aspects of German culture, seems to have been permanently ended by the First World War.

OLD-STYLE PHILANTHROPY

While in matters of charity the Captain was naturally generous, he adhered to the standards of his generation. Aside from an annual donation of about a thousand dollars to the Associated Charities of Milwaukee, he liked to make many small gifts, often anonymously and often spontaneously, to individuals or organizations with which he was personally familiar.[49] Our knowledge of the Captain's gifts, derived only from scattered notices, is undoubtedly quite incomplete. In 1892 he gave the Milwaukee Law Library Association ten years free rent in the new Pabst Building, and $1,500 with which to buy books. About 1899 he contributed $1,000 for a Young Women's Christian Association building.[50] But he won his widest acclaim as a philanthropist in this year of patriotic fervor following the

[48] In addition to the company records regarding the Pabst Theater, see Oscar V. Deuster, "The Story of the German Stage in Milwaukee," pp. 23-27, MS.
[49] *Sentinel,* Jan. 2, 1904.
[50] *Sentinel,* Jan. 2, 1904.

Spanish War by paying $8,000 for an autograph album that Lydia Ely had collected for the purpose of raising funds to complete the Soldiers' Monument on Grand Avenue. Papers as remote as the *Hartford Courant* noted the event.[51] Important among the gifts donated in the latter years of his life was that of the picture, "Silent Devotion," by Carl Marr in December 1901 to Milwaukee's Layton Art Gallery. The picture, largely a matter of antiquarian interest today, was highly valued around the turn of the century.[52] His annual gifts of Christmas baskets ran as high as a hundred or more, and his small gifts to all kinds of causes are too numerous to summarize.

In spite of the threat that it constituted to beer gardens, the Captain worked steadily for the creation of Milwaukee's magnificent park system. "I venture to say," wrote the Captain's friend, Edward Coleman, "that his goodness of heart will be more commented upon by thousands with whom he personally came in contact than his deserved success as a man." [53]

During the eighteen years he served as president of the Pabst Company, Gustav took a similar part in the philanthropic life of Milwaukee; but, just as in the case of his father and most of the successful men of the time, his activities followed his personal interests rather than any pattern dictated by feelings of responsibility for planning general community welfare. Gustav also followed his father in liking to give anonymously. In 1902, for example, he gave 350 cords of wood to the Associated Charities of Milwaukee with the request that nothing be said about it.[54] He was particularly conscious of the need for better hospital facilities, giving continually to the Milwaukee Sanitarium in amounts as large as $2,500 at a time, and helping to found the Columbia Hospital.[55] In community-fund, school, and hospital drives, he gave his time lavishly, occasionally heading the ef-

51 *Journal*, Feb. 3, 1899; *Hartford Courant*, Sept. 30, 1899. Scrapbook clippings.
52 *Journal*, Dec. 9, 1901.
53 *Sentinel*, Jan. 2, 1904.
54 *American Brewer*, XXXVI, No. 2 (Feb. 1903), 89.
55 *Sentinel*, June 16, 1907.

fort—as when he collected money for the founding of the Milwaukee Country Day School.[56]

In assessing the total contribution of Pabst and its principal owners to preprohibition civic welfare, art, education, and other such aspects of culture in Milwaukee, we must be careful to judge the men by their time. Wealthy Americans of this period did not in general regard it as their duty to give large sums for the private promotion of the pursuits that their fathers had had little chance to appreciate or enjoy. The day of heavily endowed colleges, museums, and foundations had not yet dawned. The reinvestment of capital in business was generally regarded as more socially valuable and morally righteous than was the encouragement of "nonproductive," aesthetic, or intellectual pursuits. The Pabsts seem fairly typical, in these respects, of the business leaders of the rapidly developing Middle West.

[56] Interview with Edwin Pabst, Aug. 8, 1945.

CHAPTER XI

BARGAINING WITH LABOR

THE history of labor in the Best and Pabst plants, prior to national prohibition, encompasses the whole transition from pre-industrial, handicraft conditions to the large-scale modern assembly line; from household workers toiling like brewers of the Middle Ages to unionized laborers superintending nearly automatic machinery. It illustrates the earliest successful industrial-union movement, accompanied by a long series of amicable contract negotiations. From the time brewing became big business in the 1880's, the brewery workers were in the vanguard of the trade-union movement, and the employers among the first to agree to continuous collective bargaining.

Up to the Civil War, brewing remained a "household" industry. The three or four hands usually needed to assist the partners in running a brewery generally lived with the owning family, and their wages included board and lodging. In 1850, the Bests had four workers, some of whom lived with the family in the small white house on Chestnut Street.[1] We have no way of knowing how the $62 a month that the partners paid out were divided among the men. Hermann Schlüter in his *Brewing Industry and Brewery Workers' Movement in America* says, without offering proof, that in the 1840's brewery wages ran from $4.00 to $6.00 a week without board and $4.00 to $12.00 a month with board and washing.[2]

By 1860, Best employed eight men and paid them a total of $200 a month. Some of this must have gone to workers who lived in boarding houses or their own homes. As the usual wages per day for Milwaukee laborers were about 50 cents with board and 75 cents without, the average rate of $25.00 per month at Best's would indicate fairly good pay. Board at this time cost about $2.50 per week.[3]

[1] "Wisconsin Census" [1850].   [2] Schlüter, p. 90.   [3] "Wisconsin Census" [1860].

271

After the Civil War, Best progressed rapidly toward being a big employer. By 1870, the company employed a hundred workers, including those in the office, and they earned an average yearly wage of about $500.[4] But Best's was an exceptional establishment; the brewing industry as a whole was still made up of small brewers each employing about a half-dozen men. Such small groups naturally did not feel the necessity for unionization. Furthermore, increasing beer sales, even during most of the depression in the 1870's, placed brewery laborers in an advantageous position in relation to other workers. Prices of beer were also maintained fairly well, so there was no great pressure on wages. Instead of declining 20 per cent or more as in most industries, brewery wages remained stationary and even increased in some areas. By the end of the seventies, therefore, throughout the nation brewing was an industry of relatively high wages. Rates were $10 to $13 a week as against $7.50 to $9.00 for equally skilled labor in other industries.[5]

Brewery workers earned their higher weekly pay, however, for their hours were unusually long, even for this period, and seven days work each week was the general rule. Fred Pabst, reminiscing in 1936, described the old working day that continued into the eighties.

I dare say there are many of our old timers who remember very well when the men started at four o'clock in the morning and worked until half past six, when they stopped for breakfast. At seven o'clock they went back to work and worked until twelve and then worked in the afternoon from one to six. I often wondered why these men going home at night after six didn't meet themselves coming back at four in the morning.

They worked these long hours because brewing was a continuous process in the early days. The same men who did the mashing and the brewing followed the beer into the fermenting cellar, where they

---

[4] "Wisconsin Census" [1870].
[5] Schlüter, p. 100. N. W. Aldrich, *Report on Wholesale Prices, Wages, and Transportation,* I, 173, Table 39.

pitched the yeast, started the fermenting process, did work in the lager cellars and also filled barrels in the racking room. It is true better hours could have been arranged when this condition no longer existed, but it is easy to stay in a rut. I am glad to say that our brewery was the first to discontinue the early hours before breakfast, which was quite a transition in those days, certainly a good one.[6]

THE RISE OF UNIONS

Shorter hours became the rallying cry of the first brewery workers unions which appeared in Cincinnati in December 1879 and in New York eighteen months later. These pioneer organizations met with little success in their efforts to establish collective bargaining. This was partly due to the fact that brewery workers were only semiskilled, and most of the jobs were of a routine character that could be mastered within a few days by men of average intelligence. The early unions were not complete failures, however, for many of the employers who refused to recognize the unions or bargain with them voluntarily granted most of their demands. Hours came generally to be set at twelve or thirteen per day with time off for two meals. This left a ten- to twelve-hour-daily work period. Two or more hours were usually required on Sunday, often with extra pay.[7]

In the middle eighties, the Knights of Labor, a trade-union organization including all types of skilled and unskilled workers, rose rapidly to national prominence. The Knights was one big union divided into trade assemblies representing the major types of industry. One of these was brewing. New activity leading to the formation of Brewers Union No. 1, Local Assembly 1,672, of the Knights of Labor, was started in New York late in 1884, but the movement did not reach Milwaukee until the spring of 1886.[8] Here an old relief and benefit society for brewery workers with some two hundred and fifty members, which

---

[6] *Blue Ribbon News,* June 1936, p. 3.
[7] Aldrich Report, I, 178, Table 44; Schlüter, pp. 122-27.
[8] Schlüter, p. 115.

had existed since the late seventies, formed the basis for trade-union organization after the pattern of the Knights.[9]

The year 1886 is one of the most famous years in the annals of American labor. The Knights had won great prestige among workingmen by energetic organizing and action in the short but severe depression of 1884 and 1885. As a result, when prosperity returned in the early months of the following year, the Knights gained an enormous membership. By July 1, the organization which had numbered only 150,000 at the end of the previous year counted 702,000 members.[10] The craft unions outside the Knights had also expanded at such a rate that there were about a million organized workers in the United States by the summer of 1886—far more than in any previous year of the nineteenth century.

With prices mounting and jobs becoming plentiful, laborers, organized and unorganized, demanded higher wages and shorter hours. The eight-hour movement, which had languished during the depression, took on renewed life and became a goal toward which all workers could strive in common.

Labor disputes in Milwaukee started at the beginning of 1886, but the first sign of trouble at the Best plant came with the unionization of the maltsters in March of that year. The Captain, mildly sympathetic with the labor movement at this time, readily acceded to their demands for union recognition and abolition of Sunday work. The grateful maltsters publicly thanked him in the *Milwaukee Seebote* on March 24:

We, the maltsters of the Phillip Best Brewery, feel that we owe thanks to the abovementioned firm for granting all the demands that we justly made of them, and herewith express our gratitude publicly. There was no strike in prospect, for after the maltsters in malting house No. 2 organized and elected a leader, the remaining maltsters joined the movement, and the president of our firm granted all our demands after a brief conference.

[9] *Biennial Report of Labor* [1883-84], p. 134.
[10] John R. Commons, *History of Labour in the United States,* I, 381.

Honor to whom honor is due. Honor to our leaders who led us to victory in a just cause and honor to our employer who granted our just demands.

In the name of all, G. N.[11]

The Milwaukee *Labor Review* began publication April 3 to spearhead the drive for union recognition, promising that it would not "be an enemy of capital, it will advocate ever and in all cases a just compensation to the employees—a living wage— and a living proportion of the profits of business." [12]

The rest of the brewery workers joined with the maltsters in organizing Local 7,953 of the Gambrinus Assembly of the Knights of Labor.[13] On April 21, they sent the following letter to the nine Milwaukee breweries:

DEAR SIRS:

On the above date the above assembly in special session prepared the following resolutions for your consideration:

1) In view of the strenuousness and unhealthfulness of work in the breweries and malthouses and of the excessive number of unemployed laborers in this our rich country be it

Resolved that from May 1, 1886 on the 8-hour day be recognized as the normal working day.

2) We demand that the present wage-scale be maintained and that the full monthly wage be paid on the first Monday of every month.

3) That 50 per cent wage increase shall be paid for work over 8 hours a day and for Sunday work.

4) That no workers be employed who do not belong to the Order of the Knights of Labor or who won't agree to join the Order within a month from the date of hiring, the foreman excepted.

5) That no persons whatsoever be hired who have been recommended by others. Let everyone who seeks work speak for himself.

Respectfully,

335-16 STREET   GEORGE BERINGER, *Secretary* [14]

[11] *Seebote,* Mar. 24, 1886. Scrapbook clipping.
[12] Milwaukee *Labor Review,* Apr. 3, 1886.
[13] *Daily Journal,* Apr. 21, 1886.
[14] Translated from a German newspaper clipping, dated Apr. 21, 1886. Scrapbook clipping.

The brewers, acting in concert, replied two days later:

MILWAUKEE, April 23, 1886

We have received from your representatives the resolutions prepared by you at your special meeting of April 16 and have given them thoughtful consideration; herewith we lay before you our views upon the points you presented.

No. 1 ——— [*sic*]

Without any special pressure from you we have recently reduced the working time by 3 hours and all of you know that the required work can hardly be accomplished in this time, despite the low ebb of business this season. Further, all of you as practical brewers know that not all of the work pertaining to a brewery can be accomplished, even with the employment of a greater number of people under the 8-hour system, and that it is impossible even with the best of intentions, to reduce the working time any further.

Even now when the summer season has not yet begun it is difficult enough to get all the essential work done in a 10-hour day and any further reduction would be ruinous.

Your own Orders' General Masterworkman exhorted you on April 19 to the effect that the interests of the manufacturers and workers must be duly considered before instituting anything like the 8-hour day.

Over and above this you should remember that you do not now render 10 full hours of work, inasmuch as within that time you eat your lunches, visit the beer-barrels and otherwise waste time. We hope, therefore, that you will give thought to the uniqueness of our industry, and we must for the stated reasons definitely decline to grant this demand.

2. *Retain wage-scale*

We reply to this by stating that we are in full accord and gladly grant this demand.

3. *Fifty per cent more over 8 hours and for Sunday*

Permit us to make the counter-proposal that all work beyond 10 hours be paid for in proportion to the wage, and that all Sunday work be paid for at 50 per cent pro rata over the regular monthly wages.

4. *Closed Shop*

We believe that you would not knowingly do anyone injustice, and therefore would not require of us to set up regulations in our business that would rob of their livelihood those true and tried workers who for various reasons have declined membership in your Order. To the same extent that we claim no right to dictate to a worker that he must be a Catholic, Protestant, or Jew, we believe we have no right to require associations which have no direct connections with his duties as a worker. It would be a violation of the recognized rights of personal freedom of every citizen, should we seek to compel him, against his will and convictions, to belong to the Order.

We recognize the right of the worker to organize and to promote his own interests, if his circumstances are oppressive and make the improvement of living-conditions advisable; we have therefore never denied anyone the privilege of belonging to any order or any lodge, and regard it as a rank injustice to dictate to anyone on this matter. We do not doubt that your sound sense of justice will, upon due reflection, find you in agreement with us and will withdraw a demand which cannot endure because it is basically unjust. Therefore we cannot fulfill your desire.

5. *No sponsoring of workers*

We are familiar with the reasons which have motivated this well-intentioned demand, and inasmuch as you regard it as necessary to abolish an abused practice that has developed over a period of years, and that by reason of its nature threatens to become mutually harmful, we join with you and will see to it that your desires will be fulfilled.

We hope that you will receive this expression of our views in the same cordial spirit which has heretofore pervaded the negotiation of our concerns with our employees; then there will be no danger threatening our further friendly relations.

Signed by Best, Schlitz, Jung & Borchert, Falk, Blatz, Obermann, Miller, Gettelman, and Cream City Brewing Companies.[15]

Thus began the fight over the fundamental issue—the closed shop—that was to disturb brewery relations in Milwaukee for

[15] Translated from a German newspaper, dated Apr. 23, 1886. Scrapbook clipping.

19

the next half-dozen years and general American labor relations for the next sixty. The brewers' argument was that of all other employers. They must have the right to choose their own workers in their own plants, and they would fight longer and harder over this point than over any question of wages or hours.

The next step was a conference between the union representatives and the brewers in which the union agreed to give up the eight-hour day and the closed shop in return for a substantial increase in wages. But the employers replied:

We have studied the scale of wages which you laid before us at the conference and have come to the conclusion that they are considerably too high to be acceptable to us under any circumstances.

We have the conviction that we have always paid good wages; wages that have been uniformly consistent during the last 20 years and compare favorably with those of other branches of industry, and which enable everyone to live respectably and effect savings.

The treatment of our employees, as is generally known, has always been very liberal, and no more is required of anyone than can reasonably be expected.

Therefore we do not feel definitely obliged to put a wage increase into effect, for we have the conviction, as we have already stated, that we have dealt justly with our workers: nevertheless we have concluded to demonstrate our good will and bring a sacrifice to the prevailing spirit of the times.

Therefore we submit the following essentially increased and for all local brewers binding wage scale, hoping that herewith we will give full satisfaction to all employees in all branches of our industry.

Malthouse workers	$55-60 per month
Cellar and brewhouse workers	50-55
Washhouse	45
Teamsters	45
Firemen	50-60
Peddlars	5 a month increase
Experienced coopers to receive	2.25 a day

The above wage rates are to go into effect on May 1, include unavoidable Sunday work, and in the various departments existing work shall be performed in the customary time and without any extra remuneration.

We are of the opinion that we are rewarding our employees liberally with these wages, and hope that with this accommodation we may convince you, as well as labor in general, that we are considerate, and are glad to make a sacrifice for the sake of establishing a friendly and cordial relationship between employers and employees.[16]

THE STRIKE OF 1886

The companies' wage offer was unsatisfactory, and the union threatened to strike on the first of May. This was right in the midst of the busy season for brewing, and, hoping to avert a stoppage, the employers offered a new increase in wages. The union refused this too.[17] May came with negotiations still deadlocked and, according to schedule, the strike began. The difference in rates at issue is shown in the following table.[18]

RATES AT ISSUE IN WAGE DISPUTE

Type of Work	Received	Wanted	Were Offered
Washhouse	$40	$50	$45
Cellar and brewhouse	45-50 *	55-60	50-55
Malthouse	45-50 *	55-60	55-60
Teamsters	40	50	45
Peddlars	55-65 *	65-75	60-70
Coopers	2 per day	3 per day	2.25 per day

* These ranges are due to distinction between first-class men and second-class men (*Western Brewer*, XI, No. 5 [May 15, 1886], 983).

The maltsters' basic-wage demands had been met, but not their demands for extra pay for Sundays. They were in the strongest bargaining position of any of the workers since many of the brewers, particularly Schlitz, had a considerable amount of germinating barley on the floor when the strike began. At

[16] Translated from a German newspaper, dated Apr. 27, 1886. Scrapbook clipping.
[17] *Western Brewer*, XI, No. 5 (May 15, 1886), 983.
[18] *Sentinel*, May 2, 1886.

Best's, however, the issue was academic as they were through malting for the season.[19]

All the nonoffice employees except the peddlars (salesmen-teamsters) walked out of all the breweries except Falk's. Twelve hundred men were idle, including 445 at Best, 350 at Schlitz, and 175 at Blatz. While the employers made no attempt to hire other men, they had to keep the ice machines going in order to prevent thousands of barrels of beer from spoiling. The Captain and Charles Best therefore persuaded the firemen and engineers to return by four o'clock of the first day by granting their demands both for eight hours and for higher pay.[20] The peddlars continued to make city deliveries although, on the third day of the strike, some of them were stoned or forced to return to the brewery.[21] But, all in all, things were quiet, and the relations between workers and employers surprisingly friendly. Similar strikes affecting some hundred establishments and bringing out some 12,000 men were occurring throughout Milwaukee; and on Sunday, May 2, the brewery workers joined with strikers from other industries in a monster parade to a picnic at the Milwaukee Gardens.[22] On May 3 the Falk workers were persuaded by the committee from their local that it was their duty to join the strike, and they did so.[23] Meanwhile, the brewers quietly met in the office of the Empire Brewery and resolved to make no further concessions.[24]

Only Chicago was more affected than Milwaukee by the record-breaking strikes of May 1886. Employers were alarmed over the fact that Socialists such as Paul Grottkau were attempting to give the struggle a revolutionary direction.[25] Against the advice of some of the calmer civic leaders, the governor was asked to send the militia to keep order in Milwaukee. On May 5,

[19] Sentinel, May 3, 1886.
[20] Sentinel, May 2, 1886.
[21] Daily Journal, May 3, 1886.
[22] Sentinel, May 3, 1886.
[23] Sentinel, May 4, 1886.
[24] Sentinel, May 3, 1886.
[25] Morris Hillquit, History of Socialism in the United States, p. 247.

the troops fired on a crowd of between 500 and 1,000 workers demonstrating before the plant of the North Chicago Rolling Mills at Bay View, killing six and wounding three of the crowd. The militia now took over the job of patrolling the city, and no further disturbances of any consequence occurred.

None of this excitement affected the brewery strike, the leaders of which continued to negotiate the issues calmly and sensibly. After further conferences with the brewers on May 3, the Captain met with a committee of the union and agreed to their wage demands but not to the closed shop. At nine the next morning, the committee announced that they could not accept the Captain's offer unless he discharged twenty men who had worked during the strike. This he refused to do. But later in the day the union gave way on this point,[26] and all the workers returned on the sixth. Similar agreements were reached the same day at Schlitz, Blatz, and Jung and Borchert. By the seventh, the strike was over everywhere with the workers victorious in their wage demands but not in their demands for the eight-hour day or the closed shop.[27] So unusual were union victories in these early days that the *Milwaukee Sentinel* said: [28]

The success of the employees of the breweries has been almost phenomenal.

"The conditions were hard," said a large manufacturer, "but we can only wait until our inning comes." The increase in the pay of the men is as follows:

Where at Work	Received	Get
Washhouse	$40	$50
Cellar and brewhouse	45-50	55-60
Malt house	45-50	55-60
Teamsters	40	50
Peddlars	55-65	65-75
Coopers, per day	2	3

26 *Daily Journal*, May 4, 1886.
27 *Labor Review*, May 8, 1886.
28 *Sentinel*, May 9, 1886.

This is an advance of 120 dollars per annum for each man or $162,000 for the 1,350 men. It is a large item out of the pockets of the brewers, and it is distributed among the firms as follows:

Phillip Best Brewing Company	$54,000
Jos. Schlitz Brewing Company	42,000
Val. Blatz	21,000
Franz Falk	12,000
Jung and Borchert	9,000
Fred Miller	9,000
J. Obermann Brewing Company	6,000
Cream City Brewing Company	4,800
A. Gettlemann [sic]	3,600
	$162,000

The brewers' wage agreement with the employers represented a remarkable gain for a semiskilled group. On the basis of the wages of 1860 being one hundred, principal labor groups were reported by the Aldrich Committee as having achieved the following national levels by 1887: [29]

Brewers	201.1	Metals	144.6
Lumber	170.9	Agricultural implements	149.0
Building trades	170.1	Leather	134.4
Railroads	149.1		

JURISDICTIONAL TROUBLES BEGIN

The success of the Gambrinus Lodge and local assemblies of the Knights of Labor in the brewing industry led, at Baltimore in August 1886, to the beginning of a rival union, the National Union of the Brewers of the United States, in the Federation of Organized Trades and Labor Unions, the ancestor of the American Federation of Labor. On October 2 the new organization started the publication of the *Brauer-Zeitung*.[30]

[29] Aldrich Report, I, 173, Table 39.

[30] "The brewery workers were affiliated with the A. F. of L. as the Brewers National Union. Later that year, in September 1887, the name of the union was changed to National Union of United Brewery Workmen of the United States. In 1903 the name was changed to International Union of the United Brewery Workmen of America." Lloyd George Reynolds and Charles C. Killingsworth, *Trade Union Publications*, I, 301.

There was nothing in the constitution of either group to prevent joint membership, but few if any workers would belong to competing unions. Actually, the stage was now set for all the quarrels that could grow out of dual unionism, particularly as the new Federation of Organized Trades and Labor Unions reorganized in December 1886 as the American Federation of Labor. The new Federation now started a drive for locals, whereas the Knights, by adopting policies in opposition to the desires of the skilled crafts, rapidly lost in membership. Terence Powderly, the Grand Master Workman of the Knights, was an ardent Prohibitionist, and, under his persuasion, the Knights adopted a temperance clause in their constitution. This action was certainly not calculated to appeal to the brewery workers. And when it was followed by an executive order banning beer at union picnics, the members of the Knights Gambrinus Lodge, in the summer of 1887, ceased paying their dues and joined the new Federated Trades Council of Milwaukee as Local No. 9 of the National Union of United Brewery Workmen, A. F. of L.[31] The tight-barrel coopers, who made barrels to hold liquids, followed the brewery workers in their shift of allegiance.[32]

THE BREAKUP OF THE FIRST LOCAL

The good relations between the brewery owners and the local were not affected by these shifts in national allegiance. During this period the original contract was renewed for another year, but this early tranquillity ended with the strike of the workers in the independent malthouses in the fall of 1887. The maltsters in these specialized houses were receiving only about $50 a month for seven days' work, whereas those in brewery-owned malthouses received $55 and extra pay for Sundays, or a total of over $60. The strikers asked $60 straight and free beer, which

[31] *Labor Review*, July 23, 1886; *Brewers' Journal*, XI, No. 10 (Aug. 1, 1887), 340. The charter of the National Union of United Brewery Workmen in the A. F. of L. was issued and granted Mar. 4, 1887. Schlüter, p. 212.
[32] *Brewers' Journal*, XII, No. 1 (Nov. 1, 1887), 4.

was believed to be necessary to ward off tuberculosis in the damp air of the malting room.[33] On their side, the independent Milwaukee maltsters had the fact that their pay scale was below that of other big malting centers. The owners replied, however, that their rural competitors paid still lower wages, and they could not afford to pay at the brewery level and still meet country competition.[34]

The striking maltsters made no attempt at forceful picketing, and their places were quickly filled.[35] Their only hope of bringing pressure to bear on the independent owners appeared to be to get the three small breweries that bought their malt to refrain from buying nonunion products. The brewers involved regarded it as a dangerous precedent to recognize union control over their purchase of raw materials and refused. The union therefore had to attempt a secondary boycott by trying to ban the use of beer made from "scab" malt, while at the same time their brewery members continued to make the beer.[36]

The differing seasonal variations in the brewing and malting industries made the maltsters' strike particularly hard for Local 9 which included both groups of workers. Maltsters worked from September to May and, hence, could only make demands in that season. But other parts of the breweries operated well below capacity in fall and winter, and could be shut down for a month or so with no loss in sales. While a fall strike seemed strategic to the maltsters, therefore, it was a hopeless time for the brewery workers to bring pressure through direct action. A secondary boycott never arouses much popular sympathy, and the fact that it had to be enforced against firms in which their own union members were still employed made it even less acceptable. Furthermore, the union contract called for arbitration of all disputes, but technically the owners could hold that there was no dispute involving conditions of work in the brew-

[33] Evening Wisconsin, Nov. 8 and 14, 1887.
[34] Der Herold, Nov. 9, 1887. Scrapbook clipping.
[35] Evening Wisconsin, Nov. 9, 1887.
[36] Evening Wisconsin, Nov. 12, 1887.

eries and, therefore, nothing to arbitrate. The workers' lack of experience in union action blinded them to the essential weakness of their position. Losing patience too quickly, they apparently declared their boycott without having exhausted legally the possibilities of arbitration.

The brewers were only too ready to accept battle under the circumstances. On November 25, the nine brewing firms declared the boycott a breach of Article XI of the contract, and severed relations with the union.[37] In the words of the Captain:

These men did not keep faith with us, and we don't propose to have anything more to do with them; we won't sign any more contracts, and we consider the contract cancelled.[38]

The grounds for this action were summarized in a pamphlet given to each man as he came to work in the morning. Union members were not discharged from the breweries, however, and there was no aggressive attempt to break the union.

Local 9 with 1,350 members was the strongest labor organization in Milwaukee, but probably no union could have won out under the circumstances.[39] The union now had to declare a boycott against all Milwaukee beer, without daring to call a strike of the brewery workers. Thus they moved further into the contradictory position of repudiating the product they were making.

The tight-barrel coopers joined the boycott on December 3, and two days later Richard Elsner, secretary of Local 9, broadcast the following appeal to labor in the Milwaukee *Daily Review*:

The committees in their respective breweries have been refused a conference with the bosses about the existing difficulties, declaring they would not acknowledge our union at present. Further arrange-

[37] *Der Herold*, Nov. 25, 1887 (scrapbook clipping); *Evening Wisconsin*, Nov. 25, 1887.
[38] New York State *Mediation and Arbitration Board, Second Annual Report* (1889), p. 304.
[39] Membership in 1886 as reported in the *Sentinel*, May 9, 1886.

ments will be made to bring our union upon a better basis than before.

To help us morally, I am sure all friends of organized labor will drink only union beer. Klinkert's beer is at the present time the only union beer in this city.[40] Miller's, Gettleman's [sic], and Cream City Brewery Companies are non-union malt beers.[41]

Elsner also sought to capitalize the fact that this was a period of renewed activity in the Western prohibition movement (see p. 305) by threatening in a statement to the *Evening Wisconsin* the following day:

If the bosses fight the union, every man will vote the temperance ticket. I will pack my trunk and make temperance speeches. We have 1,400 workers who all have their first Citizen's papers and can vote. They will turn temperance. We can live without beer.[42]

A continuous advertisement was run in the Milwaukee *Daily Review:* [43]

Non-Union Beer

Miller's, Gettleman's [sic], and Cream City Brewing Companys' are non-union malt beer.

Union Beer

Klinkert's beer *is the only* union beer.

But all this was just whistling to keep their courage up. The maltsters' strike had definitely failed, and benefit payments of ten dollars a week to the seventy-odd striking maltsters were exhausting the union's funds.[44]

In mid-December the A. F. of L. held its annual convention, and came to the aid of Local 9 with a national boycott on Milwaukee beer.[45] Pamphlets explaining the boycott were distributed to all A. F. of L. members. Within two weeks, the

---

[40] Klinkert was a brewing company in Racine, Wisconsin.
[41] Milwaukee *Daily Review,* Dec. 5, 1887.
[42] *Evening Wisconsin,* Dec. 6, 1887.
[43] *Daily Review,* Dec. 9, 1887.
[44] *Freie Presse,* Dec. 13, 1887. Scrapbook clipping.
[45] A. F. of L., *Report of Proceedings* [1887], p. 19.

Knights of Labor added its support. The pamphlets distributed and the resolutions passed by the various unions were written for propaganda value rather than for accuracy. They omitted the true cause of the difficulty and appealed to the public on the grounds that nonunion beer was bad or unhealthy. A typical poster read: "Milwaukee non-union beer contains more water and chemical substances than malt and hops, take care of your health!" [46] Bakers Union, No. 49, in Chicago, resolved that the unusual amount of sicknesses among its members came from drinking Milwaukee beer. [47]

The net effect of these campaigns can easily be overestimated. There were less than half a million members in the A. F. of L. and the Knights, together, out of some fifteen million workers. Many unorganized workers and practically all middle-class people resented union activities, and might actually go out of the way to buy boycotted beer. The books of the Pabst Company fail to show more than seasonal variation in volume, although the expansion of their business was so rapid during this period that it is hard to tell what should have constituted normal sales.

Up to mid-January 1888 the Brewers' Association had taken no steps against union employees who quietly worked at their jobs. But when St. Louis beer was served exclusively at the Brewery Workers' Masked Ball, one of the great annual social events of Milwaukee, the brewers decided the time had come to strike back. [48] They demanded that their employees resign from the union, and discharged at least some of those who refused. While the Best Company discharged twenty-two men, management claimed the dismissals were due to seasonal requirements. A declaration signed by 150 employees attested that Best "did not use any force at all" in getting them to cancel their union membership. [49]

[46] *Daily Review*, Jan. 9, 1888.
[47] *Daily Review*, Dec. 31, 1887.
[48] *Daily Review*, Jan. 25, 1888.
[49] *Daily Review*, Jan. 25, 1888; *Evening Journal*, Jan. 26, 1888 (scrapbook clipping).

The brewers' action virtually ended the existence of Local 9 under Elsner's leadership. Best claimed they had enough beer on hand to last two months and, presumably, most of the other brewers were equally well prepared. To strike would have been hopeless, and the workers had no choice but to give way. The *Evening Journal* editorialized:

That the brewer's union has met with a Waterloo is admitted on all sides. Public opinion in this conflict has been entirely with the bosses, who, it was admitted, could no longer countenance this organization. . . . . It is very probable that a new organization will be effected, but the main features will be support in cases of sickness, and all the bosses have promised their assistance.

Everything went on smoothly in the breweries today, and no further disruption between bosses and men is looked for.[50]

The blow to organized labor in Milwaukee was severe. Charles Nicholaus, Milwaukee organizer of the brewery workers, looking back fifty years later, wrote:

It must not be overlooked that the brewing industry was the largest in Milwaukee and its thorough unionization had a tremendous influence on the unionization of other workers. From 1885 to 1886 it was a continuous struggle to keep the organization alive. Then followed the general lock-out in 1887 which lasted for four years.[51]

As the Captain explained the situation: "The employing brewers do not want to reduce wages or increase working hours, but they intend to free themselves from the dictates of the union."[52] The executives of the United States Brewers' Association issued a circular dated February 1, 1888, calling upon its members "to do all they may be called upon to do and all that is in their power in order to sustain the brewers of Milwaukee in their opposition to the despotic rule of the outspoken anarchists who are today leading and misleading the workmen in our employment."[53]

[50] *Evening Journal,* Jan. 24, 1888. Scrapbook clipping.
[51] *Brewery Worker,* XLI, No. 35 (Aug. 29, 1936), 3.
[52] *Brewers' Journal,* XII, No. 7 (May 1, 1888), 270.
[53] *Brewers' Journal,* XII, No. 5 (Mar. 1, 1888), 174.

The union met similar defeats in the other large cities in 1887 and 1888, and although the national labor organizations continued the boycott, it coincided with a period of major advance in the sales of the shipping brewers.

CAPTAIN PABST REVIVES THE UNION

From 1886 to 1891, Pabst and Anheuser-Busch were racing neck and neck for national leadership. A few thousand barrels diverted from one to the other could decide the coveted position in these years. The A. F. of L. adroitly seized upon this situation in 1889 as a means of re-establishing the brewers union in the Middle West. The general boycott was abandoned and, aside from the "pool brewers" of New York City,[54] only Anheuser-Busch, Schlitz, and Lemp were banned.[55] By the following year, the A. F. of L. boycott was being enforced only against Pabst and Anheuser-Busch. Posters were distributed in both English and German such as the following:[56]

Patronize Home Industry

Union Men—Friends of
Organized Labor
Ask For
Erie Union Beer!

Do Not Drink

Anheuser-Busch
(St. Louis)
Pabst Br. Co.   unhealthy Scab Beer
(Milwaukee)

In this way, the A. F. of L. secured a certain amount of bargaining power even though it no longer had strength in the

---

[54] Brewery owners in New York City and vicinity who had united in 1887 in order to act together against the workers are referred to as "pool brewers." Schlüter, p. 241.

[55] A. F. of L., *Report of Proceedings* [1889], p. 41.

[56] Handbill in English and German circulated by local labor unions in Erie, Pa. Scrapbook clipping.

brewing industry. Neither the Captain nor Adolphus Busch cared much whether Schlitz or Lemp gained or lost 10,000 barrels, but they were vitally interested in the slightest deviation in each other's sales. Busch probably suffered more than Pabst because the boycott of the Knights of Labor, which was still in force, was more effective in the South which was largely Anheuser-Busch sales territory.

The United States Brewers' Association retaliated against the A. F. of L. and the Knights by resolving "that at the expiration of existing contracts no new agreements shall be made with any Brewery Workingmen's Unions." [57] But no action seems to have resulted, and Pabst's credit manager, Pierce, claimed that his company hired men without regard to union status.[58]

By the summer of 1891, Busch apparently decided that he could regain first place in the industry and also improve his position in the British syndicate negotiations (see pp. 157-58) by ending the Knights' boycott. After some negotiations, he recognized a Knights of Labor local and signed a contract; and the Knights withdrew their boycott on September 25.[59]

The Captain countered this move by making peace with the A. F. of L., and asked that an organizer be sent to Milwaukee. At a meeting on November 30, attended mainly by Pabst employees, a new A. F. of L. local was set up.[60] The original local was made up of Pabst, Miller, Falk, Jung and Borchert, Cream City, and Gettelman. But Schlitz and Blatz quickly followed suit and, at another meeting, set up a second local which united with the first under a single set of officers.[61] The teamsters and coopers at this time set up separate organizations affiliated with the National Union of United Brewery Workmen.[62]

---

[57] Circular, dated Mar. 26, 1888, issued by the U.S.B.A., *Convention Proceedings* [1888], p. 21.

[58] *Daily Review*, Sept. 26, 1888.

[59] Schlüter, p. 178.

[60] *Daily News*, Dec. 1, 1891.

[61] *Daily News*, Dec. 3 and 17, 1891.

[62] *Daily News*, Dec. 10, 11, 12, 1891.

On December 12 the A. F. of L. convention at Birmingham lifted the boycott on Pabst beer, and the Captain wrote to his old friend, Fred Kiesel: "The boycott is lifted and everything is lovely. Busch thought he had it salted for us, but he didn't quite succeed." [63]

This ended important labor troubles in the Pabst Company until 1922 when prohibition and depression upset the continual renegotiation of contracts. The Knights maintained the Pabst boycott until the spring of 1892 but, since their total membership was now only about 100,000 workers, it was a matter of no great importance. The Federated Trades Council of Milwaukee, after expressing opinions that Anheuser-Busch was at the bottom of the Knights' action, ordered the following unanimous resolution sent to President Gompers of the A. F. of L.

Whereas, the executive board of Knights of Labor in session at Pittsburgh, Pennsylvania, May 14, 1892, placed a boycott upon the Pabst beer of Milwaukee in favor of Anheuser-Busch beer of St. Louis, alleging that Pabst beer is a non-union product; Whereas, the situation relative to the employment of labor by the two breweries is as follows: The Pabst Brewing Company's beer is an exclusively made union product. All its ingredients are prepared by union labor, while the malt used by the Anheuser-Busch company, as alleged, is bought largely at malt-houses located in small towns, where non-union labor is employed at a greatly reduced figure. The Anheuser-Busch labor which is represented both in the union and the Knights of Labor operates under the jurisdiction of the International Brewers' Association. Resolved, That it is the sense of this council, that it is the duty of all organized labor to give the same protection to employees of such labor in the distribution and sale of their products that is demanded by such labor of employers in the recognition and employment of such organized labor. Resolved, That inasmuch as we know the charge that Pabst beer is a non-union beer to be utterly false and without foundation and believe that the boycott placed at Pittsburgh has been incited and instigated by and through the agents of the Anheuser-Busch Com-

[63] Letter, Dec. 15, 1891.

pany because of the rivalry existing between it and the Pabst Company, we hereby appeal in the interest of fairness to the Pabst Company as well as in the interest of organized labor which cannot prosper under the employment of such diverse and unfair methods, to the International Brewers Union to demand that the executive committee of the Knights of Labor lift immediately said boycott, and that widespread public announcement be made of the same when done.[64]

A week later General Secretary Hayes of the Knights denied that any boycott was being maintained against Pabst beer, and the critical period of unionization in Milwaukee brewing came to an end.[65]

THE STRUGGLE FOR INDUSTRIAL UNIONS

During the years from 1891 to 1919, the United Brewery Workmen and the associated Milwaukee brewers worked out the techniques of collective bargaining with great success. There is perhaps no other example in American history of a period of such harmonious relations between nine associated employers and several thousand employees. The practices and traditions developed at this time have, in general, come down to the present day.

A primary necessity for such orderly bargaining was a strong union. Brewers, as we have seen, were no more anxious to divide authority over labor conditions with a union than were other employers, but the Milwaukee firms were quicker than many in recognizing the advantage of having contented workers and a responsible union leadership that could handle inter-craft disputes. The continued renewal of union contracts, therefore, depended on the ability of the United Brewery Workmen leaders to maintain a strong and harmonious local union that not only could back up its demands with unified action, but could guarantee that its commitments would be fulfilled.

The Brewery Workmen did not achieve this position easily;

64 Daily News, May 20, 1892.
65 Evening Wisconsin, May 28, 1892.

indeed, the relatively peaceful history of their relations in Milwaukee tends to distort the story of their struggles to achieve their Milwaukee position elsewhere. Not only did brewers in St. Louis, Cincinnati, Philadelphia, and New York continue to fight the union throughout most of the nineties, but there were serious troubles within the union as well.

The first of these was the continuation of the jurisdictional fight between the A. F. of L. and the Knights. In 1893 the Brewery Workmen became Trade District 35 of the Knights of Labor, although many of the locals remained affiliated with the A. F. of L. and not with the Knights, depending largely on which group was established in the local community. After three years of rivalry for control between the rising A. F. of L. and the declining Knights, the former demanded that Trade District 35 be dissolved and the complete authority of the A. F. of L. be recognized. Adherence to this demand marked the end of the official connection of the national brewery workers union with the Knights, although some locals continued their affiliation for a short while.[66]

Between 1893 and 1908, the brewery workers fought and won a battle for industrial unionism within the A. F. of L. similar to the one that the Committee for Industrial Organization— now the Congress of Industrial Organizations—was to lose, on a much larger scale, in the 1930's. As soon as the brewery workers had demonstrated their strength, the international craft unions such as the teamsters, firemen, and steam engineers tried to separate their respective crafts from the all-embracing brewery workers union. Although the members of the crafts in the breweries steadily voted to stick with their fellow workers, the powerful national craft unions won the support of A. F. of L. top leadership. The order issued to the Brewery Workmen to release the engineers and firemen in 1902 was followed by continuous pressure from the teamsters' unions from 1904 to 1906.[67]

[66] Schlüter, pp. 216-18.
[67] Schlüter, p. 226.

20

But the engineers, firemen, and teamsters refused to leave the Brewery Workmen and they were sustained by a general vote in other branches of the national union.[68] On June 1, 1907, therefore, the A. F. of L. revoked the Brewery Workmen's charter and banned beer drinking to all union workmen.[69] The Brewery Workmen now turned to the new Industrial Workers of the World, whose socialist leanings generally accorded with the political views of the German leaders of the United Brewery Workmen. Seeing that the Brewery Workmen, at this time one of the strongest unions in the country, was quite capable of acting independently, the A. F. of L. backed down and restored the charter February 24, 1908.[70]

Trouble also arose early between the Brewery Workmen and the various skilled craft unions whose members had no connection with brewing but who still worked in the breweries. Chief among these were the building trade-unions which quarreled with the Brewery Workmen over jurisdiction, and with the brewery owners over pay. As Schlitz was adding rapidly to its equipment during these years, the main trouble occurred there. Fred Pabst thought that it might be necessary to form an employers association in addition to the trade associations in order to handle the bewildering complexity of the new labor relations. In June of 1898, he wrote to August Busch:

You have probably heard there is a great deal of friction between the Building Trades Council and Schlitz Brewing Company. In fact, a boycott has been declared vs. Schlitz as they have openly placed them on the black list which is virtually the same as a boycott. . . . . If we glory in the trouble of others and do not look at the situation magnanimously, these labor troubles will continue to increase, and become an unbearable nuisance. We were well started to form a protection association, and if the Anheuser-Busch Brewery [sic]

---

[68] *Sentinel,* June 1, 1907. Scrapbook clipping.
[69] *American Federationist,* XIV, No. 7 (July 1907), 483.
[70] A. F. of L., *Report of Proceedings* [1908], p. 71.

Association would attach their signature to the agreement, we soon could get sufficient signatures to bring the agreement into effect.[71]

The employers association was never formed, and trouble continued. In 1901, the Building Trades Council boycotted Schlitz on the question of jurisdiction over men doing plumbing work in the brewery, a hard province to define in an industry where adding water and washing form so large a part of the operations. The Federated Trades Council of Milwaukee objected to the boycott and the Brewery Workmen officially denounced it.[72] The Milwaukee Brewers' Association abrogated their agreements with the Building Trades.[73] Ultimately the A. F. of L. executive council sustained Schlitz, and the Building Trades Council gave way.[74]

During the whole period from 1891 to 1905, Pabst's relations with the Brewery Workmen had been harmonious. The high esteem in which the company was held by the A. F. of L. executives was demonstrated in the coopers' trouble of 1899. The editor of the *American Federationist* writes:

The Pabst Brewing Company is well-known as a strictly union concern employing several hundred union men, and as a fair-dealing firm, having contracts with unions of no less than thirteen trades, besides that of the brewers. The company having experienced a great increase in business, it recently became necessary for the firm to obtain an increased supply of barrels. The local Coopers' Union admitted that it was impossible for its members to produce a sufficient number, and the company then bought all the union made barrels obtainable, which purchases, however, proved inadequate to meet the demand.

In this emergency, the company asked permission to operate the machinery that at the suggestion of the union it had purchased the year previous, agreeing to employ thereon none but union men working 8 hours per day, at full union wages. The union refused to grant this request, and incredible as it may seem, suggested that the

[71] Letter, June 14, 1898.
[72] *Sentinel,* July 28 and Aug. 20, 1901.
[73] *Sentinel,* July 30, 1901.
[74] *Sentinel,* Oct. 11, 1901.

company buy barrels made by non-union men and boys, whether made by hand or machine. This refusal was followed quickly by the union in question sending circulars throughout the country in which the company was denounced as an unfair concern.

Such was the lamentable situation when information from the most reliable sources reached this office that unless justice was done the Pabst Brewing Company, all coopers employed in the Milwaukee Breweries would be locked out, all existing contracts with unions would be revoked, and that employers generally in Milwaukee would, and did refuse to enter into agreements with unions. A most thorough investigation was instituted, and the company was proven blameless.

Repeated efforts to adjust the difficulty having failed, owing to the unconciliatory attitude maintained by the Coopers' Union, the Executive Council of the American Federation of Labor has declared to the organization in question and now declares to organized labor and the public generally, that the action of the Coopers' Union toward the Pabst Brewing Company to be both irrational and unjust.

When the above declaration was made known to the Coopers' Union of Milwaukee, the A. F. of L. office was advised by telegraph by President Teney of the Coopers' International Union that the "boycott" on Pabst Brewing Company was withdrawn, and that he, President Teney, would see to it that the above is carried out. Much to the general regret, however, it is learned that the Milwaukee Coopers' Union has violated the official declaration of its own duly constituted officers, and in spite of an open avowal to withdraw its attack on the company, is maintaining its hostile attitude in every way within its power. This is as unfair as it is unjust and indefensible.[75]

A GENERATION OF HARMONIOUS RELATIONS

While New York and Philadelphia brewers continued to resist the union shop on into the twentieth century, there was no such attitude in Milwaukee. When in August of 1901 a report

[75] *American Federationist*, VI, No. 9 (Sept. 1899), 164-65.

reached Milwaukee that the Brewers' Association had issued a circular calling for a general lockout of the union because of New York and Philadelphia troubles, Gustav Pabst stated:

Our relations with our workmen are friendly and we have a year's contract with them, which we have no intention of breaking. We would be ready to renew it at any time. I have no idea where the report came from. There is certainly no way for the lockout to reach Milwaukee, as we would not join in a movement of this kind. We have no grievance against our men.[76]

The same sentiment was shared by the workers. "In Milwaukee," said Charles Nicholaus, the delegate to the convention of Brewery Workmen, "the brewery workmen are well organized, probably the best in the country. . . . . We have no fear whatever of any trouble in Milwaukee and we have not worried about the threat from the East." [77]

At the Saratoga meeting of the Brewers' Association in 1902, the employer advocates of collective bargaining won a victory and, instead of pursuing forceful antiunion tactics, the convention at the request of the national union set up a three-man board for labor arbitration with Gustav Pabst as a member, along with Otto Stifel of St. Louis and Rudolph J. Schaefer of New York.[78] The aim of this board was to work toward an over-all agreement between the members of the Association and the United Brewery Workmen.

A week later, in Milwaukee, a new three-year union contract between the workers and the Milwaukee brewers was agreed to. Six weeks before the old contract was to expire, on May 1, 1902, Gustav Pabst had led the way among the brewers in expressing his willingness to grant the eight-hour day.[79] The contract as finally agreed upon on June 20 called for: the eight-hour day for all but the teamsters; a general 10 per cent wage

---

[76] *Sentinel*, Aug. 25, 1901. Scrapbook clipping.
[77] *Sentinel*, Sept. 5, 1901. Scrapbook clipping.
[78] *One Hundred Years of Brewing*, p. 568. See also *Sentinel*, Apr. 13, 1902.
[79] *Journal*, Apr. 21, 1902. Scrapbook clipping.

increase; slack season rotation of work; and a continuance of the former arbitration clause. In return, the workers allowed the foremen to leave the union, conceded the employers' right to hire and fire if reasons for discharge were stated in writing, and agreed to substitute March for May as the termination date of the three-year contract.[80] The *Milwaukee Sentinel* discussing the contract noted:

This year the contract will contain a clause to include women who work in breweries, also the employees of the bottling department.

Brewery workers now have 8 hour day and wages on 9 hour basis so that their situation is better than that of any other trade.[81]

The unions covered by this and subsequent contracts were: Brewers Local 9, Bottlers Local 213, Teamsters Local 72, and Engineers and Firemen Local 25, all affiliates of the United Brewery Workmen, A. F. of L. The coopers and machinists were covered by separate contracts.[82]

The negotiations at the termination of the contract in 1905 were accompanied by a short strike, and much worker dissatisfaction with the terms finally agreed to on April 9 by the union leaders.[83] The increase in general prices after 1897 put a steady pressure on real wages, and at each contract renewal a problem arose regarding whether the raise granted covered the rise in the cost of living. Some of the men felt that the horizontal 50 cents a week increase was inadequate in a four-year contract. An outstanding gain for the cause of unionism was scored, however, as far as men were concerned, in the recognition of the closed shop in the bottling department.[84] This last provision, of course, opened the door to the replacement of men by nonunion women, but after two years of operation, Charles

---

[80] *Sentinel*, June 20 and 21, 1902. Scrapbook clippings.
[81] *Sentinel*, May 1, 1902. Scrapbook clipping.
[82] *Sentinel*, July 1, 1902. Scrapbook clipping.
[83] *Milwaukee County Historical News*, Apr. 9, 1905. Scrapbook clipping.
[84] *American Brewer*, XXXVIII, No. 8 (Aug. 1905), 401.

Henning vigorously denied that women were replacing men in the bottling department.[85]

WAGES PAID, 1905-1918

(Weekly)

Classification	Four-Year Contract 1905-1909	Three-Year Contract 1909-1912	One-Year Contract 1912-1913	Three-Year Contract 1915-1918
Beer bottlers	$12.00	$13.00	$15.00	....
Machine boys (bottling)	.90 (per day)	1.50 (per day)	....	....
Malthouse men	15.00	16.00	....	$18.50
Malt millers	16.00	16.50	....	....
Cellarmen	15.00	16.00	....	20.00
Brewhouse men	15.00	16.00	16.00-18.00	20.00
Washhouse men	14.00	14.50	....	....
Pitch yeast men	14.00	14.50	....	18.50
Grain driers	13.00	14.00	....	18.50
Icemen, pump men, coolers, yeast men	16.00	16.50	....	18.00
Engineers	17.00	17.50	17.50-19.50	21.50
Firemen	15.00	15.50	17.50-19.50	19.50
Boiler washers, shaving burners, condenser washers, coal passers	....	14.84	....	19.50
Teamsters	14.00	14.50	15.00-18.00	....
Stablemen	13.50	14.00	15.00-18.00	18.00
Peddlar-Chauffeurs	....	...	....	20.00
Girls	3.00	...	6.00-7.50	10.00

The contracts themselves have been destroyed. The above data is from the newspapers.[86] On May 8, 1909, a new three-year contract was negotiated after four weeks of conferences. The wage increases, as shown in the above table, were again the results of a compromise. The demands for three instead of two quarts of free beer a day and Election Day as a holiday were given up, although an additional day off each month was won for the engineers. The rotation system of slack season lay-offs was abolished and the old system, based largely on seniority, was resumed. The Brewery Workmen's locals recognized the right of the coopers and machinists to separate contracts. Per-

[85] *Sentinel,* Apr. 16, 1907.
[86] Contracts of 1905-1909 and 1909-1912 are from the *Sentinel,* Mar. 9, 1909; contract of 1912-1913 from the *Sentinel,* Mar. 11, 1912; contract of 1915-1918 from the *Sentinel,* Mar. 13, 1915. Scrapbook clippings.

haps the most interesting feature of the contract was its adoption for the first time by a referendum of the workers with the breweries closed during the voting.[87]

A strike of the building trades in May of 1909 led to the first collective contract covering all locals in American building-trade history, and presumably settled the jurisdictional disputes that had harassed the brewers since the late nineties.[88]

In the spring of 1910, the bottlers union started taking in women whose wages previously had been defined, but who had not been union members. The newly organized women demanded higher wages. Both Schlitz and Pabst at first resisted this unprecedented demand for female rights, but the union forced a compromise. A contract was negotiated for the women and girls that would become effective at the next contract date, March 1, 1912. The new women's local was recognized, and their wage demands of $6.00 a week for the first three months in the labeling department, where beginners fifteen to eighteen years old were employed, and $6.50 thereafter, and a rate of $7.50 a week elsewhere in the plant were met.[89]

The contract of March 10, 1912, contained wage increases of $2.00 to $4.00 a week, but ran for one year only. Apprenticeship arrangements were clearly defined for the first time to meet the charge that excessive apprentice labor was being used. In the brewery there could be one apprentice for every twenty men. His wages would be $12.00 a week for the first year and $12.50 thereafter. In the bottle house the ratio could be one for each two men, and the wage $9.00.[90] Thus, both the employers and the union preserved the idea that brewing was a skilled craft, and both felt they profited by it.

No mention has been found of the 1913 to 1915 contract in the newspapers or elsewhere, so we may presume that no important changes were made.

[87] *Sentinel,* Mar. 9, 1909. Scrapbook clipping.
[88] *Sentinel,* May 28 and 30, 1909. Scrapbook clipping.
[89] *Sentinel,* May 23 and 25, 1910. Scrapbook clipping.
[90] *Sentinel,* Mar. 11, 1912. Scrapbook clipping. See also *American Brewers' Review,* XXVI, No. 4 (Apr. 1, 1912), 173.

The negotiations of 1915 illustrated the advanced methods of bargaining that had been evolved in Milwaukee labor relations. After a week of conferences, the Brewers' Association framed a counter proposal to the original union demands for higher wages. This was voted on by the men, on March 7, and rejected. The Association then offered another proposal that was duly voted on and rejected March 10. With the negotiations stalled, the workers staged a one-day strike to show their support of their leaders. On March 12, a compromise was reached (see wage-rates table, p. 299). At the conclusion, the veteran labor negotiator, Charles Nicholaus, said: "There never was a more friendly feeling between the employers and employees than there is now." [91]

The final preprohibition contract carrying further wage increases was negotiated without difficulty in 1918.

The coming of prohibition ended the old United Brewery Workmen and brought this uniquely successful period of labor relations to a close. Industrial unionization had worked smoothly, in Milwaukee brewing at least, for twenty-seven years during which there had been only about a month of time lost in strikes. The chief difficulties had come with the auxiliary workers having separate craft organizations, but even these had finally worked out most of their jurisdictional conflicts. Pabst had not only led the way in forming the locals of the Union of Brewery Workmen, but under the conciliatory leadership of Gustav Pabst, the company had done much to secure continuous harmony.

[91] *Sentinel,* Mar. 13, 1915. Scrapbook clipping.

CHAPTER XII

THE PROHIBITION MOVEMENT

THE banning of a major industry of hundreds of years' standing by action of the national government was unprecedented in the history of American business up to 1918. "There is no analogy in the history of any labor organization, or any nation," wrote the officers of the brewers union in 1920, "in which hundreds of thousands of men were deliberately deprived by the state and the nation of their employment and business, without a semblance of consideration of the wishes of the people." [1] Yet this action, taken without compensation to workers or stockholders, was carried out in the nation that has been the chief respecter of private enterprise and property rights. Why should an action so unusual have occurred in apparently the least likely place?

Looking back upon the later phases of the prohibition movement, scholarly observers have seen that it was only partially a fight against liquor, and still less a campaign for temperance. No study of the liquor problem with a view to finding workable solutions to the evil of drunkenness was undertaken by American enthusiasts bent on destroying breweries, wineries, and distilleries. Their solution, complete elimination of human practices as old as recorded history, was one never attempted by any other nation. A social campaign apparently so irrational and contrary to American ideals at once raises a suspicion that the surface does not reveal the inner motives of the movement.

In the case of prohibition, conflicts deeply embedded in American culture contributed their repressed power to the crusade. The antipathy of country to city, of native to foreigner, of Protestant to Catholic, and of rigid Puritan to urbane gentleman were all mixed in varying proportion from one rural district to another. Beer, a drink so mild that its consumption has

[1] *Brewery, Flour, Cereal and Soft Drink Workers' Journal*, XXXV. No. 22 (Sept. 18, 1920), 1.

been encouraged by most civilized nations, unfortunately became entangled in these folk prejudices. Beer is regarded as a traditional native drink in all western European countries; but in America, it could be branded as German and foreign due to the fact that the mild lager made by the mid-nineteenth-century immigrants had largely superseded the stronger native product. Furthermore, in turning their attack against the saloon, a largely urban and hence partially Catholic institution, the fanatics linked beer indiscriminately with wine, whisky, and popery.

THE EARLY PROHIBITION MOVEMENT

The attacks upon "foreign" culture in Milwaukee by settlers from New York and New England in the decade of the fifties have been described in Chapter II. Then "foreign" beer was linked with German free thought rather than with Catholicism, but the challenge to a narrow and overzealous American Protestantism was the same. This early movement was reflected in the nation as a whole as a mixture of nativism and temperance enthusiasm that led thirteen states, during the fifties, to adopt some type of prohibitory legislation before the movement was lost in the larger excitement of the sectional struggle. Only seven of the acts remained on the statute books at the end of the decade.

From 1860 to 1880, only three states were continuously dry. But the prohibition movement was no more dead than were the forces that prompted it. From 1869 on, the national Prohibition party ran candidates in presidential and many state elections. In Wisconsin the movement was given political impetus by a rural Protestant order known as the Grand Lodge of the Good Templars. Unable to muster the legislative following necessary for a prohibitory act, they won a compromise in the form of the Graham Law of 1872, requiring a $2,000 bond from licensed liquor sellers on which they could be sued for any of a long list of possible civil offenses.[2]

2 Act passed Mar. 28, 1872, *Wisconsin General Laws*, chap. 127, p. 171.

This act produced organized resistance by the Wisconsin brewers who met in Milwaukee August 6, 1873, and resolved to hold the governor as well as the Republican party responsible for the Graham Law and for the "pietistical and nativist demonstrations that have been made during the last year." [3] In the ensuing election campaign in which they backed Democrat A. N. Taylor for governor, the brewers appear to have been careful to dissociate themselves from the hard-liquor interests, and to emphasize that they stood for true temperance.[4] This stand was much easier to maintain in this period when breweries in general were not involved in saloon ownership. Although one historian thinks that the Graham Law was the most important single element in the election,[5] Governor Taylor's victory was no real test of antiprohibition sentiment as Grangers and liberal Republicans, for reasons that had little or nothing to do with beer, joined with the brewers in supporting the Democrats.

The Woman's Christian Temperance Union was founded in Ohio in 1874 to work, not for temperance as its name implies, but for completely prohibitory legislation. Appealing to the increasing group of middle-class women who had the leisure and energy for social activity, the league rapidly gained a large following outside the big cities. It set about to organize the millions of Protestant churchwomen for a crusade against all liquor. It carried the fight into the public schools through a juvenile branch, and supplied for courses on physiology fanciful textbooks showing the evil effects of alcohol. The wave of prohibition legislation that struck the Middle West in the eighties was to a considerable extent a result of the work of the W.C.T.U.

In 1881 Kansas wrote an absolute prohibition clause into the state constitution, South Carolina adopted a liquor-control sys-

<hr>

[3] *Sentinel*, Aug. 7, 1873.
[4] *Sentinel*, Oct. 24, 1873.
[5] William Francis Raney, *Wisconsin: A Story of Progress*, p. 268.

tem, and Illinois established local option. Local option provisions allowed each county or township in the state to decide the liquor sales question for itself. By refusing to grant licenses, the locality could prevent public sale, but could not prevent private individuals from receiving or consuming liquor. Between 1883 and 1887, a majority of the counties of West Virginia and Maryland adopted such no-license provisions, and Georgia, Mississippi, and Missouri passed general local option laws. During the same period, Iowa, Rhode Island, and the Dakotas went totally dry. The Dakotas and little Rhode Island were not particularly important from the Milwaukee standpoint, but Iowa was one of Pabst's big markets. Finally, in 1887 the "writing on the wall" appeared when Senator Blair of New Hampshire introduced a prohibition amendment to the Federal Constitution.[6]

Neither state prohibition nor local option could prevent the shipment of out-of-state products to private consumers and, hence, had little effect on sales of hard liquor which was either ordered direct from a distiller or sold in speak-easies, then called "blind tigers."[7] State or local laws designed to eliminate the saloon, however, had a very depressing effect on beer sales. In states where the drys could not gain a majority for either local option or state prohibition, they often were able to pass high license laws requiring saloonkeepers to pay $500 to $1,000 annually. While these laws concentrated drinking in larger saloons, a good thing in itself, they also forced the brewers into the saloon business and saloon ownership, since many of the smaller proprietors had to borrow from the brewers in order to pay for their licenses. The brewery could not risk being responsible for a license where it had no control over the establishment; and, therefore, in many instances the brewery bought the property, licensed it, and leased it to the former proprietor.

A compromise solution to the liquor problem was tried in

[6] Fletcher Dobyns, The Amazing Story of Repeal, p. 227.
[7] For court decisions, see Robert E. Cushman, Leading Constitutional Decisions, pp. 217-25.

South Carolina which allowed beer to be sold by private retailers but limited the sale of hard liquors to state-owned dis-
pensaries. While similar to the systems adopted with success by
many European countries, the plan failed to function satisfactorily, partly because of the American dislike of government
business activity, a bad administrative setup, and the unenforci-
bility of such a system by a single state.[8]

APATHY OF THE BREWERS

Democratic legislatures are bound to give way to well-organ-
ized pressure groups unless counter pressures are applied. As
Professor Odegard says in his scholarly study of the prohibition
question:

Democracy without organization is inconceivable, and public
opinion that is unorganized is likely to be evanescent and ineffective. . . . . Within the matrices of the major parties minor
associations are formed which, without regard for party opinion on
other matters, carry on agitation for or against projects deemed
favorable or prejudicial to their interests.[9]

The brewers were undoubtedly too slow in organizing pressure
counter to the W.C.T.U. and other prohibition organizations.
With waves of fanatical opposition rising around it, the
United States Brewers' Association refused to be alarmed, and
voted only such trifling sums as five or ten thousand dollars a
year for publication purposes. Occasionally as much as $5,000
might be appropriated to fight a state election but, during the
nineteenth century, no continuous, large-scale, educational campaign was carried on to win public sentiment to the support of
beer.[10] While their enemies were raising an army of devoted
workers among the general public, the brewers foolishly trusted
in their passive friends and general public inertia.

[8] Frederic H. Wines and John Koren, *The Liquor Problem in Its Legislative Aspects,* pp. 161 ff.
[9] Peter Odegard, *Pressure Politics: The Story of the Anti-Saloon League,* p. vii.
[10] For appropriation in 1881, see letter from Louis Schade to Captain Pabst, July 23, 1881; for 1887 appropriation, see *Evening Wisconsin,* May 26, 1887.

To a considerable degree, the brewers were hindered by having to fight adversaries who could not be brought into the open. In so far as prohibition was an antiurban, antiforeign, and anti-Catholic movement, it could not be adequately met by rational arguments in favor of beer. Possibly the recognition of this situation accounts for the brewers' lack of interest in trying to win favorable public opinion. In 1887, at the height of the national wave of prohibition excitement, a brewers' meeting in Milwaukee, for example, called to discuss means of combating the movement, was but thinly attended. L. C. G. Brandt, the presiding officer, said:

It shows that the enthusiastic feeling is gone. I am sorry for this because there is as much danger now as there was a year ago or two years ago, and the threatened danger will increase from year to year. I suppose a good many of the delegates stayed at home, feeling a sense of security because the President of the United States, on his recent visit here, joined our society indirectly, of course.

This reference to President Cleveland's having drunk beer at Best's brewery called out applause.

We feel grateful, of course, to the President, continued Mr. Brandt, for he has aided our cause greatly, directly and indirectly. But we should not drop our efforts for all that, for there is danger around us.[11]

At no time did the United States Brewers' Association represent as many as half of the brewers, and often paid-up membership sank to one-third that number. Brewing was essentially small local business and, unless laws threatened the individual brewer's immediate locality, it was hard to get him to contribute.

National shipping breweries, such as Pabst, of course recognized their responsibilities and economic necessities; and their generous contributions to extra funds for fighting prohibition were the main reliance of the Association. Each of the large brewers had also to contribute to his local association. During

[11] *Sentinel,* Oct. 13, 1887.

the eighties, contributions to the local Milwaukee association ran about a cent a barrel, and additional personal contributions were undoubtedly made on occasion by the Captain to aid the antiprohibition movement in neighboring states.[12] But the problem of building active public support of brewing could not have been solved by money alone. The brewers needed a positive program and an emotionally appealing slogan, neither of which was developed prior to 1918.

It was due more to the failure of existing legislation and the public's growing apathy than to any effective work on the part of the liquor interests that prohibition reached a low ebb by the early nineties. The second wave of prohibition fanaticism, like the earlier one of the fifties, had receded.

Antiliquor laws were being repealed, and brewers and distillers were settling back secure in the illusion that the public, having gone through its period of experimentation, would henceforth reject measures against the use of mild stimulants. While the producers were relaxing, however, the most powerful pressure group of the whole period was being organized directly under their noses.

THE ANTI-SALOON LEAGUE OF AMERICA

The Anti-Saloon League of America, fathered by the Reverend H. H. Russell of Berea, Ohio, finally discovered the precise formula for joining all the varied motives involved in prohibition in support of a unified national campaign. Russell, apparently a religious psychopath, thought that he approached the crusade at the direct guidance of God. Addressing the League's fifteenth convention at Columbus in 1913, he said:

The Anti-Saloon movement was begun by Almighty God. . . . . It is very plain now that it was the hand of the Most High that turned my course toward that historic seat of reform [Oberlin College]. There for five years, God held me under the benign influences of the most militant college center where I could be trained

12 Annual Inventory Listings.

as a reformer and just where His guiding star would hang above the future cradle of reform. . . . . At a Conneaut, Ohio, church in the winter of 1893, a pastor introducing me to his congregation said: "There was a man sent from God whose name was John; it is equally true there was a man sent from God whose name was Russell! " In the awed silence of my heart, I was compelled to believe the statement was true.[18]

The Anti-Saloon League was organized nationally in 1895 and was a league of all temperance organizations and churches favoring prohibition. It competed with none, but offered aid to all. Its formula was to bring the power of the affiliated church groups, largely Methodist, Baptist, Presbyterian, and Congregational, against the institution of the saloon.

Charged with being a political machine, the League has answered, "The church is a machine and the League is a machine within a machine." But they continue, "The ordinary political machine is built and maintained for the personal advantage of the biggest cogs in the machine. The Anti-Saloon League is so constructed that all personal advantage is submerged to the one task of establishing sobriety in the nation." The League was organized to give church people an effective political organization to fight the liquor traffic. The existing political parties, it was felt, left to their own devices, were hand and glove with the saloon. . . . .

If there be such a thing as black-washing, this is what the League did to the saloon. Its violent language could not have been calculated to appeal to the critical faculties of even the most abstemious. The League set itself the task of creating, through the instrumentality of a powerful propaganda, an emotional abhorrence of the saloon and the liquor traffic. To the sincere dry crusader a licensed system of selling liquor or a state-conducted saloon, such as was attempted in the South and is successfully being operated in England today, would be as intolerable as a licensed system of vice.[14]

The Anti-Saloon League during the years from 1905 to 1913 put its major emphasis on the winning of local option in the

[18] Quoted by Odegard, pp. 6-7, 9.
[14] Odegard, pp. 16, 39.

21

rural districts which eliminated the saloon, its avowed enemy, and built up dry political majorities. By 1906, thirty states had local option laws, and three had special systems of liquor control. Even in Wisconsin, more than six hundred small villages and townships had abolished saloons.[15] The movement did not stop the consumption of beer, as no laws, even in the dry states, prohibited the individual from drinking, but it continually added to the number of drinking voters who had no interest in saving the saloon.

From 1907 to 1910, there was a sharp upswing in prohibition legislation. In 1907, in Wisconsin, a hundred more communities abolished liquor licenses;[16] and for the first time in eighteen years, new states voted for complete prohibition—Georgia by act of its legislature, and Oklahoma in its first constitution. In the two following years, Mississippi, North Carolina, and Tennessee were added to the dry ranks, and in North Carolina, where the act was submitted to popular referendum, prohibition won a vote of two to one.

The most effective force behind this drive seems to have been the preaching of ministers in Southern Protestant churches. Through them, the League was effectively aligning all alcohol, even in the form of beer, with the devil.

THE FAILURE OF COMPROMISE

In the early years of the century, it seemed possible that some scheme of reasonable control of the liquor business might be worked out along European lines of government rationing and sale. A committee of fifty distinguished citizens, led by such men as Seth Low, reform mayor of New York, and Charles Eliot, long-time president of Harvard, issued a series of volumes, based on objective study of the liquor question, that supported the desirability of allowing the use of light wines and beer. In the summary volume published by the committee in 1905, John

---

[15] Ernest H. Cherrington, *The Evolution of Prohibition in the United States of America,* pp. 255-56.
[16] Cherrington, *Evolution of Prohibition,* p. 291.

S. Billings condemned the type of propaganda with which the W.C.T.U. and the Anti-Saloon League were indoctrinating children in the schools.

In view of what is known as to the effects of the moderate or occasional use of alcoholic drinks upon man, much of the methods and substance of the so-called scientific temperance instruction in public schools is unscientific and undesirable. It is not in accord with the opinions of a large majority of the leading physiologists of Europe as shown by the statements printed on page 18, volume 1, of the report on the *Physiological Aspects of the Liquor Problem.* This appears to us to be a matter of grave importance.[17]

Aside from the many, though confused, motives that gave the dry crusade its fanatical character, the greatest obstacle to effective control of liquor in the United States was the general American fear of governmental power. Systems like those in England, Sweden, or Norway where saloons were strictly controlled not only required strong and uniform governmental authority, but the latter two competed with private enterprise in hard-liquor distribution. Since none of the parties to the American controversy were ready to advocate this type of action, both sides were discouraged from attempting compromises.

THE BREWERS' DEFENSE

The attack on the saloons reduced the brewers to one of two methods of defense, either divorce beer from the hard-liquor selling saloon, or improve the saloon so that it would be less open to attack. Still overconfident of their position, they failed to pursue either method vigorously. Not until after 1914 was any continuous effort made in the brewers' defensive propaganda to dissociate beer from hard liquor. And even then it was weakened by the fact that the National Wholesale Liquor Dealers Association contributed one third of the money for a common defense fund.[18]

---

[17] Frances Greenwood Peabody, *The Liquor Problem*, p. 35.

[18] *Brewing and Liquor Interests and German Propaganda*, Senate Document, No. 62, 66th Congress, 1st session (1919), I, 66.

The old-fashioned saloon was vulnerable to attack, particularly by those who never went into them and hence imagined far worse conditions than actually existed. As John Koren, writing as an investigator for the Committee of Fifty, wrote of the Chicago saloons:

What is it one sees inside of the saloons? Not a riotous company intent upon reducing itself to intoxication, but, instead, a well-behaved little group of men who play cards together, read, smoke, and drink a glass of beer.[19]

But this was not the picture built up in the minds of the non-saloon-going public by the W.C.T.U., and later by the Anti-Saloon League.

The brewers undoubtedly put too much faith in contributions to party funds and in getting behind the right candidates. Fred J. Kiesel, for example, wrote Gustav Pabst on June 28, 1900:

From all I can learn Dubois will surely be the next senator for Idaho. I think it could be for the interest of the brewers to secure his cooperation—he is aggressive and able—if you think well of it— send me $1000-$5000. I think it will be the best investment you ever made. Wire to me at Ogden when you receive this.[20]

Such minor campaign contributions were no doubt needed to help counteract the expenditures of the Anti-Saloon League, but they did not necessarily affect the opinion of the general public; in a sense they were defensive, not aggressive expenditures.

After 1881 various agencies representing brewing opinion subsidized newspapers to print favorable articles, but here again the campaign pointed to no aggressive or positive program for reforming the liquor situation. In addition, the brewing appeals could not combat the campaigns of the Anti-Saloon League in such areas as the rural South. The brewers' literature, whether

---

[19] John Koren, *Economic Aspects of the Liquor Problem*, p. 214.
[20] Letter, June 28, 1900.

in newspapers or pamphlets, would not normally circulate there as it did in the larger towns, hence it was unavoidable that the country *v.* city nature of the issue became intensified.

After almost a generation of easily holding their own against the prohibition forces, it was hard in the prewar years to make the brewers aware of the cumulative force of the Anti-Saloon League campaign. As late as August 30, 1907, Charles Henning of Pabst told a *Sentinel* reporter that Milwaukee brewers were not represented at a meeting at Cincinnati to adopt measures to check local option in the South.

As far as I know no Milwaukee brewery was represented at any such meetings. What is more, I have not heard any Milwaukee brewer express himself one way or the other on legislation in the south unfriendly to the brewery interests.[21]

By 1909, the brewers were intensifying their efforts, although it is hard to say they were really alarmed. They relied increasingly upon reform of the saloon as the best means of combating the activity of the League. In 1908, Hugh Fox, secretary of the United States Brewers' Association, wrote:

Control, and not elimination, is the key to the solution of the saloon problem. . . . . The encouragement of beer-houses is most desirable. My own belief is that the system can only be operated successfully when brewers actually *own* and *operate* the places where their product is sold. At present, brewers finance most of the saloons but do not operate them or even actually control them. . . . . If the saloon keeper was the agent or employee of the brewer, he would have no interest in selling spirits.[22]

That a similar idea was shared by liberal sources outside the beer trade was indicated in articles such as that of *The Nation* entitled "Awakening of the Brewers."

The responsible agent in the liquor-selling business is not the man behind the bar, but the man behind the brewery. The direct respon-

---

[21] *Sentinel,* Aug. 30, 1907. Scrapbook clipping.
[22] Hugh Fox, "The Saloon Problem," *Annals of the American Academy of Political and Social Science,* XXXII (July-Dec. 1908), 532, 536.

sibility of the brewer for the character of the liquor traffic is not well recognized.[23]

But the brewers were not ready to go so far as either their secretary or *The Nation* urged in assuming complete responsibility for brewery-owned saloons. The Milwaukee brewers as a compromise developed the "Wisconsin idea" of vigilance committees to clean up or close disreputable establishments. The committee set up a bureau to take responsibility for the conduct of retail liquor selling in so far as violations of the law were concerned, but this was only one angle of the problem.[24] Meanwhile, the Liberty League and the Model License Leagues, supported by the brewing interests, were stirred to fresh activity.

In 1908 Gustav Pabst contributed an article to the nationally read *Cosmopolitan* magazine as one of a series on the prohibition question. The gist of his appeal was that: "The aim of civilization is to make men better and stronger by the exercise of will power, not by imposing arbitrary rules upon them. Temperance is civilization and intelligence. Prohibition is tyranny." [25] The editor allowed him to use his $200 compensation as a prize for the best letter discussing the *Cosmopolitan* articles.[26] The number of letters favorable to beer and unfavorable to statutory prohibition supported Gustav in his hope that the movement was losing ground.

The American Brewer advocated a program for making the drinkers more aware of the danger threatening them and mobilizing them to combat prohibition.

The American Brewer long ago suggested the formation of an organization of advocates of the moderate use of alcoholic beverages to successfully fight the prohibition agitation. Since that time dealers and merchants' leagues, liberty leagues, liberal Sunday leagues and so forth have been formed in various states; but still the concurrence of the great mass of the consumers is lacking. . . . .

---

23 *The Nation*, LXXXIX, No. 2306 (Sept. 9, 1909), 227-28.
24 *U.S.B.A. Year Book* [1910], p. 145; [1911], p. 177.
25 *Cosmopolitan*, XLIV, No. 6 (May 1908), 559.
26 *Cosmopolitan*, XLVI, No. 6 (May 1909), 719, 720.

The American Brewer has also suggested that saloon-keepers and dealers distribute the abundant, excellent literature fighting prohibition among the consumers.

The final purpose is not to educate the consumers, who of course, are found in the ranks of the anti-prohibitionists, but to induce the consumers who underestimate the importance of the agitation of its adversaries and who are quite indifferent, to take active part in the battle against the fanaticism of the abstinence movement and to join the organization, which, as a temperate society is most able to offset the extreme demands of the prohibitionists.[27]

As a result of all of this activity some territory was won back from local option in 1910 and 1911 and once more the brewers grew optimistic. In 1910 President Carl J. Hoster told the members of the Association:

The convention concludes the most important year in our organization in that we feel that since the last convention we have finally succeeded in breaking the backbone of the prohibition wave.[28]

And in 1911, he assured them: "It is, I believe, true that the Prohibition movement is on the wane." [29] Gustav Pabst took the same view in his annual report to the stockholders.

THE PROHIBITION FORCES CLOSE IN

This period of false hope was abruptly ended in 1913 and the battle entered its final stage. Through the Webb-Kenyon Act passed by Congress in that year, Prohibitionists finally discovered a device for exercising the Congressional commerce power "uniformly" as required by the Constitution, and at the same time preventing the importation of liquor into dry states. The Supreme Court had ruled in 1890 that liquor or other goods coming into a state were not subject to the local police power until the original containers were broken open, or the goods sold. For a number of political reasons not directly connected

[27] *American Brewer*, XLII, No. 6 (June 1, 1909), 274-75.
[28] *American Brewer*, XLIII, No. 7 (July 1, 1910), 343.
[29] *American Brewer*, XLIV, No. 11 (Nov. 1, 1911), 558.

with prohibition, it was possible to get the Republican Congress promptly to pass the Wilson Act, of 1890, making liquor subject to the state police power "upon arrival in such a state." In 1898, however, the Supreme Court nullified the effect of this law by ruling that "upon arrival in such a state" meant delivery to the consignee. If the latter were an individual at his home address, further action by state authorities would require a search warrant and invasion of the sanctity of the home. The Webb-Kenyon Act of 1913 avoided these constitutional difficulties by simply providing that shipments of intoxicating liquors into any state for use contrary to law should be prohibited. President Taft vetoed the bill on constitutional grounds; but after Congress had readily repassed it, the Supreme Court held that this withdrawal of the protection of the Federal commerce power was constitutional.[30] It must be remembered, however, that no state prohibited the consumption of liquor so that the door was still open for purchase for private use.

The most important event of 1913 in the prohibition struggle, however, was the shift of the Anti-Saloon League from its campaign for local option to continuous and heavy pressure for a Federal constitutional amendment. At its jubilee convention, commemorating the twentieth anniversary of Russell's conception of the idea of the League, Wayne B. Wheeler, at that time superintendent of the Ohio league, said:

We welcome you . . . to the launching of the most beneficent and far-reaching movement since the civil war. As Moses said to the children of Israel that they should go forward, just so the time has come for the moral forces of this great nation to march on against the last bulwarks of the enemy. A great national evil has been localized and quarantined. Over two-thirds of the saloons of America

---

[30] For discussion of cases: *Leisy* v. *Hardin*, 135 U.S. 100 (1890); *In re Rahrer*, 140 U.S. 545 (1891); *Rhodes* v. *Iowa*, 170 U.S. 412 (1898); *Clark Distilling Co.* v. *Western Maryland Railway Co.*, 242 U.S. 311 (1917). See Cushman, *Leading Constitutional Decisions*, pp. 217-25.

are now in ten states. They are localized more today than slavery was when the last stage of the conflict was reached. The people are growing restless. Like the muttering of a great storm you can hear the determined demand from every quarter to attack the enemy all along the line for national constitutional prohibition. I do not know how you may feel about this, but I would die rather than run from such a conflict.[31]

THE LAST STAND OF THE BREWERS

The United States Brewers' Association responded at once to this new threat. Annual dues were raised from one to three cents per barrel.[32] Under the direction of Percy Andreae, a public-relations counsel reputedly so able that he was paid $40,000 a year, a National Association of Commerce and Labor was organized.[33] This Association worked with the Brewers' Association through a joint committee.[34] Propaganda was commenced emphasizing the independence of brewing from the whisky interests and emphasizing the value of the family beer garden on the European model. In countries like Sweden, beer was not regarded as an intoxicating liquor, and there seemed no reason why the same distinction could not be established here. Max Henius told the brewers' convention the following year that Denmark did not tax beer with under 2¼ per cent alcohol, by weight, and that thereby it had become the most popular drink. He urged the brewers to get behind a similar plan in the United States.[35]

The continued support of organized labor was one of the brewers' principal reliances in holding the thirteen states necessary to defeat the amendment. Trade-union liberty leagues were organized, and the progressiveness of the industry in recognizing the unions and voluntarily providing workmen's compen-

[31] Quoted by Odegard, pp. 149-50.
[32] Senate Doc., No. 62, 66th Congress, 1st sess., I, 1072.
[33] Senate Doc., No. 62, 66th Congress, 1st sess., I, 64, 68, 264.
[34] Senate Doc., No. 62, 66th Congress, 1st sess., I, 934.
[35] Max Henius, *Danish Beer and Continental Beer Gardens,* p. 9.

sation plans was emphasized. In 1914, the labor committee reported to the United States Brewers' Association:

The brewery workers' unions have done a magnificent work during the past year in regard to assisting the brewers to fight the battle against prohibition. Their work has not only been zealous and active but it has been intelligent and efficient, and they certainly deserve great credit for what they have done.[36]

The Association's defense program, however, failed to live up to its early promise. No real break was made with the hard-liquor interests who contributed to common funds, and although many bad saloons were eliminated no essential change in the economic relations of these establishments was attempted. This failure to take real positive action made the speeches of Andreae and the literature of the National Association of Commerce and Labor and the Liberty League seem somewhat meaningless to many liberals. "After making . . . . allowances," Hugh Fox warned the Brewers' Association of Massachusetts at their annual dinner in 1915, "I think we must concede that the brewers have lacked vision and perspective in their public relations." [37] *The New Republic* editorialized this same year: "The most cross-grained and arid of prohibitionists seem radiantly wise alongside the special pleaders of the liquor trade." [38] The attempt to boycott firms advocating prohibition, pursued from 1909 to 1915, undoubtedly produced an unfavorable reaction.[39] The close tie that had naturally been formed with the German-American Alliance turned out to be a liability as the war situation progressed, and the Alliance fell under suspicion of disloyalty. Similarly, exposure by a Senate committee of the perfectly legitimate investment by leading brewers in the *Washington Times* made in 1918, with Arthur Brisbane hired as editor, made a bad impression on a public prepared to put the worst interpretation on any activity by Germans.[40]

[36] *American Brewers' Review*, XXVIII, No. 12 (Dec. 1914), 575.
[37] "Our Constructive Policy," an address delivered by Mr. Hugh Fox.
[38] *The New Republic*, Oct. 2, 1915, p. 219.
[39] Senate Doc., No. 62, 66th Congress, 1st sess., I, 145, 219.
[40] Odegard, p. 263.

In spite of the increased activity of the brewers, nine states were added to the dry column in 1914 and 1915. Gustav Pabst, in his first address as president of the United States Brewers' Association at the convention in 1916, warned his colleagues of the seriousness of the situation and forecast the dangers of complete prohibition.

There has been such a vast improvement in saloon conditions that the great majority of them are now decent and law-abiding, but the traditions of the past have given opposition to the saloons an impetus which it is difficult to overcome. . . . .

So far as can be reasoned from experience gathered through generations of experiments, backed by all the force there is in law, the abolition of the legalized traffic in alcoholic liquors would mean its replacement by an unregulated manufacture and sale so extensive and of such a character as not only to exclude the possibility of diminishing the actual drink evil, but certain to intensify its worse forms.[41]

THE LEAGUE VICTORIOUS

By this time the Anti-Saloon League had developed the most powerful "reform" lobby in American history. As in many pressure groups, its leaders were not deterred by considerations of either fair dealing or democracy; nothing counted except to win. In March 1916, for example, they forced prohibition on the District of Columbia without regard for the will of the people of the district, holding their congressional majority in line by threatening reprisals against any who faltered in this perversion of democracy.[42] We shall see, presently, how the President of the United States had to secure necessary war legislation by communicating directly with the League rather than with the people's representatives.

The congressional elections of 1916 proved to be the crucial

[41] *U.S.B.A. Yearbook* [1916], pp. 2, 5.
[42] Odegard, p. 161.

test of the strength of the League and of the weakness of the brewers. Wayne Wheeler said:

All the energy we put into the 1914 campaign boiled and bubbled with hotter fire in the campaign of 1916. We laid down such a barrage as candidates for Congress had never seen before, and such as they will, in all likelihood, not see again for years to come. . . . . On election night the lights burned late in our Washington office. Elsewhere our state workers were getting the returns. . . . . We knew late election night that we had won. Many hours before the country knew whether Hughes or Wilson had triumphed, the dry workers throughout the nation were celebrating our victory. We knew that the Prohibition Amendment would be submitted to the states by the Congress just elected.[43]

The United States' entrance into the war made the League's victory even more certain. The brewers' German ancestry could now be used to brand the liquor business as pro-German, and its leaders as traitors. John Strange, a dry leader and former lieutenant-governor of Wisconsin, said at the beginning of 1918:

We have German enemies across the water. We have German enemies in this country too. And the worst of all our German enemies, the most treacherous, the most menacing are Pabst, Schlitz, Blatz and Miller. They are the worst Germans who inflicted themselves upon a long-suffering people.[44]

Only in the light of this unreal atmosphere of war hysteria is it possible to understand the complete sweep of the dry forces between 1917 and 1919.

Prohibition of the manufacture of beer and wine was only dropped from the Food Control Bill of August 1917, which banned distilling, by the direct intercession of President Wilson with the League leaders. After an exchange of messages with the Chief Executive, and a conference with the Democratic floor leader of the Senate, the Prohibitionists agreed to relax their

[43] Quoted by Odegard, p. 163.
[44] *Journal,* Feb. 13, 1918.

insistence on a total dry victory so that necessary wartime legislation might go through Congress without undue delay.[45]

But even after this display of League power, and with almost the certainty that an amendment would be submitted to the states, Gustav Pabst felt some confidence. At the 1917 convention of the U.S.B.A., he noted that:

Recent editorial expression of the public press throughout the length and breadth of the land clearly indicates that there is a great and growing sentiment in this country in favor of the manufacture and sale of licensed wine and beer.[46]

It can be said that right up to the end the brewers never lost hope that beer would not be included in the final prohibition legislation, and that they never realized the full power of the League.

Before the Food Control Bill had passed Congress, the Eighteenth Amendment was introduced in the Senate, but the special session adjourned without House action, and the measure had to wait for the assembling of the new and drier Congress in December 1917.

The speed with which the amendment went through the House and Senate in the last half of December may be explained partly by the war and partly by the fact that most members knew how they were going to vote and seemed to want to get the business over with. Although the amendment passed the House 282 to 128 and the Senate, 47 to 8—it has been estimated that it could not have been passed by secret ballot [47]—the debate was perfunctory. Only Senator Heflin of Alabama seriously raised the question of state rights which was to be the major barrier to enforcement. The proceedings literally left the wet forces dazed. "The wets seemed scarcely to have observed their own defeat," writes Charles Merz, "no demonstrations of hostility took place in the wet centers of the country. The press

45 Odegard, p. 168.
46 U.S.B.A. Yearbook [1917], p. 166.
47 Odegard, p. 173.

of the larger cities reflects small interest in the question, either in its letter columns or in its news." [48]

The war literally obscured the whole prohibition question, driving it to the inside pages of the newspapers. Not only was the amendment ratified while the soldier voters were away from home, but while the attention of the citizenry was away from home also.

While the Anti-Saloon League was waging its superbly efficient campaign to put the amendment through the state legislatures, Congress took wartime action against beer and wine. Bad crops and food and labor shortages were the basis and excuse for this legislation introduced in September 1918. Canada had taken local action for complete prohibition in eight out of nine provinces, but none of our European allies had prohibited beer, and even the enemy, far worse off for food, had only cut the strength and quantity of the brew.[49] European sanity had no effect upon Congress. That the "wartime" pressure was not really due to war needs is shown by the "emergency" rider to the Agricultural Stimulation Bill, prohibiting brewing after May 1, 1919, and sale after July 1, 1919, passed fourteen days after the armistice had ended the fighting.

When the Eighteenth Amendment went to the states, twenty seven were already dry. Only twelve had regular sessions of the legislature in 1918—of these, eight passed the amendment. Seven other states called special sessions and ratified. A large number of legislatures convened for the first time on January 1, 1919, and the necessary three fourths were quickly secured, even Wisconsin ratifying on January 15 and 16 by large majorities in both Houses.[50]

The methods of the League are well illustrated in Wisconsin. R. P. Hutton, the new state superintendent of the League, put

---

[48] Charles Merz, *The Dry Decade*, pp. 36-37.

[49] Quebec had 2.5 per cent beer throughout the war. Leslie Gordon, *The New Crusade*, p. 245. See also Arthur Shadwell, *Drink in 1914-1922; A Lesson in Control;* and Ernest Barron Gordon, *The Dry Fight in Europe and Its Relation to America.*

[50] Odegard, pp. 174-76.

emphasis on the Republican primaries for the state election of September 1918. He told the League's 1919 convention:

We used a million book pages of literature per month. We put on a country schoolhouse campaign . . . . We put factory experts to speak in the factories and got the companies to pay the men for listening. We built up a Council of One Thousand to back us— business and labor leaders. . . . . We enlisted the Hemlock Hardwood Lumber Association in its entirety. We sold the factories billboards and posters which were changed bi-weekly, and a monthly educational scientific tract in tabloid form which went into the pay envelopes. We organized the drys in every county. We helped to select dry legislative candidates who could get votes. We listed the two-thirds of our voters who habitually failed to vote in the primary, divided them into blocks of five, put a dry corporal over each five, and got 138,000 of these stay-at-homes to the polls on the primary day, September 3rd, knowing who was the dry candidate for senate and assembly, and absolutely pledged to vote for them. We staged the biggest demonstration in Madison the state had ever seen. We ratified! and in the archives at Washington, Wisconsin was one of the thirty-six. We put it over.[51]

One notes in this explanation the important fact that many business interests had been led temporarily to support prohibition, usually with considerable hope that it would lead to increased industrial production. But efficient expenditure of money also counted heavily in the League's favor. By 1918, it was estimated that the League was spending $2,500,000 annually through an organization that neither the brewers alone nor the combined liquor interests could equal.[52] The brewers lacked friends ready to contribute, as the Rockefellers, Kresge, and other businessmen did to the League. And they also lacked the army of small contributors who gave annually to the League as they would do to a church mission. The League had a public of many hundreds of thousands of devoted followers, whereas the great army of men and women who stood for

51 Quoted by Odegard, pp. 179-80.
52 Odegard, p. 181.

civilized drinking failed to co-operate with the brewers for their mutual protection.[53]

The final touches were added to prohibition by the passage of the Volstead Act in October 1919, defining intoxicating beverages as those containing over one half of 1 per cent alcohol. President Wilson vetoed the bill on the ground that it confused wartime restrictions with the enforcement of the amendment, but the steam-roller dry majorities in both Houses overrode the veto without serious consideration of the President's objections.

As explained at the end of Chapter IX, our detailed history of Pabst ends with prohibition. The following four chapters merely recount the major events in the history of the company from 1920 to 1946 in order to show the connection between the material in the body of the history and the current situation.

[53] Odegard, pp. 183 ff.

CHAPTER XIII

FRED PABST TAKES CONTROL

WHAT were the thousand-odd brewers, to say nothing of over 150,000 wholesalers and retailers, to do with their plants and equipment? Could they be converted to other products, or must they be sold? In general the smaller brewers and the retailers sold out, but most of the big shippers decided to try to keep their plants in operation making whatever products they could. In both cases, the transition was eased by the postwar boom from 1919 to 1920 which produced soaring real-estate prices and a sellers' market for nearly every commodity.

By the end of 1919, the Pabst Company was in excellent financial condition, and prepared for the worst. Cash on hand stood at $634,000, readily marketable securities at $417,000, securities having a specialized market at $1,213,000, net bills receivable at $1,279,000, and inventory at about $1,000,000. Against these ready assets of over $4,500,000, the company owed only $345,000 on current liabilities, and $1,246,000 in long-term bonds. Pablo and Tonic sales had totaled over $550,000 in 1918, and brought $127,000 in profits, so that the beginning of a future business already existed.

But there was also a dark side to the picture. Pablo and the Tonic made a profit because they were to a large extent carried along by the production and selling costs of the beer. To make these or other nonalcoholic beverages the main basis of the business required the invasion of new markets already occupied by well-established concerns and newly competed for by many of the erstwhile brewers as well. Since the company might liquidate at no more than about a 20 per cent loss, there were grave doubts in the minds of some of the stockholders regarding whether the experiment should be risked. Neither Gustav nor Fred Pabst, however, wanted to close the brewery. Both were strongly sentimental in their attitude toward the old employees and toward the business which had been in the family for four generations. Fred Pabst, particularly, felt sure that the common sense of the American people would lead eventually to a repeal of the Eighteenth Amendment. Accordingly, the two brothers determined to carry on making whatever appeared likely to offer a chance for success, renting the parts of the plant that they could not use.

Apart from the development of new products, the decision to carry on raised problems about the liquidation of saloon and restaurant real estate, and about the form of management of the new enterprise. To solve these problems, in December 1920, two corporations were established: the Pabst Corporation to carry on production, and the Pabst Realty Company to hold or liquidate the "outside" properties. The Pabst Brewing Company was then placed in liquidation. Its plant and equipment were exchanged for 50,000 one-hundred-dollar par-value shares of the new Pabst Corporation. The brewing company's other properties went to the realty company in return for 4,000 of its no-par-value shares. The book value of the assets received by the Pabst Corporation was some $5,700,000. The book value of the realty company's new assets was around $4,100,000. The low real-estate figure was due to the fact that about $2,000,000 worth of property had already been sold in 1919 and 1920 and the proceeds paid out in liquidating dividends to the stockholders of the Pabst Brewing Company.

FRED PABST TAKES OVER

Gustav Pabst became president of the operating company, Henry Danischefsky, vice-president, and Henry Stark, secretary and treasurer. The new management was not ideally suited to the task ahead. Henry Stark was in his sixties and in poor health. Henry Danischefsky was a real-estate specialist and former contractor who could be of service to the realty company, but was inexperienced in production and selling problems. While Gustav Pabst had had many years of experience

FRED PABST

with all angles of the brewing business, his main interest had
been in production, and he had had little personal experience
with the new types of marketing problems that would now con-
front the company. To add to the difficulties, Stark died on
March 14, 1921. H. W. Marsh, of the Marsh Refrigerator
Service Company, became secretary-treasurer, and Edward
Loebl, of the traffic department of the brewery, became assistant
secretary.[1] Once again, as in the period of the nineties, the company seemed to need more seasoned top executives than were
available in its own ranks.

For one such executive, however, one experienced in both the
marketing and the making of food products, the company did
not have to look far. This executive was Fred Pabst. In 1921 he
returned to industrial business, after more than fifteen years in
agriculture, to try once again as he had as a young man to steer
the family company through a difficult period. He suggested to
his brother that they separate the two major activities and
that one man head the real-estate organization and the other
the manufacturing company. Persuaded by his brother-in-law,
W. O. Goodrich, and other close friends that this was a wise
plan, Gustav Pabst on December 23, 1921, resigned from the
presidency of the Pabst Corporation, and he and Henry Danischefsky devoted themselves exclusively to the realty company.

This left production and marketing of new products up to
Fred Pabst. He built up his new organization with the aid of
H. W. Marsh and Hugo Kuechenmeister from the Marsh Company. Marsh now became vice-president of the production company and Kuechenmeister became treasurer. Loebl joined them
as secretary. The company had but three directors: Fred Pabst,

[1] The Marsh Refrigerator Service Company was the successor to the Milwaukee
Refrigerator Transit Company. This organization had been set up in 1903 at the
time of the Elkins Act to allow Pabst to make favorable railroad arrangements without incurring the penalties for rebating. In 1906, however, the United States Circuit
Court held that the arrangements between the Refrigerator Company and certain
railroads were in fact a violation of the law. The Refrigerator Transit Company was
accordingly dissociated more distinctly from the brewery, and Marsh became its
president. See *United States* v. *Milwaukee Refrigerator Transit Co. et al.,* 142 Fed.
247 (C. C. E. D. Wis. 1905); 145 Fed. 1007 (C. C. E. D. Wis. 1906).

W. O. Goodrich, and H. W. Marsh—and the latter was relatively unfamiliar with its business. In fact, the only officer at the head of the organization who had been with the company for any length of time was Loebl. Of the twenty home-office executives who in 1915 received salaries of $200 a month or more, only seven were still active in the company in 1921. Of the eight home-office salesmen employed in 1921, only two had been with the company since 1915. In the brewhouse, still the chief productive unit, Fred Bock had been succeeded by his former assistant, Charles Elich. There were, however, two important men of long experience who continued to serve the company: F. H. Squier as advertising manager and Dr. Alfred J. Schedler as head of the all-important laboratory, at the largest salary paid to anyone but Fred Pabst.

Fred Pabst appears to have developed good morale in the new organization. One officer of the company writes:

Anyone discussing Mr. Pabst with the older employees of the Brewery is impressed by the peculiar quality of affectionate loyalty shown toward him. There is almost a possessive quality in it, among both men and women. Analysis brings forth stories of kindnesses, not on the part of an employer toward an employee, but rather those of a friend to his friends. Sickness, death and trouble of any kind within the ranks of those employed in the Milwaukee brewery have always called forth his sympathy and interest. Many of his employees tell how he called upon them when they were in the hospital, or how he wrote to them when they were forced to spend a time in convalescent homes or in the country after serious illnesses. When he has a fine harvest of corn on the farm he still sends in a load of it to share among the employees. When a milk strike in Milwaukee brought worry and fear to young parents for the welfare of their babies, he sent milk from his farm for all brewery employees who had children in need of it. It is his rare ability to put himself in the other fellow's place in all the crises of life that have won for him an unswerving loyalty from all who work around him.

His interests in the welfare of others extend outside the ranks of company employees. For many years he has been a member of the board of directors of the Milwaukee Urban League, and has also given much of his time to the furtherance of the Negro cause.

THE STRUGGLE FOR WORKING CAPITAL

Lack of working capital was a severe handicap to the company during the twenties. Payment of Pabst Brewing Company liquidating dividends totaling 33⅓ per cent of the common stock and separation of over $4,000,000 worth of real estate from the operating company had deprived it of two thirds of the resources of the old organization. Furthermore, stockholders continued to sell their shares, and rather than let these fall into the hands of outsiders, Fred and Ida Pabst or the company bought them.

STOCKHOLDERS AS OF DECEMBER 29, 1921, AND AUGUST 8, 1922

	Shares Held December 29, 1921	Shares Held August 8, 1922
Emil Schandein (Jr.)	960	960
Estella W. Schandein and Emil Schandein (trustees for Emil Schandein)	1,800	1,800
Ella S. Frank	2,160	2,160
Louise F. Ott	667	667
W. O. Goodrich	20	.....
Fred Pabst	11,287	16,409
Marie Pabst Goodrich	10,227	.....
Elsbeth Pabst (represented by trustees)	8,920	.....
Emma Pabst Soehnlein	666	666
H. W. Marsh	1	1
Mrs. Ida Pabst	.....	5,124
Total	36,707	27,787

The 8,920 shares of Elsbeth Pabst, the Captain's granddaughter, were purchased in 1922 from the First Wisconsin Trust Company, which was acting as trustee, for $356,000 in notes. Although an effort was made to sell some or all of this stock to existing Pabst stockholders, there were few takers in the depressed market of 1922, and almost 8,000 shares remained in the treasury. While this increased the value of the remaining stock, it placed a further drain upon the working capital of the company during the years when the notes were being paid off.

The situation was eased somewhat in December 1923, when Fred Pabst sold the cheese division of Pabst Holstein Farms with $704,775 worth of assets, chiefly in the form of bulk cheese inventory, to the Pabst Corporation in return for the latter's notes, payable over five years. But as operations showed a loss in the following year, due to the beginning of new lines of production, inventory again had to be lowered to meet the notes as they became due.

The end of 1924 marked the lowest ebb in company financial affairs. The net worth of the company stood at only $2,745,000 and current assets at $1,618,000, inclusive of $190,000 of deferred liabilities. There were distinct indications, however, that things were about to take a turn for the better. But before they did, there were still more changes in management.

In September 1924, H. W. Marsh resigned as vice-president and general manager to return to the Marsh Refrigerator Service Company. He was replaced by Frederick A. Pabst, Fred Pabst's eldest son, who had become a director in the preceding January after the resignation of W. O. Goodrich in June 1922. Fred J. Postel, an engineer who had previously been made assistant manager, took Marsh's place on the board. The business now, more than ever before, was the responsibility of Fred Pabst and his wife and sons. Among them they owned 74.45 per cent of the stock; they had to sink or swim with the company. Fortunately they swam. The year 1925 resulted in a net profit of $227,849.33, and by the next year, company prospects were good enough to justify the negotiation of a million-dollar bank loan for additional working capital. Temporarily, at least, the major problems had been solved.

GENERAL FINANCIAL DATA, 1921-1927

	1921	1922	1923	1924	1925	1926	1927
Capital	$3,670,700	$2,891,800	$2,963,800	$2,946,800	$2,877,400	$2,875,700	$2,875,700
Surplus	139,633	154,094	129,441	241,350	13,500	660,522*	813,537
Dividends	......	......	......	......	......	......	......
Current assets	869,237	1,297,693	2,104,983	1,774,621	1,617,625	2,848,867	3,086,032
Deferred liabilities	......	200,000	830,000	685,000	190,000	139,994	113,915
First mortgage bonds funded debt	......	......	......	......	......	......	1,500,000
Gross profit from operating	73,548	219,346	221,588	492,053	774,847	1,541,043	1,833,322
Other income, including rents	288,824	164,582	185,963	171,343	334,678	129,800	109,943
Selling expense	251,256	84,104	147,967	456,516	530,122	1,000,000 (estimate)	1,348,923
General and administrative expense	132,735	145,921	178,902	175,965	192,634	236,218 (estimate)	276,297
Profit or loss before special charges	21,708	153,003	80,682	140,427	386,770	434,605	317,646
Special charges	117,925	289,998	107,641	150,229	158,922	227,277	158,094
Net profit or loss	139,633	136,094	26,959	119,313	227,849	207,328	159,552

* Due to book profit on purchase of 8,920 shares at a discount.

Pabst's profits from 1925 on were the result of a gradual development of new products, increasing knowledge of their manufacturing techniques and sales possibilities, and general business prosperity. Four distinct courses had been open to the company in 1919. They could manufacture soft drinks including "near beer"; malt extracts and syrups for medicinal, baking, and home use; cheese or other processed foods; or they could convert to entirely new lines like machinery manufacturing, one of Milwaukee's great industries.

During the first years, the company followed all four courses in order to test all possibilities. Twenty-five thousand dollars were invested in acquiring from the Continental Engineering Company the exclusive right to manufacture, subject to royalties, a device for continually turning the poppet valves on gasoline engines so as to make wear more even and to avoid the necessity of frequent valve grinding. A Pabst subsidiary, the American Rotating Valve Company of Milwaukee, was thus established and housed in the brewery buildings. As almost all automobile companies would have to make use of a successful device of this type, the potential market was enormous; but the invention did not prove commercially successful, and in 1924 its further development was abandoned.

The Fred Pabst Company was another venture in metal manufacturing built around patents for seamless welding and patented pipe connections, or "nipples." In 1922 the stock of this company was sold to the Pabst Corporation for $100,000. Up to 1929, this subsidiary had made a total net profit of roughly $9,690. In that year it was dissolved, and its only asset, the stock of the Frank Wiedeman Company, the company that made the pipe nipples, was transferred to the Pabst Corporation. The corporation valued this stock, plus a $5,000 note from the Frank Wiedeman Company, at $134,000, which Price, Waterhouse regarded as conservative. Even by 1932 this investment was still valued at a net of $104,000, although it was not paying dividends. These experiments with metal manufacture, of no great importance in themselves, were typical of the efforts of the big breweries to find all possible means of adjustment to the new situation.

Much more akin to the company's tradition and experience was the manufacture of "near beer," tonic, and malt syrup. These perpetuated much of the old work of the brewery, but all the new beverages put together failed to utilize the full capacity of the brewery or more than 25 per cent of the bottling capacity. Near beer or malt cereal beverage, as it was called, was simply the old Pabst beer that was brewed now with an extra thick wort, fermented slowly at an unusually low temperature until it gained about 1 per cent alcohol, and then diluted to bring it down to the legal ½ per cent limit. Later the process was changed to that of brewing a regular 3 or 4 per cent beer, and then dealcoholizing it by a patent process. The same care was used in buying materials as had been practiced in the days of real beer, but no near beer ever won any great popularity. The nonalcoholic beverages whose sales were boosted by prohibition were largely those which mixed well with hard liquors; and despite a small cult of near-beer and alcohol drinkers, beer in general did not meet this requirement.

The favorite prohibition beverages such as ginger ale and various fruit syrups could be sold through the same outlets as near beer. They were also relatively stable because of their high sugar content, and could be shipped or stored either in bottles or jugs in the warm months without refrigeration. From these standpoints, they made an excellent addition to the near-beer business, helping to fill up carload lots where the beer orders alone were inadequate. On the other hand, the bulk of such drinks as ginger ale and cream soda in small bottles ran so high in relation to value, that they could scarcely stand the cost of transportation by rail. The companies specializing in these products have built profitable national sales only by shipping concentrates in bulk and carbonating and bottling at local centers. Fred Pabst was not prepared to undertake this latter development, but after weighing the pros and cons, he decided anyway to try the soft-drink business. On May 31, 1923, for $45,000 the Pabst Corporation bought the property, good will, trade-marks, formulas, and processes of the Sheboygan Beverage Company, and undertook the production of ginger ale, cream soda, and other soft drinks and syrups.

Malt syrup used much the same parts of the old brewing equipment as did near beer. In the early days of prohibition, Pabst drew malt syrup from the brew kettle, without hopping, and then evaporated it to a thick concentrate containing about 80 per cent solids. Bakers and pharmaceutical firms were the customers, but the demand was necessarily small compared to the number of breweries seeking to fill it. After some two years of experimentation with the possibilities of this variety of syrup, hops were added, both in the brewing and by injecting a hop concentrate after the evaporation process, and a syrup was produced suitable for use in homemade fermented beverages which rapidly found a wide market. As the popularity of malt syrup increased, the Pabst Corporation applied its policy of developing quality to this product, and superseded its standard Blue Label malt syrup with a new Black Label brand that contained all the elements of a specially fine beer. In addition to the Black Label, a Pabst Label malt syrup and unlabeled malt syrups for dealers who would can it or bottle it under their own trade-mark were produced.

Pabst's Milwaukee competitors, Schlitz, Blatz, Miller, Gettelman, and Cream City, produced malt syrup, near beer, or both. A new Capital Brewing Company was also formed in Milwaukee to enter the malt-syrup business. While some large firms like Schlitz made other products as well, malt syrup was the mainstay of most brewers who continued to operate during these trying years.

The fourth major product undertaken by Pabst, one that was to rank in manufacturing importance with malt syrup, was processed cheese. While other brewers converted to cereal beverages, soft drinks, candy, and machinery production, as well as to malt syrup, Pabst was alone in starting the large-scale processing of cheese. This was a result of Fred Pabst's personal interest in the development of fine cheeses. He had been experimenting with cheese manufacture for many years through a corporation known as Pabst Holstein Farms that he established on his extensive property at Lake Oconomowoc, some thirty miles west of Milwaukee. In conjunction with Dr. Schedler and the laboratory staff, processes were developed for readding the whey which is ordinarily lost in cheese making, pasteurizing the resulting mixture, and producing a "processed" cheese that was both more nutritious and more durable when packaged in small quantities than the old-style cheese. In December 1923, when Fred Pabst sold his Holstein Farms equipment and supplies to the brewery, the old "icehouses" (refrigerated fermenting and storage houses) I-IV were converted for cheese processing and storage. Employees in this division rose from 33 in December of 1925 to 128 by December of 1926, and 176 by the following March.

The cheese was prepared for marketing under Pabst brand names in three forms: (1) Pabst Wonder Process Cheese which included American, Brick, Pimento, Swiss, and Limburger pasteurized loaf cheese; (2) a special new cheese called Pabst-ett; (3) pasteurized package cheese which was sold as bulk cheese through brokers. Pabst-ett, prepared partly from aged imported Cheddar in keeping with the traditional Pabst emphasis on quality, put up both in round packages of about half a pound and in separately wrapped small portions, was pushed as the principal cheese product. By the year ending October 31, 1930, the sales of cheese had reached 9,072,800 pounds of Pabst-ett, 3,502,200 pounds of loaf cheese, and 1,223,370 pounds of package cheese.[2]

The production of all these cheeses came to be burdened with

[2] General Foods contract, p. 2.

an additional expense for royalty payments. On February 25, 1927, the United States District Court for the Eastern District of Wisconsin rendered a decision sustaining Kraft Cheese Company patents so basic to cheese preservation and involving such obvious processes that all other manufacturers were forced to pay Kraft a royalty on cheese production.[3]

An additional manufacturing expense that Pabst voluntarily assumed was due to the company's insistence upon extra-high standards of quality. Pabst's raw cheeses were aged for many months longer than those of its competitors, with the result that inventory charges ran very high.

Along with these major productive efforts, Fred Pabst was always on the alert for new specialties. Experiments were made in the production of levulose, from artichokes, a type of sugar then claimed to be harmless to diabetics, but costs could not be reduced sufficiently for commercial success. The Department of Agriculture has continued similar experiments down to the present day, but the price of levulose is still too high. Water from one of the brewery's deep artesian wells was bottled under the label, Artesia Water, but, due to difficulties with the well, this experiment was also abandoned.

Even with cheese production on a large scale, all these various manufacturing operations failed to take up the facilities of the brewery, and about half the floor space was rented to other companies. This brought in a net return of $75,000 to $100,000 a year. Although some products made more than this in certain years, for the prohibition period as a whole rental was the best source of income.

[3] *Kraft Cheese Company* v. *Pabst Corporation*, 17 F. 2d 787 (E. D. Wis. 1927).

PROFIT AND LOSS AND SURPLUS ACCOUNT, 1926-1929 *

	1926	1927	1928	1929
Cheese division:				
Pabst-ett	$ 7,345	$ 14,393	$ 32,828	$256,781
Processed cheese ..	107,858	68,869	61,897	101,591
Malt-syrup division:				
Black label	......	65,832	15,812	40,839
Other labels and				
bulk	346,844	287,380	230,728	105,575
Beverage division:				
Cereal	17,536	46,025	63,336	114,181
Tonic (2% and				
½%)	88,408	23,946	12,133	8,558
Carbonated &				
Artesia	......	......	......	25,532
Total products	236,413	144,992	134,643	274,836
Rentals	87,643	78,407	94,860	99,834
Sundry income,				
unallocated	21,773	23,296	16,444	22,197
Sundry expense	75,153	36,158	46,331	196,783
Excess capacity expense.	20,523	20,463	19,230	21,073
Total before tax.......	250,154	190,074	180,387	179,012
Federal income taxes..	33,450	20,637	20,077	23,826
State income taxes.....	19,269	10,860	9,523	15,068
Net profit	197,435	158,577	150,786	140,118
Add to surplus, Jan. 1.	11,317	186,327	338,435	483,069
Adjustment to surplus.	2,094	6,469	6,152	8,558
Dividends	......	......	......	86,274
Total surplus to date.	$186,327	$338,435	$483,069	$538,354

* Italics indicate losses or deductions. Figures do not include subsidiaries other than Pabst Sales Corporation.

LABOR PROBLEMS

Due mainly to the smaller number of workers needed in the bottle house, Pabst's new operations never required more than about half the number of employees used in brewing real beer. Foremen in general stayed on, but during late 1919 and early 1920, when American factory employment reached a peak never to be surpassed until 1940, and jobs could be had for the asking, many old employees, uncertain of the future of "near beer" and malt syrup, drifted away to other industries.

PLANT EMPLOYEES * [4]

Location	June 15, 1924	June 15, 1929	June 15, 1932
Brewhouse and Cellars.............	19	36	50
Engineering Department	10	11	12
Boiler Room	13	11	10
Syrups and Canning Departments....	5	11	19
Cheese Department	88	144	96
Malthouse	...	...	28
Bottle House	64	93	88
Miscellaneous	34	75	62
Total	233	381	365

* Exclusive of drivers, peddlars, city salesmen, and mechanics for delivery service.

To cover most of the new types of brewery operation, the International Union of United Brewery Workmen was expanded under the title of the Brewery, Flour, Cereal, and Soft Drink Workers of America, and the A. F. of L. executive council granted it jurisdiction over all cereal workers.[5] The Milwaukee brewers entered into one-year contracts with the new organization in 1920 and 1921, providing for higher wage levels necessitated by the inflation that reached its peak about the time the first contract was being signed in May of 1920.

By spring of 1922, however, the Milwaukee brewers decided to force the union to accept a wage reduction and to give up the closed shop. There were many causes for this decision to terminate a thirty-year-old relationship. The Milwaukee Employers Council modeled on those formed in other cities after the First World War was carrying on a vigorous campaign for the "open shop." They put great pressure on the brewers to fall in line and to help make Milwaukee a completely open-shop city.[6] The country was in deep depression and the brewers were losing money in their efforts to sell new products. Pabst, which had never before failed to make a profit in any year for which

---

[4] Comparative pay roll distribution sheets.

[5] *Brewery, Flour, Cereal and Soft Drink Workers' Journal* (from now on referred to as the *Brewery Worker*), Mar. 3, 1923.

[6] *Brewery Worker*, Feb. 13, 1926.

records exist, showed substantial losses in 1920, 1921, and 1922. Furthermore, the brewery workers were now mainly young employees who had taken the places of the veterans of the pre-prohibition days, and management did not feel the same sense of obligation to these newcomers.

Unsuccessful negotiations between the Milwaukee brewers and the five locals of the brewery union dragged on until late in April 1922 when a strike was called against all the Milwaukee brewers, except Blatz which had signed the union contract. The national executive council of the union ordered out the workers at the Pabst, Schlitz, and Miller branches and agencies all over the country, and listed Pabst, Schlitz, Miller, Gettelman, Cream City, and the Milwaukee Waukesha Agency as firms unfair to union labor.[7] Blatz, Independent, Premier Malt Products Company—the firm Pabst merged with in 1932—Anheuser-Busch Sales Company, Ballantine, and Ebling were specially cited by the council as fair.[8]

While Miller settled with the union in the fall of 1923, the striking workers were replaced at Pabst and Schlitz, and the A. F. of L. boycott continued year after year. The effect of the boycott on Pabst sales is impossible to determine. In 1923 and 1924, the company lost less money than in 1922, due probably to increasing general prosperity, and in 1925 made the biggest profit of the prohibition period.

In the middle of 1925, Schlitz and Cream City, in the hope of gaining an advantage over their competitors, signed union contracts. While Fred Pabst and Gettelman held out until early in 1926, Schlitz action had broken the united front and the other brewers were forced to enter again into closed-shop contracts with the unions.[9]

The two-year contract which became effective on April 1, 1926, was basically similar to those which have been regularly

[7] *Brewery Worker,* May 13, 1922.
[8] *Brewery Worker,* Sept. 29, 1923.
[9] *Brewery Worker,* Mar. 14 and June 6, 1925, Jan. 30, 1926.

renewed from that day on. While the closed shop was recognized, the employer had complete authority to hire and fire union members. When no men could be supplied by the union, temporary permit cards were to be granted to nonunion workers. The eight-hour day, compulsory arbitration, and a number of welfare provisions were included. Wages for all fully qualified workers, except women, firemen, and engineers, ran from $29 to $31 for a forty-four-hour week. Women, employed only in the bottle house, received $20, firemen, $33, and engineers, $36.[10]

For a period of generally declining trade-union strength, this contract was, from the labor standpoint, a very advanced and satisfactory agreement. Wage rates, for example, were above the 65 cents an hour average calculated by the National Industrial Conference Board for skilled and semiskilled labor in manufacturing industries for the second quarter of 1926,[11] although basic weekly wages due to only a forty-four-hour week ran a little below the board's general estimate of $31.27. Compulsory arbitration by two representatives each from the employer and the union, with a fifth chosen from the outside by these four if necessary, was a provision unusual in American labor history. No strikes have been called by the union officials in the Milwaukee brewing industry since the adoption of this form of contract.

MARKETING PROBLEMS

Aside from the labor troubles of the mid-twenties, production of Pabst's new foods and drinks never raised serious difficulties. Marketing the new products, however, presented problems altogether different from those encountered in the selling of beer. Each major new product required a separate sales organization, as each was sold to different types of outlets. Near beer and

---

[10] Articles of Agreement between Pabst Corporation and Local Union, No. 9, of the International Union of United Brewery Workers of America, dated Apr. 1, 1926.
[11] M. Ada Beney, *Wages, Hours and Employment in the United States, 1914-1936,* p. 53.

soft drinks were sold to suppliers of drug stores and drink stands, as well as to the hotel and restaurant trade with which the beer salesmen had been familiar. But the much smaller volume in each case meant that it was necessary to cover the country with fewer branches, fewer agents, and fewer salesmen. Only about six Pabst branches remained out of the forty-odd existing before prohibition; and as we noted earlier, the profit margin after shipment was so small on these products that it was very difficult to combat local competition.

Malt syrup in turn was sold to a special group of jobbers, wholesalers, and bottlers that were not in general associated with either the soft-drink or food markets.

Cheese products had to be marketed through still other local distributors who supplied grocery stores and delicatessens, and who were already handling the cheeses of either Kraft or Borden, Pabst's biggest national competitors.

With the necessity of bucking larger specialized competitors in each market, Pabst's principal administrative problem became the securing of competent sales managers. The men trained in beer selling found it difficult to readjust, and new men had to be brought in to head the three new divisions. Whereas beer had been sold on a discount basis governed largely by local competitive conditions, a single national price for a given volume came to be recognized as essential in the new lines. In 1926 Pabst's board of directors resolved that there should be "no price deductions, special discounts or allowances . . . . unless . . . . authorized in writing by the president or vice-president," and fixed discounts based on volume seem to have been the rule thereafter.[12]

The most important change in marketing came with the addition of the cheese division in 1924 and the beginning of a large-scale selling campaign. Sales expenditures, which until this time had been geared to small volume, were now tripled in the first year. The selling staff was increased 150 per cent and

[12] Directors Record, June 29, 1926.

23

the home-office force was doubled. On June 18 the Pabst Sales Company was created to avoid local taxes on the total assets of out-of-state corporations that might be levied on the cheese stor-age houses that the company had to construct in various states. Pabst had once more become a big business.

SELLING EXPENSES, 1921-1924

	1921	1922	1923	1924
Salesmen's salaries and commissions	$39,189	$30,120	$41,120	$110,542
Salesmen's expense	24,580	14,888	21,469	42,541
Peddlars and collectors wages, commissions, and spendings	36,901	16,626	10,668	4,694
Wilson Co. brokerage expense	......	......	......	31,850
Branch sales or operat-ing expenses	65,819	8,435	......	16,007
City sales dept.	......	......	8,232	6,287
General sales dept.	......	......	7,613	26,156
Bad debts	......	......	......	16,344
Advertising	25,882	6,480	26,083	71,817
Signs and Views	17,142	1,173	6,486	......
Samples	955	316	1,582	11,528
Malt syrup	1,223	1,986	......	......
Consigned stock	......	......	9,920	31,217
Freight	33,909	3,054	12,450	*70,428
Miscellaneous	5,656	1,026	2,344	17,105
Total	$251,256	$84,104	$147,967	$456,516

* Includes returns on empties, and loss of bottles.

The risk taken in investing nearly $2,000,000 in this expan-sion seemed amply justified at the end of the first year. By the end of 1925, gross profits from operations were 250 per cent above those of 1923; and for the first time since prohibition, there was a net profit from manufacturing.

Toward the close of 1925, large advertising campaigns for Pabst-ett were begun. On August 12 Pabst entered into a $40,000 agreement with the Street Railways Advertising Company of New York City for a one-year display in the streetcars of New

York and Brooklyn.[13] On September 2, a $24,000 billboard and newspaper campaign in the principal West Coast cities was arranged for with Klau-Van Peterson-Dunlap-Youngreen, Inc.[14] In 1926 the throttle was opened still wider. Additional bank credit permitted another doubling of selling outlays, which reached the million-dollar level that year. Extensive local advertising was continued through Klau-Van Peterson-Dunlap-Youngreen Company with Pabst-ett as the featured product. From June to November, inclusive, the agency was commissioned to spend $21,000 for "sustaining advertising" in the principal Middle Western cities, an outlay reckoned as equal to about 15 cents per dozen packages sold in this area.[15] This was followed by an agreement with the same agents for December and January covering advertising in *The American Weekly, The Saturday Evening Post, Liberty, The Progressive Grocer, Chain Store Age,* and various newspapers, as well as a special three-month newspaper campaign for the Chicago market starting in November. The total cost of this promotion was set at $100,000.[16]

The 1927 advertising campaign went far beyond that of the previous year. For cheese advertising alone, the board resolved to spend at the rate of 15 cents per dozen Pabst-etts sold, up to a total of $300,000 for the year, under the direction of W. R. Patterson, a marketing specialist, who had recently come from the Canada Dry Ginger Ale Company to head the cheese division. For malt-syrup advertising, an additional $50,000 was to be spent under the direction of Joseph Dribben, the advertising manager of that division.[17]

The cheese sales responded well to this advertising pressure. In 1927 Pabst-ett and bulk cheese for the first time showed net profits; and the losses on loaf cheese were reduced so that the

13 Directors Record, Aug. 25, 1925.
14 Directors Record, Nov. 3, 1925.
15 Directors Record, June 10, 1926.
16 Directors Record, Nov. 30, 1926.
17 Directors Record, May 18, 1927.

loss on the entire cheese division was only about $50,000, a very fair result considering the highly competitive nature of the market and the fact that the Pabst campaign was only three years old. The following year, these losses were cut still further to about $25,000.

Advertising seems to have been relatively ineffective in the case of malt syrup, the company's main profit maker. There was a gradual decline in the profits of the syrup division from $347,-000 in 1926 to $215,000 in 1928 due mainly to increasing national and local competition.

One may wonder why the policy of pushing a nonprofitable division was pursued, while the most profitable division of the business was falling behind. The answer is at least twofold. Some officers and directors feared that the malt-syrup business would be interfered with, ultimately, by adverse legislation, and that it formed an unstable basis for a permanent business; secondly, Fred Pabst was deeply interested in the cheese business personally and preferred to build the future of the company around that division.

FINANCING EXPANSION

New methods of budgeting and accounting were introduced in planning the 1926 sales campaign. Each area around a key town or city was studied separately for each product. Salesmen were asked for specific estimates of how much increase could be expected as the result of certain advertising and promotional expenditures. Under the supervision of R. C. Zimmerman, a college-trained accountant, an exact system of sales cost accounting was introduced. By allocating costs and returns separately to each of the many products and areas, it was possible to see strong and weak situations with some accuracy.

This careful planning paid dividends. In the year 1926, profits before special charges reached $435,000, reminiscent of the old days of beer brewing. Even after setting up a special tax reserve and deducting a considerable book loss on the sale of equipment no longer in use, the net profit was nearly as great as the year before and, considering the capital involved, as good as the twentieth-century average for brewing operations.

The company also considerably improved its financial situation at the beginning of 1927 by using a $1,500,000 bond issue to fund most of the short-term indebtedness, which had risen sharply with the expansion of business. The First Wisconsin Company, the security affiliate of the First Wisconsin National Bank, rated the company very highly as a risk. It estimated the buildings as "having a sound value of between four million dollars ($4,000,000) and five million dollars ($5,-000,000)," and that if the half of the old space then used by the Pabst Corporation for its business were rented, it would bring in a net of $200,000 a year. Consequently, the bankers took a 5½ per cent first-mortgage bond issue maturing at the rate of $150,000 a year from March 1, 1930, to March 1, 1939, at a net of 97 to the Pabst Corporation.

By 1928 and 1929, the company appeared well established in its new lines of business. Its sales volume of over $6,000,000 a year was almost as large as that of the average prewar years of the brewing business. Capital and surplus had risen to about $3,800,000, and net profits totaling $832,000 had been earned for the five years, 1925-1929, an average rate of 4½ per cent. For operations begun under the compulsion of a confiscatory law in new and highly competitive lines of business, the success achieved must have been satisfying to the Pabst management.

EXPANSION OF THE SYRUP BUSINESS

Pabst's group of officers had changed but little between 1924 and 1929. In 1925 Hugo Kuechenmeister had been succeeded as treasurer by J. H. Moore, formerly with the Wisconsin Tax Commission, and in 1926 Rudolf Pabst, Fred Pabst's second oldest son, had been elected second vice-president. That was all. The stockholders had also remained about the same. The only important change being that Fred Pabst had gradually distributed a good share of his and his wife's stock among their seven children, so that by 1929, the younger Pabsts collectively held nearly 10,000 shares and their father and mother, only 12,484. The three-member board of directors, which had been the rule since the resignation of Gustav Pabst and Henry Danischefsky at the end of 1921, was expanded to seven members in 1927 by the election of Rudolf Pabst, Edward Loebl, J. H. Moore, and W. R. Patterson. On October 29, 1929, following the resignation of Fred J. Postel from the board, August Pabst became third vice-president and James R. Nicholson, fourth vice-president. At the next stockholders meeting, February 4, 1930, the new vice-presidents were elected members of the board of directors. Nicholson resigned December 8, 1930, but Fred Pabst's sons continued as vice-presidents until the merger with Premier Malt Products Company in 1932.

While the business was doing well, on the whole, there were some difficulties in the situation. To begin with, processed foods and soft drinks operated on a much narrower margin than beer brewing. Of the $6,256,000 net received from sales in 1929, raw materials alone took $3,792,000 and other direct manufacturing costs raised the total to $4,620,000, or a hazardous 73.85 per cent of sales. This meant that selling, administrative, and all other expenses, which in the days of beer had averaged over 60 per cent of the total costs, now had to be taken out of the remaining 26.15 per cent before there was anything left for dividends and profits. Pabst manufacturing costs were undoubtedly higher than most of its competitors due to the traditional insistence on quality. Since the company would not consider reduction in quality, the only road to lower costs was through larger volume.

This would require no new outlays for plant as the firm still had excess capacity. Malt syrup and cereal beverage production, particularly, could be largely increased without requiring additional facilities. The syrup business had declined about 40 per cent in 1929 due to the loss of a large customer, and there was clearly a need for boosting this division of the business.

Furthermore, the existing volume of syrups and cereal beverages had never required enough malt to justify the operation of the malthouse, so that malt had to be purchased, while the empty building swelled the excess plant capacity that had to bear annual upkeep and depreciation. As the power needed for malting could be largely supplied from excess steam produced for the rest of the plant, there would be a large saving in the cost of malt if volume could be raised to a point that provided efficient use of the gigantic malting equipment.

Just at this time an opportunity was presented to expand the syrup volume to the required extent and to acquire, at the same time, a going sales organization. The Puritan Malt Extract Company was a recently developed Chicago organization for selling malt syrup purchased from independent producers. By 1929, the business had been built up by the Magnus brothers to a volume of nearly $3,500,000. A sale was finally arranged as of January 1, 1930, at a price of $1,192,179.18 of which $537,-693.51 was good will and the remainder, largely inventory. Joseph E. Magnus was made general manager of the Pabst Corporation and a member of the board, and was allowed to retain a number of his key men in order to follow up the Puritan customers.

BUCKING THE STORM

As events proved, this major expansion in a promising direction came at an unfortunate time, yet very few businessmen looked for any prolonged depression, even after the market collapse of October and November 1929. Prosperity seemed "just around the corner," and the patriotic, as well as the wise, business policy appeared to be to carry on as if nothing had happened. The stock market recovered rapidly in the first half of 1930, and many indications pointed to the probability that the recession would be no more serious than that of 1921.

To take advantage of the new setup, an unprecedented advertising campaign totaling over $500,000 for malt syrup alone, and $1,028,000 for all products combined, was undertaken through Batten, Barton, Durstine and Osborn. Full-page advertisements in local papers were used to "break" new markets for both cheese and malt syrup. Salesmen's and sales-department salaries rose from $232,000 in 1929 to $587,000 in 1930. "Dealers' helps," similar to the old-time Signs and Views which Pabst had not previously used in the syrup business, totaled $122,000. This was business on a dollar scale beyond anything ever attempted by the Pabst Brewing Company.

SELLING EXPENSES, 1929-1931

	1929	1930	1931
Salesmen's salaries and commissions.	$232,270	$587,436	$513,156
Salesmen's expenses	145,407	152,971	295,008
Brokerage and commissions	47,650	92,586	38,160
Traveling		236,945	48,350
Branches sales or operating expenses.	13,796	43,488	12,568
Bad debts	28,842	40,871	84,504
Advertising	358,506	1,028,184	778,349
Exhibition expense	7,028	14,205	
Samples	56,282	45,505	35,127
Bonus and prize promotion		50,152	42,896
Demonstrations	2,779	9,281	18,262
Dealers' helps		122,472	96,646
Free goods	73,843	83,812	
Institutional department	12,676		
Co-operative marketing allowance..		10,485	
Spoilage	19,820	53,933	129,347
Telephone and telegraph	8,001	21,247	46,240 (includes postage)
Freight	32,918		
City delivery	32,074	27,362	45,520
Storage	9,395	21,256	20,356
Miscellaneous	35,026	60,830	29,532
Total	$1,116,313	$2,703,021	$2,234,021

A monthly newspaper called the *Pabst-Pep Sales Booster* was started in the middle of 1930 as a means of stimulating efficiency and enthusiasm in the sales force. The following letter, by J. E. Magnus in the December 15 issue, re-emphasized the necessity of salesmen "selling" distributors on the merits of Pabst products:

This is a repetition of a story that has been told to you many times, but I do not think it can be told too often. Pabst products are being supported aggressively at all times by advertising campaigns and other merchandising means. Our greatest weakness lies in the fact that we do not have a full complement of enthusiastic distributors who are in turn getting enthusiastic retailers to move the merchandise into the hands of the consumers.

If our salesmen are well informed on our products and take pains to educate our jobbers to the fullest possible extent and see that they are well informed and that their salesmen are fully informed, those salesmen will in turn educate the retailer to an appreciation of Pabst Products and get sales pressure from them to move the goods into the hands of the consumer.

Considering the fact that 1930 was a year of relative depression, the market responded well to all of this selling pressure. Net sales reached $9,880,000, and the sales of malt syrup exceeded those of Pabst and Puritan, combined, in 1929 by $281,000. Possibly the price paid, a $700,000 increase in selling expense over the total of the two companies for 1929, even though it produced a net loss of $11,000 would have been a good investment had prosperity returned as expected.

In 1931 the company again had to decide whether to continue fighting to hold the expanded market or to retrench. To do the latter at a time when a host of journalists and economists were predicting recovery for early 1931 meant to lose most of the anticipated gain from the capital invested in the good will of Puritan Malt. The Pabst management, therefore, decided to push ahead and to run counter to the market trend.

While the Puritan purchase built volume for malt syrup, cheese sales were still below the break-even point, due to particular difficulties in marketing. Outside of the largest cities, many of the distributors to whom the company sold were agents also for one of its competitors. This is always costly and trouble-

GENERAL AND FINANCIAL DATA, 1928-1932

	1928	1929	1930	1931	1932 *
Capital	$2,875,700	$2,872,900	$2,872,800	$2,872,800	$2,872,800
Surplus	947,870	983,658	874,380	261,655	481,576
Dividends	....	86,274	3,000	....	....
Current assets	2,925,533	2,599,874	3,369,176	2,075,581	1,944,504
Deferred liabilities ..	80,000	60,000	197,912	643,956	1,187,973
First-mortgage bonds funded debt	1,500,000	1,349,000	1,200,000	1,050,000	898,000
Net sales	6,562,848	6,256,015	9,880,217	6,939,917	3,562,496
Production and operating expenses ...	....	....	6,663,597	4,864,494	2,356,456
Gross profit from operating	1,394,201	1,636,300	3,216,621	2,075,422	1,206,040
Other income including rents	159,577	192,525	161,980	147,929	58,481
Selling expense	956,486	1,116,313	2,703,021	2,334,021	904,841
General and administrative expense ...	287,815	291,047	425,856	296,291	156,991
Profit or loss before special charges....	299,507	421,465	249,724	306,961	202,688
Special charges	148,721	334,500	360,792	297,513	162,767
Special credit to income	....	....	....	....	100,000
Net Profit or Loss	160,757	86,965	111,068	604,474	139,921

* To July 31.

some; yet it was economically unthinkable for Pabst to set up a sales organization simply for the distribution of cheese products. A partial way out was found through the expansion of the General Foods Sales Corporation's marketing facilities in 1930. General Foods offered Pabst an opportunity, at this time, to enter into a marketing agreement that would provide about seven hundred local "wagon" distributors for Pabst cheese products, and, at the same time, help General Foods support its new big organization. A four-year agreement was signed, effective January 1, 1931, that guaranteed to Pabst the maintenance of a set number of wagon distributing routes and the services of the drivers in arranging for window displays, advertising material, and demonstrations. Pabst, in return, agreed to spend on advertising an amount equal to at least ten cents per dozen packages of Pabst-ett sold. This arrangement also allowed Pabst to abandon the cheese storage houses that had been erected by the

Pabst Sales Company in order to aid local distributors.[18] The Pabst Sales Company, itself, also ceased to function.

Even though Pabst's net sales in 1931 of $6,940,000 were larger than in any prohibition year except 1930, the immediate results were bad. Gross sales in the cheese and beverage divisions dropped $2,000,000, which accounted for a net loss on these divisions' operations of $517,000. Malt syrup sales also declined $1,200,000 and showed only a paltry profit of $63,000. A sharp decline in price rather than volume was the cause of the slump in both divisions. As the depression deepened, prices broke even faster than expenses, since many of the latter were contracted for well in advance.

RESULTS BY DIVISIONS, 1928-1932

Sales	1928	1929	1930	1931	1932 *
Cheese	$4,650,500	$4,711,079	$5,156,263	$3,150,092	$1,168,508
Malt syrup	1,985,958	1,250,135	4,976,501	3,738,101	2,434,091
Beverages	299,375	732,624	671,351	706,699	313,663
Total above	$6,935,833	$6,693,838	$10,804,115	$7,594,892	$3,916,262
Less freight and allowances	372,985	437,823	923,898	654,975	353,766
Net sales	$6,562,848	$6,256,015	$9,880,217	$6,939,917	$3,562,496

* To July 31.

BENDING BEFORE THE WIND

By the end of 1931, neither Pabst nor most other American corporations were prepared to buck the depression any longer. Salvation lay in bending before the storm by cutting expenses and adjusting to a smaller volume of business. This was done with remarkable success in the early months of 1932.

J. E. Magnus relinquished the general managership, and J. H. Moore resigned as treasurer at the end of 1931. A new economy regime was introduced symbolized by R. C. Zimmerman, the controller, becoming an officer of the company, and Einar Oyaas, from the General Mills Company, becoming treasurer. The new board—composed of Fred Pabst; his sons, Fred A.,

---

[18] General Foods contract.

Rudolf, August, and Robert; Loebl; and Zimmerman—showed the complete elimination of "outsiders."

Production costs and salaries were cut in every direction, inventories were reduced to essential minimums, and advertising was apportioned with the greatest care. The termination of the General Foods contract, by mutual consent, allowed both companies to eliminate unprofitable outlets, and brought Pabst a $100,000 cash payment by way of compensation. The result was a minor miracle; for the first seven months of 1932, all three divisions showed a substantial gross profit from operations, and the company made a total net profit of $140,000. Prorated on a monthly basis, this rate of approximately $20,000 a month was better than the new company had ever averaged in any previous year. Sales volume was also holding up remarkably well. In spite of diminished advertising and abnormally low prices, net sales revenue was coming in at the rate of $6,100,000 a year. The company had weathered the depression.

PREPARING FOR REPEAL: THE PREMIER MERGER

By the middle of 1932, a growing political movement for the amendment of the Volstead Act and the legalization of mild beer made it appear probable that Congress would act favorably on these matters regardless of the outcome of the national election. As a result, all brewers who had remained in operation were thinking in terms of resuming their old activities.

By arranging for the termination of the leases on the excess plant capacity, Pabst was prepared from the production standpoint to resume large-scale brewing operations, but the company would have to borrow working capital to finance sales expansion and to create a new selling force with suitable branches and agencies. At this point the men who had carried one of the old Illinois breweries through prohibition by producing malt syrup approached Fred Pabst with the suggestion that the two companies should merge.

The Premier Malt Products Company, descendant of the De-

BALANCE SHEET AS OF JULY 31, 1932 *

Assets

Cash in Banks and on hand............................ $ 545,881
Cash Surrender Value Officers' Life Insurance.............. 120,963
Accounts receivable, less reserve for loss on bad accounts..... 622,822
Inventories:
    Finished goods 152,835
    Raw materials and supplies........................ 481,047
                                                $1,923,548

Due from stockholders and employees................... 151,884
Investments and advances:
    Frank Wiedeman Company......................... 127,271
    Milwaukee Grains & Feed Corporation................   33,912
    Sundry investments and notes.......................   68,794
    Advances to Pabst Realty Company..................   34,723
                                               $ 416,584

Capital Assets at book value:
    Land 542,338
    Buildings, machinery, autos........................ 2,151,676
                                               $2,694,014

Good will 537,694
Deferred charges 126,476

    Total assets $5,698,316

Liabilities

Current liabilities (includes wages, commissions, taxes, installments on notes, etc.)............................... $ 496,514
Deferred liabilities:
    Ida Pabst .... $ 500,000
    Land contract   37,000

                                               537,000
Funded debts 1,048,000
Reserves (mainly for cases and bottles)................... 294,916
Capital stock $2,872,800
Surplus, including $467,745 arising from purchase
   of capital stock........................... 449,086

                                            3,321,886

    Total liabilities $5,698,316

* This statement, made at the time, differs slightly from the later, adjusted Price, Waterhouse statement.

catur Brewing Company, had adequate working capital, a large
sales force, many branches, and a group of able executive officers headed by an engineer and inventor, Harris Perlstein.
Premier did not have a big brewery, however, nor a beer with
a national reputation. Each group had what the other lacked,
and Fred Pabst, in his middle sixties, was not averse to relin-
quishing executive leadership to officers of proven ability. As a
result, Fred Pabst and his sons agreed to join forces with
Premier.

CHAPTER XIV

PREMIER AND THE MERGER

THE companies that merged in 1932 were by no means strangers to each other. From about 1912, the Decatur Brewing Company, an ancestor of Premier, had been an agent for the distribution of Pabst beer, and the arrangement had only been terminated by the coming of prohibition in 1919. Later, Harris Perlstein, of Premier, and Fred Pabst had come to know each other well when Perlstein was president and Pabst a director of the National Malt Products Manufacturers Association. The firms manufacturing malt syrup in the twenties—Fleischmann, Premier Malt Products Company, Anheuser-Busch, Pabst, Schlitz, Wander, Ruppert, Ballantine, and dozens more—had formed this trade association, and many well-known figures, both within and without brewing circles, sat around the directors' table. Probably it was Perlstein's services as president of this association for several years that showed Fred Pabst what manner of man and executive he was; and, doubtless, it was through that contact that Perlstein came to admire Fred Pabst's steady character.

THE BREWERY AT DECATUR

The Decatur Brewing Company, while relatively small in size, was almost as old as the Pabst company.[1] The business had been started in 1855 by John Koeler and Adam Keck who soon after sold it to Edward Harpstrite. Just as Jacob Best, Sr., is the earliest known direct ancestor of present-day Pabst management in the Mettenheim-Milwaukee line, so Edward Harpstrite begins an uninterrupted succession of chief executives in the Decatur-Peoria line. In 1862 Harpstrite took as a partner a twenty-eight-year-old Decatur tobacco manufacturer, Henry

[1] In addition to the company records, see *One Hundred Years of Brewing*, p. 314; and clipping from *The Decatur Review*, Oct. 5, 1936.

Shlaudeman. Harpstrite must have been impressed by the general ability and ingenuity of his young German friend, as Shlaudeman had had no experience with the brewing business. In any case, Harpstrite guessed right. Shlaudeman turned out to be not only a good production boss, but also an able technical man. Perhaps it was his early training as a copper- and tinsmith that fitted him to invent a beer cooler, similar to the famous Baudelot, and to follow this with a hot-air pitching machine and a safety-valve apparatus for bunging chip casks.

The Harpstrite and Shlaudeman business progressed after the fashion of hundreds of other small-city breweries, making satisfactory profits from a volume held down by the limited size of the market area. When Harpstrite retired on October 1, 1884, the brewery became a Shlaudeman family business in the hands of Henry and his two sons, Frank and Harry. Four years later they incorporated it as the Decatur Brewing Company with Henry as president, Frank as vice-president, and Harry as secretary-treasurer.

As with other successful local brewers whose own businesses could not be expanded further without undertaking the expenses and risks of shipping, the Shlaudemans devoted their extra energy to various near-by enterprises. Henry Shlaudeman became a director of local ice, coal, milling, and public-utility companies, and, in the late nineties, he was made president of the Citizens National Bank of Decatur. In 1900 he was succeeded in this latter post by his younger son, Harry. The elder Shlaudeman continued as president of the brewery until 1903 when, at the age of sixty-nine, he reluctantly turned his job over to Frank. Retiring shortly afterward to the friendlier climate of southern California, he lived to be eighty-nine.

Frank Shlaudeman managed the business successfully through the difficulties that harassed all breweries in the twentieth century. When Decatur adopted local option in 1912, a large part of his market disappeared and production fell to under 30,000 barrels a year.[2] To compensate for this, he ar-

2 Interview with A. J. Ostendorf, Sept. 11, 1945.

ranged to become a distributing agent for Pabst whose product
was easier to market outside of Decatur. The Pabst agency was
successful enough for Shlaudeman to discontinue his own brewing in 1914.

THE RISE OF PREMIER

With the spread of prohibition, many breweries began looking for new products to manufacture. The wartime shortage of
sugar opened up an avenue of new activity which Shlaudeman
was not slow to realize. Malt syrup, long used by bakers, was
now urged strongly by the United States Department of Agriculture as a general substitute for cane sugar. With a wholesale
price of seven cents a pound and a pleasant honey-like flavor,
it was finding acceptance by food manufacturers and house-
wives. Looking about for advice in entering this new field,
Shlaudeman in 1918 came to the firm of Singer-Perlstein Company, consulting chemical engineers.

Philip A. Singer, a chemical engineer of considerable prominence in the cereal field, had formed a partnership in 1917 with
Harris Perlstein, a young graduate of Armour Institute of
Technology in chemical engineering, who had proved his met-
tle while associated with Singer on several jobs during the preceding three years. They first hung out their shingle in Milwaukee, but within a year they had so many important clients,
including some in places as far away as Australia and South
Africa, that they decided on a more central location in Chicago.

The sugar shortage found Singer and Perlstein ready not only
with knowledge of the ordinary processes for making malt
syrup, but also with a specially developed process for the manufacture of maltose, a syrup derived from the action of malt
diastase on corn, rice, or other starchy substances.

Since certain stages in the making of malt syrups, including
maltose, are similar to the making of wort for beer, breweries
were attracted to the possibilities in this field, and several, like
the Decatur Brewing Company, turned to the Singer-Perlstein
Company for technical aid. Decatur Brewing Company began

24

to turn out syrup in 1918, using the trade name Premier Malt Products Company. Two principal brand names were adopted, "Premose" and "Blue Ribbon." Use of the latter brought a protest from Pabst, who had, however, not begun the manufacture of malt syrup at the time, and resulted in litigation which was ultimately won by Decatur.[3]

With Anton Spaeth running the sales end, Decatur prospered in this new business. Wanting larger output but unable to convince Shlaudeman that he should make further investment in "brick and mortar," Spaeth in 1920 formed a group to establish an Eastern plant, under an arrangement with the Decatur Brewing Company. The Singer-Perlstein Company was engaged to locate, establish, and manage the plant; and Singer and Perlstein, individually, were persuaded to join the group of owners. Premier Malt Products of Ohio, Inc., was formed to re-equip and operate as a syrup plant the former brewery of John Buehler at Steubenville, Ohio; and Singer and Perlstein placed Robert Clark, who had worked for them as a superintendent of construction, in charge.

While the establishment of Premier of Ohio meant a narrowing down of Singer's and Perlstein's engineering activity in the syrup field to Decatur and Steubenville, it was, at this stage, only a side venture for them, and the Singer-Perlstein Company carried on with its general consulting activities. Likewise, Spaeth continued his position as vice-president of Decatur Brewing Company.

Success of the Decatur and Steubenville operations, and the desire of Frank Shlaudeman to retire from active leadership of the Decatur firm, led to a merger of the two firms in 1924 in a new organization: the Premier Malt Products Company (Delaware). With the formation of the new company it was decided to replace the cramped quarters at Decatur and Steubenville with a new plant capable of growing with the market. Taking advantage of the chance to buy some large well-located factory

---

[3] *Pabst Brewing Co.* v. *Decatur Brewing Co. et al.,* 284 Fed. 110 (C. C. A. 7th 1922).

buildings at Peoria Heights, a suburb of Peoria, equipment was installed to concentrate manufacturing in this northern Illinois center. In 1925, when operation of the new plant commenced, the Steubenville plant was relinquished, but, because of the need for its output, operation of the Decatur plant continued for some time thereafter.

The merger and the building of the Peoria plant brought an end to the Singer-Perlstein Company's activities. The engineering office in Chicago was closed, Singer was elected president and Perlstein treasurer of the new company, and both moved to Peoria to assume their duties. Before construction at the new plant could be finished, however, Singer became ill and the combined job of completing the construction and of running the business fell on Perlstein's shoulders.

Due largely to the ability of Harris Perlstein, Premier much more than lived up to the directors' hopes for its expansion. Perlstein continually made innovations that improved the quality and cut the cost of the company's product, and he also attracted to the company an unusual number of able young men. At the same time the regional distributors, most of whom had been appointed by Anton Spaeth, equipped with the best product on the market, from the dealers' standpoint, turned in orders in steadily increasing volume. In 1927 the company made another major addition to productive capacity by buying the assets of Bosch Food Products Company, then operating a malt-syrup plant in the former Leisy Brewery in Peoria, and promptly enlarging the plant. This purchase also provided Premier with a malthouse, and gave the company three manufacturing plants in the Peoria area.

The leadership of this rapidly growing enterprise reflected a fusion of the former managements. Frank Shlaudeman retired from active management, but became a director. From 1924 until 1927, Singer served as president, Spaeth as vice-president, Clark as secretary, and Perlstein, who was the most active force and in effect general manager, held the title of treasurer.

In 1927 Spaeth retired from active management, although he remained on the board until his death in 1931; Singer became chairman of the board; Perlstein, president; Clark, vice-president; and Charles T. Buehler, son of the former Steubenville brewer, secretary-treasurer. The retirement of Singer in 1928 led to the abandonment of the office of chairman and was accompanied by the splitting up of the secretary-treasurership. James G. Shakman, a well-trained technical and production man of unusual talent who had been Perlstein's classmate at Armour Institute and who had joined the Premier organization in 1927, became treasurer. This group of officers guided Premier until the merger with Pabst in the fall of 1932.

PREMIER MALT SALES COMPANY

In 1927 it also began to be evident that the system of regional franchises, under which advertising and sales activities were largely determined by the individual distributors, would not permit a unified national sales effort. Perlstein advocated and carried through the acquisition of the various distributing companies, partly by cash purchase and partly through payment with stock—an arrangement which retained the organization and co-operation of the distributors, and turned out happily for them in later years. Premier Malt Sales Company, organized as a wholly owned subsidiary on December 19, 1927, began business in January 1928, with offices in Chicago. Perlstein was president of the sales company as well as of the manufacturing company, and F. E. Solfisburg, who had been one of the owners of the distributing company which had formerly operated out of Chicago, became vice-president and sales manager of the sales company.

Now effective advertising and selling on a national scale became possible, and a vigorous program was pursued. Premier Malt Products Company quickly became the largest firm in its field. The picturesque Ben Bernie was placed on the radio, and "Blue Ribbon Malt"—as Bernie put it, "The Mosta of the Besta"—became a household word.

THE MOVEMENT FOR REPEAL

Although the Premier business grew until the assets of the firm were worth over ten million dollars, and its sales volume surpassed that of any of its competitors, Harris Perlstein never lost sight of the possibility of the return of legal beer. When that happened he wanted to be ready to enter the national market with a well-known brand.

The early twenties offered little hope for a change in the Volstead Act. The antiprohibition forces gained strength slowly, as the principal evils of prohibition—speak-easies, bootleggers, and political corruption—were not immediately obvious. Organized labor, to be sure, had never relaxed its opposition to prohibition in general, and the Volstead Act, which prohibited beer, in particular. But if the Prohibitionists had been more moderate and farsighted they might have quieted the labor opposition and furthered the cause of temperance by an amendment to the Volstead Act permitting 2.75 per cent beer. At this time, however, the drys were confident of defeating all moves for modification, and refused to listen to any proposals for change.

The only other powerful organization against prohibition, the Association Against the Prohibition Amendment, had been formed in April of 1919, by a group of the country's richest men. Its ranks were steadily enlarged as it became apparent that in most areas prohibition was not increasing the sobriety of industrial labor, and that the loss of tax revenues from liquor necessitated higher income and corporation taxes. But not until about 1926 did this organization gain its strongest backers. From then on, a group of big businessmen such as executives of Du Pont, General Motors, and Standard Oil became the largest contributors of money to the association. Among the brewers, whose checks were much smaller than those of some of the leading industrialists, the largest individual contributions came from Fred Pabst.[4]

[4] Dobyns, p. 9.

Among the other national organizations working for repeal were the Women's Organization for National Prohibition Reform, the Moderation League, the Voluntary Committee of Lawyers, and the Crusaders. In June 1932, all these antiprohibition groups, plus the American Hotel Association, joined in the United Repeal Council.[5]

As long as prosperity lasted, modification of the Volstead Law was the principal hope of the reformers, but as industrial stagnation and mass unemployment forced Americans to think more seriously about national affairs, immediate legalization of beer in order to provide jobs and government revenue became popular in both political parties, and complete repeal appeared a possibility.

From time to time, Premier had considered the acquisition of brewing property for future beer production and more attention was given to this subject as the tide against prohibition ran stronger. While one or more local breweries might readily be bought, Perlstein and his associates felt that their nationwide sales organization and their leading position in the malt-syrup trade could only be used to maximum advantage by a tie-up with one of the former nationwide shippers. The most logical of all the possibilities in this direction would be an arrangement with Pabst.

When events convinced Harris Perlstein that the time had come to act, he turned, with typical simplicity and directness, to his fellow director of the National Malt Products Manufacturers Association, Fred Pabst, and suggested merging their companies. The personal friendship that had grown up between the two men while serving on the association's board of directors was an important element in the final decision to combine their enterprises. The joining of the chief malt products firm, with the once greatest beer producer, in order to provide additional resources for expansion, may seem so obvious a business arrangement as to require little explanation, but personal factors

[5] Dobyns, p. 122.

HARRIS PERLSTEIN

working in reverse fashion have often prevented just such logical steps. The personality of Fred Pabst leads one to believe that
had he not liked Perlstein as a man, nothing on earth would
have persuaded him to merge the businesses.

Even after the desirability of a merger had been agreed upon
by the two leaders, the combining of Pabst and Premier involved some difficult decisions. In the first place, it was not certain that beer would be legalized. Without beer production,
Premier would gain no great advantage from a merger with a
Milwaukee cheese and malt-syrup company. If, on the other
hand, the expected happened and beer became the chief product
of the combined enterprise, the Pabst company had a much
greater potential value. To take care of this situation, the name
of the Premier Malt Products Company was changed to the
Premier-Pabst Corporation, and a complex division of common
and preferred stocks was worked out. Three classes of 5 per
cent cumulative preferred were to have first claim on earnings.
The 40,000 shares of Class A were divided evenly between the
stockholders of the two companies; the 71,000 shares of Class B
would go to Premier stockholders and an equal amount of
Class C to those of the Pabst Corporation. In addition to the
preferred stocks, 335,462 shares of Class B common and 11,086
shares of voting Class A common were divided between the
two groups of stockholders in agreed amounts. The Class C
preferred would not have a claim to dividends unless the manufacture of beer was legalized. If the period of legal manufacture
extended over five years, however, the Class C claim was to
become permanent. Directors could not declare dividends on
the common until all the preferred requirements had been met.
The fulfillment of the conditions necessary to Class C dividends
would assure Pabst stockholders of an annual return of over
$450,000 a year from preferred, apart from any dividends on
the common. Since this sum would be about equal to the average net earnings of the old Pabst Brewing Company for the
five full years preceding prohibition—a firm employing about

three times the capital of the later Pabst Corporation—the Pabst negotiators could congratulate themselves on having made an excellent bargain.

All of these arrangements required appraisals, reincorporations, and prolonged discussion. But on October 28, 1932, the final agreement was signed and shortly thereafter the businesses were formally joined as the Premier-Pabst Corporation.

PLANNING FOR REPEAL

Meanwhile, due to the foresight of Fred Pabst, preparations for beer production in the historic Milwaukee brewery were well advanced. In October 1930, he had started acquiring new storage tanks, kegs, and other equipment necessary for brewing. He terminated the leases of tenants using the space that had not been needed during prohibition, "It's a risk, I know," he told a reporter, "however, public opinion is a pretty good barometer. It is my own firm opinion that beer will return in the not distant future, and I am willing to take the chance." [6] The advanced state of Pabst preparations is indicated by the fact that while by 1933, when both breweries were producing beer, the Schlitz properties were assessed at almost as high a value as those of Pabst, a year before beer production commenced, Pabst had had buildings and machinery rated at 30 per cent more than its rival at the foot of the hill. [7] As a result of these preliminary expenditures legalization of beer on April 7, 1933, found Pabst better prepared than its former competitors.

While reconversion to brewing posed relatively few production problems for Pabst, the winter of 1932-1933 was one of great suspense in regard to the status of beer pending the repeal of the Eighteenth Amendment, and its permanent status should repeal fail of ratification. Pabst, Perlstein, and Schedler went to Washington for lengthy conferences with brewers and legislators. A bill was introduced to nullify the Volstead Act and

[6] *The New York Times,* Oct. 4, 1930.
[7] *American Brewer,* LXVI, No. 8 (Aug. 1933), 74.

to relegalize beer in the fall of 1932, but it appeared likely that the alcoholic content would be limited to 2.75 per cent by weight. The Pabst group, together with other brewers, thought this percentage too low to ensure satisfying and stable beer. On December 9, 1932, Perlstein wrote to Henry T. Rainey, majority leader in the House, pointing out that if it were agreed that 3.2 per cent beer was still nonintoxicating, there were important advantages in establishing this maximum. The beer would be more popular and, hence, bring in more tax revenue to the government, whereas the higher alcoholic content would require the use of more grain and thus aid the farmer. On December 12, Rainey replied, "I quite agree with you. There is no substantial difference and if 3.2 per cent beer is not intoxicating that is the percentage beer we ought to have. You are right about it—the better the quality of the beer the more revenue we get and that is the major reason for the attempt to enact this legislation at the present time." Other legislators also agreed with the brewers' contentions, and the Cullen-Harrison Bill, passed on March 22, 1933, legalized 3.2 per cent beer.

The repeal amendment was not agreed to by the necessary three quarters of the states until December 5, 1933, but to most Americans the return of legal beer on Friday, April 7, in accordance with the Cullen-Harrison Bill, symbolized the end of the dry era. In all the traditional brewing centers, crowds waited at the breweries for the first glasses of the new beer. Grocery and delicatessen stores delivered cases to homes before breakfast on Friday morning. Old restaurants and beer halls reopened, old customs were revived, and, most important of all, thousands returned to brewery work.

CHAPTER XV

THE REVIVAL OF BREWING

IN 1933, old-time brewers surveyed a business scene in which subtle but important changes would prevent a return to the conditions of the "good old days." Beer, coming back as a depression panacea, was more heavily taxed by both federal and state governments than ever before in time of peace. The relations between brewers and sellers of beer were strictly regulated by both federal and state authorities, and in most states breweries were not allowed to own or control retail outlets. Section 2 of the repeal amendment stated: "That transportation or importation into any State, Territory, or possession of the United States for delivery or use therein of intoxicating liquors, in violation of the laws thereof, is hereby prohibited." Before prohibition no state had ever levied an excise tax on beer, but, backed by this provision, every state and the District of Columbia ultimately imposed such taxes ranging from 32 cents to $4.65 per barrel, with the general average a little over $1.00.[1]

Moreover, many states added to the brewers' new problems by passing burdensome regulatory laws. Containers, credit terms, labels, deposits, and many other details were subjects of state legislation. California, for example, in 1935 suddenly limited the size of outdoor beer signs to 720 square inches, outlawing $100,000 worth of Pabst equipment and about half as much for both Anheuser-Busch and Schlitz.[2] Other states made more fundamental attacks on national beer distribution. Indiana set up politically controlled distributing monopolies that exacted special license fees from out-of-state brewers, while Pennsylvania in 1935 not only placed a discriminatory license

[1] *Brewers' Almanac*, 1946, pp. 12-16.
[2] *Premier-Pabst Sales Co. et al.* v. *State Board of Equalization et al.*, 13 F. Supp. 90 (D. C. S. D. Cal. Cen. Div. 1935).

tax on the sale of "imported" beer, but required that the officers, directors, and 51 per cent of the stockholders of distributing corporations be residents of the state. Pabst and the other large shippers attacked the validity of such discriminatory laws and fought them right up to the federal Supreme Court, but by broad interpretations of the Twenty-first Amendment, the right of the states to adopt virtually any form of regulation was upheld.[3]

On the national scene the Cullen-Harrison Bill of 1933 contained little more than a provision for a $5.00 per-barrel tax on 3.2 per cent beer, and the requirement of a brewing permit from the Bureau of Industrial Alcohol; but it was generally understood that additional legislation would soon be passed regulating the conditions of the trade, and that brewers would be wise to refrain from any investments in retail property.[4] The regulations came late in the year 1933 with the adoption of the NIRA Brewers Code, followed by the Federal Alcohol Administration Act of 1935. The latter act, which placed the administration of alcoholic industries in the Bureau of Internal Revenue, prohibited brewers or distributors from subsidizing retailers in order to establish exclusive outlets. The Brewers Code, adopted in December 1933, placed no controls on methods of production or prices but strictly defined the methods of selling. No beer could be sold on consignment, or on the basis of secret rebates or allowances. Brewers could not buy licenses for retailers, lend money, or supply equipment beyond one-hundred-dollars worth of signs per year for each outlet. No prizes or premiums could be distributed except advertising novelties of a nominal value. No contract could be made for the exclusive sale of one brand of beer.[5]

[3] *Premier-Pabst Sales Co. et al.* v. *McNutt, Governor, et al.*, 17 F. Supp. 708 (D. C. S. D. Ind. 1935); *Premier-Pabst Sales Corporation* v. *Grosscup et al.*, 12 F. Supp. 970 (D. C. E. D. Pa. 1935); aff'd 298 U. S. 226; *State Board of Equalization of California* v. *Young's Market Co.* (1936), 299 U. S. 59.

[4] The federal tax on all beer of $5.00 up to June 30, 1940, was raised to $6.00 on July 1, 1940; to $7.00 on Nov. 1, 1942; and to $8.00 on Apr. 1, 1943.

[5] *American Brewer*, LXVI, No. 12 (Dec. 1933), 15-16.

Following the overthrow of the NIRA by the Supreme Court, similar conditions were established by Regulation 6 of the Federal Alcohol Administration Act. The new regulations continued the prohibition on ownership or control of retail outlets or equipment but permitted the supplying of retailers with signs to a value of not over ten dollars, in use at any one time, advertising specialties up to ten-dollars value annually, newspaper cuts for local advertising, and up to two gallons of beer for samples. These regulations are substantially in effect at the present time.

Still, had the Captain been alive he might even now have repeated his favorite remark, "All is well and the goose hangs high." The purchase of retail outlets, the area in which the Pabst policy of insisting on quality above all else had run into difficulties in the earlier years, now promised to be a problem of the past. No longer could brewers of inferior beer, through lawful control of all outlets, keep the fine shipping beers out of their local market.

There were other advantages in the new legal arrangements. From 1911 to 1914, the last years before the rapid rise of prohibition legislation, nearly 33,000,000 people had lived in territory where sale of all liquor was prohibited by local option, and 13,000,000 to 14,000,000 in bone-dry states. With the return of beer in 1933, local option for beer was only enacted in areas with a population of 21,700,000, and soon repealed in many of these, so that the bone-dry population fell to around 8,000,000. In the new era no state-wide legislation, prior to 1944, prohibited beer. Thus the brewers' market was much larger than before.

Meanwhile, new technical and economic developments helped the large shipping brewers to service their unprecedented markets. The motor truck greatly facilitated the supply of middle-distance cities. The metal keg, in the use of which Pabst had pioneered, ultimately proved superior to the wooden ones for shipping purposes. The number of brewers had been reduced from almost 1,400 in 1914 to about 700 in 1934. As Harris Perlstein summed it up:

Our breweries are fewer, they are bigger, they serve a wider territory. That is the natural result of several developments, including the building of hard roads and the perfection of motor trucks. Before prohibition storage branches were a long haul away in point of time by means of the picturesque brewery wagon. Today such locations would be a few minutes haul for a high speed truck and we do not have branches close to the breweries except sometimes in very large cities.[6]

Increased use of advertising and the trend toward more home consumption were also favorable to the large brewer who could afford to keep his product continuously before the public.

But probably as important as any of these factors in the period after 1933, and from a business standpoint one of the most significant developments in the entire history of brewing, was the introduction in 1935 of beer in cans. As we have seen in the case of Pabst, the greatest disadvantage faced by the shipping brewers in competition with local brewers was transportation cost. The can, because of its small shipping weight, efficient use of space in packing and loading, and its elimination of the cost of returning empties, could go far toward removing this disadvantage.

The brewing industry was peculiarly free from anything approaching monopoly. Unlike soft drinks, beer could not be shipped in concentrated form for local bottling, but had to be transported from the brewery in its dilute, finished form. Thus, even with advances in transportation and the advent of the can, the major market still went to local and regional shippers. Yet the total market was now so large that development of a big business was possible for the few national shippers. The general figures for the industry from 1933 until wartime rationing of grain in 1944 also indicated an almost steady increase in the proportion of the national market shared by the largest brewers.

[6] *Brewers' Technical Review*, X, No. 9 (Sept. 1935), 315.

In 1911, a representative prewar year, the three largest American brewers produced about 7 per cent of the total beer sold, whereas in 1941, the last year relatively unaffected by war conditions, they marketed over 14 per cent of the national total.[7] In parallel was the decline in the number of brewers from over 700 in 1934 to under 500 by 1943, as competition eliminated many of the poorly managed or inefficient breweries.

Repeal of prohibition revived the state and local brewers' associations such as those in Chicago, Milwaukee, Illinois, and Wisconsin. These associations quickly, though temporarily, assumed special functions in the enforcement of the NIRA codes. The old parent organization, the United States Brewers' Association, however, which had carried on all during prohibition, failed at first to receive adequate support from the industry. Out of some 700 brewers in 1934 less than 150 belonged to the United States Brewers' Association and a preponderance of these were located in the Eastern area.[8]

Harris Perlstein shared the conviction of some of the more forward-thinking brewers that not enough was being done to protect the industry from a renewal of dry activity, and that a positive program of public relations must be undertaken. Failing to secure action in that respect and indignant over the failure of the U.S.B.A. representatives on the code authority to protect the right of Pabst to a hearing before certifying an alleged code violation to the Department of Justice, Pabst withdrew from the association in 1934. Anheuser-Busch subsequently followed suit and as a result, by 1936, two of the three largest brewers were outside the association.

August A. Busch, Jr., now joined Harris Perlstein in organizing a large number of the independents in a new association that they named Brewing Industry, Inc., with Busch as president and Perlstein as treasurer. In addition to the United States Brewers' Association and Brewing Industry, Inc., there was

[7] Anheuser-Busch figure is from *Western Brewer*, XXXVIII, No. 5 (May 1912), 233; Schlitz figure from Wisconsin tax reports; 1941 figure based on reliable estimates.
[8] U.S.B.A., *Convention Proceedings* [1934], p. 15.

also an American Brewers Association, formed by some near-beer manufacturers during prohibition, and continued for real beer after repeal, and later the United Brewers Industrial Foundation (changed in name to the Brewing Industry Foundation in 1942) set up by the U.S.B.A. "to interpret public interest to the brewers and the brewing industry to the public."

From the beginning Messrs. Busch and Perlstein regarded Brewing Industry, Inc., as a stopgap measure until an appropriate industry program could be developed on which the various factions could agree and the brewing groups could be brought together in one organization.[9] With the help of Bernard Lichtenberg and his Institute of Public Relations, Busch and Perlstein through Brewing Industry, Inc., developed and demonstrated a program of industry self-regulation, and then used this as a springboard for unification. The first step toward national unity was the merger in March of 1940 of Brewing Industry, Inc., and the American Brewers Association into American Brewing Industry, with Harris Perlstein as president. The following year the new association was merged with the United States Brewers' Association and harmony was restored to the industry. In 1944 the Brewing Industry Foundation was absorbed by the parent body which changed its name from the United States Brewers' Association to the United States Brewers Foundation, Inc. Harmony was again threatened during the war by the rise of a new rival group, the Small Brewers' Committee. Despite the existence of this committee, however, the United States Brewers Foundation included in its membership the makers of over 80 per cent of the beer output of the country, together with the most important producers of materials and supplies for the brewing trade.

MODERN MANAGEMENT

While the stock in the Premier-Pabst corporation was closely held, no individual controlled anywhere near a majority. The

[9] Busch urged co-operation: *American Brewer*, LXIX, No. 4 (Apr. 1936), 23; Perlstein urged co-operation: *American Brewer*, LXXII, No. 2 (Feb. 1939), 23

Fred Pabsts and their sons owned the largest block of voting stock in the possession of one family, but the business was no longer a "family company." As a result, management was more professionalized and impersonal than in the days of either the Captain or Henry Shlaudeman.

At the head of the company whose executive officers were now in Chicago were Harris Perlstein, as president, and Fred Pabst, Robert Clark, James G. Shakman, and F. E. Solfisburg as vice-presidents. Perlstein also served as president of the Premier-Pabst Sales Company. This was the wholly owned subsidiary corporation which had been founded, December 17, 1927, as the Premier Malt Sales Company. Besides Perlstein, F. E. Solfisburg, the parent company's vice-president in charge of sales, and Charles T. Buehler, its secretary-treasurer, served in these same capacities in the sales company. (See Chronology, pp. 427-29, for assistant secretaries and treasurers.)

On December 20, 1938, the stockholders of Premier-Pabst Corporation voted to return the name of Pabst Brewing Company to the business and to simplify its capital structure. The Class A preferred stock was substantially unchanged, but each share of Class B preferred was to be exchanged for 75/100 of a share of new convertible preferred and 1½ shares of new common, and each share of Class C preferred for 55/100 of a share of convertible preferred and 1½ shares of common. Class A and B common were to be exchanged for the new common at the rate of 2½ shares of new stock for each share of the old. Thus the company would have only one type of common and two types of preferred.

Fred Pabst was now named chairman of the board of directors of the Brewing Company. The death of both Solfisburg and Clark in 1939 left Shakman as the only vice-president. Ivin E. Harris, who had been in the selling end of Premier since 1927 and had advanced to the position of assistant sales manager under Solfisburg, was made vice-president and general sales

manager of the Pabst Sales Company (the former Premier-
Pabst Sales Company, renamed in December 1938, following
the renaming of the parent company). At the same time Edwin
L. Morris, formerly of Swift who had joined Pabst in February
as director of sales promotion, was made vice-president of
the Pabst Sales Company in charge of advertising and public
relations.

In 1941 Fred Pabst's son, Rudolf Pabst, assistant secretary of
both the brewing and sales companies, received the additional
title of secretary of the sales company, but resigned the next
year to enter the Navy. On his return from service in 1945, he
became president of the newly acquired Hoffman Beverage
Company of Newark, New Jersey, and vice-president of the
Pabst Brewing Company. Edward H. Fiedler, who had handled
the legal work of Premier and Pabst as a partner of the firm of
Daily, Dines, White and Fiedler for many years, in 1942 became vice-president and general counsel of both the brewing
and the sales companies. The next year R. C. Zimmerman,
formerly controller of the Pabst Corporation and since 1941
assistant treasurer of the brewing company, was made "assistant vice-president in charge of the Milwaukee plant." Lester
Jones, who had grown up with Premier, was given the same
title for Peoria operations. From 1933 and 1934 on, A. J.
Ostendorf and E. B. Thornton, respectively, served as assistant
treasurers, and in 1939 Thornton also became assistant secretary. Between 1942 and 1945 the sales company expanded its
list of officers to include E. B. Thornton as assistant secretary-
treasurer, J. G. Gazzolo, office manager, as assistant treasurer,
and Dorothy Fiedler, E. H. Fiedler's sister, as assistant secretary.

The Hoffman Beverage Company was bought for cash on
December 18, 1945, becoming a wholly owned subsidiary, and
a group of old-time Pabst executives were put in charge. Along
with Rudolf Pabst as president were Edward H. Fiedler, vice-
president, and E. B. Thornton as secretary and treasurer. This

25

same group plus Harris Perlstein and James G. Shakman made up the board of directors of the subsidiary. John T. Rice, attorney for Hoffman, and George W. Fraser, Hoffman controller, were named assistant secretary and assistant treasurer, respectively, and on April 26, 1946, were given these same offices in the brewing company.

Thus the parent company and its two active subsidiaries had twenty-seven offices held by sixteen individuals as against a maximum of five officers in either Pabst or Decatur at any time prior to 1920. While the company was doing more than three times as much business as the Pabst and Decatur brewing companies combined had ever done in any of the earlier years, the increase in officer personnel was due more to modern ideas of setting up functional divisions under the immediate charge of officers of the company, and of rewarding executives with officerships, than to the mere increase in volume.

Management in 1946, even on the nonofficer levels, stemmed from the older Pabst, Premier, and Hoffman personnel with only a few men brought in from other companies. The board of directors also reflected this policy. In that year it consisted of Fred Pabst, chairman, Charles T. Buehler, Edward H. Fiedler, Frank T. Miller, Rudolf Pabst, Harris Perlstein, James G. Shakman, Robert Shlaudeman, and Bernard A. Spaeth. Shlaudeman and Spaeth, representing the inheritance from the old Decatur Brewing Company, and Frank T. Miller, a Peoria attorney, were the only nonofficers on the board. Collectively, Pabst's directors represented, either personally or through close family connections, a majority of the voting stock and the company therefore was not troubled by conflicts arising from the separation of ownership and control.

PLANNING FOR INCREASED VOLUME

From the production, sales, and income standpoints, management was extraordinarily successful in the years between repeal and the close of the Second World War. Production of

Pabst beer rose from 700,000 barrels in 1933 to 1,000,000 in 1934, 1,500,000 in 1936, 2,000,000 in 1941, 2,400,000 in 1942, and to well over 3,000,000 to lead the industry in 1946. Although annual dividends were paid on the common, except for 1934 and 1935, and over $5,000,000 worth of preferred stock was retired, the value of the company by 1946 had more than doubled.

CAPITAL, SURPLUS, AND PHYSICAL EQUIPMENT, 1933-1946

As of December 31	Capital Stock and Surplus	Land, Buildings, Machinery, and Equipment at Cost, Without Depreciation
1933	$12,666,464	$8,236,809
1934	13,478,478	9,224,688
1935	13,920,038	9,129,123
1936	14,436,744	9,719,176
1937	15,181,582	10,432,734
1938	16,655,984	10,885,675
1939	15,173,118*	11,313,756
1940	14,818,987*	11,669,401
1941	16,119,290	12,720,471
1942	17,370,658	13,315,399
1943	18,698,282	13,587,883
1944	20,198,425	13,890,155
1945	21,067,060*	20,786,995
1946	27,258,782	22,972,928†

* Preferred stock retirements: 1939, $3,200,000; 1940, $800,000; 1945, $1,283,480.
† Total figures used to show rate of investment. The depreciated figure for 1946, for example, was $11,888,563.

Just as in the early years of expansion under Captain Pabst, the net increase was continually reinvested in enlarging the business. In addition to an investment of over $2,000,000 in 1932 and 1933 in storage cellars and other equipment necessary to prepare the Milwaukee plant for the resumption of beer brewing, the 100 per cent increase in business from 1933 to 1936 necessitated continual investment in kegs, shipping boxes, bottles, and cans. The grain elevator on Commerce Street in Milwaukee, close to the Schlitz plant, was expanded twofold in 1937 so that all the malt used in Pabst beer could be made in the historic plant that since 1901, at least, had been the world's largest brewery-owned malthouse. By 1941 Pabst-Milwaukee was producing more beer than ever before in its history, and additional facilities again had to be provided.

The development of brewing at Peoria necessitated the building of a new stockhouse and bottle house there in 1934 and additions to the bottle house between 1937 and 1941. By 1941 Peoria had a 1,000,000-barrel capacity as against over 2,000,000 for Milwaukee. Special facilities for the manufacture of ale, to keep its manufacture separated from that of beer, were installed. In order to ensure uniformity of the beer produced at the two breweries, malt was sent from Milwaukee and the mineral content of the local water was adjusted to that of Milwaukee. In 1938 a new corn mill was also built in Peoria to supply corn grits for Pabst beer and syrup products. The mill was of a special type worked out by members of the Pabst and Allis-Chalmers staffs. Fine grinding was necessary, and the germ of each kernel which would introduce oil into the beer had to be removed. The oil extracted from the separated germ was sold as a separate product, as was the "hominy feed" made of the residue from the milling of the grits.

Acquisition of the Hoffman Beverage Company in December 1945 gave Pabst a modern brewery as well as an established soft-drink business. Hoffman had made soft drinks in Newark for over thirty years. Its brewery, added in 1934, was one of the newest and best equipped on the Atlantic seaboard. Before Pabst acquired the Hoffman properties, its technical staff had passed on them and decided that with certain additions and changes the Hoffman brewery would be well adapted to the production of the same Blue Ribbon beer as was being made at Milwaukee and Peoria. The necessary alterations and improvements were quickly begun, and by May 1946 the Newark brewery was ready for its new task. The Hoffman Beverage Company then went out of the brewing business, the brewery

being operated directly as a unit of the Pabst Brewing
Company.

Divested of its beer-manufacturing operations, the Hoffman
Beverage Company was back where it had started from, producing with model facilities its well-known and highly regarded soft drinks for the New York area. Before the war,
Hoffman had made a varied line of soft drinks, but, with the
sugar shortage, had limited its output to ginger ale and sparkling water. Consumer surveys showed that people in Greater
New York regarded these as the finest of their kind. The
Hoffman reputation in soft drinks matched the Pabst reputation in beer. Pabst therefore not only retained the Hoffman
Beverage Company as its soft-drink subsidiary but threw new
energy into its operation, and began to plan for its future when
wartime restrictions should be eliminated.

Hoffman Beverage also served Pabst in another capacity.
Though no longer making beer, its big fleet of trucks thoroughly covering the New York market suited it well to the job
of distributing Pabst Blue Ribbon at wholesale in that area.

Due largely to the purchase of the Hoffman brewery and
soft-drink properties, investment in land, buildings, and equipment which had increased some $5,500,000 between 1933 and
1944 was increased by almost $7,000,000 in one year. The money
for the purchase of the Newark company which was doing
about a $10,000,000 annual business came partly from the sale
of liquid assets held in the Pabst surplus account and partly
from short-term loans that were quickly repaid from earnings.

With the government restrictions imposed on the ownership
of retail outlets by breweries, the tendency of brewing companies, as well as other large American corporations, has been
to dispose of all surplus real estate. Due to the smallness of the
old Decatur business, and to the separation of the Pabst Realty
Company from the Brewing Company in 1920, the present
company held very little real estate in 1933, but even that
amount was reduced until, by 1945, Pabst held less than $25,000
worth of real estate not used in production or distribution.

IMPROVED OPERATIONS AND NEW PRODUCTS

Except for the introduction of the metal keg and the can, the improvements in brewing operations since 1933 have been refinements rather than fundamental changes. Manufacturing costs fell from 1933 to 1941, but this was a result of increased volume of production rather than of important changes in method. Labor costs per barrel which in the 1890's had been less than half the cost of materials, and which had remained less than the latter figure right up to 1919, now slightly exceeded it. Wage increases, the larger number of employees needed for the increased percentage of packaged beer, and declining grain prices brought about this change. Even though wages stayed high, declining grain prices from 1935 to 1941 joined with increased production in diminishing unit costs. A shipping brewer had also to add the expense of transportation, which remained fairly constant up to the war, and in 1939, for example, cost Pabst $2,750,000 for railroad freight, and $400,000 for trucking, or an average of $1.91 per barrel for all beer produced.

Among the improvements in methods of production from 1933 to 1946 were more power machinery, faster bottling operations, better refrigeration, increasingly exact control of temperature, and better grading of barley, with pilot plant tests of the various grades and types to secure more uniform malting. More careful laboratory checking of all stages of the brewing process also helped to avoid variations in the beer. In fact, the old-style brewmaster, once the most important man in the brewery, had been largely superseded by specialized technicians. On the basis of the results recorded by control laboratories in Milwaukee, Peoria, and Newark, the vice-president in charge of production, James G. Shakman, regulated the formula for the beer. To ensure uniformity, the same grains, malt, hops, and type of water were used at all plants, while the local brewmaster or superintendent of brewing had to see that instructions were carried out and to meet the emergencies that might call for instant, on-the-spot decisions. The blending of at least thirty-three separate brews in each sample of the finished product further ensured so high a degree of uniformity that even experts could not tell reliably which plant had brewed a particular bottle of beer.

Entirely separate from the control laboratory in Milwaukee was the research laboratory and office of experimental development run by Toly Agazim. Here a staff of five Ph.D.'s in chemistry, with twice as many assistants, on the one hand continuously studied the materials and processes used in beermaking and worked out improvements in the character of the materials that came in contact with beer, and on the other hand worked on the development of new grain products.

Guided by its research laboratory, Pabst was one of the first to initiate recovery of its surplus brewers' yeast as a highly refined product suited to pharmaceutical and food use. In addition to yeast, breweries, as we have noted earlier, produce a by-product of importance in the form of the insoluble part of the grains left as a residue in the mashing process. These "brewer's grains" are widely used in the feeding of dairy herds and other animals. Yet the importance of "brewer's grains" has often been forgotten by the public, and always overlooked by Prohibitionists charging the brewers with wasting food. In 1945 the weight of dried "brewer's grains," rich in residual proteins and several vitamins, sold for cattle feed by the Pabst Company was over 47,000 tons, or equal to 30 per cent of the total original weight of the grain used in beermaking. In addition to this, the 10 per cent of the original bulk removed in "screening" of barley to prepare it for malting was also sold for feed.

The research laboratory was also concerned with the products of the separate plants at Peoria where Pabst carried on the manufacture of its malt and maltose syrups and various dry products made from such syrups. Three Pabst plants are located at Peoria—the big brewery at Peoria Heights and, in Peoria proper, the syrup plant which includes the corn-grits mill erected in 1938 and a malthouse. The Peoria malthouse specializes in the production of diastatic, high-enzyme malt used in the products made in the syrup plant. This malt requires a different type of barley from that employed in making brewing malt at the big Milwaukee malthouse.

The products of the Peoria syrup plant are marketed by a special department of the Pabst Sales Company, known as the Industrial Products Division. Food type syrups are sold to bakers, breakfast-food and some other food producers, and tobacco manufacturers. Pharmaceutical syrups are sold to manufacturing chemists, and a desizing agent used for the removal of starch from cloth is sold to textile mills.

Pinch-hitting for sugar, as in the First World War, Premose became, in the Second World War, the main item of the Industrial Products Division. In syrup and dry form this sweetening was in great demand. The manufacturing department broke a bottleneck in its manufacture through a new method for cooking the corn (principal ingredient of Premose), and millions of pounds rolled to sugar-short industries each month.

But, for the history of brewing, the most important work of the Milwaukee research laboratory was that connected with the development of the metal keg and can. Beer acquires unwanted flavors from contact with all metallic elements in their pure form. Although the chemical reaction is too slight to measure except by microchemical methods, one part per million of iron in a bottle of beer, for example, will produce a noticeable taste. Consequently, the steel and black-iron kegs, coated with much the same pitch as that used in the wooden kegs, rushed into use to fill up the shortage after repeal were unsatisfactory. Dents in the keg resulting from rough handling would break the interior coating of pitch and bring the metal in contact with the beer. Three or four men in the Milwaukee laboratory were assigned the task of experimenting with every conceivable kind of keg lining. They successfully applied a new kind of lining to steel kegs, a heat polymerized, synthetic, resin type; and with the simultaneous development of cans for beer, the brewing industry was on its way to emancipation from the age-old sway of glass and wood shipping containers.

Like the metal keg, development of a metal can for beer presented both mechanical and chemical problems. The American Can Company tackled the job, but after solving the mechanical problems it enlisted the help of the Pabst research laboratories in testing various linings. Here the investigation Pabst was carrying on in relation to linings for steel kegs worked in particularly well. Pabst, critical of the linings first offered by American Can, warned the can company not to proceed too fast. But the sales department of the can company was anxious to move into commercial production. Finally, Dudley W. Figgis, then assistant to the vice-president and now president of the American Can Company, came to a meeting in Harris Perlstein's office. Samples of bottled and canned beer were poured into unmarked glasses and Perlstein was challenged to distinguish them. Quickly he did so. Three times the test was repeated—three times the results were the same. Perlstein argued for further research on the can linings. Figgis, impressed by what he had seen, agreed, and premature introduction of the beer can was averted. Some months later progress in perfecting the lining for beer cans had reached the point where Pabst was willing to put its beer into the new package, and beginning in July 1935 Pabst in "keglined" cans was ready for the national market.

Continental Can Company soon followed American into the beer-can field, but with a different can design and lining material. American, arguing that the can should be as compact as possible, made a regular sanitary style (flat top) can, with a baked synthetic, resinous, plastic lining. Continental brought out a "cone-top" style, closed with a regular bottle crown, and lined with a waxy compound. But the popularity of the flat top later forced Continental to add that type to its line.

The stability of brewing technology in the twentieth century was reflected in the permanence of jobs. Except for the general increase in bottle-house employment, the relative distribution of workers at the Milwaukee brewery for the busy and slack seasons of any sample year in the thirties looked much the same as in preprohibition days. Total average employment in the Milwaukee plant went up from 908 in 1934 to 2,248 in 1944, as a result of both increased production and the diminished efficiency of labor during the war (see Appendix C, p. 402).

Generally satisfactory union relations aided Pabst's continuous efforts to foster good morale among its employees. From 1933 on, two- or three-year contracts were negotiated with the International Union of Brewery, Flour, Cereal and Soft Drink Workers of America, generally at increasing wage rates. The two-year, self-renewing contract effective March 1, 1945, for example, provided for: a closed shop with temporary permit cards when union members in good standing could not be secured; the right of the employer to hire and fire; layoffs of new employees on the basis of length of service and older employees by rotation; reinstatement after leaves for illness; the outlawing of sympathetic strikes; access of union officials to the places of employment; the eight-hour day and forty-hour week with time and a half for overtime; rotation of shifts every four weeks; vacations of one week with pay after one year's service, and two weeks after three years' service; free beer in quantities to be determined by the employer; compulsory arbitration of disputes by a joint board; exclusion of foremen from the union; and wages of from $45.00 to $49.00 a week for most male employees and $34.50 to $38.50 for women.

As in the earlier period, in spite of an overwhelming vote by the workers in May 1934, in favor of just one union, separate A. F. of L. affiliated unions sought control of teamsters, firemen, engineers, and other special groups. As a result of these jurisdictional difficulties, the Milwaukee local of the Brewery Workers, in September 1946, voted by a small majority to shift its allegiance from the A. F. of L. to the C.I.O. The Peoria local, on the other hand, voted to remain independent of any national affiliation. In Newark, although the brewing department employees joined the C.I.O., the drivers and bottling employees remained in the A. F. of L.

The company made use of athletic teams, annual picnics, Christmas presents, and magazines to stimulate loyalty in the staff. The *Blue Ribbon News* was revived in Milwaukee in April 1934 with a character quite different from the prepro- hibition model. Instead of being aimed mainly at the trade, it was now a "house organ" devoted to news and events at the Chicago, Milwaukee, and Peoria centers, and later Newark, with occasional educational articles about Pabst products.

In December 1942 the company instituted a noncontributory pension plan for salaried employees receiving over $2,400 a year. The plan was designed to supplement social-security benefits, and provided not only for pension payments after the age of sixty-five for those who had been with the company twenty years or more, which together with social-security benefits would bring the total to 30 per cent or more of their former salary, but also for death benefits and severance pay- ments to those leaving the company after more than five years of service. In 1944 the plan was amended to include all salaried employees of over five years' service, and in 1946 to include, on the same basis, employees of the Hoffman Beverage Com- pany and other subsidiaries. Group-insurance plans of various types had also been introduced in all of the divisions.

To regulate and systematize contributions for civic and general social welfare, the company in 1945 established the Pabst Breweries Foundation. During 1945 and 1946, the Foundation received a total of $666,100 from the company and disbursed $338,600.

CHAPTER XVI

THE CAMPAIGN FOR THE NATIONAL MARKET

THE relative stability in brewing technology and labor relations after repeal did not extend to marketing. Here the years after 1933 were the most exciting in the history of American brewing. Not even in the early days of national shipping when Captain Pabst was trying to expand beyond the Chicago-Milwaukee axis, nor in the experimental years of bottling, did management have to make so many decisions crucial to its continued expansion and prosperity.

The future market for packaged beer was one of the major problems. "In 1933," said Harris Perlstein,

the probable future course of the beer business could be envisioned in either of two ways: (1) To look back at the business as it had existed prior to Prohibition and anticipate a renewal of many of the old situations, or (2) To assume that the general changes that had affected all consumer merchandise in the period between 1919 and 1933 would have their effect upon beer as well. Prior to Prohibition, draft beer was by all odds the principal factor. However, the American public had indicated its preference for packages in practically all lines. The old cracker barrel was no more. To the management of Pabst this meant that a similar change was indicated in the marketing of beer. They felt that draft would decrease in importance compared to packages.[1]

A corollary of the Pabst decision was that packaged beer must be backed by vigorous advertising from the very start when new drinking habits were being formed. Accordingly, Pabst invested about $2,000,000 a year in advertising in 1934 and 1935. In 1934 Pabst led all the brewers in newspaper advertising linage by a wide margin, using 77 per cent more space than Anheuser-Busch, its nearest competitor. In 1935 the other

[1] Statement to the author, Dec. 15, 1946.

brewers followed Pabst and stepped up their newspaper expenditures, but Pabst still held the lead in space.[2]

Beer advertisers had also a new public to consider. Drinking in public was no longer solely a man's prerogative. Prohibition and the speak-easy had changed that. And the new tavern with its conventional glass store-front no longer presented the "men only" atmosphere of the old saloon with its dark panels and swinging doors. For the home, the packaged beer sold in delicatessen and grocery stores was bought largely by women. Hence, the campaign that started in 1933 was pushed into exclusively feminine territory through advertisements in such magazines as *Delineator* and *Woman's Home Companion*.

The Ben Bernie radio show was continued for Blue Ribbon beer, and Bernie in return for a $4,000 a week contract agreed not to broadcast for any other product. Through such then novel devices as kidding the sponsor and inviting guest artists, he made the Pabst half hour at nine o'clock Eastern standard time on Tuesday evenings one of the most talked about radio programs in the country.

Time has emphasized the correctness of the Pabst decision to throw the weight of its advertising and promotion behind packaged beer, but throughout the thirties this policy encountered unexpected difficulties. Since few establishments were equipped to serve draught beer at the beginning of legal distribution, almost all beer was sold in bottles. During the so-called "honeymoon," from April to December 1933, brewers without national reputation shipped their beers far and wide in hope of capturing a market. Optimistic distributors became oversupplied and a great many stocks of bottled beer, some, not too well brewed in the first place, became old before they could be disposed of by retailers. As a consequence, the reputation of bottled beer suffered a setback. Draught beer, which must be sold promptly because it is not pastuerized, pleased the

---

[2] Pabst used 791,661 lines in the papers of seventy-one cities in 1934 and 645,957 in seventy-three cities in 1935. *American Brewer*, LXIX, No. 4 (Apr. 1936), 79.

public taste better, and in 1934 it began to look as though the Pabst management had guessed wrong.

Not only did packaged beer fail to hold even 30 per cent of the market in 1934, but the beer market as a whole was smaller than expected. For the year ending June 30, 1934, total domestic sales were only 32,000,000 barrels—less than half as much as in the best years before prohibition. Moreover, Pabst soon found that its wholesale jobbing organization, built up for malt syrup and cheese, was not well suited to beer distribution. From 1933 to 1939, Pabst had to seek new distributors for some six-hundred-odd local markets, about three quarters of its total number.

THE CAMPAIGN FOR THE CAN

Just as these problems of reconversion appeared to be reaching their maximum, however, a new boost was given to packaged beer by the perfection of the can. In the American Can Company's "keglined" can, ready for distribution by the summer of 1935, Pabst management saw new hope for the future—that the can could lead ultimately to far wider marketing of packaged premium beer. "We feel that since the relegalization of beer the market for beer has never been fully developed," said Harris Perlstein.

Statistics show the per capita consumption to be very much less than formerly. Of course, higher taxes have much to do with this, but there is another factor commonly overlooked. Competitive beverages have gained a great market and beer needs to be merchandised with the object of winning new customers. Beer barrelage will come up as beer obtains a larger percentage of the total beverage market.

Beer in cans offers an opportunity to stimulate and expand the market for beer. The fact that the can delivers beer in good condition and is convenient means that it will win new customers.[3]

[3] *Brewers' Technical Review*, X, No. 9 (Sept. 1935), 315. The Econometric Institute found no correlation between beer and soft-drink sales. *Memorandum to the United States Brewers Foundation, Inc.*, p. 17.

Pioneering in the introduction of canned beer on a national scale was a task calling for energy and a willingness to take risks. The Pabst "Tapacan" was introduced locally in Milwaukee and Peoria in the summer of 1935 while necessary materials including the essential can openers were being distributed to dealers and stock-piled at the plants. Encouraged by the results of these first few months of marketing experiments, Pabst swung its promotion solidly and confidently behind the can in the fall of 1935.

Pabst top management had never expected the can to completely replace the bottle. Harris Perlstein cautioned his sales organization not to count the bottle out and tried to reassure the exponents of glass that the introduction of the can would not operate to the disadvantage of the bottle, but, rather by directing the attention of the public to packaged beer and promoting its acceptance in the home, it would place beer on the same road that had been traveled by packaged food products, enlarging the market for bottles as well as cans. As cans made news of beer and brought more consumers to the industry, both brewers and bottle manufacturers would benefit. Though subsequent statistics bore out Perlstein's contention, he could not quiet the alarm that arose in brewing and glass-making circles in 1935 and the years directly following.

The can had every advantage over the bottle from the marketing and consumer standpoint, save for the elements of appearance and tradition. A twelve-ounce can is just about half the height of a bottle and the shipping weight is much less, a flat top and bottom allows the can to be stacked, there is no danger of breakage, it is easier to carry, store, and cool, and, most important of all from the consumer standpoint, there are no deposits or returns of empties. But hotels, restaurants, taverns, and the Pullman Company preferred the appearance of the bottle on their tables and helped to develop the idea that the can should be used only for "home" consumption.

Alarmed by what they considered a most serious threat to

their business, the glass companies developed the "stubby" and "steinie" short bottles, easier to ship, store, and handle than the traditional long-necked bottle. They produced the new models in quart and two-quart sizes as well as in the old twelve-ounce size, and backed them with extensive advertising. But the chief aid to the glass companies came from the propaganda of brewers who were not equipped with canning facilities. They played upon the popular idea that foods packed in glass were better and safer than those in metal. In 1936 the Schwarz Laboratories made comparative analyses of canned and bottled beers over a thirteen-week period. They found no difference in biological activity or chemical composition, finding only minor technical differences that would not have affected the enjoyment of the ordinary beer drinker.[4]

When the tumult had quieted somewhat, it was evident that beer in cans was here to stay. Its popularity varied in different markets. New York accepted it enthusiastically for home use—practically its only opportunity to try the can since most of the taverns and restaurants of that area served only draught beer. As early as November 10, 1935, *The New York Times* quoted I. E. Harris, then in charge of the Pabst divisional sales office there, as reporting that sales resistance to beer in cans had been overcome. On the other hand, by the end of 1937, after a year and a half of promotion, the can had captured less than 10 per cent of the Milwaukee market.[5] In the national market as a whole, to large degree because of Pabst merchandising, the can was established and due for a gradual increase in popularity. But most important, as Perlstein had foreseen, public interest in packaged beer had been stimulated. Consumers might argue in regard to the relative merits of bottles and cans as containers for beer—but they bought more packaged beer! New business opportunities were shaping for the bottle makers even while they worried about the can.

[4] Schwarz Laboratories, Inc., *Comparative Analysis of Bottled and Canned Beers*, p. 73.
[5] *Journal*, Dec. 31, 1937.

YEARS OF PROSPERITY

Pabst gained its share of the steady increase in total beer consumption during the business upswing from 1933 to 1937. A survey of ten cities by the Ross Federal Research Corporation late in 1935 demonstrated the general effectiveness of the Pabst advertising campaigns. Personal interviews of 2,517 people showed that of those who had seen beer advertising 50 per cent were using the product advertised, and 75 per cent of these drank Pabst. A still more positive proof of advertising effectiveness was Pabst's sales leadership of the "big three" in 1936.

In 1935 national chain radio was laid aside, not to be used again until 1943. With Pabst's help, the American Can Company was enabled to acquire the Ben Bernie show largely for promotion of its keglined cans for beer. Behind this move was Pabst's decision to place its advertising budget on a more flexible basis, which would permit gearing expenditures in various markets more directly to sales—a pattern into which chain radio, with its general spread, did not fit at the time. Greater emphasis was now put on outdoor posters, signs, and "point-of-purchase" displays (the old-time Signs and Views).

Of minor importance in total volume, but of undoubted value in maintaining the prestige of Blue Ribbon beer, was Pabst's prompt entry into the export market. The export division of the sales company, established in August 1933, ultimately secured leading firms as distributors in eighty-four nations or colonies. The practice was to sell outright to one firm in each area and let it take care of retail distribution. The best areas for sales were, as in the older period, South and Central America and the Far East where local beer brewing was either small scale or lacking. Occasionally, in areas where competition was severe, Pabst backed up its foreign dealers with neon signs, billboards, newspaper and magazine advertising, and radio programs. By 1941 Pabst sold about 60 per cent of some 200,000 barrels of beer exported from the United States.

26

In promoting various brands, from 1934 to 1940, Pabst partially repeated its history from 1896 to 1903. In both periods promotion was gradually spread behind an increasing number of brands, but ultimately concentrated on a single one. Blue Ribbon, the prestige label of the Pabst line in preprohibition days, was again applied to Pabst's first-quality beer in both bottles and kegs in 1933 and later in cans. In 1934 draught and bottle Blue Ribbon ale were introduced. Both Blue Ribbon beer and ale were priced in the middle thirties at $15 a barrel wholesale for draught and 15 cents retail for bottles. At first to meet local Milwaukee competition, followed by a spread to many markets, other Pabst labels from the preprohibition era, such as Red, White and Blue, were used to compete in the popular-priced (ten cents per bottle) field. The popularity of the Blue Ribbon Casino, with Ben Bernie as its star attraction, at Chicago's Century of Progress in 1933 and 1934 led to limited introduction of another new, popular-priced brand, "Casino." For a short time the famous old Pabst brand—Export— was applied to beer in cans, and a new name, "Old Tankard," to ale in cans. In 1939 Pabst introduced "Andeker," a new draught beer of all-malt, European type, made of a special kind of malted barley and using only imported hops. This beer, being unsuited to bottling, was sold only in kegs, and only in selected markets, at a high price. When the outbreak of the Second World War shut off the supply of European hops, Andeker was discontinued.

Just as in the preprohibition days, other brewers tried to capitalize on the Pabst reputation and extensive advertising. A New England brewery sought to gain from the Ben Bernie radio program by putting out an "Olde Maestro" beer, but was stopped by a United States District Court ruling in January 1935.[6] In 1933 Pabst also started action against the Milwaukee Brewery of San Francisco for a Golden Ribbon label, and in April 1936 the United States District Court prohibited this

---

[6] *Premier-Pabst Corporation* v. *Elm City Brewing Co.,* 9 F. Supp. 754 (D. C. D. Conn. 1935).

label as an infringement on Pabst rights.[7] The next year the *American Brewer* noted that legal action prevented a Beaver Dam, Wisconsin, brewer from using Pabst's Red, White and Blue label, trade-marked in 1899.[8]

During 1936 and 1937 the sum total of Pabst's promotional efforts seemed satisfactory. Pabst's percentage of national volume sold rose from 2.43 per cent in 1935 to 2.82 per cent in 1936, and 3.05 per cent in 1937.[9]

THE MARKET AND THE DEPRESSION OF 1938-1939

General business depression in 1938 and 1939, however, shattered any complacency that might have been developing among the Pabst executives. Hard times and unusually low prices for wine and distilled liquors checked the rapid advance of packaged beer which in 1938 and 1939 remained at about 45 per cent of a slightly diminished total national beer consumption.[10]

For the first time since the merger Pabst faced a leveling off of sales. Added to these external problems, the death of Solfisburg, the vice-president in charge of sales, led to a re-evaluation of Pabst promotional efforts.

During 1939, merchandising, marketing research, and sales-training departments were inaugurated; a limited number of direct branches were added to the distributing system; Ivin E. Harris was promoted to vice-president in charge of sales; and Edwin L. Morris was brought in to handle advertising. A new national advertising agency was also engaged, and, just as from 1903 to 1919, promotion was put largely behind Blue Ribbon in the old-style bottle. At the same time sales and

---

[7] *Premier-Pabst* v. *Milwaukee Brewery of San Francisco* (D. C. N. D. Cal. S. Div. Equity 3594-S, 1933). See also *American Brewer*, XVI, No. 8 (Aug. 1933), 38; LXIX, No. 5 (May 1936), 41.

[8] *American Brewer*, LXX, No. 1 (Jan. 1937), 52. No information in company records.

[9] Pabst Marketing Research Reports, 1939.

[10] Econometric Institute, *Memorandum to the United States Brewers Foundation, Inc.*, p. 3.

advertising expenditures were increased 42 per cent above those of 1937.

The reintroduction of branches also marked a partial return to the system employed by Pabst before 1919. But now Pabst followed the policy of restricting branch operations to its home cities plus a few of the larger metropolitan areas where satisfactory results had not been had through independently owned wholesalers. The new branches were fewer in number than in the old days and handled a smaller percentage of the total distribution.[11]

BEER SALES IN THE UNITED STATES

Fiscal Year Ending June 30	Total Tax-Paid Withdrawals, Barrels	Percentage of Total Withdrawals Packaged
1934	32,266,039	31.6
1935	42,228,831	25.0
1936	48,759,840	29.5
1937	55,391,960	38.1
1938	53,926,018	43.8
1939	51,816,874	46.2
1940	53,014,230	49.3
1941	52,799,181	51.7
1942	60,856,219	56.1
1943	68,636,434	58.7
1944	76,969,764	60.8
1945	79,590,598	65.4
1946	81,286,821	65.9

MODERN MARKETING IN OPERATION

Pabst's new marketing research department illustrated the change that had taken place in methods of business policy formation between the late nineteenth and middle twentieth centuries.[12] Captain Pabst had formed his ideas about consumer preferences, sales promotion, and market areas from random

[11] About 15 per cent in 1946.
[12] Arthur H. Cole has called this the change from rational to cognitive entrepreneurship. Arthur H. Cole, "An Approach to the Study of Entrepreneurship," *The Tasks of Economic History* (Supplemental Issue of *The Journal of Economic History*) VI (1946), pp. 1-15.

letters, conversations, and the readily discernable trends in company earnings. But by the 1930's, the national situation was too complex and the factors too varied for a top executive to depend on such hit-or-miss information. For many years, to be sure, market data of many types had been collected and used by both Fred Pabst and Harris Perlstein, but now this function of providing additional eyes and ears for top management was systematized and placed under experienced direction. The department not only conducted surveys on consumer and dealer preferences, the sales of other brewers, and the effectiveness of advertising, but it also assisted in the drawing up of sales quotas, constructed statistical series on population and income trends and other data valuable in shaping executive decisions, and executed special assignments for top management as the need arose.

From the late thirties the information developed through research in food products by Pabst's and other laboratories, and information bearing on hotel and restaurant management was passed on to operators of restaurants and hotels through the consumer service department. Miss Annette Snapper, head of the department, lectured at national and sectional hotel and restaurant association meetings and offered advice to any operator who needed help on questions as varied as better lighting, rationalization of kitchen procedures, better menus, or personnel problems.

The new officers and departments and the higher promotional expenditures, 15 per cent larger in 1940 than in 1939, seemed justified by results. A 27 per cent increase in sales volume in 1941 put total barrels sold well over the two million mark.

While the modern functional divisions and specialized jobs were new in the history of Pabst, much of the actual promotional work had to follow established patterns. In addition to the extensive use of magazine advertising, newspaper space, outdoor posting, and radio broadcasting, strong emphasis was placed on point-of-purchase display. While this activity has always been basic in beer promotion, it was elevated to new importance in Pabst planning. Also stepped up was Pabst participation in national and sectional conventions of the brewing and allied industries.

Outstanding displays at fairs and exhibitions were another old-time practice pursued by the company. The award of prizes and medals was no longer a feature of the fairs of the 1930's at Chicago, San Francisco, and New York. The promotional value came rather from the attractiveness and popularity of the company exhibits. In the Chicago Century of Progress in 1933, Pabst was well represented by the Blue Ribbon Casino, which proved to be one of the most popular dining and gathering places of the entire exposition. A major entertainment program headed by Ben Bernie constituted one of the important features, not only of the Blue Ribbon Casino but of the fair itself. Pabst also participated at San Francisco's Treasure Island, and at the New York World's Fair on Long Island in 1939 and 1940, where a six-sided Pabst pavilion covering 40,000 square feet set in a garden of maple trees served food and Pabst Blue Ribbon beer to the music of a good orchestra. Pabst was also featured in many of the other exhibitions and concessions throughout the fair grounds.

PABST AND THE WAR

The war brought personnel problems, material shortages, and special restrictions to the breweries, but no wartime prohibition. Americans had learned what Europeans had known in the earlier conflict—that beer is a valuable beverage for both military and civilian morale. Current Army regulations, which forbade the sale of intoxicating liquors, permitted beer containing not over 3.2 per cent of alcohol by weight at Army establishments. General Marshall, as Chief of Staff, and other Army and Navy authorities exerted great efforts to keep up the supply of beer. Pabst, leading all other brewers in foreign shipments, sent some 450,000 barrels to the armed forces overseas in 1945.

Early that year James G. Shakman of Pabst surveyed the beer supply problem on the Western Front as consultant to the quartermaster general. He found that as a result of careful artillery aim, breweries had been miraculously spared in cities like Tobruk, Naples, and Aachen where almost everything else was in ruins. In many cases the machinery was still adequate for turning out good beer, but without American materials they could not produce a brew satisfactory to our troops. Accordingly, Shakman recommended that beermaking ingredients be shipped from the United States, since they took up less than a quarter of the cargo space of the finished product, and that the European breweries be put into service producing a beer of specified quality. As the war came to a close, ten technicians from the United States were at work on this task.

Export for civilian consumption was enmeshed in a web of regulations. Export licenses had to be obtained from Washington and, in almost every area, import licenses from some foreign government. Rigid exchange controls made it difficult for the customers to pay in American dollars, and high customs duties, wherever local breweries existed, further hindered the trade. But from the long-run standpoint, the boost given to the Pabst name from thousands of GI's asking for it in taverns and hotels, or drinking it at government canteens and recreation centers all over the world, was bound to be of inestimable value, not only to export sales but to packaged sales at home. Following the close of the war the company had many more foreign orders than it could fill under the existing conditions of grain and transportation shortages. In view of the intensive domestic demand, only small quotas could be allotted to keep a Pabst position in each market that could be expanded when beer might again be plentiful.

Enlistments and the draft took away brewery labor while high wages and government purchasing increased the demand for beer. By the end of the war Pabst was employing almost 4,000 people. Milwaukee and Peoria brewed more beer than ever before, and the malthouse and syrup departments at Peoria speeded up the production of malt products for munition, alcohol, food, pharmaceutical, and textile manufacture. As the war continued and 1,400 Pabst employees joined the armed forces, 1,500 women, some of them wives who took the places of their husbands, were added to the pay rolls. Except for office workers these new female employees were almost all in the bottle houses, first in carton folding and inspecting, then in pasteurizing, packing, and soaking, and finally in receiving, labeling, and filling.

Besides high labor turnover, and the impossibility of quickly training new workers up to the old levels of efficiency, a 70 per cent increase in grain prices raised costs. Caught between ceiling prices on beer and government rationing of grain which held down production, the brewers' profits, after taxes, were not large. On the other hand, they had only minor problems in conversion and reconversion.

Beginning in late 1943 and continuing in 1944, in celebration of the company's one-hundredth anniversary, Pabst undertook to help boost national morale, endangered by fears of postwar unemployment, and also to gain public good will by holding a postwar employment contest. Nearly 36,000 essays, limited to 2,000 words each, were submitted. The board of judges consisted of Clarence Dykstra, president of the University of Wisconsin, Professor Wesley C. Mitchell of Columbia University, Beardsley Ruml, chairman of the Federal Reserve Bank of New York, and A. F. Whitney, president of the Brotherhood of Railroad Trainmen. The judges were assisted in the preliminary screening of the essays by the Columbia University economics department. Herbert Stein of the War Production Board won the $25,000 first prize, and Leon H. Keyserling of the National Housing Agency, the $10,000 second prize. In addition, the judges awarded fifteen $1,000 prizes. The winning plans were published in a widely distributed booklet.

THE POSTWAR MARKET

At the close of hostilities, when the government suddenly imposed restrictions more serious than those during the war, the brewers ran into difficulties not foreseen by writers on the postwar economy. On March 1, 1946, an order was issued limiting the use of grain by brewers to 70 per cent of that used in the corresponding period of 1945. However, able presentation of their case by the brewers led to the easing of the restrictions on September 1, 1946, and their complete elimination a few months later.

Looking to the postwar period of renewed competition, Pabst had not relaxed its promotional efforts when wartime prosperity and restrictions produced a sellers' market in beer. In March 1943 radio network advertising was resumed on the Columbia Broadcasting System with the Groucho Marx show. The following year Danny Kaye, Eve Arden, and Lionel Stander together with Harry James's orchestra appeared on the Pabst half hour. This first radio venture by Danny Kaye was continued during the winter of 1945-1946, with Orson Welles doing the summer show. In the fall of 1946 Eddie Cantor took over. Pabst made its radio shows and its slogan, "Thirty-three Fine Brews Blended into One Great Beer," the core of its promotional efforts. Marx, Kaye, or Cantor "point-of-purchase" materials such as pocket calendars and cardboard store displays were distributed. "Thirty-three to one" was the theme for a series of full-page color advertisements in leading magazines and for outdoor posters in 175 cities.

Successful promotion was only one factor, however, in Pabst's reconquest of national sales leadership in 1946. Another vital factor was wise planning for increased capacity and better physical distribution. Purchase of the Hoffman Beverage Company in the fall of 1945, as we have seen, gave Pabst an up-to-date Eastern plant which it was able to equip with the additional apparatus necessary for the manufacture of Blue Ribbon by May 1, 1946. Meanwhile, neither of Pabst's two major competitors had acquired any additional breweries.

The exact future trends of the postwar market situation could not readily be forecast in 1946. Packaged beer made up 66 per cent of the total volume sold, justifying the Pabst predictions of the early thirties; and the nationally advertised beers had gained sharply in public favor. Pabst was doing a record-breaking business, but Anheuser-Busch and Schlitz were still close behind, and behind them, in turn, were other large brewers like Ballantine of Newark and Liebmann and Schaefer of New York. The tendencies favoring larger producers had built up a dozen other regional firms, some old and some new, whose yearly brewing capacities of 750,000 to 1,500,000 barrels were far beyond those of preprohibition years. In addition, a large brewing enterprise as a subsidiary to wine and distilled liquor production was created in 1945 when Schenley, of distilling fame, purchased Blatz of Milwaukee. All these developments presaged new conditions of competition in the brewing industry, but it was too early to tell whether in postwar America the largest firms would grow faster than the medium large, how far mergers and purchases of regional manufacturing and distributing facilities would reduce the number of competitors, or what the advantages or disadvantages might be in Schenley's combined ownership of brewing and distilling plants. Up to 1946 the relatively limited sales territories of each of the other large brewers left Pabst, Anheuser-Busch, and Schlitz in their special and historic relation to the national market.

Whatever the course of future competition, Pabst, with its main brewery in Milwaukee and its two auxiliary modern plants at Peoria and Newark, was in a better position than ever before to compete for the national market. Neither of its two major competitors was as well situated in relation to the East— the area in which the shippers had always been weakest and had the most to gain. Management was in strong and relatively youthful hands. In addition to beer and ale, the company was fortified by its foothold in the soft-drink field and its backlog of other products. In a longer view of Pabst history, the most striking years of success might lie in the period to come rather than back in the Captain's time.

APPENDIXES

A. DIRECTORS

PHILLIP BEST BREWING COMPANY, PABST BREWING COMPANY, PABST
CORPORATION, 1873-1932

Directors	Term
Captain Frederick Pabst	1873-1904
Emil Schandein	1873-1888
Charles Best	1873-1890
Lisette Schandein (Mrs. Emil)	1889-1905
Gustav G. Pabst	1890-1921
Charles W. Henning	1893-1917
Fred Pabst	1893-1932
Ernest Borchert	1893-1899
Frank R. Falk	1893-1902
Rudolph Nunnemacker	1899-1900
Jacob Heyl	1900-1903
W. O. Goodrich	1904-1922
Henry J. Stark	1905-1921
Henry Danischefsky	1917-1921
H. W. Marsh	1921-1924
Frederick A. Pabst	1923-1932
F. J. Postel	1924-1929
Rudolf Pabst	1927-1932
Edward Loebl	1927-1932
J. H. Moore	1927-1931
W. R. Patterson	1927-1929
August Pabst	1929-1932
James R. Nicholson	1929-1930
J. E. Magnus	1931-1932
Robert Pabst	1932-1932
R. C. Zimmerman	1932-1932

PREMIER-PABST CORPORATION, PABST BREWING COMPANY, 1933-1946

Directors	Term
Charles T. Buehler	1933-1946
Fred Pabst	1933-1946
Harris Perlstein	1933-1946
James G. Shakman	1933-1946
Bernard A. Spaeth	1933-1946
Philip A. Singer	1933-1934
Robert Clark	1933-1939
F. E. Solfisburg	1933-1939
Rudolf Pabst	1936-1946
H. G. Atwood	1936-1940
Robert Shlaudeman	1939-1946
Edward H. Fiedler	1940-1946
J. T. Hunter	1942-1946
Frank T. Miller	1946-1946

NUMBER OF DIRECTORS CONSTITUTING THE BOARD

1873-1893	Three	1927-1932	Seven
1893-1903	Seven	1933-1934	Nine
1903-1920	Five	1934-1936	Eight
1920-1927	Three	1936-1946	Nine

B. OFFICERS

NUMBER OF OFFICERS, BY SAMPLE YEARS

1873 President, vice-president, secretary

1880 President, vice-president, secretary

1890 President, vice-president, secretary

1900 President, first vice-president, second vice-president, secretary, treasurer

1910 President, vice-president, secretary

1920 President, vice-president, secretary, treasurer, assistant secretary

1925 President, first vice-president, second vice-president, secretary, treasurer

1930 President, first vice-president, second vice-president, third vice-president, fourth vice-president, secretary, treasurer

1936 President, four vice-presidents, secretary-treasurer, assistant secretary-treasurer, two assistant treasurers

1946 Chairman, president, two vice-presidents, vice-president and general counsel, secretary-treasurer, two assistant vice-presidents, assistant secretary-treasurer, two assistant secretaries, two assistant treasurers

C. EMPLOYEES
NUMBER OF EMPLOYEES, 1878-1901, 1933-1946

1878	187	1897	722
1879	201	1898	683
1880	235	1899	658
1881	337	1900	669
1882	434	1901	724
1883	398	1933	2,200
1884	434	1934	1,950
1885	447	1935	1,700
1886	451	1936	2,100
1887	455	1937	2,175
1888	398	1938	1,850
1889	404	1939	1,875
1890	495	1940	2,050
1891	595	1941	2,550
1892	639	1942	3,225
1893	744	1943	3,450
1894	766	1944	4,100
1895	742	1945	3,825
1896	767	1946	5,250

D. SEASONAL VARIATION IN EMPLOYMENT, 1907-1908 *

	12/29/07-1/11/08	4/19-5/2/08		12/29/07-1/11/08	4/19-5/2/08
Peddlars	13	12	Painters	17	24
Teamsters	44	55	Boiler House	19	19
Barnmen	16	16	Steam Fitters	18	16
Smith Shop	3	3	Engineers	15	16
Harness Shop	1	1	Tinners	8	8
Wagon Shop	22	23	Machine Shop	29	27
Lager Cellar	65	65	Masons	17	11
Ferm. Cellar	25	24	Electric Shop	3	3
Brewhouse	25	24	Sign Dept.	4	3
Washhouse	50	50	Plumber	1	1
Malthouse	28	29	Laboratory	1	2
Elevators	4	4	Car Packers	24	24
Coopers	47	48	Stirnewith	2	2
Yard Coopers	103	99	Weighers	1	1
Galv. Shop	3	1	Watchmen	7	7
Millwrights	24	24			
R. E. Carpenters	3	8	*Total*	681	697
Carpenters	39	47			

* Exact listing as in Sundry Papers Scrapbook, 1873-1919.

E. SALARIES OF OFFICE STAFF, 1880 *

Brewmaster	$416.66
Foreman, Empire Brewery	208.33
General accountant and examiner †	175.00
General correspondent	166.67
Traveler	150.00
General freight agent	145.84
Cashier	100.00
Bottling department superintendent	100.00
Barley buyer	100.00
Maltster	100.00
General bookkeeper	100.00
Shipping and receiving clerk †	100.00
Collector	100.00
Bottling department bookkeeper	100.00
Traveler	83.34
Icehouse superintendent	75.00
City bookkeeper and assistant †	65.00
Department clerk, telephone operator, and assistant †	65.00
City agent	60.00
Assistant correspondent	60.00
Superintendent of Pewaukee icehouse	50.00
Assistant bookkeeper and bill clerk †	50.00
Keg bookkeeper and assistant †	35.00
Assistant shipping and receiving clerk †	35.00

* Confidential memorandum by Charles Best for listing of office help. The lists of salaries paid monthly and of other employees not noted in Mr. Best's memorandum are from salary ledger.

† These compound titles were each borne by a single individual.

THE PABST BREWING COMPANY

F. BANK LOANS, 1882-1893 *

HIGHEST AND LOWEST MONTHLY FIGURES FOR EACH YEAR
(AMOUNTS OWED TO INDIVIDUAL BANKS)

Dates	Total	Second Ward Savings Bank	Wisconsin Marine and Fire Insurance Company Bank
1882, December	$ 894,519	$ 694,519	$200,000
September	550,000	400,000	150,000
1883, April	1,136,423	936,423	200,000
October-November	600,000	400,000	200,000
1884, April	751,653	551,653	200,000
September-December	200,000	100,000	100,000
1885, February-May	250,000	150,000	100,000
September-December	None	None	......
1886, March-May	150,000	150,000	......
January and August-November	None	None	......
1887, June	397,558	386,558	......
January and October-November	150,000	150,000	......
1888, March	257,243	257,243	......
September-October	None	None	......
1889, February-April	300,000	300,000	......
May and July-December	None	None	......
1890, April	76,987	76,987	......
January-March and July-November	None	None	......
1891, December	672,802	672,802	......
April	8,892	8,892	......
1892, June	1,061,281	1,061,281	......
October	500,000	500,000	......
			Wisconsin National Bank
1893, May	1,271,472	971,472	300,000
October	700,000	500,000	200,000

* Private trial balance, 1882-1893.

G. SYNDICATE BREWERIES *
(APRIL 1891)

Capital in £

Baltimore Breweries Company 190,000
    Bauernschmidt and Marr Brewing Company

Bartholomay Brewing Company 970,000
    Bartholomay Brewing Company; Rochester Brewing Company; Genesee Brewing Company; the malthouses of E. B. Parsons and J. N. Oothout

Betz, J. F., and Son 550,000
    J. F. Betz and Son, Philadelphia

Chicago Breweries Company 1,000,000
    McAvoy Brewing Company; Wacker and Birk Brewing and Malting Company

Cincinnati Breweries 230,000
    Jung Brewing Company, Cincinnati; Crescent Brewing Company, Aurora

City of Baltimore United Breweries Company 335,000
    John Bauernschmidt; William Miller and Company; H. Strauss Brothers Company

City of Chicago Brewing and Malting Company 1,900,000
    Conrad Seipp West Side Brewing Company; F. J. Dewes; malthouses of George Bullen and Company and L. C. Huck

Denver United Breweries Company 600,000
    Ph. Zang Brewing Company; Denver Brewing Company

Detroit Breweries 160,000
    Charles Endriss; Jacob Mann; Bavarian Brewing Company; A. Goebel and Company

Emerald and Phoenix Brewing Company 470,000
    T. C. Lyman and Company, New York; F. J. Kastner, Newark

Hills Union Brewery Company 115,000
    William Hill, Newark

Illinois United Breweries 300,000
    Gipp's Brewing Company; Union Brewing Company; Gus Leisy Brewing Company; J. Kollmer and Company; Edwin Porter, Joliet; Markert and Company, Wilmington

Indianapolis Breweries Company 430,000
    C. F. Schmidt; Pihieber Brewing Company; C. Maus

Jones, Frank, Brewing Company 1,300,000
    Frank Jones, Portsmouth, New Hampshire; Jones, Cook and Company, Boston

* *Western Brewer*, XVI, No. 4 (Apr. 15, 1891), 878.

27

Syndicate Breweries—*Continued*

Capital in £

Milwaukee and Chicago Breweries 2,271,000
M. Brand Brewing Company; Bartholmae and Leicht Brewing Company; Ernest Brothers Brewing Company; Bartholmae and Roesing Brewing Company; K. G. Schmidt Brewing Company, Chicago; V. Blatz of Milwaukee

New England Breweries Company 610,000
John Roessle; Haffenreffer and Company; Suffolk Brewing Company, Boston; Stanley and Company, Lawrence

New York Breweries Company 930,000
H. Clausen and Son Brewing Company; Flanagan, Nay and Company

St. Louis Breweries Company 2,850,000
Anthony and Kuhn Brewing Company; Bremen Brewery Company; Brinkwirth-Nolker Brewing Company; Cherokee Brewery Company; Excelsior Brewery Company; Green Tree Brewery Company; A. Griesedieck Brewing Company; H. Grone Brewery Company; Hyde Park Brewery Company; Klausmann Brewery Company; Liberty Brewing Company; Miller Brothers Brewing Company; Schilling and Schneider; Joseph Schnaider; Charles G. Stifel's; Wainwright Brewery Company; Jul. Winkelmeyer Brewing Company Assoc.,—all of St. Louis; and Heims Brewery Company of East St. Louis

San Francisco Breweries Company 1,500,000
Wieland Brewery Company; United States Brewery; Chicago Brewery Company; Willows Brewing Company; South San Francisco Brewing Company; Pacific Brewery—all of San Francisco; Fredericksburg Brewery, San Jose; Oakland Brewery, Oakland; Brooklyn Brewery, East Oakland; Hofburg Breweries, West Berkeley

Schoenhofen, Peter, Brewing Company 617,000
P. Schoenhofen Brewing Company

Springfield Breweries Company 135,000
Schneider Brothers; Vorce and Blee, Springfield, Ohio

United States Brewing Company 1,100,000
Albany Brewing Company, Albany, New York; G. Krueger Brewing Company; P. Hauck and Company; Mrs. C. Trefz —all of Newark; and A. Huepfel's Sons, New York

Voight Brewery Company 200,000
E. W. Voight, Detroit

Washington Brewery Company 161,000
Albert Cary, Washington

BIBLIOGRAPHY

On the ground, presumably, that each company's records are somewhat unique and, in any case, not open to the public, business historians have omitted bibliographies. I believe that neither of these reasons warrants such omission. One of the greatest difficulties encountered by the historian, trained in the use of conventional sources but a babe in the woods among business records, is to know what to look for. Company records may be in dozens of different departments, storerooms, vaults, or warehouses. Usually there is no officer of the company who can remember where everything is. The historian, therefore, needs to know what he wants in order to know when he has probably secured everything likely to exist in a particular type of business. The Pabst records from 1873 to 1919 appear to be about as complete as can be expected in most companies, and a listing of them, together with the less complete records for other periods, may give the future historians an idea of what to look for when studying similar manufacturing enterprises. Furthermore, many companies are ready to permit properly qualified economists or historians to use their records for specified purposes. But to judge whether a company's records may be helpful for a given problem, the economist or historian must know what records exist.

The following list of Pabst records includes everything preserved from 1844 to 1919. From 1920 to 1932 it includes only the records used in our brief sketch of the prohibition years. From 1933 to 1946 information has been supplied by Pabst officers, and only the few records used directly are listed. The records do not include all the materials that may be found in a large brewing company. Pabst pay rolls and union contracts are lacking for the period before 1920. Sales data and branch records are quite incomplete. Some of these may be tucked away in the larger branch offices, although the company policy has been to send all noncurrent records to Milwaukee. More detailed data on the branches did not appear important enough to our over-all study to warrant a thorough search of the many branch offices.

RECORDS IN THE ARCHIVES OF THE PABST BREWING COMPANY, MILWAUKEE, WISCONSIN

(Complete 1844-1919; selected, 1920-1932.)

GENERAL RECORDS

Bound Volumes

Combination Record, 1873-1882. Articles of Association, Minutes of the Board of Directors, Annual Statement of Affairs. In January 1882 the Directors Record and the Stockholders Record were separated. The Stockholders Record was set up from May 20, 1873. The Directors

Record was set up from April 7, 1876. The new records, therefore, contain copies of information in the Combination Record up to January 24, 1882. 1 vol.

Directors Record, 1873-1932. Minutes of the Board of Directors. 3 vols.

Documents and papers relating to the transition from the Pabst Brewing Company to the Pabst Corporation. Bills of Sale relating to the Pabst Corporation, 1920-1932. 1 vol.

Documents, correspondence, and papers relating to the Fred Pabst Company, the Seamweld Equipment Corporation, the Frank Wiedeman Company, the Puritan Malt Extract Company, 1922-1930. 1 vol.

Letter Books—Executive Correspondence, 1874-1879; 1879-1888; 1887-1888; 1882-1891; 1884-1898; 1898-1901; 1888-1915. 7 vols.

Letter Book—Branch Office (unidentified) to Captain Pabst, 1893-1900. 1 vol.

Pabst Brewing Company in Liquidation, 1920-1921. 1 vol.

Pictures of Brewery and General Properties, 1873-1920. 3 vols.

Real Estate Purchases, 1892-1902. Listings of mortgages and payments (incomplete). 4 vols.

Stock Certificate Books, 1873-1932. 5 vols.

Stock Certificate Book, Fred Pabst Company. 1 vol.

Stockholders Record, 1876-1932. Minutes of stockholders meetings. 2 vols.

Stock Transfer Books, 1873-1932. 5 vols.

Loose Records and Papers in File Boxes and Cabinets

Contracts. General, 1890-1932; miscellaneous memorandums, 1879-1890.

Citizenship papers, commissions, passports, will of Phillip Best.

Letter files—letters received by executives, 1878; 1879; 1880; 1881; 1882-1897; 1898-1901; 1899-1903. 7 boxes.

Miscellaneous papers relating to: American Valve Rotator Company, 1920-1924; attempted syndicates, 1900-1910; Delta Cooperage Company, 1892-1919; Fermentation Gas Company, 1895-1896; Marsh Refrigerator Service Company, 1917-1919; Milwaukee Beer Company, 1898-1919; Milwaukee Grains and Feed Corporation, 1931-1932; major legal actions involving the company, 1882-1932; The Pabst Theater, 1895-1932; trade-mark registrations and infringements; Frank Wiedeman Company, 1929-1931; Pabst Dietary Products Inc., 1928-1930.

Mortgage papers, partnership agreements, records of loans, 1846-1866.

Miscellaneous photographs.

Real-Estate Records

Brewery—Deeds, Abstract of Titles, 1844-1932. 20 boxes.

General, 1869-1920. 351 boxes.

Records relating to the Pabst Realty Company, Ventnor Corporation, Washington Highlands Company, 1918-1928.

ACCOUNTING RECORDS

Bound Volumes

Annual Inventory Listings, 1881-1902. 1 vol.

Annual Statement of Affairs: Book A, 1873-1890; Book B, 1891-1901 (separate sheet for 1902 in Book B).

Consolidated Profit and Loss: Pabst Corporation and Pabst Sales Company, 1928-1929. 1 vol.

Export Ledgers, 1902-1920. 19 vols.

General Ledgers, 1873-1920. 21 vols.

Private Ledger, 1873-1920. Ledger accounts for stockholders, capital stock, surplus, bills payable, mortgages, brewery real estate, stocks and shares, interest, Second Ward Savings Bank. 5 vols.

Private Journal, 1876-1920. Profit and Loss, monthly salaries of executives, dividends, notes, and deposit account in Second Ward Bank, notes due. 4 vols.

Private Trial Balance, 1881-1920. Set up on monthly basis according to accounts in Private Journal. 1 vol.

Receipts and Voucher Book, 1869-1886. 1 vol.

Reports of Accountants
   Jones, Caesar, Dickinson, Wilmot & Co., Chicago (agents of Price, Waterhouse & Co.) 1904, 1905, 1906.
   Dickinson, Wilmot & Sterrett, Chicago (agents of Price, Waterhouse & Co.) 1907, 1908.
   Price, Waterhouse & Co., Chicago (from 1915, Milwaukee), 1909, 1911-1918, 1920-1932.

Sundry Papers Scrapbook, 1873-1919. Internal Revenue and Brewers' Bonds, 1873-1876; Beer Inventories, 1875-1876; Confidential Reports on other brewing companies, 1885-1915; Address to Milwaukee Brewers' Association by Jacob Obermann. 1 vol.

Sundry Promissory Notes, 1869-1886. Miscellaneous canceled checks, receipts, some mortgage records, and certificates of deposit. 1 vol.

Tax Receipts Scrapbook, 1851-1885. 2 vols.

Tax Receipts and Invoices Scrapbook, 1887-1891. Contains receipts carrying 175 different names of individuals and business concerns, most of them retail dealers doing business with Pabst.

Internal Revenue Form Book, 1863, 1895-1919. 5 vols.

Loose records and papers in file boxes and cabinets

Monthly Trial Balances, Pabst Brewing Company, 1902-1915.

Pabst Corporation, Cheese Division, Financial Statements, 1930-1933.

Federal Income Tax Returns, 1909-1917 (incomplete).

OPERATING RECORDS

Bound Volumes

Cost Book by Brands, 1907-1918. 1 vol.
Fortnightly Time Books, 1907-1913 (in Brewhouse Records). 5 vols.
Monthly Salary Ledger, 1876-1914. 5 vols.
Monthly Salary Journal, 1890-1897. 1 vol.
Monthly Salary Ledger, Fred Pabst Company, 1929-1933. 1 vol.
Confidential Memorandum, by Charles Best. 1 vol.
Sud Books, 1894-1920 (in Brewhouse Records). 7 vols.

Loose Sheets

Comparative pay-roll distribution, 1924-1932.

ADVERTISING AND SALES RECORDS

Bound Volumes

Branch Sales Reports by Months, 1917-1919. 1 vol.
Comparative Annual Sales Statements by Brands, 1907-1916. 1 vol.
Comparative Sales by Wholesale Customers, 1914-1915. 1 vol.
Customers' Accounts—Day Book, 1849-1852. Listing of some individuals'
    accounts, most entries made in German. 1 vol.
Dealers' Accounts, 1892-1893. Unmarked for territory—evidently Kansas
    City Branch Account Book. 1 vol.
Distribution of General Selling and Management Expense, 1910-1914.
    1 vol.
Scrapbook of Labels, 1899-1930. 1 vol.
Blue Ribbon Cheer, May 1932.
Blue Ribbon News, May-December 1913; January-December 1914;
    January-February 1915; complete file, 1934-1941.
Pabst Marketing Research Reports, 1939-1946.
Pabst-Pep Sales Booster, December 15, 1930.
Pabst Times, February, December 1935.
Souvenir Booklets issued in 1877, 1883, 1891, 1896, 1905, 1906.
Special Booklets: *German Poem,* 1888; *For Members of the G.A.R.
    23rd National Encampment,* August 25, 1889; *An Invitation to Mil-
    waukee,* 1893; *50th Anniversary,* 1894; reprint from *Collier's Weekly,*
    "Always Pure," 1894; *100 Points of Perfection,* 1895; reprint of
    A Hundred Point Man, by Elbert Hubbard, 1915.
Secret Books, issued 1889-1898. *Secrets, More Secrets, Still More Secrets,
    Untold Secrets, Ominous Secrets, Wedding Secrets, Charm Secrets,
    Home Secrets, Baby Secrets.*

Loose Sheets in Cabinets

Summary of branch operations, 1902-1918.
Sales statistics (beverages), 1932.
Brewers' Association agreements, 1898, 1902.
Advertising memorandum contracts, 1879-1890.
Memorial of Milwaukee Saloonkeepers.
Union contract, April 1, 1926.

COMPANY SCRAPBOOKS

A large amount of miscellaneous information concerning the company in the form of press clippings, pictures, and promotional literature was deposited by the Pabst Brewing Company with the Milwaukee County Historical Society where it is available to all scholars. This material is referred to in the footnotes as "scrapbook clippings."

ADVERTISING SCRAPBOOKS

Samples of booklets, advertising, labels, promotion cards, and some issues of *Blue Ribbon News*. 2 vols.
Special Advertising, 1888-1917. 4 vols.
Magazine Advertising, 1911-1917. 1 vol.
Best Tonic Advertising, 1887-1917. 6 vols.

NEWSPAPER CLIPPINGS

General write-ups from various newspapers, 1879-1897; 1897-1903; 1897-1904; 1904-1906. 4 vols.
Milwaukee Sentinel, 1901-1907, 1907-1915. 2 vols.
Milwaukee Journal, 1901-1917. 1 vol.
Evening Wisconsin, 1901-1917. 1 vol.
Milwaukee *Free Press*, 1901-1912.
Milwaukee *News, Der Herold, Germania*, and out-of-town papers, 1906-1909; 1907-1915. 2 vols.
Memorial Volume on Captain Pabst, 1904. 1 vol.
On Gustav Pabst, 1907-1911. 1 vol.
On Labor from Milwaukee Newspapers, November 9, 1887–February 17, 1888. 1 vol.

MISCELLANEOUS BOOKLETS, POSTERS, AND CALENDARS

GENERAL MATERIALS

The "outside" or noncompany materials used, while listed in the footnotes, are assembled here to provide a comprehensive view of some of the auxiliary sources for business research.

MANUSCRIPTS

Deuster, Oscar V. "The Story of the German Stage in Milwaukee."
Milwaukee County Historical Society, Milwaukee.
Perlman, Selig. "History of Socialism in Milwaukee, 1893-1910." A.B.
thesis. University of Wisconsin. [In the possession of the author.]
United States Census Bureau, manuscript form, "Wisconsin Census,"
1850; 1860; 1870. State Historical Society of Wisconsin, Madison.
United States Works Progress Administration, Federal Writers Project,
Wisconsin. "Milwaukee Guide," three parts. State Historical Society of
Wisconsin, Madison.
United States Works Progress Administration, Federal Writers Project,
Wisconsin. "Notes on Biography of Captain Frederick Pabst." State
Historical Society of Wisconsin, Madison.   •
United States Works Progress Administration, Federal Writers Project,
Wisconsin. "Notes on Milwaukee Brewing." Milwaukee County
Historical Society, Milwaukee.

GOVERNMENT DOCUMENTS

Acts and Resolves Passed by the Legislature of Wisconsin, 1850.
Adulteration of Food Products. Senate Committee on Manufactures.
Senate Report, No. 516. Fifty-sixth Congress, first session (February 28,
1900).
Aldrich, N. W., ed. *Report on Wholesale Prices, Wages, and Transportation* (Aldrich Report). Senate Report, No. 1394. Fifty-second Congress,
second session (1893). 4 vols.
*Biennial Reports of the Bureau of Labor and Industrial Statistics of
Wisconsin,* 1883/84-1920.
Brewing and Liquor Interests and German Propaganda. Senate Document, No. 62. Sixty-sixth Congress, first session. (1918, 1919). 3 vols.
Federal Reporter, CXXVII, CXLIII, CXLV, CCLXXIV.
Federal Reporter Supplement, IX, XIII, XVII.
Federal Reporter, Second Series, XII, XV, XVII.
General Laws Passed by the Legislature of Wisconsin, 1872.
New York State. *Annual Report of Commissioners of Labor,* 1886-1890.
————. *Mediation and Arbitration Board, Second Annual Report.*
Albany, 1889.
Royal Commission on Customs and Excise Tariffs, Australia. *Minutes of
Evidence,* VI, Div. 1, Stimulants, 1906. 4 vols.
United States Department of Commerce, Bureau of the Census. *Census,*
1850-1940.
————. *Census of Manufactures,* 1914.
————. *Census Survey of Business, 1937-1938. Retail Survey.*
————. *Census Survey of Business, 1937-1938. Wholesale Distribution:
Beer and Other Fermented Malt Liquors.*

————. *Thirteenth Census of the United States*, Vol. VIII, *Manufactures*, 1909; *General Report and Analysis*, 1913.
United States Statistical Abstracts.
Wisconsin Reporter, XCIII.

CONVENTION REPORTS, DIRECTORIES, STATEMENTS OF MILWAUKEE BOARD OF TRADE AND CHAMBER OF COMMERCE

American Brewing Institute. *Transactions*. Vol. I-V (May 1901–March 1910). New York, 1902-1910.
American Brewing Trade List and Internal Revenue Guide for Brewers. Supplement to the *American Brewers' Review*. Chicago, 1903-1915.
American Federation of Labor. *Report of Proceedings, 1887-1920.* Cincinnati, 1888-1921.
Brewers' Almanac, 1944. New York: United States Brewers' Association, 1944.
Brewers' Almanac, 1946. New York: United Brewers Foundation, 1946.
Brewers' Guide for the United States, Canada and Mexico. Supplement to the *American Brewers' Review*. Chicago, 1896, 1898.
International Brewers' Congress II. *Report of Proceedings.* Chicago: Fred Klein Co., 1912. 2 vols.
Milwaukee Board of Trade. *Annual Report of Commerce.* Milwaukee, 1855-1856.
Milwaukee Chamber of Commerce. *Annual Statement of Trade and Commerce.* Milwaukee, 1858-1873.
New York City Copartnership and Corporation Directories. New York: The Trow City Directory Company, XXXV (1887)-LXXVIII (1930).
Milwaukee City Directories, 1851-1920.
Tovey's Official Brewers' and Maltsters' Directory of the United States and Canada. Supplement to the *Brewer's Journal*. New York, 1881, 1882, 1899, 1901-1904.
United States Brewers' Association. *Reports of Convention Proceedings,* 1883-1909; 1934-1936; 1942-1944.
United States Brewers' Association. *Yearbooks,* 1910-1920.

STATE AND LOCAL HISTORIES

Aiken, Andrew Jackson, and Proctor, Lewis A., eds. *Men of Progress, Wisconsin.* Milwaukee: Evening Wisconsin Co., 1897.
Anderson, W. J., and Bleyer, Julius, eds. *Milwaukee's Great Industries.* Milwaukee: Association for the Advancement of Milwaukee, 1892.
Austin, H. Russell. *The Milwaukee Story.* Milwaukee: *Milwaukee Journal*, 1946.

Bruce, William George. *Builders of Milwaukee.* Milwaukee: Bruce Publishing Co., 1946.

———. *The Auditorium.* Milwaukee, 1909.

———, ed. *History of Milwaukee City and County.* Chicago: S. J. Clarke Publishing Co., 1922. 3 vols.

———. *A Short History of Milwaukee, Wisconsin.* Milwaukee: Bruce Publishing Co., 1936.

———. "Memoirs of William George Bruce," *Wisconsin Magazine of History,* XVI (1932-1933), 359-82; XVII (1933-1934), 3-71, 187-227, 307-40, 402-32; XVIII (1934-1935), 42-65.

Buck, James S. *Pioneer History of Milwaukee.* Milwaukee: Milwaukee News Co., 1876-1886. 4 vols.

The City of Milwaukee Guide. Milwaukee: Caspar and Zahn, 1886.

Conard, Howard Lewis. *History of Milwaukee County.* Chicago and New York: American Biographical Publishing Co., 1895. 3 vols.

Deutsch, Herman J. "Yankee and Teuton Rivalry in Wisconsin Politics of the Seventies," *Wisconsin Magazine of History,* XIV (1930-1931), 262-82, 403-18.

Everest, Kate A. "How Wisconsin Came by Its German Element." MS., A.M., 1892. Collections of the State Historical Society of Wisconsin. Madison, XII, 299-334.

Fish, Carl R. "Phases of the Economic History of Wisconsin, 1860-70," *Proceedings of the State Historical Society of Wisconsin, 1907.* Madison, 1908. Pp. 204-16.

"German Pioneer Letters," *Wisconsin Magazine of History,* XVI (1932-1933), 428-48.

Gregory, John. *Industrial Resources of Wisconsin.* Milwaukee, 1855.

Gregory, John Goadby. *History of Milwaukee, Wisconsin.* Chicago: S. J. Clarke Publishing Co., 1931. 4 vols.

———, ed. *Southeastern Wisconsin: A History of Old Milwaukee County.* Chicago: S. J. Clarke Publishing Co., 1932. 4 vols.

Hense-Jensen, Wilhelm. *Wisconsins Deutsch-Amerikaner, biz sum Schluss des neunzehnten Jahrhunderts.* Milwaukee: Die Deutsche Gesellschaft, 1900-1902. 2 vols. Vol. II by Wilhelm Hense-Jensen and Ernest Bruncken.

Holton, E. D., and Others. *Commercial History of Milwaukee, Opening of the Chamber of Commerce.* Collections of the State Historical Society of Wisconsin. Madison, 1906. IV, 253-89.

Hooker, William Francis. *Bill Hooker's Old-Time Milwaukee and Men Who Helped Make It Great.* Milwaukee: W. F. Hooker, 1935.

———. *Glimpses of an Earlier Milwaukee.* Milwaukee: *Milwaukee Journal,* 1929.

Industrial History of Milwaukee. Milwaukee: E. E. Barton, 1886.

Kellogg, Louise Phelps. "Wisconsin Historical Landmarks," *Proceedings of the State Historical Society of Wisconsin, 1927.* Madison, 1928. Pp. 63-110.

Koss, Rudolph A. *Milwaukee.* Milwaukee, 1871.

Lacher, John H. A. *The German Element in Wisconsin,* Milwaukee: Muhlenberg Unit 36, Milwaukee Steuben Society of America, 1925.

Larson, Laurence M. *A Financial and Administrative History of Milwaukee,* University of Wisconsin Bulletin, No. 242, "Economics and Political Science Series," IV, No. 2. Madison, 1908.

Levi, Kate Everest. "Geographical Origin of German Immigration to Wisconsin." MS., Ph. D., 1898. Collections of the State Historical Society of Wisconsin, Madison, XIV, 341-93.

Magyar, Francis. "History of Early Milwaukee German Theatre, 1850-1868," *Wisconsin Magazine of History,* XIII (1929-1930), 375-86.

Merk, Frederick. *The Economic History of Wisconsin During the Civil War Decade.* Publication of the State Historical Society of Wisconsin, Vol. I. Madison, 1916.

Milwaukee Historical Advertisements. Milwaukee: Second Ward Savings Bank, 1924.

Milwaukee Illustrated. Milwaukee: W. W. Coleman, 1878.

Milwaukee Illustrated. Milwaukee: C. N. Caspar Co., 1901.

Milwaukee Sentinel. An Illustrated Description of Milwaukee. Milwaukee, 1890.

————. *Centennial Edition.* Milwaukee, 1937.

Milwaukee, Seventy-five Years a City. Milwaukee: The 75th Anniversary Committee, 1921.

Old Settlers Club of Milwaukee County. *Early Milwaukee.* Milwaukee: The Club, 1916.

Quaife, Milo M. *Wisconsin: Its History and Its People, 1634-1924.* Chicago: S. J. Clarke Publishing Co., 1924. 4 vols.

Raney, William Francis. *Wisconsin: A Story of Progress.* New York: Prentice-Hall, 1940.

Redfield, Lorraine Culver. *The Story of Pewaukee, 1836-1936.* Madison: Howard Clements Co., 1936.

Schafer, Joseph. *Four Wisconsin Counties.* Madison: State Historical Society of Wisconsin, 1927.

————. "Prohibition in Early Wisconsin," *Wisconsin Magazine of History,* VIII (1924-1925), 281-99.

————. "Sectional and Personal Politics in Early Wisconsin," *Wisconsin Magazine of History,* XVIII (1934-1935), 442-65.

————. "The Yankee and Teuton in Wisconsin," *Wisconsin Magazine of History,* VI (1922-1923), 125-45, 261-79, 386-402; VII (1923-1924), 3-19, 148-71.

Schlinkert, Leroy. *Subject Bibliography of Wisconsin History.* Madison: State Historical Society of Wisconsin, 1947.

Smith, Guy Harold. "Notes on the Distribution of German-Born in Wisconsin in 1905," *Wisconsin Magazine of History,* XIII (1929-1930), 107-20.

Still, Bayrd. "Growth of Milwaukee as Recorded by Contemporaries," *Wisconsin Magazine of History,* XXI (1938), 262-92.

———. "Milwaukee, 1870-1900: The Emergence of a Metropolis," *Wisconsin Magazine of History,* XXIII (1939), 138-62.

———. "Development of Milwaukee in the Early Metropolitan Period," *Wisconsin Magazine of History,* XXV (1942), 297-307.

Uber, Harvey August. *Environmental Factors in the Development of Wisconsin.* Milwaukee: Marquette University Press, 1937.

United States Biographical Dictionary, Wisconsin Volume. Chicago: American Biographical Publishing Co., 1877.

Usher, Ellis Barker. *Wisconsin, Its Story and Biography, 1848-1913.* Chicago: Lewis Publishing Co., 1914. 8 vols.

Ward, William W. "Early Legislation Concerning Wisconsin Banks," *Proceedings of the State Historical Society of Wisconsin, 1895.* Madison, 1896. Pp. 155-61.

Watrous, Jerome Anthony, ed. *Memoirs of Milwaukee County.* Madison: Western Historical Association, 1909. 2 vols.

Western Historical Company. *History of Milwaukee, Wisconsin.* Chicago: Western Historical Co., 1881.

Wheeler, Andrew Carpenter. *The Chronicles of Milwaukee.* Milwaukee, 1861.

OTHER SECONDARY SOURCES

Accum, Frederich Christian. *A Treatise on the Art of Brewing.* London: Longman, Hurst, Rees, Orme and Brown, 1820.

Andreae, Percy. *The Prohibition Movement.* Chicago: Felix Mendelson, 1915.

Arnold, John P. *Origin and History of Beer and Brewing.* Chicago: Alumni Association of the Wahl-Henius Institute of Fermentology, 1911.

Arnold, John P., and Penman, Frank. *History of the Brewing Industry and Brewing Science in America.* Chicago: privately printed, 1933.

Beney, M. Ada. *Wages, Hours and Employment in the United States, 1914-1936.* "National Industrial Conference Board Studies," No. 229. New York: National Industrial Conference Board, 1936.

Bergner and Engel Brewing Company. Philadelphia, 1882.

Black, William. *A Practical Treatise on Brewing.* London: Longmans, Brown, Green and Longmans, 1844.

Bowers, David Frederick, ed. *Foreign Influences in American Life.* Princeton: Princeton University Press, 1944.

Brewers' Industrial Exhibition. *Essays on the Malt Liquor Question.* New York, 1876.

Bursk, J. Parker. *Seasonal Variations in Employment in Manufacturing Industries,* "University of Pennsylvania Research Studies," No. 14. Philadelphia: University of Pennsylvania Press, 1931.

Cherrington, Ernest H. *The Evolution of Prohibition in the United States of America.* Westerville, Ohio: American Issue Press, 1920.

Clark, Victor S. *History of Manufactures in the United States, 1607-1928.* New York: McGraw-Hill Book Co., 1929. 3 vols.

Clarke, Edward W. *Brewery Bookkeeping, A Practical Treatise on Brewery Accounts Including Office Management.* Chicago: H. S. Rich & Co., 1898.

Cochran, Thomas C. "The Economics in a Business History," *The Tasks of Economic History* (Supplemental Issue of *The Journal of Economic History*), V (1945), 54-65.

Cole, Arthur H. "An Approach to the Study of Entrepreneurship: A Tribute to Edwin F. Gay," *The Tasks of Economic History* (Supplemental Issue of *The Journal of Economic History*), VI (1946), 1-15.

——. "Business History and Economic History," *The Tasks of Economic History* (Supplemental Issue of *The Journal of Economic History*), V (1945), 45-53.

Colvin, David Leigh. *Prohibition in the United States.* New York: George H. Doran Co., 1926.

Commons, John R., *et al. History of Labour in the United States.* New York: Macmillan Co., 1918, 1935. 4 vols.

Cooper, Isabella Mitchell. *References, Ancient and Modern, to the Literature on Beer and Ale.* New York: United Brewers' Industrial Foundation, 1937.

Copeland, Wilbur Fisk. *Handbook of Prohibition Facts.* New York: Funk and Wagnalls Co., 1892.

Cronau, Rudolph. *Prohibition and the Destruction of the American Brewing Industry.* New York: R. Cronau, 1926.

Cushman, Robert E. *Leading Constitutional Decisions.* Rev. ed. New York: F. S. Crofts & Co., 1929.

Dobyns, Fletcher. *The Amazing Story of Repeal; An Exposé of the Power of Propaganda.* Chicago: Willett, Clark & Co., 1940.

The Econometric Institute Incorporated. *Memorandum to the United States Brewers Foundation, Inc.—The Effect of National Prohibition on the Market for Beer During the Excess Profits Tax Base Period 1936-1939.* New York: Econometric Institute Inc., 1945.

Ehret, George. *Twenty-five Years of Brewing.* New York, 1891.

Elwell, Fayette H. *Brewery Bookkeeping and Cost Finding.* New York: United States Brewers' Association, 1935.

Faust, Albert Bernhardt. *The German Element in the United States.* New York: The Steuben Society of America, 1927. 2 vols. in 1.

Fosdick, Raymond B., and Scott, Albert L. *Toward Liquor Control.* New York: Harper & Bros., 1933.

Fox, Hugh. "Our Constructive Policy." An Address Delivered at the Annual Dinner of the Brewers' Association of Massachusetts, May 26, 1915.

———. "The Saloon Problem," *Annals of the American Academy of Political and Social Sciences,* XXXII (July–December 1908), 531-38.

George, John Edward. *The Saloon Question in Chicago.* New York: Macmillan Co., 1897.

Gordon, Ernest Barron. *The Dry Fight in Europe and Its Relation to America.* New York: Alcohol Information Committee, 1930.

Gordon, Leslie, compiler. *The New Crusade.* Cleveland: Crusaders Inc., 1932.

Gras, N. S. B. "Are You Writing a Business History?" *Bulletin of the Business Historical Society,* XVIII, No. 4 (1944), 73-110.

Hamilton, G. S. *Brewery Accounting.* London: Gee & Co., 1939.

Hansen, Emil Christoph. *Practical Studies in Fermentation.* Translated by Alex K. Miller, revised by author. London: Spon, 1896.

Hansen, Marcus Lee. *The Atlantic Migration.* Cambridge: Harvard University Press, 1940.

———. *German Schemes of Colonization Before 1860,* "Smith College Studies in History," IX, Nos. 1 and 2 (October 1923, January 1924). Northampton, Mass.: Department of History of Smith College.

———. *The Immigrant in American History.* Cambridge: Harvard University Press, 1940.

Harrison, Leonard V., and Laine, Elizabeth. *After Repeal: A Study of Liquor Control Administration.* New York: Harper & Bros., 1936.

Henius, Max. *Danish Beer and Continental Beer Gardens.* Illustrated lecture by Max Henius at Convention, Atlantic City, October 2, 1913. New York: United States Brewers' Association, 1914.

Hillquit, Morris. *History of Socialism in the United States.* New York: Funk and Wagnalls Co., 1906.

Hind, H. Lloyd. *Brewing Science and Practice.* London: Chapman and Hall, Ltd., 1938-1940. 2 vols.

Hole, S. Reynolds, Dean of Rochester. *A Little Tour of America.* London: E. Arnold, 1895.

Jorgensen, Alfred P. C., *Micro-Organisms and Fermentation.* Translated by S. H. Davies. London: C. Griffin & Co., Ltd., 1911.

Koren, John. *Economic Aspects of the Liquor Problem.* Boston: Houghton Mifflin Co., 1899.

Krout, John A. *Origins of Prohibition.* New York: Alfred A. Knopf, 1925.

Manchester, Herbert. *The Diamond Match Company.* New York: privately printed, 1935.

Merz, Charles. *The Dry Decade.* Garden City: Doubleday, Doran & Co. 1931.

Mock and Blum. *List of United States, British and German Patents Covering the Manufacture of Non-Alcoholic Beverages.* New York: Mock and Blum, 1918.

Morison, Samuel Eliot. *The Founding of Harvard College.* Cambridge: Harvard University Press, 1935.

Nowak, Carl Alfred, ed. *New Fields for Brewers and Others Active in the Fermentation and Allied Industries.* St. Louis: C. A. Nowak, 1917.
――――. *Modern Brewing.* 2d ed. St. Louis: C. A. Nowak, 1934.
Odegard, Peter H. *Pressure Politics: The Story of the Anti-Saloon League.* New York: Columbia University Press, 1928.
One Hundred Years of Brewing. Supplement to the *Western Brewer* (1903). Chicago: H. S. Rich & Co., 1903.
"Papers on Prohibition, Liquor Laws, etc." Pamphlets issued by the United States Brewers' Association, 1887-1888.
Peabody, Francis Greenwood, ed. *The Liquor Problem; A Summary of Investigations Conducted by the Committee of Fifty.* Boston: Houghton Mifflin Co., 1905.
Persons, Warren Milton. *Beer and Brewing in America, An Economic Study.* 4th ed. New York: United Brewers' Industrial Foundation, 1941.
Phelps, Edward Bunnell, compiler. *A Summary of the Possibilities and Probable Cost of the Proposed Plan for Workmen's Compensation and Old-Age Pensions for American Brewery Workmen.* New York: United States Brewers' Association, 1911.
Powderly, Terence V. *Thirty Years of Labor: 1859 to 1889.* Columbus, Ohio: Excelsior Publishing House, 1890.
Presbrey, Frank. *The History and Development of Advertising.* Garden City, N. Y.: Doubleday, Doran & Co., 1929.
Research Company of America. *National Survey of the Brewing Industry.* New York: Research Company of America, 1940-1944.
Reynolds, Lloyd George, and Killingsworth, Charles C. *Trade Union Publications, the Official Journals, Convention Reports, Proceedings, and Constitutions of International Unions and Federations, 1850-1941.* Baltimore: Johns Hopkins Press, 1944-1945. 3 vols.
Romer, Frank. *Reviewing American Brewing.* Baltimore: Crown Cork and Seal Co., 1942.
Salem, Frederick W. *Beer, Its History and Its Economic Value as a National Beverage.* Hartford: F. W. Salem & Co., 1880.
Schaefer Brewing Co., F. & M. *Our One Hundreth Year.* Privately printed, 1942.
Schlüter, Hermann. *The Brewing Industry and Brewery Workers' Movement in America.* Cincinnati: International Union of United Brewery Workmen of America, 1910.
Schwarz Laboratories Inc. *Comparative Analysis of Bottled and Canned Beers.* New York: Schwarz Laboratories Inc., 1936.
Seager, Henry R., and Gulick, Charles A., Jr., *Trust and Corporation Problems.* New York: Harper & Bros., 1929.
Shadwell, Arthur. *Drink in 1914-1922, A Lesson in Control.* London and New York: Longmans, Green, 1923.

Thomann, Gallus. *Alleged Adulteration of Malt Liquors*. New York: United States Brewers' Association, 1886.

———. *American Beer, Glimpses of Its History and Description of Its Manufacture*. New York: United States Brewers' Association, 1909.

———. *Documentary History of the United States Brewers' Association*. New York: United States Brewers' Association, 1896, 1898. 2 vols.

———. *Liquor Laws of the United States*. New York: United States Brewers' Association, 1885-1887. 2 vols.

———. *Up to Date, A Review of Some Important Phases of the Drink Question, 1888-1892*. New York: United States Brewers' Association, 1892.

Thornton, Frank Weldon. *Brewery Accounts*. New York: Ronald Press, 1913.

United Brewers' Industrial Foundation. *American Beer and Ale, A Handbook of Facts and Figures*. New York: United Brewers' Industrial Foundation, 1937.

United States Brewers' Association. *History of Brewing and the Growth of the United States Brewers' Association*. New York: United States Brewers' Association, 1937.

Wahl, Arnold Spencer. *Wahl Handy Books of the American Brewing Industry*. Chicago: Wahl-Henius Institute, 1937, 1944.

Wahl, Robert, and Henius, Max, compilers. *American Handy Book of the Brewing, Malting and Auxiliary Trades*. 3d ed. Chicago: Wahl-Henius Institute, 1908. 2 vols.

Wheeler, Wayne B., compiler. *Federal and State Laws Relating to Intoxicating Liquors*. 2d ed. Westerville, Ohio: American Issue Press, 1918.

Wilcox, W. F., ed. *International Migrations*. New York: National Bureau of Economic Research, Publication 14, 1929; Publication 18, 1931.

Wines, Frederic H., and Koren, John. *The Liquor Problem in Its Legislative Aspects*. Boston: Houghton Mifflin Co., 1897.

Wittke, Carl Frederick. *We Who Built America, The Saga of the Immigrant*. New York: Prentice-Hall, Inc., 1940.

Wolman, Leo. *The Growth of American Trade Unions, 1880-1913*. New York: National Bureau of Economic Research, 1924.

———. *The Boycott in American Trade Unions*, "Johns Hopkins University Studies in Historical and Political Science." Series 34, No. 1. Baltimore: Johns Hopkins Press, 1916.

MAGAZINES *

Advertising Experience, 1896-1902.
American Brewer, 1869-1946.
American Brewers' Gazette and Malt and Hop Trades' Review, 1877, 1878, 1879.

* Because of irregular practices in numbering the various trade journals, volumes and numbers have been omitted.

American Brewers' Review, 1893-1918.
American Federationist, September 1899; July 1907.
Beverage Journal, 1933-1946.
Brewer and Maltster, 1910-1919; 1933-1937.
Brewer and Maltster and Beverageur, 1919-1933.
Brewers Digest, 1939-1946.
Brewers' Journal and Barley, Malt and Hop Trades' Reporter (German and American Brewers' Journal), 1884-1921.
Brewers Journal–Western Brewer, 1933-1946.
Brewers Technical Review, 1934-1937.
Brewery, Flour, Cereal and Soft Drink Workers' Journal, 1918-1934.
Brewery Worker, 1934-1946.
Collier's Weekly, November 1, 1902.
Commercial and Financial Chronicle, July 2, 1910, September 17, 1910.
Cosmopolitan, May 1908; May 1909.
Modern Brewer, 1935-1939.
Modern Brewery, 1933-1935.
The Nation, September 9, 1909.
The New Republic, August 21, 1915; October 2, 1915.
Northwestern Trade Bulletin, August 21, 1879.
Printers' Ink, February 27, 1907.
The Tasks of Economic History (Supplemental Issue of *The Journal of Economic History*), 1945, 1946.
Theatre: Illustrated Monthly Magazine of Theatrical and Musical Life, 1903.
Western Brewer, 1883-1920.
Wisconsin Magazine of History, 1918-1946.

NEWSPAPERS

Evening Wisconsin, 1887-1892.
Milwaukee *Labor Review*, 1886-1887.
Milwaukee Daily Journal, 1886-1890.
Milwaukee Daily News, 1891-1892.
Milwaukee Daily News and Review, 1889-1891.
Milwaukee *Daily Review*, 1887-1889.
Milwaukee Journal, 1910-1920; 1930-1945. Microfilmed from 1910-1920; at the Milwaukee Public Library.
Milwaukee Leader, January 30, 1929.
Milwaukee Sentinel, 1837-1920. Microfilmed from 1837-1909; at the Milwaukee Public Library. Indexed from 1837-1879 by the United States Works Progress Administration, Federal Writers Project, Wisconsin.
New York Herald, January 7, 1900; January 21, 1903.
New York Times, 1930-1945.
Wisconsin Banner und Volksfreund, 1855-1866.
Wiskonsin-Banner, 1845-1855 (after April 18, 1845, *Wisconsin Banner*).

28

CHRONOLOGY

THE PABST BREWING COMPANY

1842   Jacob Best, Jr., and Charles Best established a vinegar factory in Milwaukee.

1844   Charles Best returned to Mettenheim, Germany, and brought the rest of the Best family to Milwaukee.

September 10. First real estate purchased on Chestnut Street Hill, the present site of the Pabst Brewing Company, Milwaukee.

The brewery, Best and Company, owned and operated by Jacob Best, Sr., and his sons, Jacob, Jr., Charles, Phillip, and Lorenz, was established in Milwaukee.

1845   February 22. First lager beer from Best and Company available for sale.

July. Charles Best withdrew from Best and Company.

1848   Frederick Pabst came to America from Germany.

1850   February. Lorenz Best joined Charles, establishing the Plank Road Brewery (ancestor of the Miller Brewing Company).

1851   August 6. New partnership agreement drawn up between Jacob Best, Sr., Jacob Best, Jr., and Phillip Best.

1852   July 1. First *display* advertisement for Best and Company placed in the *Wisconsin Banner*.

1853   January 14. Jacob Best, Sr., retired. Jacob Best, Jr., and Phillip Best carried on the business of Best and Company under a partnership.

1854   By this year a branch office of Best and Company had been set up on Randolph Street, Chicago.

1857   Frederick Pabst became a steamship captain on the Great Lakes.

1858   Phillip Best was commissioned a brigadier general of the First Division of the state militia.

1859   October 1. Jacob Best, Jr., and Phillip Best terminated their partnership. Phillip Best continued the business as sole proprietor.

1862   March 25. Phillip Best's daughter, Maria, married Captain Frederick Pabst.

September. First federal excise tax on beer became effective, $1.00 per barrel.

November 12. United States Brewers' Association was founded.

1864   Phillip Best took Captain Pabst into business as an equal partner in Phillip Best and Company.

1866   May 16. Phillip Best's daughter, Elizabetha (Lisette), married Emil Schandein.

October 15. The partnership between Phillip Best and Captain Pabst was dissolved, and a new partnership agreement between Captain Pabst and Emil Schandein drawn up for Best and Company.

1869   July 17. Phillip Best died.

1870   November 11. The Melms brewery was purchased by Best and Company and named the South Side Brewery. The brewery on the hill was known as the Empire Brewery.

June. Best beer was awarded a prize at the Beer Fair in Milwaukee.

1873   March 13. The Phillip Best Brewing Company was incorporated in Wisconsin; capital, $300,000. Officers were Frederick Pabst, president; Emil Schandein, vice-president; and Charles Best, secretary.

Philipp Jung was appointed brewmaster.

1875   The Phillip Best Brewing Company started bottling, but turned the department over to Stamm and Meyer of Milwaukee.

1876   Best beer was awarded a gold medal at the Centennial Exposition in Philadelphia.

1878   Best beer was awarded a gold medal at the World's Fair in Paris.

1879   Adam Klinkert became brewmaster.

October 16. The Boyle ice machine was purchased for the Empire Brewery (installed in 1880).

December 21. Fire destroyed the malthouse, elevators, and office building.

1881   February 5. The Phillip Best Brewing Company purchased bottling business of Stamm and Meyer and continued the bottling department under their own name.

August Olinger became brewmaster.

1882   Pieces of blue ribbon were tied around the necks of Best's "Select" beer.

John Metzler became brewmaster.

September 13. Contract was made with the Western Edison Light Company for construction and erection of its dynamo machines and incandescent lights at the Empire Brewery.

1884   April 15. J. F. Theurer became brewmaster.

April 26. Capital was increased to $2,000,000.

1886   Operations at South Side Brewery were discontinued.

The first trained laboratory scientist, Dr. Otto Mittenzwey, was added to the staff.

May 1. Strikes were held in Milwaukee; settlement by the brewing companies was completed by May 7.

1887   Pure yeast culture was introduced at the Empire Brewery.

Milwaukee brewers severed relations with Local No. 9, National Union of United Brewery Workmen.

1888   November 12. Directors voted to erect a restaurant and a pavilion at Whitefish Bay, which later developed into a famous amusement center.

November 25. Emil Schandein died.

1889   March 18. The name of Phillip Best Brewing Company was changed to the Pabst Brewing Company. Capital stock was in-increased to $4,000,000.

First "Secret" book was issued.

August 25-31. Captain Pabst and the company helped in the entertainment of the 23d National Encampment of the G.A.R. in Milwaukee.

Captain Pabst refused to sell to the British syndicate—the first in a series of refusals.

1890   January 22. Charles Best resigned; Gustav Pabst was elected secretary.

September 17. The Pabst Theater opened.

June 18. The Pipe Line Act was approved by Congress.

1891   March 4. Pipe line was first used to carry beer to bottle house.

Saladin pneumatic malting system was installed on two floors of the Pabst malthouse.

November. Settlement was made at Pabst with Local No. 9, International Union of United Brewery Workmen.

1892   October 25. Purchase of the Falk, Jung and Borchert Brewing Company. Capital was increased to $10,000,000.

October 31. Gustav Pabst resigned as secretary; Charles W. Henning was elected secretary.

November 1. Dr. Paul Fischer succeeded Otto Mittenzwey in the laboratory.

Captain Pabst became the first president of the Wisconsin National Bank.

The Pabst Building, Milwaukee, was erected.

1893   February 15. Ernest Borchert was elected second vice-president; Frank R. Falk elected treasurer.

The gold model of the brewery was exhibited at the World's Columbian Exposition in Chicago.

November. Pabst beer was judged highest in points by jury of World's Columbian Exposition. The Best Tonic received high award.

1894   January 31. Lisette Schandein resigned as vice-president. Gustav Pabst was elected first vice-president. Dr. Alfred J. Schedler joined staff in the laboratory.

1895   The words, "Blue Ribbon," were added to the label of "Select" beer.

November 8. The Pabst Theater reopened after a disastrous fire.

Western Shipping Brewers' Association was organized.

1898   January. The Blue Ribbon label was first used.

June 14. Excise tax on beer was raised to $2.00 per barrel.

1899   June 19. Ernest Borchert resigned; Fred Pabst was elected second vice-president.

November 11. The Pabst Hotel in New York City opened.

Pabst gave the first large order to the Diamond Match Company for advertising on book matches.

Captain Pabst bought an autograph album to raise funds for the Soldiers' Monument in Milwaukee.

1900   March 27. Trade-mark for Blue Ribbon lager beer was registered.

September 22. The Pabst Harlem Restaurant was opened in New York City.

Use of label, "Milwaukee Beer," was restricted to Milwaukee, Wisconsin, brewers by decree of the United States Circuit Court.

1901   June 6. Fire in elevator and malthouse.

June 30. Excise tax on beer was reduced to $1.60 per barrel.

1902   J. F. Theurer resigned; Frederick Bock became brewmaster.

Frank R. Falk resigned; Charles W. Henning became treasurer in addition to secretary.

July 1. Excise tax on beer was reduced to $1.00 per barrel.

1903   January. The Pabst Grand Circle Restaurant was opened in New York City.

1904   January 1. Captain Frederick Pabst died.

January 11. Gustav Pabst was elected president.

Audit of company books was made for the first time by a public accounting firm.

The Pabst Blue Ribbon Prize Team started a tour of the country.

1905   May 9. Fred Pabst resigned as vice-president.

1906   January 27. Charles W. Henning was elected vice-president; Henry Stark was elected secretary.

March. The Gargoyle Restaurant was opened in Milwaukee.

July 17. Bond issue was floated through the Wisconsin National Bank.

October 16. The company decided to use Crown Cork and Seal Company bottle tops.

1907   Blue Ribbon Beer won highest award at the International Hygienic and Pure Foods Exposition in Antwerp.

1908   Electrification of all power machinery was completed.

1909   October 25. Boiler house explosion.

1910   June 18. Capital was increased to $12,000,000; preferred stock issued.

1912   January 29. W. F. Schad was elected assistant secretary.

Western Shipping Brewers' Association was dissolved.

1913   May. First issue of the *Blue Ribbon News* came out.

October 27. The style of Blue Ribbon bottles was changed to shoulder bottles.

December 30. Directors voted to plat the Whitefish Bay property.

1914   October 23. Excise tax on beer was raised to $1.50 per barrel.

1916   Gustav Pabst was elected president of the United States Brewers' Association.

March 1. First nonalcoholic Pablo sold.

1917   January 29. Charles W. Henning retired; Henry Danischefsky was elected vice-president.

October 4. Excise tax on beer was raised to $3.00 per barrel.

December 18. Resolution for prohibition amendment was adopted by Congress.

1919   February 25. Excise tax on beer was raised to $6.00 per barrel.

May 1. Brewing of beer was prohibited.

July 1. Sale of beer was prohibited.

1920   December 4. The Pabst Corporation was organized. Capital $5,000,000. The Pabst Realty Company was organized.

December 24. The Pabst Brewing Company was dissolved.

1921   March 14. Henry Stark died; Edward Loebl was elected assistant secretary.

April 12. H. W. Marsh was elected secretary-treasurer.

December 23. Gustav Pabst and Henry Danischefsky resigned, Fred Pabst became president of the Pabst Corporation; H. W. Marsh, vice-president; Hugo Kuechenmeister, treasurer; and Edward Loebl, secretary.

1923 December 31. The Pabst Corporation acquired the business of the Sheboygan Beverage Company. The Pabst Corporation acquired the cheese division of the Pabst Holstein Farms.

1924 September 29. H. W. Marsh resigned; Frederick A. Pabst was elected vice-president.

1925 August 25. Hugo Kuechenmeister resigned; John H. Moore was elected treasurer.

1926 November 30. Rudolf Pabst was elected second vice-president.

1929 October 29. August Pabst was elected third vice-president; James Nicholson elected fourth vice-president.

1930 January 2. The Pabst Corporation bought the Puritan Malt Extract Company, Chicago.

December 8. James Nicholson resigned as fourth vice-president.

1931 February 2. Frederick A. Pabst was elected executive vice-president.

February 9. R. C. Zimmerman was made controller.

November 6. John H. Moore resigned; Einar Oyaas was elected treasurer.

1932 November 6. Premier Malt Products Company voted to merge with the Pabst Corporation.

1933 March 1. Name of Premier Malt Products Company was changed to Premier-Pabst Corporation, and the name of Premier Malt Products Sales Company was changed to Premier-Pabst Sales Company.

April 1. Officers of Premier-Pabst Corporation were Harris Perlstein, president; Fred Pabst, Robert Clark, James G. Shakman, vice-presidents; Charles T. Buehler, secretary-treasurer; Melba V. Walker, assistant secretary; A. J. Ostendorf and Edward Loebl, assistant treasurers. Officers of Premier-Pabst Sales Company were Harris Perlstein, president; F. E. Solfisburg, vice-president; Charles T. Buehler, secretary-treasurer.

April 7. The Cullen-Harrison Act, passed March 22, legalized beer. Excise tax was set at $5.00 per barrel.

August. Export Division of the sales company was established.

December 5. Twenty-first Amendment was ratified.

December. Brewers Code of NIRA was adopted.

1934   Premier-Pabst Corporation withdrew from United States Brewers' Association. Brewing Industry Inc. was formed.

Industrial Products Division was set up in Peoria to market auxiliary products.

February 20. F. E. Solfisburg was elected vice-president and E. B. Thornton was made assistant treasurer of the brewing company.

1935   National radio network advertising was discontinued.

February 19. Melba V. Walker resigned as assistant secretary of the brewing company. George W. Stewart was made assistant treasurer of the sales company.

March 20. Metal kegs were first adopted by Premier-Pabst.

July. Pabst beer in "keglined" cans was first marketed.

August 29. Federal Alcohol Administration Act was passed.

1936   May 29. E. B. Thornton was made assistant secretary and assistant treasurer of the sales company.

July 28. E. B. Thornton was made assistant secretary of the brewing company.

October 21. The United Brewers Industrial Foundation was formed.

1937   March 9. Rudolf Pabst was made assistant secretary of the brewing company.

1938   A new corn-grits mill was built at Peoria.

December 20. The name of Premier-Pabst Corporation was changed to Pabst Brewing Company, and the name of Premier-Pabst Sales Company was changed to Pabst Sales Company.

1939   February 22. Fred Pabst resigned as vice-president and was named chairman of the board of the brewing company.

May 20. F. E. Solfisburg died.

June. Marketing research department and consumer service department of the sales company were established.

June 20. James G. Shakman was elected vice-president of the sales company.

August 18. Ivin E. Harris and Edwin L. Morris were elected vice-presidents of the sales company.

October 4. Robert Clark died.

1940   March. American Brewing Industry was formed by merger of Brewing Industry, Inc., and the American Brewers Association. Harris Perlstein was elected president.

March 12. Rudolf Pabst and Dorothy Fiedler were made assistant secretaries, and J. G. Gazzolo was made general office manager of the sales company.

June. The slogan "Thirty-three Fine Brews Blended Into One Great Beer" was first used in national advertising.

July 1. Excise tax on beer was raised to $6.00 per barrel.

1941   January. American Brewing Industry and the United States Brewers' Association were merged under the name, United States Brewers' Association.

March 11. Edward C. Loebl resigned as assistant treasurer and R. C. Zimmerman was made assistant treasurer of the brewing company.

September 22. Charles T. Buehler resigned as secretary, and Rudolf Pabst was elected secretary of the sales company.

1942   September 21. Rudolf Pabst resigned as secretary of the sales company and assistant secretary of the brewing company. Charles T. Buehler was elected secretary of the sales company.

October 22. Edward H. Fiedler was elected vice-president and general counsel of the brewing company.

November 1. Excise tax on beer was raised to $7.00 per barrel.

December 18. Pension plan for salaried employees was set up.

1943   National radio network advertising was resumed.

March 9. Edward H. Fiedler was elected vice-president and general counsel of the sales company.

April 1. Excise tax on beer was raised to $8.00 per barrel.

December 1. Pabst Postwar Employment Awards were announced.

December 18. R. C. Zimmerman and Lester Jones were made assistant vice-presidents of the brewing company.

1944   March 14. J. G. Gazzolo was made assistant treasurer of the sales company.

September. Brewing Industry Foundation (formerly the United Brewers Industrial Foundation) and the United States Brewers' Association were merged under the name, United States Brewers Foundation.

1945   December 18. Hoffman Beverage Company was acquired as a subsidiary by Pabst Brewing Company. Officers appointed were Rudolf Pabst, president; Edward H. Fiedler, vice-president; E. B. Thornton, secretary-treasurer; John T. Rice, assistant secretary; and George W. Fraser, assistant treasurer.

December 21. Pabst Breweries Foundation was set up.

1946   March 12. Rudolf Pabst was elected vice-president of the brewing company.

April 26. John T. Rice was appointed assistant secretary, and George W. Fraser was appointed assistant treasurer of the brewing company.

INDEX

A

Accounting. *See* Audits; Cost accounting

Administration. *See* Management

Advertising, 32-35, 61-64, 130, 184, 213-25, 350, 360, 369, 384-85, 391
  agencies, 129-32, 219, 237, 342-44, 348, 391
  appropriations and expenditures, 131-36, 184, 215, 219-22, 237, 342-43, 348, 350, 384-85, 392-93
  campaigns, 134-35, 213-20, 225, 237-38, 342-44, 347-49, 389
  records, 410
  regulation of, 367-68, 389
  scrapbooks, list of, 411
  See also Costs; Policy; Public relations

Advertising media, 61, 129-38 *passim*, 211-25, 237-38, 389, 428-29
  booklets, 132-33, 215, 396, 410-11, 424
  in general use, 64, 390-91
  magazines, 131, 135-36, 213-15, 217-21, 343, 385, 389, 393, 411
  motion pictures, 222
  newspapers, 32-35, 61-64, 129-32, 134-36, 214-21, 343, 384-85, 389, 393, 422
  outdoor, 132, 219, 222-23, 343, 366
  radio, 360, 385, 389-90, 393-94, 397, 428-29
  special, souvenirs, etc., 131, 134-36, 139, 184, 214-25, 230, 238, 242-43, 246, 367, 393-94, 397, 411, 425
  See also Expositions; Signs and Views

Agazim, Toly, 379

Agencies, Agents. *See* Sales promotion

Agreements. *See* Partnerships; Price agreements; Trade associations; Trade-unions

Agricultural Stimulation Act (1919), 322

Aiken, Andrew Jackson, and Proctor, Lewis A., 95n.

Alcohol Administration Act (1935), 367-68, 428

Aldrich, N. W., 272-73n., 282n.

Ale, 12-13, 15-18, 21, 27, 30, 33-34, 44, 52, 71-72, 73n., 123, 376, 390

Allis-Chalmers Manufacturing Company, 261, 376

Allowances, 141-42, 184, 225-27, 341
  See also Discounts; Rebates

American Brewer (first published), 113

American Brewers' Association, 371, 428

American Brewers' Gazette (first published), 113

American Brewing Industry, 428-29

American Can Company, 381, 386, 389

American Federation of Labor (A. F. of L.), 282-83, 286-301, 338-39, 382-83

American Rotating Valve Company, 332

Andeker beer, 390

Anderson, W. J., and Bleyer, Julius, eds., 78n., 255-56n.

Andreae, Percy, 317-18

Anheuser, E., and firm (St. Louis), 67, 71-73, 121

Anheuser-Busch Brewery Association (St. Louis), 60, 71-74, 119, 134, 137-38, 146, 149, 152-53, 155, 181n., 184, 233, 244, 289-95, 355, 366, 370, 384, 398

Anheuser-Busch Sales Company, 339

Anneki, Percy S., quoted, 229-30

Anti-Saloon League of America, 308-24 *passim*

Appendixes, 400-406

Artesia Water, 336-37

Ashland, Wis., branch, 167-68, 172-73

Asiatic market, 246-47, 389

Assets, 325-26, 330-31, 350, 353, 361
    See also Capital
Atwood, H. G., 401
Audits, 185-86, 198-99, 202, 226, 242, 425
Australian market, 178, 246-47, 357
Awards, 64, 134, 137-39, 206, 221-22, 394, 396, 423, 425-26, 429
    Pabst postwar employment, 396-97, 429

B

Baker, Edwin D., 38-39
Baker Law (1907), 227
Ballantine, P., and Sons (Newark), 72-74, 339, 355, 398
Banks
    early, 43-44
    firm and, 85-86, 329, 345, 404, 426
    firm members and, 49, 260-61, 424
Barley, 13, 102-3, 119, 204, 378-80, 390
    supply, 5, 22, 26-27, 33, 66, 75, 98, 118-19, 192, 208
Barstow, Governor William A., 39-40
Batten, Barton, Durstine and Osborn, advertising agency, 348
Bauer, A. H., 113
Bavarian beer (name), 130-31, 216
Beer
    brands of, 139, 141; new, 214-18; *see also* names of individual beers
    free, 21, 141, 226, 253, 266, 283-84, 299, 382
    halls and gardens, 40-41, 317; *see also* Outlets
    history of, 11-12
    packaged *vs.* draught, 384-86
    See also Costs; Marketing; Prices; Sales; and names of types of beer
Benefits to workers. *See* Bonuses; Insurance; Pensions; Vacations; Workmen's compensation
Beney, M. Ada, 340n.
Benkard, Christian, 221
Berger, Victor, 254

Bergner and Engel Brewing Company (Philadelphia), 56-57, 72-74, 147-48
Bernie, Ben, on radio, 360, 385, 389-90, 394
Best, Charles (Frederick Charles, son of Jacob, Sr.), 8-9, 31-32
    brewery started, 18-19, 422
    comes to the U.S.A., 4-7
    established Plank Road Brewery, 22
    founder of freethinking society, 36-37
    vinegar factory, 4, 9, 11, 19, 32n., 422
    withdraws, 32, 422
Best, Charles Frederick (son of Frederick Charles), 94-97, 109, 121, 154, 280
    early training, 67, 95n.
    offices, 67, 260, 400, 423
    personality, 86
    quoted, 113, 118n., 125, 142, 165-69, 403
    resigns, 82, 424
    stock held, 67, 81, 94
Best, Chris and Margaret, 4n.
Best, Elizabetha (Lisette; daughter of Phillip). *See* Schandein, Elizabetha Best
Best, Eva Maria (Mrs. Jacob, Sr.), 7, 23
Best, Henry (son of Phillip), 67
    stock held, 67, 80-81, 189
Best, Jacob, Jr., 7-9, 24, 36, 422
    brewery started, 18-19, 422
    comes to the U.S.A., 4
    opposes prohibition, 38-40
    partnership, 22-23
    retires, 45-46
    vinegar factory, 4, 9, 422
Best, Jacob, Sr., 3-7
    brewery started, 19-21, 355, 422
    comes to the U.S.A., 4-7, 355
    death, 36
    leadership in community, 35
    political activities, 35-36
    por., *facing page* 22
    retires, 22-23, 55

Best, Lorenz (son of Jacob, Sr.), 7, 31
  brewery started, 18-19, 422
  death, 32
  withdraws, 22
Best, Margaret (daughter of Jacob, Sr.). *See* Schoeffler, Margaret Best
Best, Maria (Mrs. Phillip), 7, 26
Best, Maria (daughter of Phillip). *See* Pabst, Maria Best
Best, Phillip (son of Jacob, Sr.), 7, 16, 20-21, 48-49, 53, 63-64, 422-23
  comes to the U.S.A., 3-4
  death, 50, 423
  description and personality, 19, 35
  founder of freethinking society, 36-37
  home, 58-59
  leadership in the community, 35-36, 42-43, 67
  made brigadier general, 36, 422
  offices, 42-43
  partnerships, 18-19, 22-23, 49, 422-23
  political activities, 35-36
  por., *facing page* 48
  quoted, 6, 24-26
  retires, 49-50, 55
  runs brewery alone, 45-46, 422
Best, Sophia K. (Mrs. Frederick), viii
Best and Company
  becomes Phillip Best Brewing Company, 66-67, 423
  capital supplies, 19
  established and operations begun, 18-22, 422
  sites, 11, 26-27, 422
Best, Phillip, Brewing Company
  incorporated, 66-67, 423
  named Pabst Brewing Company, 70, 424
  officers and stockholders, 80
Best Tonic. *See* Tonic
Beverages, nonalcoholic, 209, 332-34, 337, 340-41, 346-50, 376-77, 379-80, 399
  See also Marketing; Profits; Sales; and names of such beverages
Bibliography, 407-21
Bigelow, H. M., 232; quoted, 153-55

Billigheim, Joseph, 165, 167-68, 170
Billings, John S., quoted, 310-11
Birkholz, Richard, 127
Black Label malt syrup, 334, 337
Blair, Senator John J., 305
Blancke, Charles F., 237
Blatz, Valentin, 55-56, 58, 68, 85, 154-55, 158
Blatz, Valentin, Brewing Company, 31, 54-56, 57n., 64, 71-73, 85, 129, 146-58, 225, 230, 277, 280-82, 290, 320, 334, 339, 398
Blind tigers, 305
Blue Ribbon ale, 390
Blue Ribbon beer, 177, 187, 191, 206, 216-18, 220-23, 225, 241-42, 376-77, 385, 389-91, 394, 397-98, 425-26
  bottling house, 201
Blue Ribbon Casino, 394
Blue Ribbon Commercial Company, 245
Blue Ribbon Distributing Company, 245
Blue Ribbon or Label malt syrups, 334, 358, 360
Blue Ribbon News, 220, 240-41, 383, 426
Bock, Frederick, 208, 328, 425
Bock beer, 33-35, 62-63, 216-17
Bohemian beer (name), 216-17, 242
Bonds, 195, 325, 331, 345, 350, 426
Bonuses, 94, 168, 194, 348
Booklets, 132-33, 215, 396, 410-11
  See also Secret Books
Booms. *See* Business cycles
Borchert, Ernest, 83, 115, 188-90, 192, 400, 425
  stock held, 189, 194-95
  See also Falk, Jung and Borchert
Borden Company, 341
Bosch Food Products Company, 359
Bottled beer, 123-28, 137, 204, 387-88, 390
  statistics (1881-93), 124
  See also Marketing; Profits; Sales; names of such beer

Bottling, 120-28, 201-2, 242, 378
  by agents, 125
  by branches, 175, 244
  capping and corking, 124-126, 201
Bowen, E. H., quoted, 179n.
Boyle ice machine, 97, 108, 423
Branches, 160, 165, 170-75, 177, 188,
    221, 226, 250, 341, 391-92, 422
  bottling by, 175, 244
  list of, 173
  management of, 165
  vs. agencies, 165-73, 237-40
  See also Profits; Sales
Brands. See Beer, brands of
Brandt, L. C. G., quoted, 307
Braun, John, Brewing Company, 31
Brewers
  Milwaukee (1850), 27; (1860), 54;
    (1866-72), 56; syndicate, 406
  United States (1872-74), 56-57;
    (1877), 73; (1895), 74; syndi-
    cate, 405-6
  See also individual firms
Brewers Code (NIRA), 367, 370, 427
Brewers Fire Insurance Company of
    America, 53
Brewer's grains, 14, 107, 379
Brewers Union No. 1, 273
Brewing industry, 12, 71-74, 114-23,
    250, 252, 265-68, 271-72, 366-71,
    397-98
  regulation of the, 17, 366; by
    brewers, 371
  See also Brewers; Competition;
    Milwaukee brewing industry;
    Trade associations
Brewing Industry, Inc., 370-71, 428
Brewing Industry Foundation, 371,
    429
Brewing institutes and schools, 112-13
Brewing technology, 11-18, 20-21, 27,
    75, 77-78, 100, 102-28, 202-9, 378-
    79
  carbonation, 18, 106, 120-22, 127,
    201, 204, 207-8
  fermentation, 12, 15-18, 106, 110-12,
    120, 207
  filtering, 106, 122, 204
  kraeusening, 18, 106, 120, 122

  laboratory control, 114-15, 201, 208-
    9, 378-79
  malting, 13-14, 102-6, 118, 120, 204,
    221, 424
  mashing, 14, 105-6
  pasteurization, 111, 114-15, 124, 126,
    201
  ruh stage, 18
  sparging, 14
  stabilizing, 102, 114-15, 120-21, 207
  suds, 202-3
  temperature, 13-14, 17, 105, 107,
    110, 126-27, 204, 378
  wort, 14-15, 17, 105-6, 111, 118
  See also Bottling; Inventions; Ma-
    chinery; Research; Science
Brewmasters, 15-16, 29, 88, 114-15,
    117-19, 124-25, 191, 193, 378-79
  See also Bock, Frederick; Fueger,
    Max; Jung, Philipp; Klinkert,
    Adam; Metzler, John; Olinger,
    August; Theurer, J. F.
Brigel, Leo, quoted, 146-47
Brisbane, Arthur, 318
Bruce, William George, viii; quoted,
    41, 85n., 256n.
Bruncken, Ernest, and Hense-Jensen,
    Wilhelm, 6n., 266n.
Bryan, William Jennings, 259
Buck, James S., 48n.
Buehler, Charles T., 360, 372, 374,
    401, 427, 429
Buehler, John, 358
Buildings, 45, 58-60, 375-77
  early, 19, 28-29
  Empire Brewery, model of, 137, 425
  value, 45, 345, 353
  See also Plant expansion; Real es-
    tate; Outlets
Bursk, J. Parker, 251n.
Busch, Adolphus, 72, 232, 290-91;
    quoted, 134, 150-51, 229
  See also Anheuser-Busch Brewery
    Association
Busch, August A., 294-95
Busch, August A., Jr., 370-71
Business cycles, 4-7, 182, 251
  booms, 27-31, 184, 338

depressions, 29, 43-47, 61, 72, 81-88,
93, 95-96, 138, 146, 157, 191,
210, 220, 228, 232, 241, 260,
267-68, 272, 274, 291, 329, 338,
347-52, 366, 391-92
prosperity, 6, 28-29, 44, 65, 88,
232, 274, 332, 339, 347-49, 362
See also Panics
By-products, 14, 107, 376, 396
Byrne, Thomas A., 145n.

C

Cagniard de La Tour, Charles, 110
Canadian market, 47, 178, 246
Canary Islands market, 178
Canned beer, viii, 123, 369, 380-81,
386-90, 428
Capital, 7, 19-21, 27, 67, 250, 329-32,
345, 423-24, 426
stock, 67, 84, 191-96, 326, 329-30,
363, 372, 374-75, 426
value, 29, 49, 54, 66-67, 80-81, 84-
85, 90, 96, 157, 182-83, 196,
202, 325-27, 330-31, 375
See also Working capital
Capital, British. See Syndicates
Capital of other brewers, 27, 42, 54,
250
Carbonation. See Brewing technology
Carey, Martin, 244n.
Caribbean market, 178, 246-47
Carnegie, Andrew, 91; quoted, 83
Carpenter, Emma, stock held, 189
Carpenter, Morgan, 23
Carré ice machine, 112
Cary, Alfred L., 155, 406
Casino beer, 390
Catholic Total Abstinence Society, 37
Central American market, 178, 247,
389
Central National Bank (Milwaukee),
260
Century beer, 215-16
Cheese, 262, 330, 332, 335-37, 341-44,
348-51, 363, 386
See also Profits; Sales
Cherrington, Ernest H., 310n.

Chicago, 12, 31, 79-80, 146-49, 198,
212-13, 280
branches, 78, 116-17, 171-75, 186,
188, 237-38, 250, 422
Chinese market, 178, 246-47
Chronology, 422-29
Churchward, Lord, 157-58
Cincinnati, Ohio, 79, 146-47, 152
branch, 238
Clark, Robert, 358-60, 372, 401, 427-28
Clark, Victor S., 19n.
Clausen, H., Brewing Company (New
York City), 57n., 73, 148, 406
Cleveland, President Grover, 307
Cleveland, Ohio, branch, 238
Closed shop, 277-78, 281, 298, 338-40,
382
See also Open shop; Trade-unions
Cole, Arthur H., viii, 392n.
Coleman, Edward, quoted, 269
Commons, John R., and others, 274n.
Competition, 29-32, 40, 53-66, 71-74,
100, 128, 135, 137-39, 142-43, 145-
51, 159-62, 183-85, 188, 197-98,
226-32, 284, 334, 369-70, 390, 398
monopolistic, 30, 64, 150, 159, 230
See also Position in industry;
Prices
Congress (formerly Committee) of
Industrial Organizations (C.I.O.),
293, 383
Consolidation. See Mergers; Syndi-
cates
Consumers, 10, 35, 44, 86, 142-43,
210, 256, 310, 389
service department, 393, 428
surveys, 377, 393
Consumption (beer), 55
national, 54, 71-74, 180-81, 386
seasonal variation, 12, 116
Continental Can Company, 381
Continental Engineering Company,
332
Convention reports, 413
Conventions, 224-25
Cooperage, 75-77, 97, 202, 368, 378,
380-81

Co-operation
among brewers, 53, 147, 205, 225, 294-95, 306-8, 313-15, 350-51, 365-67, 371, 385-86
with trade-unions, 317-19
See also Price agreements; Prices, maintaining; Trade associations

Coopers' Union, 295-96

Corn, corn meal, 26, 75, 119-20, 122, 204, 376, 380

Cost accounting, 95-101, 183, 344-45
records preserved, 409

Costs
advertising, 131-36, 184, 215, 219-20, 222, 237, 342-43, 347-48, 350, 384-85, 392
bottling, 124
cooperage, 75-77
ice: artificial, 97-98, 109; natural, 77, 98, 109
labor, 98-100, 124, 282, 378
living, 93, 298; early, 5 6
production, 27, 77-78, 97-100, 160, 185, 336, 346, 352, 378
raw material, 98
selling, 140-41, 160, 165, 185, 225-27, 341-42, 348, 350, 391-92
transportation, 61, 74-75, 77, 90, 98, 100, 107, 160-64, 168-69, 175-77, 181, 342, 348, 378
See also Salaries; Wages

Court action
state, 60, 245, 366, 367
United States, 225, 315-16, 327n., 336, 358, 366-68, 390-91, 425

Cream City. See Milwaukee

Cream City Brewing Company, 277, 282, 286, 290, 334, 339

Credit, 20-21, 43, 85, 343
to dealers, 140-42, 175, 226, 228

Cromwell, William Nelson, 258-59

Crown Cork and Seal Company, 126, 201, 426

Cuban market, 178, 246-47; plant, 191

Cullen-Harrison Act (1933), 365, 367, 427

Cushman, Robert E., 305n., 316n.

D

Danischefsky, Henry, 194, 326-27, 346, 400, 426-27

Danzinger, S., 166

De La Vergne ice machine, 109

Dealers, retail, 148, 165-66, 181-82
See also Outlets

Dealers, wholesale, 165-66
foreign distributors, 389
regional distributors, 359-60, 386, 398

Debts, 22, 46, 196, 353
bad, 93, 342, 348
See also Loans; Mortgages

Decatur Brewing Company, 352-59, 374
merged with Premier Malt Products Company, 358

Decisions, business, 3-4, 7, 11, 16, 19, 22-23, 31-32, 45, 48-49, 55, 59, 67, 82, 88-90, 97, 108, 113, 123, 126, 131, 134, 143, 155, 193, 326, 334, 338, 341, 347, 349, 354, 362-63, 384-85

Delbrück, M., 113-14; quoted, 106

Delta Cooperage Company, 77

Denver, Colo., branch, 238

Depreciation, 96-97, 145, 193, 198, 202

Depressions. See Business cycles

Detroit, Mich., branch, 238

Deuster, Oscar V., 268n.

Deuster, P. V., 264

Dewey, Governor Nelson, 35

Directories, list of, 413

Directors, 193, 367
names, 67, 327-28, 346, 351-52, 374, 400-1

Discounts, 65, 140-43, 145, 150, 174, 184, 213, 225-29, 341
See also Allowances; Marketing; Rebates

Dividends, 83-85, 94, 182-83, 195, 326, 329, 331, 337, 346, 350, 363

Dobyns, Fletcher, 305n., 361-62n.

Doppel Braeu beer, 215-17

Downer and Bemis Brewing Company (Chicago), 57, 72-73

Drama, 40-41, 257, 266-68
Drawback beer, 216
Dribben, Joseph, 343
Dykstra, Clarence, 396

E

Earnings, reinvestment of, 23-24, 66, 83, 85, 257, 270, 375
Eberts Brewing Company (St. Louis), 152
Ebling Brewing Company (New York City), 339
Ehret, George, Brewing Company (New York City), 57, 72-74, 147-48, 167, 210
Eighteenth Amendment, 305, 321-22, 326, 361, 364, 426
Electrification, 110, 201, 423, 426
Elich, Charles, 328
Eliot, Charles, 310
Elkins Antirebate Act (1903), 181, 327n.
Elsner, Richard, 288; quoted, 285-86
Empire Brewery, named, 61, 423
Employees, 249-55, 382-83
    benefits; see Bonuses; Insurance; Pensions; Vacations; Workmen's compensation
    number of, 27, 29, 54, 94, 99, 251-52, 271-72, 335, 337-38, 382, 395-96, 402-03
    relations of, with management, 91-95, 117, 168-71, 239-40, 253, 297, 301, 328, 344; see also Trade-unions
    in the Second World War, 396
    See also Labor; Salaries
Employers association, 294, 338
Employment. See Labor
Entrepreneurship, 67, 97, 108, 207, 214, 332, 384, 392n. See subheads under Pabst, Frederick; Pabst, Frederick, Jr.; Pabst, Gustav; Perlstein, Harris; Singer, Philip. See also Decisions; Forecasting; Innovations; Leadership
Erasmus, quoted, 11-12
Excise taxes. See Taxation
Exhibitions. See Expositions

Expansion, business, 23-29, 58-61, 82-83, 287, 342, 358-59
    See also Mergers; Plant expansion
Experimentation, 16, 102, 106-8, 110-11, 118-22, 191-92, 202, 207-9, 333-36, 379-81, 387-88
    See also Laboratory control; Research
Export lager (name), 122, 216-17, 242, 390
Export markets, 31, 52-54, 75, 177-79, 246-48, 389, 394-95
Expositions, fairs, and exhibitions, 61, 136-39, 206, 208, 221-23, 241, 255-56, 348, 390, 394, 423, 425-26
    See also Awards

F

Fairs. See Expositions
Falk, Frank R., 195, 400, 425
    offices held, 83, 189-90
Falk Brewing Company, 56, 277, 280, 282, 290
Falk family, stock held, 189, 194-96
Falk, Jung and Borchert Brewing Company, 59, 82-83, 115, 424
Faraday, Michael, 112
Farming by Captain, Fred, and Gustav Pabst, 261-62
Farnaris, R. F., 177-78
Faulkner, H. D., 155
Faust, Albert Bernhardt, 7n.
Federated Trades Council of Milwaukee, 283, 291, 295
Federation of Organized Trades and Labor Unions, 282-83
Fermentation. See Brewing technology
Fiedler, Dorothy, 373, 428
Fiedler, Edward H., 373-74, 401, 429
Fifth Ward Savings Bank (Milwaukee), 49
Figgis, Dudley W., 381
Filtering. See Brewing technology
Finance capitalism, 260
    See also Syndicates

Finances, 19-21, 45-46, 83-86, 182, 194-96, 344-45
statement of (1873-93), 84; (1894-1918), 183
See also Assets; Capital; Investments; Policy
Fine, G., 22, 37
Fires, 82-83, 87, 200, 267, 423, 425
First Wisconsin Trust Company (Milwaukee), 329, 345
Fischer, Paul, 113-14, 207-8, 424
Fleischmann Yeast Company, 355
Flintoff, John, 113
Food Control Act (1917), 320-21
Forecasting business conditions, 45, 86-90, 144, 307, 315, 319, 326, 347, 349, 352, 361, 364-65, 384, 386-87, 398
See also Entrepreneurship
Forth Worth, Texas, agency, 237-38, 244-45
Fox, Hugh, quoted, 313, 318
Frank, Ella S., stock held, 329
Frank Wiedemann Company. See Wiedemann, Frank, Company
Fraser, George W., 374, 429
Fred Pabst Company. See Pabst, Fred, Company
Freight rates, 61, 161-62, 167-69, 181
Frey, Jacob, 60
Fueger, Max, 16
Fuel, 15, 27, 29, 77
Fuller, Charles H., advertising agency, 219
Fuller, Chief Justice Melville W., 225

G

Galland pneumatic system, 103
Gambrinus, statue of, 58-59
Gargoyle Restaurant, 243, 426
Gazzolo, J. G., 373, 428-29
General Foods Sales Corporation, 350, 352
George, John Edward, 146n.
German-American Alliance, 318
German and American Brewers Journal, The (first published), 113
29

Germans, 71
in and near Milwaukee, 4-5, 7, 10, 12, 29, 36-38, 40-41, 54-55, 78, 91-92, 255-56, 266
and prohibition, 37-38, 303, 318, 320
Gettelman Brewing Company, 277, 282, 286, 290, 334, 339
Gompers, Samuel, 291
Good Templars, Grand Lodge of the, 303
Good will (business), 83, 124, 334, 347, 349, 353
Goodrich, Marie Pabst (Mrs. William O.), 192
stock held, 329
Goodrich, William O., viii, 192-93, 260, 327-30, 400
stock held, 329
Gordon, Ernest Barron, 322n.
Gordon, Leslie, comp., 322n.
Government. See Laws; United States Government
Government documents (state and United States), list of, 412-13
Graham Act (1872), 53, 303-4
Grassmann and Orth, 45, 61-62
Gregory, John Goadby, 263n.
Gross, Theodore, quoted, 233-36
Grottkau, Paul, 280
Gruber, William, 116-17

H

Hallgarten and Company, 196
Hansen, Emil Christoph, 110-12
Hansen, Marcus Lee, 3n.
Harpstrite, Edward, 355-56
Harris, Ivin E., 372-73, 388, 391, 428
Havana, Cuba, branch, 246
Hawaiian market, 178, 247
Heflin, Senator J. Thomas, 321
Heim, Ferdinand, quoted, 108
Heinemann, Frederick, 45, 62
Henius, Max, quoted, 317
Henning, Charles, 82, 189-91, 193-94, 229, 237, 250, 400, 424-26
quoted, 298-99, 313
stock held, 82, 189

Hense-Jensen, Wilhelm, and Bruncken, Ernest, 6n., 266n.

Hepburn, W. P., 206

Hermanns-Soehne, 37

Hessen-Darmstadt, Germany, 5, 24

Heusner, W. W., quoted, 243-44

Heyl, Jacob, 400
stock held, 189

Hillquit, Morris, 280n.

Hirsch Syndicate, Ltd. (London), 233-36

Histories, state and local, list of, 413-16

Hofbraeu beer, 216

Hoffman Beverage Company (Newark), 59, 373-74, 376-77, 383, 397, 429

Hole, Rev. S. Reynolds, quoted, 224-25

Hollyhock Farm (Oconomowoc, Wis.), 262-63, 265

Hooker, William Francis, quoted, 211

Hops, 14-15, 27, 66, 75, 98, 106, 122, 146, 192, 334, 378, 390

Horse breeding, 261-63

Hoster, Carl J., quoted, 315

Houghton, Mich., branch, 165, 173-75

Hours of work, 14, 93, 203, 249, 251, 272-81 passim, 295-98, 340, 382

House organs, 348-49, 383, 426

Housing, industrial, 254-55

Hunter, J. T., 401

Hursley, Doris Berger (Mrs. Frank), 254n.

Hutton, R. P., quoted, 322-23

I

Ice, 17, 77-78, 107-9, 162-63
See also Costs; Machinery, Refrigeration

Idanha Company, 260

Illustrations, list of, x

Immigration, 5-10, 12, 71, 255-56, 266-67, 303
effect on beer consumption, 54

Incentives, 70, 95-96, 168, 348
See also Bonuses

Incorporation, 66-67, 237, 245, 423

Indianapolis, Ind., 152
branch, 173

Industrial Workers of the World (I.W.W.), 294

Industrialization, growth of, 71

Innovations, 12, 95, 106, 112, 126-27, 214, 216, 359, 368-69
See also Inventions

Insurance
employees, 253, 383
fire, 53, 87, 200

Interest rates, 23, 85

Internal Revenue Act (1890), 127
See also Taxation

International Brewers Association, 291-92

International Union of Brewery Workmen (later, of Brewery, Flour, Cereal and Soft Drink Workers), 282n., 338-40, 382-83

Interstate commerce, 67, 316, 366-67

Inventions, 102-6, 122, 125-27, 204, 207-8, 332, 356-57
See also Innovations

Investments, 329, 353
in local enterprises, 85, 257-61, 332-33
in outlets, 143-45, 196-99, 211-13, 257-58
See also Buildings; Earnings; Expansions; Mergers; Policy

Iowa market, 305

J

Jones, Lester, 373, 429

Jones, W. D., and Company, 245

Juneautown, Wis., 8

Jung, Ernest, 115n.

Jung, Philipp, 115-16, 119-20, 125, 189, 194, 423

Jung and Borchert Brewing Company, 277, 281-82, 290
See also Falk, Jung and Borchert

Jung Brewing Company, 189, 405

K

Kansas City, Mo., 147
branch, 140-41, 172-73, 175, 187, 238

Kansas-Nebraska Act (1854), 36

Kathrens, Joseph R., 214, 216-17, 219, 224
Kaufmann & Company (Cincinnati), 56-57
Keck, Adam, 355
Keg beer, 117, 139-40, 185-86, 227-28, 242
Kegs, metal, 380-81, 428
Kellogg, Louise Phelps, 257n.
Keyserling, Leon H., 396
Kiesel, Fred, 291; quoted, 312
Kilbourn, Byron, 24
Kilbourntown, Wis., 8, 33
Klau-Van Peterson-Dunlap-Young-reen, advertising agency, 343
Klinkert, Adam, 116, 119-20, 423
Klinkert Brewing Company (Racine, Wis.), 286
Kloster Braeu beer, 216
Knights of Labor, 273-79, 282-83, 287, 290-93
Knox, Philander C., 230
Koeler, John, 355
Konta, Alexander, 232
Koren, John, quoted, 312
Koss, Rudolph A., 4n., 37n.
Kountz Brothers, 132
Kraeusening. See Brewing technology
Kraft Cheese Company, 336, 341
Krekel, Theodor, 170
Kuechenmeister, Hugo, 327, 345, 427

L

Labor
accidents to, 252-53
living conditions, 253-54
saving, 102, 107
seasonal variation, 203-4, 250-51, 287, 299, 402
supply, 5-6, 10, 74, 76-79, 322
turnover, 396
women's, 298-300
working conditions, 249-53
See also Costs; Employees; Hours of work; Trade-unions; Wages
Laboratory control, 113-15, 201, 208-9, 378-81, 393

Lager. See Beer
Langworthy, A. J., quoted, 8-10, 19-21
Latin American market, 246-47
Laws affecting beer
state or local, 37-40, 53, 67, 187, 220, 227, 303-6, 308, 310, 366-67
United States, 50-52, 126-27, 181, 206, 227, 230, 315-16, 319-22, 324, 352, 361-62, 364-68; see also Eighteenth Amendment; Twenty-first Amendment
Layton Art Gallery, Milwaukee, 269
Leadership in the community, 35-36, 42-43, 67-69, 92, 249-50, 264-65
Lemp, Hilda. See Pabst, Hilda Lemp
Lemp, William J., Brewing Company (St. Louis), 57n., 72-74, 146, 150-53, 181n., 230, 232-33, 289-90
Liabilities, 22-24, 325, 330-31, 350, 353
See also Bonds; Debts; Mortgages; Stockholders
Liberalism, 6, 24, 35-37, 277
Licenses to export beer, 395
Licenses to sell beer, 37-38, 50, 65, 143, 169, 171, 227, 245, 305, 309-10, 366-67
Lichtenberg, Bernard, 371
Liebig, Justus, Baron von, 110
Liebmann Sons, G., Brewery (Brooklyn, N.Y.), 57, 398
Liquid Carbonic Acid Manufacturing Company, 201
Liquidation, 326, 332
Loans, 23, 46, 85, 377, 404
to outlets, 68, 141, 143, 145, 166, 198, 240, 305
Location
advantages of Milwaukee, 4-10, 79-80
theory, 7, 74
Loebl, Edward, 327-28, 346, 352, 400, 426-27, 429
Lord and Thomas, advertising agency, 136
Los Angeles, Calif., agency, 227
Losses, 96, 168, 174-75, 186-88, 199, 330-31, 339, 342-44, 348-49, 351

Lotz, H., quoted, 103-5
Low, Seth, 310
Luening's Conservatory of Music, 266

M

Machinery, 88, 378
  bottling, 125-26, 200-2, 251
  capping and corking, 125-26, 201
  drying, 107
  ice, 97-98, 107-10, 112, 423
  malting, 103-5, 200-2, 424
  pasteurizing, 114-15, 201
Magazines, list of, 420-21
  See also Advertising media
Magnus, Joseph E., 347, 351, 400;
  quoted, 348-49
Maizone, 204
Malt, 13-14, 75, 97, 104-5, 118-20,
  122, 146, 204, 347, 376, 378, 380
  "scab," 284
Malt cereal beverage. See Beverages,
  nonalcoholic
Malt extracts, 131-32, 332
  See also Tonic
Malt Mead, 216
Malt syrup, 209, 332-34, 337, 341-44,
  346-49, 351-52, 357-58, 362-63, 379-
  80, 386
Malting. See Brewing technology
Maltose, 379
Management, 61, 70-101, 188-94, 326-
  38, 371-78, 398-99
  changes, 19, 22-23, 45, 49, 67, 189,
    330, 345-46, 351-52, 354, 358-
    60, 372-74, 391
  committees, 194
  control by board of directors, 374
  delegation of authority, 92-93, 191
  executive leadership, 58, 100
  family, 19-23, 67, 80-83, 189, 330,
    372-73
  functional, 167, 190, 194, 374, 393
  institutional, 194, 372
  need for more executives, 49, 189,
    327
  problems, 80, 190-92, 327, 340-41;
    departmental, 116-17
  relations with subordinates, 91-95,
    117, 168-70, 239-40, 253, 328-
    29, 344
  use of specialists, 115-23, 343

Manchester, Herbert, 216n.
Manuscripts, list of, 412
Marketing
  beer, 29-32, 65-66, 139-43; bottled,
    125, 175-79, 187-88, 220, 228,
    385-88
  cheese, 341-44, 349-51
  malt syrup, 341, 347-49, 380
  nonalcoholic beverages, 340-41
  problems, 340-44
  regulation of, 366-68, 377
  See also Branches; Markets; Out-
    lets; Sales; Sales organization
Markets, 368-69
  foreign; see Export markets
  local, 28-31, 61, 67-68, 79-80, 237,
    386
  national, 30-31, 67, 74-75, 79-80, 86,
    99, 116-17, 128-46, 150, 173,
    180-81, 210, 237, 241-42, 305,
    368-70, 377; campaign for, 384-
    99
  protection of, 50, 67
  sellers', 33, 325, 397
Marsh, H. W., 327-30, 400, 426-27
  stock held, 329
Marsh Refrigeration Transit Com-
  pany, 327, 330
Marquand, F., 131-32
Marshall, General George C., 394
Mashing. See Brewing technology
Mason, John W., quoted, 126
Mass production, economies of, 61,
  98-102
Mechanization, 97-98, 102-10, 378
  See also Machinery
Medals. See Awards
Melms, Charles T., 31, 50-51, 59-61,
  68
  widow of, 60
Melms, C. T., Brewery Company,
  54, 56, 59-60, 423
Memphis, Tenn., agency, 170
Merchants and Marine Insurance
  Company, 261
Mercier, Louis, 211
Mergers, 59-60, 82-83, 347, 352-54,
  358-59, 362-64, 423-24, 427
  See also Subsidiaries; Syndicates
Merk, Frederick, 44n., 55n.

Merritt, Charles E., quoted, 161
Merritt, William, quoted, 140-41
Merz, Charles, quoted, 321-22
Metal manufacture, 332-33
Mettenheim, Germany, 3-4, 7, 9, 19, 50, 422
Metternich, Prince Klemens, 6
Metzler, John J., 118-22, 142, 423
Mexican market, 53, 178, 247
Meyer, Fred E., 123
Meyer, John B., 60
Miller, Frank T., 374, 401
Miller, William, viii
Miller Brewing Company, 22, 56, 168, 227, 233, 277, 282, 286, 290, 320, 334, 339, 422
Milwaukee, Wis.
  advantages of, 5-10, 42, 78-80
  beer-exporting center, 55
  culture, 40-41, 265-68
  description of, 8-10
  growth of, 40, 68-69, 255-56
  homes, 8, 254
  industries other than brewing, 42, 68-69, 254
  population, 25, 29, 55, 79, 255-56, 267
  social life, early ("German Athens"), 40-41
Milwaukee and Chicago Breweries, Ltd., 72, 158
"Milwaukee Beer," use of label forbidden, 225, 425
Milwaukee Beer Company, 245
Milwaukee Board of Trade and Chamber of Commerce, 42, 68
  list of statements, 413
Milwaukee Brewers' Association, 228-29, 231, 295
Milwaukee brewing industry, 9, 27-30, 42-56, 68-72, 141-42, 146-47, 181-82, 256, 266-67, 338-40
  See also Brewers, Milwaukee
Milwaukee County Historical Society, viii, 411
Milwaukee Employers' Council, 338-39
Milwaukee German Society, 263

Milwaukee Grain and Feed Corporation, 353
Milwaukee Mechanics Mutual Insurance Company, 260
Milwaukee Refrigeration Transit Company, 261, 327n.
Milwaukee Saloonkeepers Association, 65
Minneapolis, Minn.
  branch, 173-75
  outlets, 198, 213
Mitchell, Wesley C., 396
Mittenzwey, Otto, 113-14, 424
Mock and Blum, 209n.
Moerlein, Christian, Brewery Company (Cincinnati), 57, 72-74, 146
Mohrhardt, F. A., 166
Monopolistic competition, 30, 64, 150, 159, 230
  See also Competition
Moore, J. H., 345-46, 351, 400, 427
Morale, 91, 100, 382-83, 396
Morison, Samuel Eliot, 12n.
Morris, Edwin, viii, 262n., 273, 391, 428
Morrison, A. Cressy, viii, 132-34, 138, 213-14; quoted, 131, 190
Mortgages, 20, 23, 42-43, 45-46, 143-44, 195, 198-99, 331, 345, 350
Mueller, Oscar, 119, 250
  stock held, 189
Mueller, Theodore, viii
Music, 40-41, 257, 266, 268
Musical Society of Milwaukee, 265

N

National Association of Commerce and Labor, 317-18
National Brewers Academy, 113
National Industrial Recovery Administration (NIRA), 368
  Brewers Code, 367, 370, 427
National Malt Products Manufacturers Association, 355, 362
National Union of the Brewers of the United States, 282
National Union of United Brewery Workmen, 282n., 283, 290-301, 424

National Wholesale Liquor Dealers Association, 311

Near beer. *See* Beverages, non-alcoholic

Neukirch, Franz, 33, 60; quoted, 5-6

New Orleans, La., 147; agency, 237

Newark, N.J., plant, 376-78, 398

New York City, 55, 79, 147-48, 165, 198, 210-12, 237-38, 388, 425
  branch, 173-74

New Zealand market, 247

Newport News, Va., branch, 238

Newspapers
  clippings from, list of, 411
  list of, 421-22
  See also Advertising media

Nicholaus, Charles, quoted, 288, 297, 301

Nicholson, James R., 346, 400, 427

Nonalcoholic beverages. *See* Beverages, nonalcoholic

Nunnemacker, Rudolph, 155, 400

O

Obermann, J., Brewing Company, 56, 189, 277, 282

Oconomowoc, Wis., 261-62, 265, 335

Odegard, Peter, quoted, 306, 308-09, 317-24

Odell, Robert R., quoted, 157-58

Old Tankard ale, 390

Olinger, August, 116-17, 120, 423

Omaha, Neb., branch, 238

Open shop, 338
  See also Closed shop; Trade-unions

Operating records, list of, 410

Ostendorf, A. J., 356n., 373, 427

Ott, Louise F., stock held, 329

Outlets, 65, 143-45, 196-98, 226-28, 238
  beer halls, 28, 31-34, 40-41, 45, 61-62, 365
  drug stores, 139, 341
  food stores, 139, 341, 365, 385
  hotels, 139, 141, 196, 198-99, 210-13, 223, 238, 257-58, 341, 387-88, 425

loans to, 68, 141, 143, 145, 166, 198, 240, 305
  regulations of, 366, 377
  restaurants, 137, 198-99, 310-13, 221, 238, 241, 257-58, 341, 365, 387-88, 394, 424-26
  saloons, 32, 58, 65, 139-46, 197-99, 210, 226-28, 241, 305
  taverns, 139, 385, 387-88
  See also Advertising media, special; Branches; Profits; Signs and Views

Oyaas, Einar, 351, 427

P

Pablo (beverage), 186, 209, 325, 426

Pabst, August (son of Fred Pabst), 346, 352, 400, 427

Pabst, Edwin (son of Gustav Pabst), 261n., 270n.

Pabst, Elsbeth (granddaughter of Captain), stock held, 329

Pabst, Frederick (Captain), 58-60, 64, 70-101, 103, 107-8, 119, 126-27, 153, 160-65, 167-69, 191-92, 204-5, 221, 267, 424-25
  ancestry and early career, 46-49
  comes to the U.S.A., 422
  death, 85, 192, 245, 425
  entrepreneurship, 53, 58, 85-86, 90-93, 115, 129, 131, 144-45, 155-58, 160-61, 165, 179, 181-82, 190-91, 210-12, 237-38, 244-45, 259
  home, 61
  interests outside business, 258-61, 265-69
  lake captain, 48, 63-64
  leadership in the community, 67-68, 92, 264-65
  marriage, 46, 48, 422
  offices held: in firm, 67, 400, 423; other, 68, 85, 256, 260, 263-65, 424
  partner of Phillip Best, 49, 53, 55, 423
  partner of Emil Schandein, 49, 423
  personal investments, locally, 257-58
  personality, 58, 91-92
  philanthropy, 268-69

political affiliations, 263-64
por., Frontispiece
prohibition, opposes, 308
quoted, 76, 88-90, 92-94, 117, 133-34, 144-45, 147, 155, 157, 168-71, 188, 191, 200, 205, 222, 229-30, 244, 259, 264, 285, 288, 291, 368
relations with employees, 91-95, 117, 253; *see also* subhead trade-unions and
stock held, 67, 80-82, 189
trade-unions and, 274-75, 280-81, 285, 288-92
Pabst, Frederick, Jr. (Fred; son of Captain), viii, 3, 189-93, 261n.
entrepreneurship, 335-36, 364, 393
interests outside business, 261-63, 265-66, 268; social welfare, 328-29
marriage, 223, 262
offices held: in firm, 189-92, 197, 260, 262, 327-28, 351, 372, 374, 400-1, 425, 427; other, 77, 266, 328-29, 355
and Perlstein, 362-63
personality, 192
philanthropy, 328-29
por., *facing page* 326
prohibition, opposes, 364-65
quoted, 197, 223, 239-40, 272, 294-95, 364
relations with employees, 239-40, 253, 328
resigns, 193, 426, 428
runs the business, 325-54
stock held, 82, 189, 329-30, 345-46, 372
and trade-unions, 339
Pabst, Frederick A. (son of Fred), 330, 351, 354, 400-1, 427
Pabst, Gustav G. (son of Captain), 182, 191-94, 200, 208, 224, 232, 315, 325-27
entrepreneurship, 200-1, 208, 245
interests outside business, 194, 224, 261-63, 265-66, 268-69; politics, 265
marriage, 232
offices held: in firm, 82, 158, 189-90, 192, 237, 326, 400, 424-25; other, 256, 260-61, 265, 297, 319, 426

personality, 191-92
philanthropy, 269-70
por., *facing page* 192
prohibition, opposes, 319, 321, 361
quoted, 92, 143-44, 149-50, 192, 200, 210, 235, 297, 314, 319, 321
relations with employees, 253, 297, 301
resigns, 327, 346, 424, 427
stock held, 82, 189
Pabst, Hilda Lemp (Mrs. Gustav), 232
Pabst, Ida Uihlein (Mrs. Fred), 223, 262, 268, 329, 353
stock held, 329, 346, 372
Pabst, Maria Best (Mrs. Frederick), 46, 48, 422
Pabst, Marie (daughter of Captain). *See* Goodrich, Marie Pabst
Pabst, Robert (son of Fred), 352, 400
stock held, 372
Pabst, Rudolf (son of Fred), 345-46, 352, 354, 373-74, 400-1, 427-29
stock held, 372
Pabst Breweries Foundation, 383, 429
Pabst Brewing Company (Delaware)
named, 372, 428
Pabst Brewing Company (Wisconsin)
liquidated, 326, 426
named, 70, 424
See also Pabst Corporation (successor)
Pabst Brewing Company of New York, 237-38, 245
Pabst Building (Milwaukee), 223, 257-58, 268, 424
Pabst, Fred, Company, 332
Pabst Company of Omaha, 245
Pabst Corporation
incorporated, 326
merged with Premier Malt Products Company, 363-64
Pabst Grand Circle Restaurant, 212
Pabst Harlem Restaurant, 212, 425
Pabst Heat, Light and Power Company, 257
Pabst Holstein Farms, 262, 330, 335, 427

Pabst Hotel: Milwaukee, 257; New York City, 211

Pabst Kaiserhof Restaurant, 213

Pabst Malt Extract. *See* Tonic

Pabst Mining Company, 260

Pabst Park, 223

Pabst Realty Company, 326, 353, 377, 426

Pabst Sales Company, 342, 351, 373, 380, 428

Pabst Theater, 223, 266-68, 424-25

Pabst-ett (cheese), 262, 335, 337, 342-44, 350

Paddock, B. B., quoted, 244-45

Panics (1837), 43; (1857), 28-29, 43-45; (1873), 43, 66; (1893), 157, 188, 210, 260; (1907), 219; (1929), 347

Parrish, D., 153

Partnerships
  Jacob Best, Jr., and Phillip Best, 23, 422
  Jacob Best, Sr., and sons, 18-19, 422
  Jacob Best, Sr., Jacob Best, Jr., and Phillip Best, 22, 422
  Phillip Best and Frederick Pabst, 49, 423
  Frederick Pabst and Emil Schandein, 49, 423

Pasteur, Louis, 15, 110-11

Pasteurization. *See* Brewing technology

Patents, 112, 126, 204, 209

Patterson, W. R., 343, 346, 400

Peabody, Francis Greenwood, quoted, 311

Pensions, 253, 383, 429

Peoria, Ill.: branch, 172-73, 175; plant, 359, 373, 376, 378-80, 387-88, 396, 398, 428

Perlman, Selig, quoted, 267

Perlstein, Harris, viii, 354, 358-64, 381, 387-88
  early career, 357-58
  entrepreneurship, 358-59, 361-62, 387-88, 393
  offices held: in firm, 372, 374, 401, 427-28; other, 359-60
    organized Brewery Industry, Inc., 370-71
    personality, 355
    por., *facing page* 362
    quoted, 365, 369, 384, 386

Phelps, Edward Bunnell, comp., 252n.

Philadelphia, Pa., 55, 79, 147-48, 165 branch, 238

Philanthropy, 68, 250, 266, 268-70, 383

Philippine Islands market, 246-47

Pierce, John S., 166, 171-72, 239, 250, 290; quoted, 78, 116-17, 142-43, 161-63, 169-71

Pilsner beer (name), 122

Pipe Line Act (1890) and pipe lines for beer, 127, 424

Pittsburgh, Pa., branch, 172-75

Plank Road Brewery (ancestor of Miller Brewing Company), 22, 31-32, 422

Plankinton, John, 256

Plant expansion, 24, 26-29, 86-91, 102-10, 199-202, 375-77

Point of purchase materials. *See* Advertising media, special; Signs and Views

Policy (general), 67
  advertising, 32, 390
  labor, 273, 278-79, 285, 287-88
  price, 72
  production, 72, 114-15, 390
  retailers', 148

Policy, Best-Pabst, 193
  advertising, 32, 35, 61, 129-30, 135-36, 213-14, 217, 343, 389-91
  co-operation, 147
  economy, 89, 177, 183-85, 226, 349-52
  employees, benefits to; *see* Benefits
  employment, 91-92
  establishing, 70
  expansion, 59-61
  flexible, 83
  forming, 192
  innovations, 381
  investment, 58-59, 144, 196-99
  labor, 281, 287-90, 294-97

long run and short run, 90
marketing, 70, 142-45, 175, 188, 213, 225-27, 241, 341, 360, 368, 389
plant, single or multiple, 89, 244-45
price, 72, 147, 149-50, 168-70, 181
product, 16, 21, 114-23, 181, 204, 220, 332-36, 344, 379, 390
salary, 93-94, 250
sales promotion, 137-38, 213, 393; see also advertising, above
subsidiaries, 245
technology, 107-8
wage, 93
See also Decisions; Entrepreneurship
Political pressure, 37-39, 51-54, 206, 259, 303, 306, 308-10, 397
See also Prohibition
Politics, participation in, 35-40, 263-65
Pools, 148, 289
See also Competition; Syndicates; Trade associations
Population
of beer-producing cities, 79
national, 71, 79
See also Milwaukee, population
Porter (beverage), 12, 21
Position in the brewing industry, 44
export business, 179, 248, 389
local, 27-28, 54-56, 226-27
national, 31, 54-56, 59-61, 71-74, 80, 98-101, 114, 134, 180-81, 184-85, 289-90, 359, 361, 364, 389, 397-98
See also Competition
Postel, Fred J., 330, 346, 400
Powderly, Terence, 283
Power, 29, 104, 108, 110, 164
See also Electrification
Premier Malt Products Company (Ohio), 59, 339, 346, 352-60, 362-64, 427
incorporated, 358
merged with Pabst Corporation, 362-64
Premier Malt Products Company of Ohio, Inc., 358
Premier Malt Products Sales Company, 360, 372, 427-28

Premier-Pabst Corporation, 363-64, 371-72, 427-28
renamed Pabst Brewing Company, 372
Premier-Pabst Sales Company, 372-73, 427-28
Premose, 358, 380
Presbrey, Frank, 132n.
Preservatives, 120-21, 204-6
Prestige, 28, 31, 65, 68, 145, 184, 196, 210, 213, 220, 225, 238, 241, 246, 295, 389-90, 394
of Milwaukee beer, 42-53
See also Leadership; Position in industry
Preusser, Christian, quoted, 7
Price agreements, 147, 150-51, 228-30
Price wars, 65, 146-51, 228-29
Price, Waterhouse & Co., 202, 226, 332, 409; quoted, 185-86, 198-99, 201, 242
Prices, general, 96, 146, 185, 226, 298, 378
Prices of beer, 22, 27, 30, 51, 72, 77, 129, 146-51, 175, 181, 185, 226-31, 241-42, 272, 390-91
maintaining, 30, 64-66, 100, 146-52, 174, 228-31
taxation effects, 51-52, 65-66, 231
See also Policy; Price agreements; Price wars
Product differentiation, 65n., 225
Production, 44, 79, 118-21, 202-3
per worker, 100
regulation of, 51, 397
seasonal variation, 12, 18, 31, 203-4, 284
volume, 21, 23-25, 27-28, 30, 54-56, 64, 71-74, 87-89, 99, 124, 256, 375-76, 378, 395-96
volume, national, 30, 56-57
volume, other brewers, 27, 54, 56, 71-74, 79, 181, 256, 370
See also Brewing technology; Seasonal variation
Products, during prohibition, 332-37
See also By-products; Marketing; Policy; and names of products

Profits, 23, 27-28, 59, 83-85, 93, 151,
158, 174, 182-88, 330-32, 337, 342,
344-45, 350, 352, 396; (1904-18),
186
bottled beer, 124, 128, 177, 186-87,
199, 217, 220, 228, 241-42
branch, 168, 173-75, 186, 188, 242,
341
cheese, 337, 343
fall in, 231, 341
keg beer, 185-86, 242
malt syrup, 337, 344
nonalcoholic beverages, 186, 325,
337, 346-47, 351
of other brewers, 151, 396
outlets, 168
real-estate, 198-99, 258, 336-37, 345
in relation to: competition, 151,
184; costs, 185; expansion, 59,
83-85; investments, 143-44, 198-
99, 258; sales, 27-28, 184; wages,
93
stable, 182-88
See also Earnings, reinvestment of
Prohibition
becomes law: local and state, 187,
303-6; national, vii-viii, 209,
291, 301-24, 333, 336, 339, 356-
57, 385; see also Eighteenth
Amendment
liberty leagues, 314, 317-18
local option, 38, 305, 309-10, 315-16,
356, 368
movements toward: local and state,
37-40, 52-53, 286; national, 202,
206, 209, 220, 241, 253, 266,
302-3
opposition to: by brewers, 304-5,
306-8, 311-24, 361-62, 364-65;
by others, 37-40, 50, 306, 310-
11, 361-62
repeal of, 370; see also Twenty-first
Amendment
Public relations, 63, 68, 133-34, 224-
25, 265, 269, 312-13, 317, 393, 396
See also Advertising
Puritan Malt Extract Company, 347,
349, 427

Q

Quality, 72, 100, 102, 114, 116-18, 121,
148, 150, 167
Best-Pabst: beer, 28, 53, 121-22, 142,
145, 181, 217-18; cheese, 335-36
emphasis on, 70, 100, 116, 122-23,
181-82, 184, 192, 204-7, 241,
346, 365, 368
See also Policy; Prestige

R

Radio. See Advertising media
Railroads
early, 31, 42-43, 60
effect of, on beer business, 123
See also Freight rates; Rebates;
Transportation
Rainey, Henry T., quoted, 365
Raney, William Francis, 304n.
Raw materials, 74-75, 78, 96, 131, 284,
346, 376-78
See also Barley; Corn; Hops; Rice;
Malt; Yeast
Real estate, 77, 143-45, 196-99, 257-58,
326-27, 329, 377
See also Outlets; Policy; Profits
Rebates
on beer, 141, 226-27, 229
railroad, 161, 165, 181, 327n.
Records in the Pabst Company
archives, 407-11
Red, White and Blue beer, 216, 390-
91
Redfield, Lorraine Culver, 77n.
Refrigeration, artificial, 17, 78, 97-98,
107-10, 112, 162, 378
See also Ice
Regan, James B., 211
Regulation, 17, 366
advertising, 367-68, 389
brewing industry, 17, 366; by
brewers, 371
export (Second World War), 394-
95
marketing, 366-68
outlets, 367-377
production, 51-52, 397
wages, 340

Religion
and the arts, 40
and prohibition, 37, 302-3; *see also* Anti-Saloon League; Women's Christian Temperance Union
Research
cheese, 335
consumption, 377, 393
fermentation, 110-12
food products, 393
institutes, 112-13
malt and malt products, 379-80
marketing, 391-93, 428
yeast, 110-12, 379
See also Laboratory control
Restaurants. *See* Outlets
Reynolds, Lloyd George, and Killingsworth, Charles C., 282n.
Rice, 75, 119-20, 122, 204
Rice, John T., 374, 429
Richmond, Va., branch, 238
Risk. *See* Decisions, business; Entrepreneurship; Investments
Rockefeller, John D., 91, 95
Romer, Frank, 126n.
Ross Federal Research Corporation, 389
Ruh stage. *See* Brewing technology
Ruml, Beardsley, 396
Ruppert, Jacob, Brewery Company (New York City), 57, 73-74, 108, 355
Russell, H. H., 308-9 (quoted); 316

S

St. Louis, Mo., 55, 78-79, 146-49, 152
St. Paul, Minn., branch, 172-73, 175, 238
Saladin pneumatic malting machine, 103-5, 107, 200-1, 424
Salaries, 27, 93-94, 165-66, 172, 193-95, 219, 249-50, 328, 342, 348, 352, 403
Sales, beer, Best-Pabst, 24, 55-56, 99, 139-42, 156, 180-82, 184, 188, 226, 243-44, 345, 350-52, 361, 386
bottled beer, 117, 176-77, 187-88, 219, 246-47; by states, 176
branch, 174, 188, 342, 348
by brands, 216
decrease in, 44, 46, 58, 138, 187, 226-27, 386, 391
export, 177-79, 246-47, 389, 394
increase in, 28, 44, 55-56, 72, 83, 86-87, 100-1, 129, 132, 135, 138-39, 142, 158, 177, 227, 238, 351-52, 393
keg beer, 139, 177, 219; by states, 176
in relation to: advertising, 135; business cycles, 58, 86, 138, 182, 251, 391; costs, 272, 346; employment, 44, 250; expositions, 138; outlets, 139, 145, 226-28; plant improvements, 87; quality, 116, 142, 148
seasonal variations in, 287
Sales, beer, general, 29, 44, 54-56, 72-74, 139, 142, 156, 181, 184, 232, 267
increase in, 54, 139, 142, 188, 232, 272
national, 72, 86, 123, 148, 158, 180-81, 305, 391-92
Sales, other products
cheese, 335, 343, 349-51
malt syrup, 349, 351
nonalcoholic beverages, 216, 325, 333-34, 340-41, 346, 349, 351
Sales organization, 160-79, 340-42
agencies, 129-32, 165-71; *vs.* branches, 165-73, 237-40
agents, 125, 139-40, 145, 160, 163, 165-71, 177-79, 221, 229, 231, 341; relations of management with, 168-70
branch managers, 165, 167, 170, 173, 221, 226
collectors, 166, 342
credit manager, 166
peddlars, 140, 165, 280, 342
representatives, 122-23, 140-41, 172
sales managers, 341, 358, 372
salesmen, 116, 139-40, 328, 341-42, 344, 348-49
subsidiary sales companies; *see* Pabst Sales Company; Premier Malt Sales Company; Premier-Pabst Sales Company

traveling agents, 92-93, 139, 145, 151, 160, 165-71, 238-40; list of, 239
See also Branches; House organs
Sales promotion, 129-46, 177-78, 240-41, 341-42, 344, 391-92, 397
outlets, 135, 139-40, 214-23, 230, 246, 393-94, 397
prizes, 348, 367
spendings by salesmen, 65, 140-43, 145, 165, 174, 184, 213, 225-27
See also Advertising; Allowances; Discounts; Expositions; Rebates; Signs and Views
Saloons. *See* Outlets
San Francisco, Calif., 198, 212; agency, 237
Schad, W. F., 194, 426
Schade, Louis, 306n.
Schaefer, Rudolph, Jr., 297
Schaefer, F. & M., Brewing Company (New York City), 57, 73, 398
Schafer, Joseph, 40n.
Schandein, Elizabetha (Lisette) Best (Mrs. Emil), 267
death, 195
marriage, 49, 81, 423
offices, 82, 189, 400, 425
stock held, 81, 189, 195
Schandein, Emil, 21, 49-50, 58-61, 63-64, 85, 88, 102-03, 118, 119n., 165, 239, 264
death, 70, 81, 424
leadership in the community, 67-68, 263-64
marriage, 49, 81, 423
offices held: Pabst, 67, 81-82, 400, 423; other, 260, 263, 266
partner of Captain Pabst, 49, 423
personal investments, local, 257
personality, 81
quoted, 108, 121, 147-48, 167
stock held, 67, 80-81
Schandein family, stock held, 329
Schedler, Alfred J., viii, 113-14, 192, 208-9, 328, 335, 364, 425
Schenley Brewing Company, 398
Schleip, Eugene, 237
Schlitz, Joseph, Brewing Company (Milwaukee), 54, 56, 57n., 60, 67,

71-74, 85, 129, 137-38, 142-43, 145-56, 167, 181n., 184, 197, 201, 223, 225, 227, 233, 256, 277-82, 289-90, 294-95, 300, 320, 334, 339, 355, 364, 366, 370n., 375, 398
merger proposed, 151-56
Schlüter, Hermann, quoted, 271-73, 289n., 293
Schmidt, F. E., 93n., 131-32
Schmitt, E., quoted, 122-23
Schoeffler, Margaret Best (Mrs. Moritz), 32
Schoeffler, Moritz, 32, 37
Schultz, Ferdinand, viii, 6n.
Schurz, Carl, 36
Schwarz, Anton, 112-13, 121
Schwarz Laboratories, viii, 112, 388
Science, contributions of, 102-8, 110-14, 204-9
See also Brewing technology; Experimentation; Research
Scrapbooks, list of, 411
Seager, Henry R., and Gulick, Charles A., Jr., 230n.
Seasonal variation in consumption, 12, 116
employment, 203-4, 250-51, 287, 299, 402
production, 12, 18, 31, 203-4, 284
sales, 287
Second Annual Brewers Congress, 52
Second Ward Savings Bank, Milwaukee, 49, 85-86, 260, 404
Secret Books, 132-33, 410, 424
Seipp & Lehmann (Conrad Seipp Brewing Company) (Chicago), 56, 72-74
Select beer (name), 130-31, 177, 187, 216-17, 423, 425
Shadwell, Arthur, 322n.
Shakman, James G., 360, 372, 374, 378, 395, 401, 427-28
Sheboygan Beverage Company, 334, 427
Shipping brewers, definition, 30
Shlaudeman, Frank, 356-58
Shlaudeman, Harry, 356
Shlaudeman, Henry, 355-56, 372
Shlaudeman, Robert, 374, 401

Signs and Views, 135-36, 138, 184, 218-19, 221-22, 342, 348, 389
Singer, Philip A., 357-60, 401
entrepreneurship, 358
Singer-Perlstein Company, 357-59
Sittig, Eugene, 113
Slogans, 133-34, 238, 356, 360, 397
Small Brewers' Committee, 371
Snapper, Annette, 393
Socialism, 254, 280, 294
Soehnlein, Emma Pabst (daughter of Captain), stock held, 329
Soft drinks. *See* Beverages, non-alcoholic
Solfisburg, F. E., 360, 372-73, 391, 401, 427-28
Sons of Temperance, 37
South American market, 178, 247, 389
South Side Brewery
closed, 88-91, 95, 97, 424
named, 61, 423
Spaeth, Anton, 358-60
Spaeth, Bernard A., 374, 401
Spalding, E. M., quoted, 164
Speak-easies, 305, 361, 385
Spendings by salesmen. *See* Sales promotion
Spent grains. *See* Brewer's grains
Sports, 68, 194, 262-63, 265
Squier, Fred H., 194, 219, 222, 224, 241, 328
Stabilizing beer. *See* Brewing technology
Stamm, G. T., 123-24
Stamm and Meyer, firm of, 123-25, 423
Stark, Henry J., 193-94, 250, 326-27, 400, 426; quoted, 91
Stein, Herbert, 396
Steiner, N., quoted, 169
Steubenville, Ohio, plant, 358-59
Stevens Point, Wis., branch, 165, 173, 175
Stewart, George W., 428
Stifel, Otto, 297
Still, Bayrd, viii, 256n.

Stock. *See* Capital
Stock raising, 261-63
Stockholders, 67, 80-83, 94, 182, 188-89, 194-96, 329-30, 345-46, 363, 367, 374
Strange, John, quoted, 320
Stricken, Jacob, quoted, 170
Strikes, 274, 279-88, 298, 300-1, 339-40, 424
See also Trade-unions
Subsidiaries. *See* American Rotating Valve Company; Blue Ribbon Commercial Company; Blue Ribbon Distributing Company; Continental Engineering Company; Hoffman Beverage Company; Jones, W. D., and Company; Milwaukee Beer Company; Pabst Brewing Company of New York; Pabst Company of Omaha; Pabst, Fred, Company; Pabst Sales Company; Premier Malt Sales Company; Premier-Pabst Sales Company
Suds. *See* Brewing technology
Sugar, 14, 121, 357, 380, 383
Surpluses, 67, 84, 96, 331, 337, 345, 350, 353, 375, 377
Surveys, 389, 393, 395
Swan, W. G., quoted, 161
Syndicates, brewery, list of, 405-6
British, 72, 80, 148-49, 151-59, 232-36, 290, 424
proposed, 151-59

T

Tables, list of, xi-xii
Taft, President William H., 316
Tapacan (beer), 387
Tariff, 50, 52-53, 395
Taverns. *See* Outlets
Taxation of
beer: federal, 50-53, 65-66, 126, 231, 366-67, 422, 425-27, 429; state, 12, 245, 366
whisky, 52, 71
Taxes, income, 337, 409
Taylor, A. N., 304
Technology. *See* Brewing technology

Temperance movement, 283, 286, 302-6, 309-11
societies and meetings, 37-39
Temperature. See Brewing technology
Texas taxation, 245
Theater. See Drama; Pabst Theater
Theurer, J. F. (Fritz), 102, 106, 121-22, 127, 204, 207-8, 209n., 214-15, 423
quoted, 215
retires, 191, 207, 425
stock held, 82, 189
Thomann, Gallus, 50n., 113n.
Thompson, J. Walter, advertising agency, 136, 217-19, 237
Thornton, E. B., 373-74, 428-29
Thornton, Frank Weldon, 183n.
Tonic, Best (beverage), 131-36, 186, 213, 215-16, 220, 325, 425
Tovey, John, 113
Trade associations, 42, 52, 65, 113, 228, 230-31, 246, 256, 294-95, 311, 317-18, 338, 370-71
committee, 50-52
See also United States Brewers' Association
Trade-marks, 129, 133-34, 177, 217-18, 222, 225, 390, 423, 425
Trade periodicals, 113
list of, 420-21
Trade-unions, 271-79, 338-40, 382
apprentices, 300
arbitration, 284-85, 297-98, 340, 382
boycotts, 284-96 passim, 318, 339
closed shop, 277-78, 281, 298, 338-40, 382
collective bargaining, 273-301
contracts, 254, 283, 285, 291-301 passim, 338-40, 382
jurisdictional disputes, 282-83, 293-94, 301, 383
liberty leagues, 317-18
lock-outs, 288, 296-98
open shop, 338
prohibition, attitude toward, 317-18
wage agreements, 282
women in, 300, 340
See also Hours of work; Wages

Transportation, viii, 9, 22, 25-26, 60-61, 163-64, 199-200, 202, 206-7, 368-69
early, 5
problems, 160-64
See also Costs; Freight rates; Railroads
Treat, Curtis M., 211
Trusts, 72, 151
See also Syndicates
Tucker, Horace, quoted, 162-63
Twenty-first Amendment, 365-67, 427

U

Uihlein, August, 77
and brothers, 72, 153-55, 223
Uihlein, Ida. See Pabst, Ida Uihlein
Underwood, F. L., 157
United Brewers Industrial Foundation, 371, 428
United States Brewers' Association (later United States Brewers Foundation, Inc.), 50-53, 125, 205-6, 248, 265, 287, 288, 290, 297, 301, 306-7, 313, 315, 317-19, 370-71, 422, 428-29
name adopted, 52
United States Constitution. See Eighteenth Amendment; Twenty-first Amendment
United States Government, relations with the brewery industry, 51-52, 126-27, 205-6, 377, 394-97
See also Court action; Laws; Taxation
Urbanism, growth of, 71

V

Vacations for workers, 382
Vinegar, 22, 33
factory, 4, 9, 11, 19, 32n., 422
Volstead Act (1919), 324, 352, 361-62, 364-65

W

Wachsner, Leon, 267
widow of, 268
Wages, 76, 88, 249, 251, 253-54, 271-84 passim, 297-301 passim, 338, 340, 378, 382
early, 5-6, 27